P9-BIV-415

THE GRAPHICS OF COMMUNICATION

COMMUNICATION

FOURTH EDITION

THE GRAPHICS OF COMMUNICATION
FOURTH EDITION

TYPOGRAPHY · LAYOUT · DESIGN · PRODUCTION

ARTHUR T. TURNBULL · RUSSELL N. BAIRD
Ohio University

HOLT, RINEHART AND WINSTON
New York   Chicago   San Francisco   Atlanta   Dallas
Montreal   Toronto   London   Sydney

This book was set entirely, both text and display, in Zapf Book, a typeface designed in 1975 by Hermann Zapf, a noted German designer and calligrapher. Among the more than forty other faces Zapf has designed are Palatino, Melior, and Optima, which are much used for both books and commercial graphics. As is the case with all type designs by Zapf, Zapf Book shows distinction without eccentricity and concern not with single letters, but with their fusion into a working text.

Zapf Book was named for its designer by the International Typeface Corporation, which introduced the typeface in 1976. The face is available in four weights, light, medium, demi, and heavy, all of which are used in this book (see Appendix B, "Specifications for This Book").

Acquiring Editor   Roth Wilkofsky
Managing Editor   Pamela Forcey
Production Manager   Nancy Myers
Art Director   Louis Scardino
Text Design   Lana Giganti
Cover Design   A. J. D'Agostino
Page Makeup   Marion Feigl
Mergenthaler V.I.P. (Variable Input Phototypesetter) Composition and Camera Work   Progressive Typographers, Emigsville, Pennsylvania
Printing and Binding   Von Hoffmann Press, Inc., St. Louis, Missouri

Library of Congress Cataloging in Publication Data

Turnbull, Arthur T
    The graphics of communication.

    Bibliography: p.
    Includes index.
    1. Printing, Practical.   I. Baird, Russell N.,
joint author.   II. Title.
Z244.T86   1980   686.2'2   79–19850

ISBN 0–03–021666–4

2   3   4   5   032   9   8   7   6   5   4

Preface

This fourth edition of *The Graphics of Communication* reflects the tremendous changes in all aspects of printed communication that have occurred in the last few years, especially the startling technological changes.

All print media—and the schools of journalism and communication involved in preparing young persons for careers with those media—have been forced to set aside traditional procedures and build their operations around the totally new technology now involved in word processing and mass communication. With the computer at its center, an explosion of technological innovations has burst upon us more quickly and with far greater force than we previously had imagined could be possible. Some of the changes were reported in the third edition, but what was the exception at that time is now the rule—or already out of date. It has now been established, without any doubt, that a good foundation of technical knowledge is essential for anyone wishing to use visual means of communication effectively.

In order to meet the needs of students in the technical area, two chapters have been added, Chapter 7 describing electronic copy processing systems and Chapter 8 providing basic how-to information involved in working with electronic input devices.

The movement of type composing and page layout from the shop of the compositor to the office of the editor means that there are new skills that must be learned; tasks that formerly were the compositor's are now the editor's. Thus a third new chapter, Chapter 12 on the preparation of mechanicals for photo-offset lithography and other photomechanical printing systems, has been added.

We continue to be convinced that a foundation of technical knowledge cannot be separate and distinct from the understanding of theoretical aspects of communication, an understanding that is also essential for all professional communicators. Exploration in the area of human information processing has been closely paralleling the startling innovations in technology; as technology has opened new vistas for graphic communication, theoretical explorations have served to provide a better, more solid basis for decision-making in the preparation of pieces of graphic communication. The theoretical and the practical have become so intertwined that the old trade approach to a course dealing with printing technology is no longer feasible. The processing of information in the human mind cannot be separated from the processing of information in the computer; the methodologies of both are so similar that what we can learn from one can be helpful in working with the other.

To put the theoretical and technical aspects of communication in better perspective, we have reorganized chapters in order to have the historical survey serve as a basis for a quick overview of all aspects of production in the first chapter. We hope that teachers and students alike will find the new organization to their liking. The chapter on newspaper design is totally new, reflecting recent changes in approach for newspaper appearance.

. . .

We again owe tremendous debts of gratitude to scores of individuals and firms who graciously provided material for this edition and previous editions. Many illustrations have been added to this edition, especially in the three new chapters and the chapter on newspaper design, and most of these were contributed by newspapers, equipment manufacturers, printers, and others associated with graphics-related industries. Although credit is given wherever such material appears in the text, we wish to add our special thanks here for these valuable contributions.

We would also like to acknowledge special debts of gratitude to the following persons who provided valuable materials and information: James A. Geladas, *Dubuque Telegraph Herald*; Frank Gillian and Cy Wainscott, *Cleveland Plain Dealer*; John Good and Reid McBride, Lawhead Press, Inc.; John Goodwin, freelance illustrator; Robert J. Harrison, *St. Petersburg Times*; Gus Hartoonian, *Chicago Tribune*; Ralph Kliesch, Ohio University; Robert Lockwood, Call-Chronicle Newspapers, Inc.; Chuck Lyons, *San Angelo Standard-Times*; James Morris, *Troy Daily News*, Troy, Ohio; Sandra Puncekar, American Newspaper Publishers Association/Research Institute; Charles Scott, Ohio University; John J. Tuohey, *U.S. News & World Report*; Robert Vereen, *Hardware Retailing*; Bill Wilt, *Newsday*; and Paul Zindell, *Hudson Register-Star*, Hudson, New York.

We are also grateful to the following, who read the manuscript of this edition and made valuable suggestions: William Biglow, Southern Illinois University at Carbondale; Bert N. Bostrum, Northern Arizona University; Mario R. Garcia, Syracuse University.

And finally, for her imaginative suggestions and helpful contributions far exceeding those required of a publisher's editor, the authors extend to Pamela Forcey of Holt, Rinehart and Winston their sincerest thanks. Her touches of excellence enhanced the third edition and have contributed much to this edition.

A. T. T.
R. N. B.

Contents

8 Processing Copy Electronically 137

Appendixes

THE GRAPHICS OF COMMUNICATION

COMMUNICATION

FOURTH EDITION

1 Graphic Communication: Present and Past

Graphic communication is a process of conveying messages by means of visual images, which are usually on a flat surface.

Two kinds of images, pictures and visual symbols, are used. The term "pictures" includes photographs, paintings, and drawings. Words are represented graphically by variously shaped patterns called the *letters* of the alphabet. These letters and the words that they form are called *symbols* because nothing about them can be related to certain objects or ideas that they signify. A symbol represents something else by reason of convention—that is, agreement among its users.

Pictures, on the other hand, usually show objects or things pretty much as they are. However, on occasion, pictures may also be used as symbols. One can imagine pictures symbolizing such holidays as Thanksgiving or the Fourth of July. These picture-symbols are as arbitrary in terms of relating directly to their referents as are word symbols in terms of what they refer to, and they must be learned in the same way that language is learned.

Pictures and written language serve quite different functions in graphic communication, but they do share a remarkable similarity. In addition to those times when we are examining visual images, our senses, including our vision, control our behavior directly. We see something blocking our way, for example, so we avoid it. The visual sense serves animals in this way. Visual images, on the other hand, make it possible for humans to consider things other than in the here and now. We can even deal with the imaginary, things that are completely divorced from reality. We can, for example, draw pictures of ghosts and write about them.

Another similarity between the two types of images is worth noting. The receiver of a visual message who seeks to understand the message must read it. *Reading* may be defined as extracting information from visual images, which means that both the pictures and the words are read. It is easy to see how this applies to words; the eye scans along a written line, making frequent stops to take in a few words. Only four or five words can be handled at each of these stops.

This is a small area, as you can confirm by looking at the area encompassed by four words in a line in this text.

A picture area is usually much larger than such a word area. In order for the reader to extract information from this much larger area, the eye must scan a picture, making frequent stops to take in information. The information taken in at all the stops is then synthesized into a meaningful whole in much the same way that meaning is extracted from the words that make up a sentence.

Of the two types of images, word-symbols are more basic to effective graphic communication. Language is, after all, the primary means of human communication, and words play an important role in thinking and decision making. This is not to say that thought is impossible without words; it is more accurate to say that language facilitates thought.

Thinking is the result of brain activity involving symbol codes in the form of neural energy patterns. These patterns are activated by external word-symbols (such patterns might also be activated by direct contact with the real world or by pictures). The results of thinking are then converted back into word codes for purposes of communication.

The written word is an extension of the spoken word. Transforming speech into writing unfortunately bypasses facial expression, tonal inflection, and gestures, which are vital in face-to-face communication. Thus, it becomes necessary in presenting a written message to make up for this loss by putting words in as effective a visual form as possible.

Printing is the means of reproducing visual images for mass communication. It is the presentation or form of the printed message that concerns us in this book. However, a word of caution is necessary. Form is inextricably involved with message content—the meanings or ideas being communicated. As Henry James once wrote, form and content are inseparable in a work of art. The writer works with a vocabulary of words and a *syntax*, which refers to the ordering of words into structures that show the word relationships. The writer has certain ideas in mind, and structures the word codes so that they will give rise to the same thoughts in the reader's mind.

The designer of printed messages also works with a vocabulary, consisting of points, lines, shapes, textures, and tones. And like the writer the designer can organize these elements into a structure or form to direct the reader's thought processes (Figure 1-1). We refer to the syntax of design at various points in the text and most specifically in Chapters 6 and 14. The effectiveness of a printed message, then, is the result of the writer and designer expressing a common meaning.

The importance of form or design may be primary or secondary, depending on circumstances. In general, the importance of form or

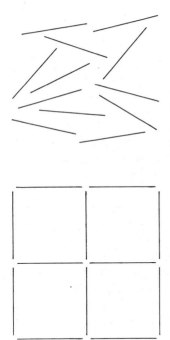

1-1 How many lines are there in the group at the top? The same number of lines is used in the organized structure below, but here the number is immediately apparent.

design is reduced as reader interest in word content increases. Readers will overcome formidable graphic obstacles to get information they strongly desire. For example, the want ads are dull in appearance, yet they are among the best-read parts of a newspaper. Also, students study monotonous lists of scores in small type to find the results of the hometown school's football game. The interest in the content is so great that graphic form is cast in a secondary role.

In complete contrast to these cases is the wastebasket fate of much printed material. Tests have shown the importance of form; material of the same content has been received, read, and acted on in one form, but discarded in another. Also, a newspaper story may gain readership from one edition to another simply by a change in headline size or placement on a page. And the addition of a second color may dramatically increase response to a direct-mail piece.

These examples, along with the general fact that any reader is offered much more than can ever be assimilated, indicate that the techniques for improving formal presentation are too important to be ignored.

The graphic designer must combine communication and creativity. To the extent that the designer's task is to present a message in an esthetically pleasing form, there may be some justification for calling the designer's work *graphic art*. We prefer the term *graphic communication* because the designer must be primarily concerned with communication, rather than art. The design of printed material should never be an end in itself—a means of self-expression for the designer. Content may dominate form, as has been noted, but form should never dominate content.

Graphic Communication Today _____

Graphic communication is a major sustaining force of our economic, political, and cultural existence. We scrutinize the acts of our government by means of the printed newspaper. We pay our printed bills with printed money, checks, or credit cards. We learn about consumer goods through printed advertising and take them home in printed cartons and printed shopping bags.

Our day is brightened by magazines, books, and greeting cards. We broaden our knowledge through textbooks and technical or professional journals. Great works of art, past and present, come to us from far-off museums as accurate reproductions. We travel about guided by printed road maps. Libraries, bookstores, supermarket and drugstore display racks, home bookshelves, and attics and basements are crammed with printed materials. So are wastebaskets that are emptied each night into trash cans. But the unending deluge of printed matter can be expected to continue tomorrow—and each day thereafter.

Naturally, the public can be expected to be selective in what it reads; it is a matter of self-defense. It follows that designers of printed materials need every skill and technique to prevent their handiwork from going to the wastebasket unread. Competition for the reader's time is keen. Messages in newspapers, for example, must vie for attention not only with television, magazines, and other newspapers, and scores of one-shot printed pieces, but also with internal competition. Since few of us read everything in a newspaper, each page, story, illustration, and headline must battle for readership with all the other pages. Only the publications and individuals who offer the best in content and form can win out in such a competitive struggle.

The process of getting words and pictures into print proceeds through three successive stages: (1) planning, (2) copy preparation, and (3) production or printing. This is true whatever the material—newspapers, magazines, books, advertisements, or direct literature.

In the second stage the word "copy" refers to both the verbal and pictures. We could just as well have called this stage "copy and art preparation." In some respects this might be a better term, since not only are photographs taken and pictures drawn but a drawing showing how words and pictures are to be arranged is also made, to serve as a blueprint for production. Such a drawing is called a *layout*. An example is shown in Figure 1-2.

Planning Stage Most people, if asked, "Which of the three stages makes the most creative demands?" would say the second stage. And why shouldn't they? After all, it is in this stage that the words and pictures are prepared and a drawing made of their formal arrangement, such as Figure 1-2. And we generally credit writers and artists with high levels of creativity.

But consider. If you're talking with someone, and you want to make a point, a plan of what you are about to say must precede your statement. If you don't know ahead of time—however brief a period—what you are about to say, how can you say it? If you were asked to letter or draw a capital letter alphabet, you would have to have in your brain neural codes: first, to tell you what the letters look like; second, their order; and third, to direct your muscular activity in putting them on paper as visual symbols.

The most significant creative activity, in other words, comes in the planning stage. The organization of content and form is decided at this time, before the words are written and the pictures are made, or they are combined together in a layout. The process of deciding such

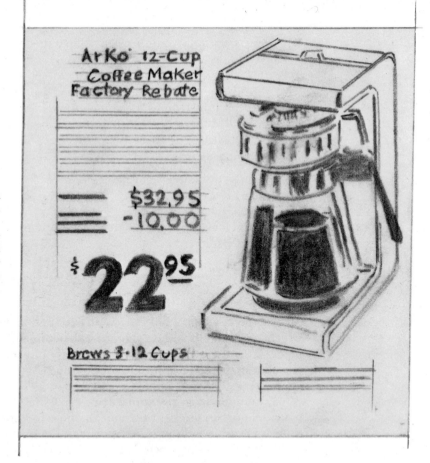

1-2 This layout, a production blueprint, shows picture and type positions. The headlines are lettered, and parallel lines indicate the placement of lines of smaller type.

matters is called *visualizing*. Both writer and designer should be involved in this process.

Visualizing is primarily a thinking process. The ideas to be communicated are given to the writer and designer and together they plan how the finished material will appear to the reader. Different possible arrangements of visual images are "seen in the mind's eye," until the one that most effectively conveys the ideas is selected. And although visualizing is not a layout exercise, the designer may "doodle" miniature sketches to aid the thinking process. Figure 1-3 shows two such sketches that preceded the layout shown in Figure 1-2.

1-3 Experimental miniatures that preceded the layout shown in Figure 1-2. The one on the right was developed into the layout.

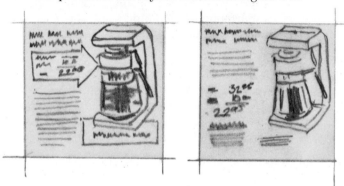

The designer must make other decisions in the planning stage, which primarily concern the printing and production techniques involved in the third stage. These technqiues are complicated, and in order to utilize them to the fullest, the designer must have a sound working knowledge of their limitations and capacities. Only in this way can the designer discharge these two major responsibilities:

1. Present a visually effective message
2. Control the costs

Preparation Stage

Once plans for the printed materials have been set, three functions must be carried out:

1. Words must be prepared
2. Pictures—if to be used—must be prepared
3. A layout must be prepared

All of these tasks must be completed, although there is no set order in which they must be done. The order depends on the type of printed material. In the book field, for example, the finished manuscript and pictures are sometimes turned over to the designer before a layout or design is begun.

In the newspaper and magazine fields the designer faces somewhat unique conditions. The format of these publications is continued from issue to issue. By *format* is meant such things as size, shape, width of columns, typefaces to be used, and relative amounts of words and pictures. These determinants of overall appearance are decided upon in the planning stage for most other printed materials. Because of these preset conditions of format, we treat newspapers and magazines separately. Newspaper design is covered in Chapter 16, and magazine design is covered in Chapter 15.

The design of advertisements and direct literature usually offers the designer a freer hand. In these cases each printed unit "starts from scratch." The three stages are more in evidence for each ad and for each piece of direct literature, since none of them has a predetermined format. Some direct literature in the form of folders is unique in that it is three dimensional as opposed to two-dimensional ads or publication pages. Folders are large sheets folded down to one size, as shown in Figure 1-4. Folders present special design problems that are presented in Chapter 17, "Designing Other Printed Literature."

Design principles

Regardless of the type of literature—book, magazine, newspaper, advertisement, or direct—the principles of effective design are unchanging. Because the designer has a freer hand in designing advertisements, we discuss these principles in Chapter 14, "Design: Combining Pictures and Words," with specific attention focused on advertisements.

1-4 Two sides of a large folder—a single sheet folded to a smaller size. Can you decide how it was folded down to produce a logical presentation? (*Courtesy* Reader's Digest. *Lawrence Welk is a Ranwood Records recording star*)

However, the design of printed literature does not always involve both pictures and words. A great deal of information in print is presented using words alone. This does not imply that formal arrangement is thereby deserted. A strictly verbal printed message may be pleasing or unpleasing to the eye. The principles involved in using type alone are considered in Chapters 5, "Elements of Good Typography" and 6, "Using Type Creatively."

Copy preparation

Early on in his or her career, the person whose work involves getting visual images into print faces two particularly vexing problems:

1. Fitting the number of words to the allotted space on the layout
2. Fitting pictures to the allotted space on the layout

As this person gains experience, these problems become easier to solve, but they must be solved in the preparation stage, before production. If the pictures or the words do not fit, either the layout must be changed or the number of words or sizes of pictures must be altered. In either case, considerable cost can be involved. How such problems are handled is covered in Chapters 9, "Preparing Words for Printing: Traditional Methods," and 11, "Preparing Illustrations for Production."

Production Stage

In the production stage the visual images—words and pictures—are arranged together according to the layout and are printed. In the planning stage the designer had to incorporate into the plan information about the production methods to be used. The designer would then have to follow through, working closely with production people, to assure that his or her "job" would turn out as visualized. The designer's task would parallel that of an architect being on the construction site to see that the building that the architect planned, and for which he or she drew blueprints, turned out as visualized.

The designer must have specific knowledge in these production areas: (1) printing processes; (2) type composition; (3) selection of paper or other printing surface; and (4) paper folding, binding, and finishing.

Printing processes

There are a number of different printing processes. The selection of the method best suited to the job at hand has more to do with the designer's proper discharge of his or her responsibilities than any other factor. A decision in this area has a marked effect on all other areas of production and even in the preparation of words and pictures, as we shall see.

The designer is used to working with images on paper. Words are composed on paper. Paintings and drawings are done on paper; even the layout is prepared on paper. Photos generally appear on paper, although they may be in the form of transparencies (much like color slides). In any event, transparencies can be imagined as being on paper.

The finished printed piece will be made up of these same images appearing again on paper, or possibly some other surface in one, two, or more colors. To make printing possible, some sort of image carrier, called a *printing plate* is needed. When it has been placed on a printing press and inked with the proper color, the printing plate transfers the images it carries to the printing surface.

At least this is the case with the three processes that are most widely used in mass communication. There are additional processes, but in every case printing requires preparation of the intermediate image carrier. The selection of the printing process, kinds of presses, and preparation of image carriers are discussed in Chapter 3, "Graphic Reproduction Processes and Presses."

Type composition
The processes and techniques involved in converting written words into type as they will appear to the reader are termed *type composition* or *typesetting*. The primary considerations facing the designer in this area are

1. Legibility of the typeface
2. Design possibilities
3. Selecting the composition method

Type legibility Since language is the primary means of human communication, legibility of the face or faces selected is of greatest concern. The term *typeface* refers to the design style of the characters of an alphabet. There are literally thousands of different typefaces, and some are more easily read than others.

Design possibilities When a number of words are composed together, they take up a portion of the layout space. The area they occupy will take on a shape, a tone, and a texture. This depends principally on the typeface, size of the type, length of the lines of type, word spacing (space between words), letterspacing (space between letters), and line spacing (space between lines).

Remember—shape, tone, and texture are part of the designer's vocabulary. This means that the shapes formed by areas of type composition can be arranged to interact with the shapes of picture elements to deliver a visually effective message.

These same factors—typestyle, size, line length, word spacing, letterspacing, and line spacing—also have an effect on legibility. A certain copy area shape, tone, or texture may be desirable, but if a trade-off is believed necessary, it should always favor legibility. The effect of these factors on legibility is discussed in Chapter 5, "Elements of Good Typography." Type and its relationship to design are discussed in several places but most specifically in Chapters 6, "Using Type Creatively," and 14, "Design: Combining Pictures and Words."

Selecting the composition method Printing from movable metal type was invented in 1450. In the next 500 years the process of getting words into type remained relatively unchanged. After the writer finished the copy, it was edited and then marked with typesetting instructions and sent to the compositor, who probably worked for a printer. The compositor might also have worked for a "type house," or a company that set the type and forwarded it to the printer, or may have worked in a newspaper composing room.

A wedding of photography and computer technology gave birth to new typesetting methods in the mid-twentieth century. These methods made it possible to set type by exposing one character after another on photographic paper or film at incredible speeds. Before three decades had passed, *phototypesetting* had become the principal means of type composition.

One of the most significant changes brought about by the growth of phototypesetting has been the effect on the role of the writer, particularly in the newspaper and magazine fields. No longer does the writer type out words on a typewriter. Rather the writer now operates keys on a typewriterlike keyboard and words appear on a televisionlike screen. The machine of which the keyboard and screen are a part is

1-5 An editorial staff writer at a VDT. (*Courtesy* Detroit News)

called a *VDT* (video display terminal). See Chapters 7 and 8 for further discussion. Assisted by a computer control, the writer can change the copy in any way desired by using the proper command keys. Once finished, the copy can then be sent from VDT to a computer memory.

In an alternative method, the copy is typed on special paper in a special typewriter. Corrections can be typed in and/or marked with a special pen. Then the copy is electronically scanned and sent to a computer memory.

An editor at any time later can order the copy back from the computer memory and make further changes on a VDT. The copy can then be returned to the computer memory, from which it can then be sent to a phototypesetter for composition. Figure 1-5 shows a writer operating a VDT.

At the time the copy is written, instructions are also written on the VDT or on the special typing paper and sent along with the copy to the computer concerning such matters as typeface; line length; letter-, line, and word spacing; and so on. The typesetter adapts the writer's copy to these requirements.

What was traditionally the preparation assignment—writing the words—is becoming a broader assignment: preparation-composition. As we stated earlier, these developments are most notable in the publishing fields. However, increasing numbers of businesses and organizations that have printing needs are assuming the composition function and are installing phototypesetting equipment.

This means that the writer of today—wherever he or she works—as a reporter or magazine writer, as an advertising-promotion writer, or as a publicity-public relations writer, should not only know how to write but also know typography and electronic word processing as well. The new processes stand ready to make the writer a typographer.

Composition in the editorial office, and "in-house" composition (done in the offices of other businesses and organizations requiring printed materials) make sense. Phototypesetting equipment is modern in styling, befitting the writer's setting in office surroundings, and less bulky and industrial looking than the metal type-producing equipment used by the traditional printer.

But of greatest importance is the fact that phototypesetting is faster, less expensive, and more versatile in the sense that it is capable of doing more with the "look" or appearance of type in print. Certainly this is a feature that should be kept as close as possible to the preparation stage.

Typographic terminology, the new and traditional methods of composition, and the machines involved are discussed in Chapter 4, "Type and Typesetting." In Chapters 7, 8, and 9 applications of the newer and older methods are discussed.

Selection of paper

Printing can be done on other surfaces than paper and the choice of surface is based on the selection of the printing process. However, our major concern in this text is with the use of paper in printing. The designer is faced with selection from a wide range of kinds and colors of paper. The choice of the right paper for the job involves many factors, which are discussed in Chapters 17, "Designing Other Printed Literature," and 18, "Paper: Selection, Folding, Binding, Finishing."

Paper folding, binding, finishing

Even after paper has passed through a printing press and has received the printed images, production is still not complete. Final processing requires converting large single sheets into separate pieces as they will be seen by the reader. The large sheets must be folded and bound to become books or booklets, which are then trimmed (cut) on three sides. If the final printed piece is to be in the form of single sheets, these must be cut from the press sheet; if the piece is to be in the form of folders, these must be cut from the press sheet and then properly folded.

Much *web printing* (printing from rolls of paper) involves, at least in part, *folding*, *binding*, and *finishing* on the press. This is particularly true in the case of newspapers, magazines, and books.

Finishing involves a number of special treatments that are discussed along with folding and binding.

Graphic Communication Yesterday _____

Our current fast, efficient methods of graphic communication have resulted from our ability to solve several perplexing problems. The first of these was the need for a set of symbols that singly and in groups could visually represent both real objects and mental concepts. A workable alphabet made this possible. Then we needed suitable materials on which these symbols could be viewed and retained for long periods of time, even permanently. Video tubes and a wide variety of papers have given us almost limitless flexibility for the display and storage of information. Long ago, the invention of ink made it possible to put symbols on paper; centuries later, movable type, type-composition machines, and printing presses made it possible to reproduce visual messages in great quantity. A need for illustrations to supplement the symbols was satisfied with the invention of photography and photoengraving techniques. And finally, the need for a machine that could substitute for the mental functions of human beings themselves—a device with the capability of making logical decisions and of storing information in its memory—was met with the introduction of computers. The combination of computer capability and photographic techniques forms the base of the current technological revolution in graphic communication.

Evolution of the Alphabet

Picture drawings on the walls of cave dwellings, the earliest evidence of graphic communication, date back some 50,000 years. Spoken language is much older—at least 1 million years old, according to anthropologists.

Written language is an extension of spoken language and has been a part of human life only since the dawn of history, 5,000 to 6,000 years ago. The boundary between historic and prehistoric is drawn where the ability to record language in visual form became a part of human civilization.

The alphabet evolved from pictures, and through the centuries spoken language probably became quite proficient. But spoken language suffered a major constraint—knowledge could only be passed from generation to generation by word of mouth. Pictures could not represent ideas when they were seen by two or more people, because pictures are capable of two or more interpretations. Was a picture of a dog *any* dog, *the* dog previously referred to, *his* or *your* dog, or an animal (an abstraction), for example?

Over the years, object pictures became stylized pictographs and eventually came to represent ideas rather than simply objects. The Egyptian hieroglyphics, forerunner of our alphabet, utilized pictographs as well as ideographs. In addition, some symbols served as phonograms—that is, they represented voiced sounds. A single word, for example, might be phonetically spelled out, shown in pictographic or ideographic form, and accompanied by a "determinative symbol" to indicate whether a certain pictograph represented a concrete object or an idea. Several hundred characters were required.

Certain northern Semitic tribes sensed the usefulness of the phonographic and adopted the concept. They used 22 of their own pictographs to represent the sounds of their language. For example, "aleph," the first letter, was the pictograph for an ox and "beth," the second letter, represented a house.

The Greeks borrowed the Semitic alphabet in the ninth century B.C. They kept the same letter order and adapted some of the letter names to Greek; aleph became alpha, and beth became beta, for example. Hence the root meaning for our word "alphabet." Some Greek adaptations are shown in Figure 1-6. Some of the Semitic letters represented no sounds in Greek and became the vowel sounds *a, e, i, o,* and *u.*

The Etruscans took the Greek alphabet to the Romans in the ninth century B.C. Only minor adjustments were needed to adapt to the Latin sounds. When completed, the Roman alphabet consisted of 23 letters; the remaining three letters were added later to bring the total to the present 26.

Writing with the Roman alphabet has existed some 3,000 years. Yet modern printing dates back only 500 years. It seems remarkable

aleph   alpha

beth   beta

gimel   gamma

daleth   delta

he   epsilon

1-6 The Semitic letters at left were adapted by the Greeks. The letter names were given Greek pronunciations.

that printing was so slow in developing, but there are several reasons. Among the early Romans the higher social classes retained writing as a special right and did not encourage its use among the less privileged. The task of producing the needed quantities of literature was assigned to slave scribes, who wrote on expensive vellum or parchment made from animal skins. The Chinese developed a paper much like that of today in the first century A.D. but it did not reach Europe until the fourteenth century.

After the fall of the Roman Empire, the church dominated the social structure of the Middle Ages, diverting attention from such worldly affairs as mechanical inventions. The need for written materials produced in quantities was met by church scribes. Finally, with the coming of the Renaissance and the shift in attention from the religious to the humanistic, there was a rebirth of learning. Common people wanted to know and to be known—they wanted to read and write. Thus the stage was set for the development of printing.

The Invention of Printing

The development of printing from movable metal type is credited to Johann Gutenberg of Mainz, Germany (Figure 1-7). Printing from wood blocks had existed for many years before Gutenberg. In this process nonprinting areas were carved from a block of wood to leave words or

1-7 Johann Gutenberg (1400–1468), founder of modern printing, and the Gutenberg press, based on the wine press of the time. The lever-operated screw lowered the platen to press the paper against the type. (*Reprinted from* A New History of Stereotyping *by George A. Kubler by permission of the Certified Dry Mat Corporation*)

pictures standing in relief, to be linked and pressed on paper. It was a slow, tedious process. Gutenberg found what were, for his day, satisfactory solutions to each major problem of printing: (1) a system of movable type that allowed characters to be arranged in any order and reused as needed, (2) a method of making these pieces of type in quantity both easily and accurately, (3) a method of holding type in place for printing, (4) a system of making the type impression on paper, and (5) an ink that would provide legible impression from type to paper.

Gutenberg used brass molds to produce his pieces of type, and with their use modern printing was born. Those who followed Gutenberg had only to devote their talents to devising typeface styles or designs, faster presses, speedier composition methods, and other printing processes to meet the needs and tastes of contemporary life. Gutenberg's process, printing from a raised surface, has come to be called *letterpress.*

Printing spread rapidly across Europe from Mainz, and artisans in different countries brought about worthy improvements in typefaces as they created designs that were reflective of their backgrounds. Many of these designs are still widely used. Yet, aside from type design, the printing art remained largely unchanged until the 1880s.

Improvements in Presses

Gutenberg's printing press was a simple wooden structure, as shown in Figure 1-7. The first major change in this bed-and-platen press came in the second decade of the 1800s with the substitution of a cylinder for the platen. A revolving cylinder picked up sheets of paper, held them tight around its circumference, and carried them over a moving-type bed. The cylinder and moving bed were steam powered, which made faster press delivery possible. This development probably could not have come sooner, since before this time the making of paper was a slow, tedious hand process. The first practical papermaking machines were introduced in the early 1800s.

Meanwhile the needs of a rapidly growing nation required more and faster distribution of the written word. The real breakthrough in printing came with the rotary press. The operation principle of the rotary press was: one cylinder would hold the type in place around its circumference; as it rotated, the type would be inked; sheets of paper would be held by another rotating cylinder and pressed against the type and then released. Such presses—known as *type-revolving* presses—once were in use, but the process of securing the individual pieces of type in place on the cylinder was tedious and prevented running the presses at their full potential speeds.

Stereotyping and modern rotary presses

If the rotary principle could be retained for speed and another means of securing the type images could be found, the rotary press would be more feasible.

Stereotyping proved to be the answer. Flat stereotype plates had been in existence since the 1830s. They were made by placing a cardboardlike mat over a form of type and subjecting the mat and the type to sufficient pressure to make a mold of the form in the mat. Molten type metal was then poured over the mat. After the metal cooled, a duplicate of the type form, called a *stereotype*, was available.

A means of developing curved stereotype plates was perfected and first used in the 1860s. These plates were formed to fit around what came to be called the *plate cylinder*—counterpart to the type cylinder. In this manner, full newspaper page stereotypes could revolve at tremendous speeds, making impressions on paper as they turned. To be fully efficient, rotary presses using stereotype plates had to be improved (1) to make it possible to feed paper from a continuous roll of paper instead of sheets, and (2) to make it possible to print on both sides of the paper web (roll) at one time. Web-fed rotary presses are among the most widely used rotary presses today.

Improvements in Typesetting

The development of presses moved ahead while improvement in typesetting lagged; in fact, most type was set by hand until 1890. Earlier efforts at speeding up this production bottleneck were only modestly successful. Hand composition presented three problems: (1) time and effort to get pieces of type from storage and set them into lines; (2) the tedious problem of letter- and word spacing to fill out lines to be flush on the right; and (3) the distribution of type back to storage.

A complete solution to these problems came with the introduction of the Linotype, invented by Ottmar Mergenthaler, a German-born watchmaker working in Baltimore. The Linotype was based on a new principle—the casting of entire lines of type by injecting molten type metal into brass molds. The operator worked at a typewriterlike keyboard. As the operator activated keys, the molds, called *matrices* (plural of matrix), one for each character, fell into line, with expandable spacebands between words. When a line of mats and spacebands was nearly to the proper length, the spacebands were made to expand, and the line became full length. Then casting with the molten metal was done, after which a mechanism returned the mats to storage. Each line was new type, as contrasted to hand-set type that was used over and over—an added bonus.

Three other hot metal typecasting machines followed the Linotype. The Intertype, introduced in 1913, was similar to the Linotype in appearance and function, and like the Linotype it was a linecasting machine. The Monotype, which first appeared in 1898, got its name from the fact that it cast individual letters instead of line slugs. The Ludlow Typograph, introduced in 1909, produced larger sizes of type on a line. Mats were assembled by hand and then cast. All these hot metal typecasting machines are still in use today, but their production is secondary to that of phototypesetting.

Standardizing type measurement

It was not until about the time that the typecasting machines were being introduced that a standard measurement for type was introduced in this country. Before that, hand-set types lacked a uniform system. Type from one founder could not be mixed with that from another; spacing materials (e.g., spaces to be placed between lines of type) would vary in widths. The introduction of the point system made for uniformity of materials and facilitated the acceptance of the new machines. The point system has also been applied in the measurement of phototypesetting materials.

Reproduction of Photographs

The only picture images that were available to letterpress printers until the 1870s were woodcuts. Zincographs, metal reproductions of line drawings, later came into use, but they did not provide a means of reproducing continuous tone illustrations such as photographs or paintings. Zincographs, which afterwards became known as line engravings or linecuts, were produced by making a photographic negative of a line drawing placed in front of a camera. The negative was then exposed to a plate of zinc made light-sensitive with a chemical coating. Where the light exposed through the negative placed on the zinc struck the coating, it (the coating) hardened. The plate was then placed in an acid bath that ate away the unprotected (not light-hardened) portions of the plate, leaving the drawing standing in relief.

Zincos were faster to make than woodcuts (blocks of wood on which images stand in relief) and were sturdier and better able to take the pressure of direct printing and of stereotyping. Moreover, they gave the artist greater freedom since he could draw his image on paper instead of on a block of wood.

Ten years later halftones or halftone engravings, metal plate reproductions of continuous-tone illustrations, made their appearance. The process was similar to that of making line engravings except that a glass screen with cross-hatched lines was placed in front of the film when a negative was made of the continuous-tone art (photograph or painting). The screen broke the varying tones into tiny varying-size dots, which stood in relief after the plate was etched (placed in the acid).

Photography has played an important role in graphic communication. We have seen its application in making letterpress image carriers, photographs are one form of the two types of visual images; we have discussed the application of photography to type composition. Later we will see how it has made possible printing processes other than letterpress.

Development of Other Printing Processes

There are two other major printing processes in addition to letterpress. All three are commercial adaptations of what were originally graphic arts techniques in the fine arts field. Letterpress is an adaptation of making manifold copies from woodcuts. The other two are now considered.

Offset lithography

The word "lithography" comes from the Greek for "stone writing"; the process is an adaptation of the graphic arts technique of drawing with a grease crayon on stone. The stone is sponged with a special water-base solution, and then inked. The greasy image holds the ink; the wet stone rejects it. Paper is then placed on the stone, pressure is applied, and the image transfers to the paper. The technique was developed in 1798, but the first practical commercial application—direct lithography—came in about 1890, when a sheet of zinc replaced the stone as an image carrier. The carrier was attached to a plate cylinder. As it rotated it was wet, and then it was inked. Paper was pressed against the plate cylinder from a second cylinder called the *impression* cylinder.

Lithography picked up its more common name, *offset printing*, later. When direct presses were operating it had been noticed that occasionally a perfect image appeared on the impression cylinder when a sheet missed being fed through and then would appear with amazing clarity on the back of the next sheet through. This gave rise to the idea of a cylinder covered with a rubber blanket to receive the image from the plate and then to "offset" it onto paper. Three cylinders comprise an offset press—plate, blanket, and impression.

Gravure printing

Engraving is the graphic arts technique from which the gravure printing process evolved. Engraving originated in the fifteenth century. Goldsmiths, who incised designs in gold plates and filled in the lines with a black ornamental substance, discovered that their designs would print on paper. Thereafter, artists cut images into metal plates, usually copper, inked the plate, and then wiped it clean. When pressed to the plate, the paper drew out the inked images.

The commercial application, which occurred first in Germany, involves a rotary press with an impression cylinder and a plate cylinder that revolves in ink and is then wiped clean. The paper is pressed to the plate cylinder by the impression cylinder.

Photographic applications About the time the lithographic and gravure principles were applied to presses, photography was adapted as a means of making plates or image carriers for the two processes. Type could be treated as line black and white drawings and continuous-tone pictures could be treated as halftone material.

2 Why and How We Read: Human Information Processing

In any human communication situation the source is uncertain to some degree about the effect the message will have on the receiver of the message. Writers and designers predict what their readers' responses, if any, will be. Even the most seasoned speakers and actors frequently confess to stage fright before a performance.

Suppose you are the source of a printed message and that you have no idea about structuring the message to your readers. You know nothing about them or how they go about reading. All you know is that they are capable of x number of equally likely responses, including none at all. In such a situation you would be unable to predict your readers' reactions. But if you did predict, as the source always tries to, you would have one chance in x of being correct, since all responses would be equally likely to occur.

Fortunately, things are never that bad. You probably will know something about how to structure the message and also something about the readers. And if you feel that you do not know enough, you will seek further information. The purpose of information, therefore, is to reduce uncertainty.

As you acquire additional information, you will learn more about structuring the message and about the readers, thereby increasing the odds for correctly predicting their responses. In seeking information you learn something you did not know before.

One might assume from what has been said that the source has a more difficult task in the communication process than the reader. This is not necessarily so. As the source, you at least know what you want to say; that is, you know what meaning you want to impart—the ideas the reader is to acquire. In addition, you have at your disposal a verbal vocabulary and a vocabulary composed of visual elements. And you have a verbal and a visual syntax. By syntax we refer to the ordering of the verbal and the visual elements to show their relationships so that the intended meaning is correctly interpreted by the reader.

The reader lacks these advantages, and must figure out the meaning for himself or herself. The reader's role in the process is not passive. The responses of the reader to the vocabulary elements and the syntaxes are not automatic. In other words, the reader is engaged in a decision-making process—deciding what meanings are being signaled.

If any of the elements, visual or verbal, are foreign to the reader's experience, correct interpretation will be difficult. For example, "The effect of a properly written and properly designed printed message is synergistic" is an accurate statement. Its meaning, however, is obscure unless the reader happens to know the meanings of the words "properly written," "properly designed," and "synergistic."

The receiver suffers two additional, significant disadvantages. First, you as the source can formulate the message at your own pace. You can rework the message if you are not satisfied with the original form. The reader, on the other hand, must decide on its meaning as he or she views it and generally cannot ask for further clarification—that is, the reader cannot give you feedback. Second, the interpretation of the message involves use of the memory system. Remember, information in the message must fall within the reader's field of experience. People have a remarkable capacity to store and retrieve information; however, there are some rather restrictive limitations on the human memory system, as we shall see later.

Reading and Information _____

The more the source knows about how the receiver reads, the more effectively can the visual images be selected and arranged. Reading was previously defined as *extracting information from visual images*, and it was pointed out that pictures as well as words are read. However, what may have been an adequate definition is certainly no explanation. Reading is a complex process. Readers do not sit back and passively receive messages through their eyes. In fact, the eyes play a minor role in comprehending a message.

Only in recent years have we begun to understand the reading process. This understanding has been made possible by contributions from information theory, communications theory, psychology, and linguistics. In the following discussion of some of these contributions, no attempt is made to be comprehensive, but those facts are selected that seem essential for an understanding of what reading is all about.

Information Theory One of the major contributions toward understanding reading has come from studies of communication systems in the form of a precise definition of information. Information takes a number of different forms as it moves through a channel between the source and receiver.

For example, suppose an advertiser hands a typed out commercial message to a radio announcer who delivers it to a listener. The channel includes the commercial copy, the voice of the announcer, the microphone, the radio transmitter and the radio waves it generates, the listener's receiver and speaker, and the latter's listening apparatus. At different times the message is variously shaped letters on the copy sheet; neural impulses in the announcer's brain; sound wave patterns as the announcer speaks; electromagnetic energy of a certain frequency at the microphone; another frequency as it moves via radio waves to the receiver where it is again altered to cause the speaker to generate sound wave patterns; finally these are picked up by the listener's ear to become neural energy in the listener's brain.

Despite these changes in form, information has remained unaltered. What, then, is it? *Information is the reduction of uncertainty* in the mind of its user. This is another of those adequate definitions that requires explanation. We need to examine the concept further.

Suppose you toss a coin. Will it fall heads or tails? Obviously, there is uncertainty. How it falls will reduce the uncertainty. Perhaps it is better to say that there are two possible alternatives. Previously it was stated that the reader is engaged in decision making, which is, after all, a matter of selecting among alternatives.

The amount of information and number of alternatives are closely related. Suppose you roll a die. It can stop with any of its six sides up. You receive more information when the die stops than when the coin fell. What if you toss two coins together. There are four alternatives: HH, TT, TH, and HT. But if you toss three coins, there are eight alternatives: HHH, TTT, and so on.

By now you should sense that the relationship between the amount of information received and the number of alternatives is not direct, because:

one coin toss selects from two alternatives
two tosses select from four alternatives
three tosses select from eight alternatives

The relationship can be expressed as a measurement of information called a *bit*, which is equal to one half the alternatives at any time. Thus:

one bit resolves the uncertainty between two alternatives
two bits resolve the uncertainty among four alternatives
three bits resolve the uncertainty among eight alternatives

Can you compute how many bits are needed to resolve the uncertainty among 64 alternatives? Read no further until you have attempted an answer.

Suppose 64 cards are spread before you, numbered 1 through 64. You are to pick the one I have in mind. Consider a bit as a "Yes" or a "No" answer to any question you ask. After all, one either does or does not acquire each bit. Your most efficient approach is to start with "Is it between 33 and 64, inclusive?" If you get a "No," next ask "Is it between 17 and 32, inclusive?" And so on. You need to ask a total of six questions. You could, of course, make a "wild guess" and ask "Is it 11?" and get a "Yes." You asked a 6-bit question and got a 6-bit answer. On the other hand, if you got a "No," you might have to make as many as 62 more guesses.

Information and redundancy

Redundancy exists whenever information is available to the reader from two or more places. A message is redundant if it contains more information than it needs to. In terms of information theory, uncertainty or number of alternatives can be reduced in two or more ways. All of this implies that a shorter message could deliver the same information.

The English language in print offers an excellent example. Sequences of letters are redundant; some letters show up more frequently than others. The letters *e*, *t*, *a*, *i*, *o*, and *n* are most frequent, whereas *z* and *x* seldom appear. Does any letter other than *u* follow *q*? It has been estimated that English is more than 50 percent redundant.

What about redundancy in pictures? A major purpose of redundancy is to save readers time and difficulty in understanding what they read by increasing predictability. Tests have characterized predictable shapes in this manner:

1. They tend to be symmetrical.
2. They involve straight lines or lines changing in a regular manner.
3. They tend to involve few angles.

Studies of eye movements over photographs reinforce these conclusions. Readers of a photograph of Baja California taken by astronauts concentrated on the less regular portions of the coastline and quickly passed over the more even portions as well as the even-toned and even-textured areas of the interior.

From the graphic communicator's point of view there are practical advantages in a purposeful control of redundancy. It means that the communicator can assist the reader in comprehending the message. The communicator could, for example, say in pictures (photographs) what is said in words, as in Figure 2-1, or could show in a chart (a picture-drawing) what is said in the text. Or the communicator might also consider a trade-off of expediting quicker delivery of the message by showing an irregularly shaped photograph, with the background removed so it is not seen as a rectangle. People tend to be more attracted to irregular shapes than to rectangular ones.

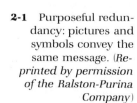

2-1 Purposeful redundancy: pictures and symbols convey the same message. (*Reprinted by permission of the Ralston-Purina Company*)

Human Information Processing _____

In the past quarter century, information theory has had a strong impact on the field of psychology. We have already discussed how the theory has made it possible to measure information. With this as a tool, psychologists have been able to discover many things about how and why we communicate with the outside world. Psychologists have incorporated their discoveries into what has been called "information processing theory." We draw on this theory in the discussions that follow.

Why We Read

Basically, we read because we have to. Humans and animals come into the world with their brains "prewired" or programmed to (1) seek out information, (2) select from the total and put into proper form what is potentially useful to make their way through life, (3) organize the information into a memory store, and (4) retrieve information from memory for use in decision making. It seems that we are destined to monitor the environment so that we can decide what is good or bad for us, what is cause and what is effect, in order to survive.

Traditionally, psychology has usually referred us to motives, primary or innate and secondary or learned, as the reasons for behavior. Information processing theory, on the other hand, considers human beings as rational, making decisions on how to respond to things and events based on the information at hand. This basic attribute is often thrown out of focus by the way in which the related terms "motives" and "emotions" are used.

A frequent criticism is often made of communicators, particularly advertising and public relations people, that they "play on people's emotions." The implication is that people are not only rational but also emotional and that the two natures are in opposition. Emotion (or motive) is often used as an explanation for behavior. Why did Smith violently attack Jones? The answer, "Out of anger," is believed to be an explanation. Treated this way the two terms take on a psychological reality that divorces them from rational or thinking (decision-making) processes. Do motives explain, or do they attach labels to behavior?

When there is an "emotional" response to a thing or an event, it is because the person involved decided on the behavior by processing the information available. Many printed messages are persuasive and make appeals to the subjective or "emotional" nature of people. In such cases, picture images are particularly effective, as opposed to words, which could throw a hard, cold light on readers' rationalizations for their behavior.

Cognitive Structure

What happens when we look at something? Light waves that may carry information strike the eyes, where the information is converted to neural energy. The information-bearing neural impulses move on to the brain, where a decision is made concerning what we are looking at. In order to decide, the brain must compare the information to something it has previously learned and stored in informational codes in memory. Would you know what lees are? Probably not, unless you had previously learned what they are.

If what is decided seems to be demanding of further information, the brain will direct the eyes to search out further information. As the new information comes in, the brain will utilize it, comparing it to information in memory in order to comprehend the situation. Or, being aware of what our current knowledge store is and what our expectations for the future are, the brain may in effect tell the eyes, "Forget it; it isn't relevant."

We speak of the eyes seeing, the ears hearing, the fingers feeling, and so on. This is not the case, however. It is the brain that sees, hears, and feels. Enclosed in total darkness and devoid of feelings of its own, the brain is a decision-making instrument that decides what we experience and learn, what our attitudes and motivations will be.

These activities of the brain are called *cognitive* processes by psychologists. Certain aspects of these processes are of especial concern to the graphic communicator. How do we learn to know what something is when we experience it—a dog or a cat, or for that matter, letters of the alphabet? Or a word, such as "animal," which covers both dogs and cats? Or any other word, which only stands for something else? What a word stands for need not be something tangible, existing in the real world. It could be a ghost, democracy, or the idea of "the" or of "_____s" attached to a singular to make it plural.

How is this knowledge, learned from our experience, organized in memory? Most of the time it seems readily accessible. If I show you a pencil and ask what it is, your answer is prompt. Your brain obviously did not have to search in a random fashion through all past experiences to find a "match-up" with what you see. Your brain was able to locate quickly what was needed because information from past experience is neatly categorized and organized in a systematic way. This organization is called *cognitive structure.*

Perceptual learning   The building of cognitive structure begins with perpetual learning, which is the process by which we (1) determine what the things and events in the world around us are and (2) organize them into our understanding of the world. The process is ongoing throughout life, which means that our understanding changes. Because the process is inherent within us, we are rarely aware that it is taking place. And yet, when we see or perceive a house, a tree, or any object at all, real or imagined, or when we recognize a friend, a decision has been made by the brain that leads to our perception.

Therefore, in terms of information theory, a perception is the reduction of uncertainty about what things and events that confront us are. However, we cannot perceive the world as it really is. Our senses are grossly inadequate. The world exists as a dynamic whirl of energy in a universe of energy; but the energy form we call light waves that

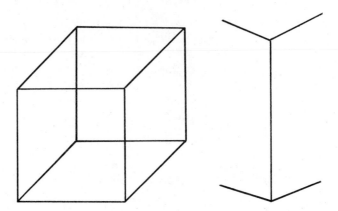

2-2 *Left:* The Necker cube. Without change in perspective, this figure has reversing depths. *Right:* What is it? An open book you are holding? Or an open book someone facing you is holding?

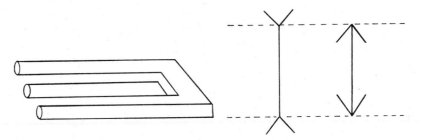

2-3 *Left:* What about the middle prong? Does it exist? This figure cannot be properly perceived. That is, the brain cannot make a decision about what the eyes see. *Right:* The vertical shafts are the same length. Do they look it? The dashed lines prove that they are.

our eyes can detect gives but little hint about what things really are. That our perceptions can only be "best guesses" about what we look at is shown in Figures 2-2 and 2-3. The several ambiguous shapes can be seen in more than one way. It is as if when we look at them, the brain "can't make up its mind."

Category formation Perceptual learning leads us to the formation of categories and discoveries of interrelationships among them. Just as no two fingerprints are exactly alike, so it is with all things and events. But in order to give structure and meaning to our experience we abstract from a thing or an event those features in which the experience resembles other things or events and group them in a category. To call something a chair is to note its similarities to other chairs and ignore any differences. These similarities are called *defining features.*

The defining features may relate to visible features such as size and shape. Consider a child learning to distinguish the letters of the alphabet. Once the patterns formed by curved and straight lines are mastered, the patterns can be stored in memory. Perception is thus necessary for recognition. The next time the child sees a certain pattern, he or she can match it against the one previously learned.

The defining features are not necessarily visual; they may be semantic. When we abstract defining features at this level we suggest interrelationships among categories. You can distinguish visually between a knife and a fork. When both the knife and fork are categorized as tableware, you know something of the interelationship and you are at a higher level of abstraction.

The semanticist S. I. Hayakawa's "abstraction ladder" offers an excellent explanation of abstraction at higher levels.[1] An increasing order of abstraction is revealed as we move from Bessie, a specific cow, through the following: Bessie — cow — livestock — farm assets — assets — wealth. We abstract from Bessie the defining features that allow us to categorize her as a cow; from the cow category we abstract those features (some visual, some semantic) that she has in common with other animals that can be called livestock, and so on.

Defining features serve as information because they reduce uncertainty; that is, they are there or they are not, just as the card previously mentioned was either between 33 and 64 inclusive or it was not.

We generally attach words to our categories, although categories may exist without words. We have no single word for the idea of "place to sit." If you needed to sit and rest during a hike in the woods, would you refuse to sit on a rock or a log because it was not labeled "chair?" On the other hand, many words, particularly the more abstract, have no reference to things in the sensory or nonmental world. In a way, a centaur or a farm asset is as real as a tree because both depend on thinking about something.

Images: concrete and abstract

As we have seen, word symbols lie along a continuum from the concrete to the highly abstract. Concrete words are those that most directly refer to things or events in the real world. The word "cow" on Hayakawa's ladder would be an example.

Pictures can also be considered to lie along a similar continuum. Photographs, especially in color, would be the most direct reference to the real world. Other types of illustrations—such as paintings and drawings—generally tend to be less direct. They are rendered in varying degrees of abstraction.

---

[1] S. I. Hayakawa, *Language in Thought and Action* (New York: Harcourt Brace Jovanovich, 1964), pp. 177 – 179.

By abstraction we mean first the enhancement of those features of a category that best identify it (make it recognizable), and second, the suppression of those features which are not generic to—that is, not basic to—comprehending it (perceiving its relationships to other categories). Photographs may, as Arnheim has said, " . . . prejudge observation by singling out accidentals as readily as essentials."[2] Figure 2-4 includes an example of an illustration which the artist has, through selective presentation of features, made more informative. Note that a degree of concreteness remains in the drawing.

2-4 The drawing in this advertisement is at a low level of abstraction. (*Courtesy Reliable Basement Waterproofing Company*)

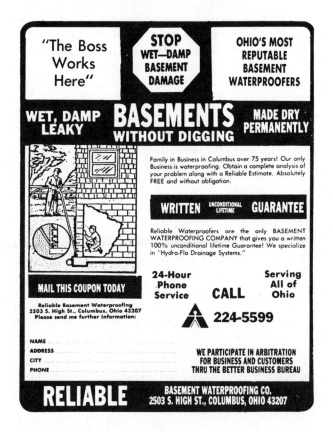

The distillation process of abstraction can be further extended, as shown in Figures 2-5 and 2-6,—the corporate symbols of the ABC Radio American Information Radio Network and of the Crown Zellerbach Corporation, respectively. Both images are far along the continuum from direct representation; but they relay information.

---

[2] Rudolf Arnheim, *Visual Thinking* (Berkeley, Cal.: University of California Press, 1969), p.175

2-5 Highly abstract drawings are far removed from being representational. They become word-like: they become symbols. (*Courtesy ABC News*)

2-6 Symbolic drawings can deliver messages about universal forces of which we are not always conscious. (*Courtesy Crown Zellerbach*)

The universe is a collection of energy—pushes and pulls that structure what we sense. When we look, we sense (perceive) more than the things or events that are shaped by these forces. We have sensations of the forces themselves, giving rise to feelings of how the things or events interact with each other and with ourselves. We are largely unaware of these and most other cognitive activities. For example, we do not conclude that when someone moves twice as far from us that that person becomes half as tall. The brain calculates the adjustment. The compositional forces that we sense are the very essence of what we see. They are instantly sensed; they account for the arousal potential of illustrations and seem to be an ingredient in esthetic interpretation.

The high degree of abstraction in Figures 2-5 and 2-6 removes most directly concrete information, leaving the visual shapes as a statement of these essential organizing forces. In Figure 2-5 the shape is composed entirely of arrows, which are themselves symbols of force direction. Note that there are white as well as black arrows. The white ones signify inflow of information; the black ones indicate the dissemination of news information.

The symbol in Figure 2-6 indicates stability through its weighty look. The company initials C and Z are delineated by the overall shape and the white lines. Finally there is the abstract suggestion of paper running through a printing press. The company is a supplier of printing paper.

The graphic communicator faces delicate choices in finding the proper level of abstractness. Will a true-to-life photograph serve best? Perhaps the subject can be highlighted and the background subdued or eliminated. Can circles or pointing devices be superimposed on the reproduction of the photograph to draw attention to defining features? Perhaps a diagram—the most abstract of illustrations—can most effectively deliver a complicated message that could only be presented verbally in a dull recitation of facts and figures.

In Figure 2-7, the words deliver a thoughtful discourse about the nutritional value of the potato and the fact that people mistakenly accuse it of being fattening. Why a painting, with its abstractness? The same situation could have been photographed. The playing down of the real aspects that a photograph would deliver removes a too direct contact with the reader concerning a touchy subject. And the "140" on the scale will not rankle the grossly overweight person while capturing the attention of those whose excess poundage is modest.

The Human IPS Three basic subsystems characterize any information-processing system (IPS)—for example, a computer. They are (1) input, (2) information processing, and (3) output. So it is with a human, who is also an IPS. Through our eyes we receive information in the form of light waves;

this is the input. Information is processed in the brain. An integral part of the processing is memory, as is also the case with a computer. And continuing the metaphor, decisions are made by comparing incoming information with stored information, followed by output, with the hoped for comprehension of the message.

The term "comprehension" refers to understanding the content or meaning of the message. Throughout the centuries people have debated the meaning of "meaning," but to little avail. So, let us define "meaning" in terms of information processing, as "the reduction of uncertainty to the point that the receiver feels satisfied that he or she understands." But, you say, we have defined the term "perception" as "the reduction of uncertainty." That is true, and in everyday language the terms are often used synonymously. Both perception and comprehension result from the cognitive processes. Perhaps this will make it

Don't blame potatoes.

How did it happen?

One day you were swell-slim-you and the next day the scales were tipping toward an unmentionable figure. And automatically you assume the culprit was that delicious baked potato you succumbed to last night.

Not likely.

Carbohydrate foods, like the potato, are necessary to maintain a well-balanced diet. And, at a surprisingly low 90 calories, a medium-size baked potato provides you with good nutritional returns. Potatoes are a good source of vitamin C (close to 1/2 the recommended daily allowance). And they also give you vitamin B₁, niacin and iron.

So, blame it on those extra midnight snacks or the jogging you were going to do, but didn't. But please, please don't blame it on potatoes.

The potato. Something good that's good for you.

2-7 A representational photograph could not have delivered this message as effectively. (*Courtesy The Potato Board*)

clear. In theory, if the source did his or her job properly and all uncertainty is reduced at the receiver end, only one "meaning" can result. Source and receiver will be of one mind. If the message should be, "The chief ordered the police to stop all gambling," what is the meaning? Each letter, each word can be perceived, but two interpretations are possible. Meaning is not in the images on paper; it is in the mind.

Information stored in memory

Before we consider information processing, we should first discuss the order and structure of previously acquired information that is stored in memory. It is important to discuss this aspect of memory, since, as you will recall, one takes in what is judged to be relevant information and matches it against that which is in memory.

Previously, we gave the barest hint of this form and structure when we said that we learn what belongs in a category and what relationships exist among categories. We now expand on this idea.

Any thing or any event has certain irreducible properties that identify it; we called these "defining features." A knife is called a "knife" and a fork is called a "fork" because of these irreducibles. However, both terms belong to another category labeled "tableware," which also has irreducible properties. Thus, an event or thing can be in more than one category or set. The term "set" is widely used as a synonym for category.

When we refer to something in terms of its position in a higher (more abstract) category or set—for example, referring to a cow as livestock—we are indicating what a cow has in common with chickens, hogs, horses, and so on. A higher set is termed a *superset* or *superordinate* category. If we refer to something in terms of its position in a lower (less abstract) category or set—for example, referring to a cow as a Jersey cow—we are indicating how this set differs from the more general or abstract "cow." A lower category or set is called a *subset* or *subordinate* category.

The structure of stored information can, therefore, be considered from the standpoint of (1) the whole formed by the relationships of subordinate components or (2) the part in relationship to the whole. For example, suppose you are asked:

1. Are canaries yellow? You would surely say yes.
2. Do canaries breathe? You may be required to search your memory and need more time to say yes. The answer is more deeply embedded in memory.

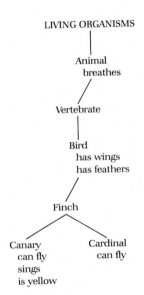

2-8 Hypothetical and partial memory network relating the canary to other living organisms. We can more efficiently process information when we organize it in hierarchical fashion—from low-level to high-level abstraction.

Figure 2-8 shows a partial memory network. To answer question 2 requires a time-consuming search to the superset "animal" where the defining feature or attribute "breathes" is found. Time tests on actual subjects have shown that search at higher levels takes more time.

Categories, together with their attendant features, seem to be stored in memory. When the printed images—words or pictures—are perceived, there is a neurophysiological reaction within the total network of knowledge. The features are thought to exist in the form of rules of description.

We can think about reading in terms of sets, subsets, and rules. The probable features of letters—straight and curved lines and angles —are abstracted at the lowest level; at a higher level they are combined, according to the rules, to be perceived. Beyond the letter level, further abstraction rules make possible word identification. Syntactic and semantic rules at a very high level of abstraction allow us to string words in higher order structures—phrases, clauses, sentences, and paragraphs to signal meanings.

Short-term memory   Our earlier discussion of the structure of previously acquired information involved storage in what theorists refer to as long-term memory or LTM. Let us turn our attention to short-term memory, STM, which also plays an important role in processing information.

Suppose you have just looked up a telephone number. Before you can dial, you are interrupted. The delay may be brief, but you have to look up the number again. Or possibly you might have forgotten the number, even though there was no apparent delay. It would seem that there is a type of short duration memory.

Short-term memory is no more a location or a place in the brain than is long-term memory. Before we proceed to look in further detail at STM and its relationship to LTM, we should make it clear that memory is a process or subsystem within the total IPS. By means of the total system we select, acquire, and retain information and utilize it in perceiving and comprehending the world in which we live. Terms such as these, together with others such as "reading" and "learning," are all aspects of the same system viewed from different angles.

As soon as information enters the IPS, an abstraction process begins. The total memory system, STM and LTM, does not reflect what impinges on the senses. Information first enters a subsystem of the STM called the Visual STM or Sensory Store, where it persists perhaps for a second or so. In this brief time, pertinent information is abstracted by the brain, making perceptual decisions.

From the Sensory Store the abstracted information moves to STM. Either at the time the information is sensed or while it is still in sensory storage, visual information is transformed into neural codes. Picture images, it is believed, are normally transformed into iconic or visual codes. Word images are transformed into either (1) an auditory or semantic code, or (2) a visual or iconic code. When words are in an auditory code, language rules—semantic, syntactic, and orthographic

—can be applied to reduce uncertainty—that is, to determine meaning.

Some situations are easier to resolve if word symbols are transformed into an iconic code, allowing the reader to image what is presented verbally. Can you answer this question: How many windows are there on the ground floor of your home? To answer, you would probably image your home, and as you moved about on the ground floor (all in imagination), you would count the windows. This would indicate that we are capable of storing visual experience. Whether visual codes are in LTM is an unresolved question. Perhaps objects and events previously seen exist in LTM in descriptive rules form (as are categorical relationships) and these rules are sent to STM to construct images for purposes of match-up with incoming information. It might be noted that both verbal and visual coded information was used in answering the previous question.

The duration of information in STM is relatively brief and the capacity of STM is limited to five to eight unrelated units—such as random letters. When we read words, the eye takes in information only at stops or fixations. Four or five meaningfully related words (perhaps 25 to 30 letters) can be seen, held in STM, and processed—that is, be interpreted to be cues for reducing uncertainty—in one second by an efficient reader. Then the eye jumps to another fixation. It is during these jumps, called *saccades*, that processing or match-up with LTM information occurs.

Thus, processing of verbal information in auditory codes proceeds serially. It is theorized, on the other hand, that pictures, transformed into visual codes, can be handled by parallel processing. One has to move one's eyes along lines of type with words falling within an area of narrow focus. Information from pictures is not limited to this narrow area. Such visual images can be more quickly recognized.

We have already established, however, that recognition is not comprehension. Printed messages are usually intended to be comprehended. Thus pictures can seldom deliver a message alone. Great care is therefore needed in their application. We earlier pointed out that pictures are an important aid in highlighting defining features and that they may be substituted for words when "emotional" appeals to the reader are involved. You may feel that words are "logical tools" and might well prefer that the emotional reasons for your response not be subjected to the cold logic of words. It might also be noted that what are termed emotional reactions are in themselves information from the autonomic nervous system; this information occupies a portion of STM and limits the space that can be utilized for comparing incoming information with LTM information.

3 Graphic Reproduction Processes and Presses

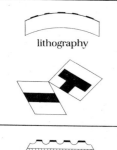

lithography

letterpress

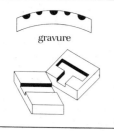

gravure

3-1 The three basic printing processes. *Offset lithography:* printing from a flat surface. *Letterpress:* printing from raised surfaces. *Gravure:* printing from depressed areas.

Modern technology has produced so many methods for getting words and illustrations into print that the selection of the most appropriate method has become one of the earliest and most difficult hurdles to be cleared on the way to effective mass communication with graphic materials.

The three most common and versatile printing methods are *offset* (photo-offset lithography), *letterpress,* and *gravure.* Other processes, such as *screen, photogelatin, flexography, thermography,* and *letterset,* are highly specialized or are variations or combinations of the three basic systems. In addition, there are what might be called *duplicating* or *copier* systems used primarily for duplicating material that has already been printed by one of the other methods.

Fundamentals of Offset

Offset is a chemical process of printing that gets images on paper by utilizing the fact that grease and water do not mix. A flat plate, usually made of aluminum, is photographically exposed and treated so the image area will receive a greasy ink and the nonimage area will receive water and repel the ink. On the press, the plate never touches the paper; the process gets its name because the ink from the plate is first offset onto a rubber surface that squeezes the ink into the paper.

Offset presses are *rotary,* that is, the type image is rotated as printing occurs. As can be seen in Figure 3-2, the plate is wrapped around one cylinder that contacts another cylinder covered with a rubberized *blanket* which, in turn, pushes the image into paper as the paper passes over an *impression* cylinder. As each impression is made, more water is applied to the nonimage area and more ink, repelled by the water on the nonimage area, is applied to the image area only.

Both sheet-fed and web-fed (from a roll rather than sheets) presses are in common use for offset.

Prepress Operations

Because platemaking and other preliminary steps in offset are *photographic*, any method of type composition can be used for offset printing. Hand lettering, pastedown letters, strike-on (typewriter) letters, phototype, proofs from metal type, or any other letter images can be pasted in position ready for photographing. Any drawings made up of lines, dots, or other patterns can be positioned and photographed along with pasteup type, or separately if necessary. Type and line illustrations are called *line copy*; photographing line copy is called making a *line shot*.

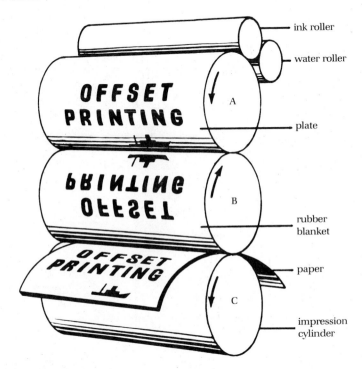

3-2 Principle of offset press operation. As plate cylinder A rotates, it is coated with water in the nonimage area and greasy ink in the image area. The ink image is transferred to the rubber blanket on cylinder B and then to the paper as the paper passes between the blanket and impression cylinder C. (*Reprinted from* Printer 1 & C, *Navy Training Courses, U.S. Government Printing Office*)

Photographs and other continuous-tone artwork (that is, originals that contain the variations in tone from light to dark) must be separately photographed to produce a dotted image in negative form.

All negatives—those resulting from photographing the pasteup plus those made from continuous-tone illustrations—are taped (stripped) onto a sheet of opaque paper called a *mask*. This assembly of negatives in position is called a *flat*. The stripper then cuts a window for each image area, and the image areas in the negatives are transferred to a plate by exposing bright light through them, a process called *burning*. Sometimes the plates are *double-burned*, triple-burned, and so on, in order to superimpose type over the illustrations

3-3   Principal steps in offset lithography.

(Reprinted from Printer 1 & C, *Navy Training Courses, U.S. Government Printing Office)*

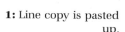

1: Line copy is pasted up.

5B: Plate is coated. (Steps 5A and 5B are eliminated when pre-sensitized plates are used.)

2: Pasteup and halftone copy are photographed separately.

6: Flat is placed over plate and plate is exposed to light (burned) through negatives.

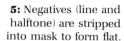

3: Negatives are developed.

7: Plate is developed.

4: Negatives are then opaqued to eliminate undesired clear spots.

8: Plate is covered with special grease-receptive lacquer that makes image areas accept ink.

5: Negatives (line and halftone) are stripped into mask to form flat.

9: Plate is put on press cylinder.

5A: Plate is cleaned.

 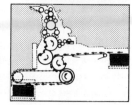

10: Paper receives ink while being fed between rubber blanket and impression cylinder.

or to obtain precise positioning. For example, when a description of a photograph is to be extremely close to the photograph, a separate flat containing the photograph may be used. The exposure of the original flat is therefore the first burn and the one for the halftone would be the double burn.

To avoid double burning, the screened negative made from a photograph sometimes is exposed on photopaper to create a screened photoprint called a *Velox;* this print can then be placed on a pasteup as if it were a drawing containing dots and lines.

For printing involving more than one color, separate pasteups, flats, and plates are required for each color. The pasteups are usually referred to as *mechanicals,* and the basic one (*key*) is done on paper or light cardboard whereas the others are done on clear acetate. Correct positioning of each color is assured with the use of *registration* marks on each mechanical (see Chapter 12).

Advantages and Uses
Offset is now the basic system of printing in the United States because it has some distinct advantages over its traditional competitors. These advantages include:

1. The ability to use all kinds of cold type methods for type composition, thus keeping cost to a minimum.
2. The ability to reproduce type clearly and distinctly. One of the ways to identify offset is to look at type under a glass; other systems produce a less precise letter image.
3. The ability to produce quality reproduction on a wider variety of paper surfaces. The squeezing action of the rubber blanket gets ink into the crevices of rough paper stock better than other processes can.
4. Cost-free reproduction of line illustrations and less costly reproduction of photographs and other continuous-tone illustrations. Because it prints from a flat surface, offset does not require acid etching of engravings for illustrations.
5. Efficient press operation; rotary presses are faster than other types, and thus, flat offset plates are ideal for rotaries. Some processes require special preparation or adaptations of type and plates in order to use rotary presses. Also, except for adjusting the ink-water balance, time-consuming makeready is avoided.
6. Easy storage of plates, flats, and mechanicals. Prepress materials for other processes are often too bulky to make storage feasible.
7. Adaptability to computerization. Cold type composition and photographic steps in production have permitted offset printers to incorporate computer assistance faster and in more production steps than some other systems.

3-4 Preparation of a book by offset lithography.

(Courtesy Vail-Ballou Press)

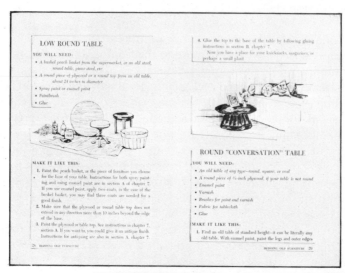

Type and line illustrations are pasted in page form, creating what are called mechanicals.

Each mechanical is placed in front of a large camera and photographed to make negatives.

Page negatives are stripped into a mask to form a flat, in this case containing 64 book pages.

The images on the negatives in the flat are transferred to an aluminum plate by beaming light through them (burning).

The developed plate carries positive-reading images of all pages in the flat.

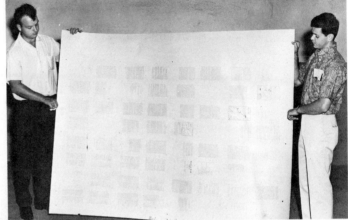

On press, the plate transfers images to the blanket cylinder, which then lays the ink on paper.

These advantages of offset have made it the most common method of producing newspapers, magazines, illustrated books, and miscellaneous brochures of all types. For students preparing for a career involving any printed medium of communication, offset is the process they should know best. As writers, editors, or graphics specialists for a newspaper or magazine, they are very likely to find that their publishers have chosen offset as the best production method for their publications. Or if their career is in advertising, public relations, or publishing organizations and their work involves the selection of printing methods, they will find that offset must be seriously considered for most of their work.

Instances in which the selection of offset would be almost certain include:

1. Short-run (under 1,000) pieces that involve type and illustrations.
2. Any number of copies that require reproduction of many photos on rough or cheap paper and good quality of reproduction is desired.
3. Any piece of printing composed mainly of drawings such as charts, diagrams, and cartoons.
4. Any moderate to medium-long run printing requiring good photo reproduction plus the size and speed of web-fed rotary presses. As runs exceed 100,000 copies, rotogravure becomes competitive; at a million copies or more, rotogravure tends to replace offset totally.

Many special factors can influence the choice of a printing process, and we can present only generalized conclusions here. In many instances printers whose expensive equipment for other processes is idle will price their work in that process below normal in order to keep their equipment from remaining idle. In some areas, a printer using what normally would be the better process may not be available. In any case, the versatility of offset requires that it be given careful consideration when any printing is being planned.

Fundamentals of Letterpress _____

Because it is the traditional system of printing, letterpress perhaps requires less explanation than other methods. A number of characteristics and ramifications of the system, however, should be noted.

It takes only a moment's thought to realize that letterpress can be defined as a direct, mechanical system of printing from raised surfaces. But the words "mechanical" and "raised" point to characteristics that are of considerable significance to anyone who is either preparing material for reproduction by letterpress or considering the system's quality and cost levels.

3-5 In letterpress printing, metal type and photoengravings must be locked into page forms for printing direct from the type and engravings.

Prepress Operations

For printing to be done directly from a raised surface, words and illustrations must, in some way, be "carved" or molded in relief in a substance sufficiently hard to withstand wear from constant applications or pressure. It should also be apparent that equality of pressure for all elements against the sheet being printed becomes a matter of necessity for a high level of quality in this process.

These two requirements point directly to five matters of importance to users of the letterpress process:

1. Traditionally, words and letters have had to be cast in metal to be reproduced.
2. Illustrations must be separately manufactured in plate form to be reproduced.
3. For fine quality of reproduction for photographs, a smooth, coated paper is required.
4. Time and skill are required in "making ready" a press form so that the pressure of each element against the paper is equal, thus giving an even application of ink.
5. Traditionally, letterpress has required the casting of curved metal plates as a duplicate of an original page of type and engravings in order to use presses with higher speeds.

Let us look at each of these items to see how they are of importance to the journalist who works with the letterpress process.

Type composition

In traditional letterpress shops, the mechanical preparation of copy starts with a skilled technician, the *compositor,* who may operate a machine, such as the Linotype, Intertype, Monotype, or Ludlow type-caster, or may even set by hand the pieces of type stored in *cases* (drawers). Type cast from molten metal is called *hot type* and its use has been fundamental to letterpress printing for centuries. Compositors of hot type have served extensive apprenticeships, are strongly unionized, and are relatively well paid. Thus, hot type composition has been a costly part of letterpress printing for many years.

Automation of hot type composition has been effected in many plants through the use of tape-driven machines; tape that is punched by a typist drives the casting machines much in the fashion of the old player piano. Perhaps of most importance, however, has been the introduction of photochemical prepress methods for rotary letterpress, thus permitting cold type composition (see the section on wrap-around plates).

Plates for illustrations

The need to have a raised surface for printing all kinds of illustrations by letterpress has also been an important factor in any comparison with other processes.

The traditional letterpress method for reproducing illustrations is to create acid-etched metal plates on which the nonprinting area is cut away in acid baths, leaving the image area in relief. Even the simplest pen-and-ink drawings require the manufacture of separate metal plates called *line* engravings; photographs or other illustrations containing continuous tonal variations require a complicated procedure of breaking the image into dots on the plate surface, plus the subsequent complicated acid etching that makes the dots stand in relief and thus be able to carry ink to the paper. These plates are called *halftone* engravings.

The special plates needed for all illustrations are one of the costly aspects of letterpress printing; they also tend to restrict somewhat the use of illustrations. Because each line drawing or photograph is a separate added cost, and because the cost for each illustration increases with the size of the illustration, there has been a tendency to use fewer and smaller illustrations than otherwise.

Procedurally, photoengravings in letterpress require working with still another production specialist, the engraver. The time allowance for the engraver's work has to be coordinated with the printer's deadlines. In some operations, notably those of newspapers, the printer also operates an engraving department, thus reducing scheduling problems.

Some electronic machines are now in use that make plastic or metal plates for letterpress illustrations without acid etching. Most of these machines employ the principle of an electric eye scanning the illustration and sending electronic impulses to a hot needle that etches dots or lines on the plate surface. Some of the restrictions in size and number of illustrations tend to be reduced in situations where these machines are installed; the cost of their operation tends to be fixed, thus making the unit cost less with added use.

Paper requirements The relief characteristic of letterpress printing necessitates the use of extremely smooth paper in order to get good reproduction of photographs. For high fidelity in reproduction, the dots in a halftone engraving must be extremely small; these tiny raised dots are lost or smudged in the hills and valleys of the coarse surface of cheaper papers. Consequently, the hard, smooth finish of more expensive papers must be provided for fine photographic reproduction. When coarse papers must be used because of cost, the engravings are made so that their dot structure is much larger, with a resultant loss of quality. Many magazines offer excellent examples of the beautiful reproduction of photos that can be achieved in letterpress printing on smooth papers; newspapers, because they are printed on the cheapest kind of paper, offer examples of poorer picture quality.

Importance of makeready in letterpress printing Theoretically, type set for letterpress printing is *exactly* 0.918 inches high, and all plates are mounted at *exactly* the same height. Perfect impressions depend on this exactness. But perfection, of course, is seldom attainable. Compensating for the imperfections in type and plate height, as well as other factors affecting pressure, is accomplished through a procedure called *makeready*. Makeready is vital to letterpress printing because it establishes the level of reproduction quality. Fine presswork can be obtained only by carefully adding tissue paper under low areas and by cutting away packing where impressions are too heavy. This work on the press cylinder is time-consuming and costly, but it makes possible the finest kind of printing. Other printing systems that do not rely on a raised surface for putting ink on paper do not require a makeready operation.

Special Requirements of Rotary Letterpress Letterpress presses can be either *platen, cylinder,* or *rotary*. The fastest of printing presses is the rotary press, which is so designated because the plates and/or type rotate on a cylinder as they carry ink to the paper.

Stereotyping Until recently the only way to use the rotary principle in letterpress was first to put the type and plates together in a flat form, and then duplicate that form on the surface of a curved plate that would fit around a plate cylinder. This was usually done through *stereotyping*, a method of duplicating that uses a papier-mâché or fiber board mat to

3-6 The three basic kinds of printing presses.

(Reprinted from Production in Advertising and the Graphic Arts by David Hymes, by permission of Holt, Rinehart and Winston)

Platen press. Printing surface (form) must be raised.

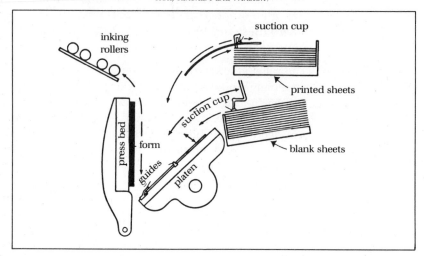

Cylinder press. Printing surface (form) must be raised.

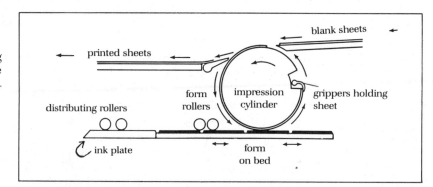

Rotary press. Printing surface (plate or plates) may be raised, flat, or gravure.

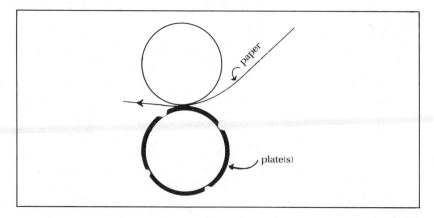

serve as a mold for a casting in molten lead. In stereotyping, the mat is placed over the page form and subjected to great pressure, forcing the relief areas of the form to be depressed in the mat. When molten lead was put on the mat in a cylinder-casting box, the lead would contain, in cylindrical form, the relief printing image of the original form. Stereotyping made modern newspaper production possible; the speed with which modern metropolitan newspapers are printed would not be possible if printing had to be done fron a flat form.

Wraparound plates

The necessity of stereotyping, although it has been a boon to newspaper printing for decades, has been somewhat of a hindrance to letterpress printing in competition with other processes. Some loss of quality that occurs during the duplicating process, plus the need to maintain a stereotyping department, have served as disadvantages. However, new techniques to permit rotary printing by letterpress without stereotyping have become available in recent years. The most significant of these techniques are those that permit the use of cold type as well as eliminate the need for stereotyping. In these systems, page pasteups are photographed and the negatives thus created are used to expose the printing image on a single thin, flat sheet of magnesium or other metal, or plastic. The metal or plastic sheet is then shallow etched to create a relief image. This lightweight, pliable plate can then be wrapped around a "saddle" and used on the printing cylinder of a rotary press.

One of the more spectacular systems for making these plates involves the use of laser beams. The Gannett Company, the publisher of a large chain of newspapers, announced in 1973 that it had successfully tested such a system. According to Gannett, its system successfully passed field tests under normal operating conditions. A series of multiple laser beams, directly from photocomposed pasteups, produced lightweight, combination metal and plastic plates at the rate of one every two minutes and performed satisfactorily in runs of up to 200,000 impressions.[1]

Platemaking systems such as these seemed to be an indicator that many newspapers would continue to be produced on letterpress presses much longer than had been forecast by many experts in the 1970s. Not only do they enable the use of the latest photocomposing systems, but they permit the owner of expensive rotary presses to forgo purchasing offset presses.

Advantages and Uses

One of the primary advantages of letterpress printing is that it is the traditional method of printing in this country. Since its invention by

---

[1] "Gannett Confirms Testing of Laser-Plate," *Graphic Communications Weekly*, October 9, 1973, p. 3.

3-7 Principal steps in stereotyping for rotary letterpress printing.

Metal type and engravings are locked in page form.

Stereotype matrix is pressed against the page form.

Flexible mat that has been pressed forms a mold for casting.

Curved printing plate being removed from casting machine.

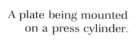

A plate being mounted on a press cylinder.

Gutenberg in the fifteenth century, letterpress has served as a primary system for mass production of words and pictures. Consequently, presses and prepress equipment for letterpress can be found in most print shops and many publication production departments. The heavy investment in this equipment has slowed the move to discard it, and in some places no other printing method is available.

Throughout its history, letterpress has demonstrated its capability to produce excellent quality work in black and white or in color on flatbed cylinder presses that can be adjusted and made ready to suit the quality demands of the most fastidious user of printing. Letterpress also retains an advantage in the production of type-only periodicals with moderate press runs. Once hot type is produced on linecasting machines, the type can be put in a page form and then on a press without further reproduction steps. Offset and other processes require that their cold type be photographed, stripped into a mask, and then exposed on a plate before printing.

The necessity for making acid-etched engravings for all illustrations used with hot type remains a disadvantage in comparison with offset, but in publications work, particularly, the disadvantages associated with hot type composition are steadily being eliminated. Many newspapers, for example, though they have converted entirely to cold type and related prepress preparation, have been able to retain their expensive rotary letterpresses by making raised-image plates for them by photochemical methods.

Although many observers and prognosticators in the printing industry have concluded that letterpress is suffering from a terminal illness and that its demise will occur shortly, such predictions are still premature. The elimination of hot type composition is well on its way (linecasting machines are no longer being manufactured in the United States), but that should not be confused with an elimination of the printing process. Printing from a raised image remains a viable system of printing that must be understood by those planning careers involving the preparation of printed material.

Fundamentals of Gravure

The terms *gravure* and *intaglio* are used to describe the printing process in which images are transferred to paper from ink-filled depressions in a surface rather than from inked lines in relief or material on a flat surface.

A typical application of the process in its simplest form is the engraving of calling cards or formal invitations. The lines to be printed are cut into the surface of a plate. The plate is coated with ink and then wiped clean, leaving ink only in the depressed areas. When paper

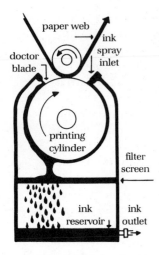

3-8 Principle of rotogravure press operation.

is pressed against the plate, it picks the ink out of the depressed areas, thus coating the image in relief on the paper.

The simple engraved invitation can, however, be considered only a distant relative of the fine reproductions of photographs and works of art that can be achieved by gravure printing. These are the result of adding photography and rotary web-fed press operation to the process, thus creating *rotogravure*.

High-speed rotogravure presses work on the same principle as the one with simple engravings. Basically, it is a matter of filling wells with ink, scraping the excess ink from the surface, and applying paper to plate with pressure (Figure 3-8).

The rotary press prints directly from an acid-etched copper cylinder using a watery, fast-drying ink. As the cylinder revolves, it goes through an ink bath and is then scraped clean by a steel knife called a *doctor blade*, thus leaving ink only in the wells of the image area. The ink is sucked into the paper surface when the paper is brought into contact with the plate.

Prepress Operations

All prepress operations that relate to copy preparation are the same for gravure as for offset. Cold type composition is pasted up to form mechanicals that are photographed. Separate continuous tone originals are also photographed, but without a screen and with low-contrast film as compared with high-contrast film used for the mechanical.

Gravure's unique capability in the reproduction of photographs stems from the different use of a screen for getting tonal gradations in these reproductions. The screen itself is different; instead of being made up of intersecting opaque lines on film, it is formed of intersecting clear lines. The use of this screen is also different.

First, the screen is placed over a sensitized gelatin transfer sheet, called a *carbon tissue*, that is big enough to cover a full printing cylinder, and light is exposed through it. The gelatin on the sheet is thus hardened in the screen pattern, because the lines forming the screen are clear. Next, a film positive of the image area is placed over the cylinder and light is exposed through it. Areas that are to carry full ink (type, for example) thus get no light through the film positive, leaving the gelatin coating soft except for the lines created by the screen. Nonimage areas get total exposure to light and total hardening of the gelatin; middletone areas would get medium exposure and medium hardening, and so on. Finally, the gelatin coating will determine the amount of ink the cylinder will apply. When acid is applied to the cylinder surface, it creates depressed areas of varying depths: in nonimage areas no depression is formed, type areas are depressed to full depth, middle tones are depressed to middle depth, and so on. When

3-9 Preparation of cylinders for rotogravure.

Laying down carbon tissue on a copper-plated cylinder.

In foreground, a cylinder is painted with asphalt in areas not covered by carbon tissue, so acid will not etch in those areas. In background, a cylinder ready for etching.

Etching a cylinder. Etching depths range from 5 microns for light tones to 35 microns for dark tones.

ink is applied, it is carried to the paper in varying amounts according to the depth of the etching.

Advantages and Uses

The picture sections of Sunday newspapers, mail-order catalogs, magazines, reproductions of paintings, and a great variety of product containers and wrappings are among the items printed by the gravure process. The chief asset of the process, reproducing highly faithful copies of photographs and paintings (both monotone and color), is possible because the thin ink in the wells of the plate spreads enough during printing to virtually eliminate any screen or dot pattern. In addition, variations in tone result from the thickness of the ink deposit instead of from a dot pattern, and photographs are reproduced with a special quality that cannot be otherwise achieved.

Type reproduction by photogravure is another matter. Type matter and illustrations are transferred together through a prescreened carbon tissue to the plate. Type matter is therefore screened. Because of this and the watery consistency of gravure inks, the text material of a gravure job is less sharp than it would be if prepared by other systems. One of the means of discovering whether or not a piece has been printed by gravure is to check the fuzziness of the type matter.

The use of gravure in commercial printing has expanded with the call for more printing on materials such as cellophane, new plastic films, and foil. New composition methods, a boon for offset, have also aided gravure. Expected improvements in platemaking also promise much for the future of gravure. One of these improvements is electronic engraving, which skips the chemical etching step in platemaking. The process, developed in Germany, is coming into increasing use in Europe and the United States. This system involves scanning of color separation prints and electronic activation of a diamond stylus that mechanically engraves the copper plate. *Inland Printer/American Lithographer* predicted in 1973 that the 10 percent share of the country's printing business then held by gravure would increase to 20 percent by 1983.[2]

Recent trends have indicated that *Inland Printer's* estimate could have been even more optimistic, especially in the magazine field. In the late 1970s several magazine giants announced either total or partial conversions to gravure, including *Reader's Digest, National Geographic, McCall's, Redbook, Ladies' Home Journal,* and the reborn *Life.* Although most of the changeovers to gravure were at the expense of letterpress, some of the work had previously been done by web offset. In all cases, the press runs were in the millions.

---

[2] "Printing, Where Have We Been, Where Are We Going," *Inland Printer/American Lithographer,* October, 1973, p. 33.

In summary, rotogravure is best suited for high-quality reproduction of photographs, in large press runs (minimum of 100,000), with the advantages becoming most pronounced when press runs reach a million copies. The high cost of plating and etching cylinders makes short runs uneconomical, and the fuzziness of type reproduction caused by the prescreening of cylinders reduces its effectiveness for type-only uses.

Fundamentals of Screen Printing

Screen printing, which is based on a principle completely different from the three most common printing methods thus far discussed, is simple but highly specialized in its uses.

The only equipment needed for the most elementary kind of screen printing is a wooden frame, some silk or other stencil material, a material to block the pores in the stencil material, a squeegee, and paint or ink. The silk, which is stretched tightly over the bottom of the frame and fastened to the frame, constitutes the printing form. A solid area is printed by pushing ink through the screen onto the paper. To form a nonimage area, it is necessary only to block the pores of the

3-10 Principal steps in screen printing. Stencil is cut by hand or produced photographically. Stencil is fixed to underside of stretched fabric and backing sheet is peeled off. Squeegee forces ink through stencil to paper underneath. (*Courtesy Masta Display, Inc.*)

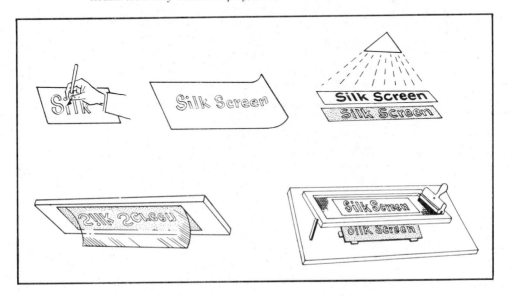

screen. With an image area and nonimage area created in the screen, printing is accomplished by pushing thick ink or paint with a squeegee from one end of the frame to the other.

Prepress Operations

The most common method of preparing screens involves the use of transparent paper that has been bonded by a film of lacquer. This paper can be used as a tracing medium by placing it over the material to be reproduced. A cutter then traces the outline of the material with a knife, cutting and stripping the paper from the image area. The sheet is then bonded with a solvent to the screen and the backing paper is pulled away, leaving the lacquer film to plug the screen in all nonprinting areas.

Some stencils, however, are prepared by hand painting with a brush, by photographic development, and with lithographic crayons. The first is especially suited for stipple and drybrush effects and requires a great skill from the painter. The second creates photographic reproductions that resemble an artist's drawings for self-expression; stencils so prepared result in beautiful work but are not suited for long, commercially feasible runs.

Advantages and Uses

Posters, displays, and fine art reproductions are perhaps the best-known uses of the silk-screen process, but it serves many other purposes. Because virtually any surface of any thickness may be printed on by this process (bottles, decalcomanias, machinery dials, wallpaper, and fabrics, to name a few), silk screen is considered whenever a printing job presents difficult problems with other processes.

The process has decided limitations. Although halftones can be reproduced by silk screen, the other processes offer much better results. One of the basic advantages of silk screen is that heavy opaque layers of ink can be laid down. This, however, produces a disadvantage because drying becomes difficult. The overall slowness of production is still one of the process's drawbacks, but it is being overcome through recent improvements. New heavy presses have capacities up to 6,000 impressions per hour, and supplementary equipment will feed this production automatically into wicket, jet-air, or oven-kiln dryers that greatly reduce drying time.

Silk screen printing is growing rapidly, especially in the packaging field, and owes its increasing use to its versatility. So-called impossible printing jobs often become completed screen-process jobs.

Photogelatin Printing (Collotype)

Although photogelatin printing differs from photo-offset lithography because it does not require a screen for the reproduction of halftones and is a direct process, it is similar in that it is photographic, chemical, and planographic.

Prepress Operations

Except for the omission of the screen as continuous-tone negatives are made, the first steps of photogelatin production are the same as those of photo-offset lithography.

Line work and photographs are handled separately and then stripped into position in a mask. After any needed retouching or opaquing is completed, the mask is placed over the plate in a vacuum frame and light is directed through the negatives. Plates used in this process are coated with a thin film of light-sensitive gelatin. As the light goes through the negatives and strikes the plate, the gelatin coating undergoes a chemical change that makes it moisture-repellent according to the amount of light received. It is this characteristic that makes photogelatin unique.

Instead of achieving variations of tones by a dot pattern or by the depth of ink receptacles, photogelatin get its tonal range according to how much water the plate repels. In clear areas (not light-struck) the plates take a full coating of water that completely repels the thick ink. In areas struck by full light, all water is repelled and all ink received. Exact reproduction of the tones between these extremes is obtained as varying amounts of ink adhere to varying exposures on the plate.

Advantages and Uses

Photogelatin printing is equal to or better than any of the other processes for the exact reproduction of photographs, paintings, and the like. Because it is a screenless process, it can produce true duplicates of the original. This is especially apparent, for example, in copies of old documents made by photogelatin—every flaw or symptom of age is faithfully reproduced. Photographs duplicated by photogelatin and glossed with varnish cannot be told from the original and can be used as original copy for the other printing processes.

Advertisers who want to show their products in the very finest detail consider the photogelatin process. Book publishers who want especially good reproduction of illustrations in a quality book turn to it. Some catalogues and sales or public relations presentations are also done by this process. Photogelatin becomes an alternative to other printing methods whenever faithful reproduction of photographs or works of art is essential. Its use is restricted mainly because it is slow and because plates cannot be carried over from one day to another, thus limiting the number of impressions. The cost involved in making a new plate daily for a long press run tends to make other systems cheaper for large jobs; with other printing systems the cost per copy goes down substantially as the number of copies increases.

Most photogelatin presses in the United States accommodate large plates (40 by 60 inches), but they produce only about 800 impressions an hour. Although the rate of turning out small printed pieces can be increased by putting several pieces on one plate, the photogelatin process is still slower than other systems.

Fundamentals of Flexography

Flexography is in actuality a form of letterpress printing. Flexible rubber plates with the printing image in relief are taped or strapped to a printing cylinder of a web-fed rotary press. Called *aniline* printing in its earlier days, flexography differs from letterpress because it uses special fast-drying aniline-based inks and the rubber plates.

Prepress Operations
The rubber plates used in flexography are made from molds of letterpress plates; therefore, copy preparation for prepress operations is exactly the same as for letterpress printing.

Advantages and Uses
Flexography is used extensively for packaging because it can lay down large areas of solid color fast and efficiently. Milk containers, cardboard boxes, gift wraps, and brown bags are very common examples of articles prepared by flexography, but flexography is also used for a wide variety of printing on foil, plastic films, and tissue paper.

Photographs can be reproduced much better by flexography than by the screen process, but flexography is not a competitor with the three basic processes for fine quality reproduction of photographs.

Fundamentals of Letterset (Dry Offset)

The printing method known as either *letterset* or *dry offset* would probably be best described as offset letterpress because it is a combination of those two basic processes. Shallow letterpress plates deposit their image on a blanket cylinder and printing occurs from the blanket. It is offset printing without water and letterpress printing that incorporates the indirect printing principle of offset.

Advantages and Uses
Although the greatest commercial use of letterset is in packaging, it is also used by some newspapers and has the same potential uses of the two processes it combines. Letterset has the advantage of avoiding dampening problems that can hamper offset while retaining the advantages that come from planographic printing.

Fundamentals of Thermography————————

Also a combination of methods, thermography starts with copies printed by offset or letterpress, but with special nondrying inks, and adds a powder to the image area. When the powder is fused to the ink by heating it, the image on the paper is in relief, just as it is with traditional engraved printing.

Advantages and Uses

Thermography is a less expensive substitute for copper and steel engraving; it is used for printing stationery and formal invitations—whenever the impression of genuine engraving is desired or special raised images are the aim.

Computerized Imaging Systems: Jet and Electrostatic Printing————————

Most current efforts to improve printing systems are being directed toward the development of totally computerized systems, systems that would start with the digital information in a computer and end with a printed image, skipping all traditional typesetting and page composition steps.

As pointed out elsewhere in this text, the digitizing and storing of all information used in printing is possible, including the graphic elements such as photos and drawings. It is also possible to position those elements on pages through the computer. In other words, all prepress functions are within the capability of the computer; the "front-end" operations in printing have all been perfected.

Presses, however, are still huge, cumbersome, noisy, inefficient, and expensive. It is no wonder that the American Newspaper Publishers Association and other interested parties are devoting much of their resources and time to the development of new imaging systems. Most encouraging of these experimental systems are *jet* and *electrostatic* printing.

Fundamentals of Jet Printing

Fundamentally, in jet printing the digitized information in a computer is used to direct ink through minute nozzles to form alphanumeric or dot patterns as they spray an image on paper. Neither large rotating cylinders nor pressure is needed to form the printed impressions, just a web of paper rolling under a jet or jets.

One of the jet printing systems that has received considerable attention has been the A. B. Dick Videojet system. It uses only a single nozzle guided by a computer so it oscillates over the paper to deposit ink, much as the electron gun produces an image on a cathode-ray or television screen. Another system, the Dijit Printer, uses a full bank of nozzles to form tiny jets of ink into necessary images by way of computer programming.

Advantages and Uses

The advantages of pressureless printing are immense and obvious. Printing on delicate breakable surfaces that cannot be printed on by traditional systems becomes feasible, the wear of plates pounding against paper and impression cylinders is eliminated, and prepress operations are totally automated.

In its current experimental stage, jet printing has been used for printing on containers and packaging materials and for addressing the millions of federal income tax forms as they emerge from a web press running at 700 feet per minute. Some typewriters using the jet principle have been introduced. The forecasts for a wide variety of uses of jet printing including the printing of newspapers and other publications are optimistic.

A linkage of jet printing with facsimile transmission may make this current optimism seem pale when compared with future reality. In newspaper and magazine publishing, for example, this might be the ultimate solution to pressroom and distribution problems. With all text and graphics gathered and arranged in page form in metropolitan editorial offices, pages could be sent by facsimile to one or several computerized jet printing facilities where the required number of copies could be printed as close as possible to their ultimate destination. Or for book publishing, consider this solution to the problems of determining print orders, storing of copies, and periodic updating. Authors could compose their work on any computer input device (a typewriter that writes on magnetic tape or perforates paper tape, for example). The work, after being fed into a computer, could be drawn out and edited to the publisher's satisfaction and returned to the computer in page form. Orders for the books could be directed, not to the publisher, but to any satellite jet printing plant located near a bookstore or near the customer. The printer could then call the computer and, in return, receive facsimile page transmission in sequence; these pages would automatically emerge ready for binding and distribution locally. Only those books sold would be printed; warehouse storage and remainders (unsold books) would no longer exist.

Fundamentals of Electrostatic Printing

Electrostatic printing relies on the attraction of positive and negative electrical charges to each other to achieve printing: a powder with one type of charge is attracted to an image area with the opposite charge.

One such system developed by Electroprint Corporation resembles jet printing to a great extent. With holes in a bar that are controlled by a computer, charges are transferred according to a program through holes into a cloud of ink, causing ink droplets to be deposited on the paper.

Another system developed by the Stanford Research Institute involves the use of a screen stencil through which powder is applied to the printing surface via electrostatic attraction. This system, therefore, resembles screen printing, but, instead of a squeegee forcing ink through the screen, an electrostatic charge is used to suck the powdered ink (toner) to the printing surface.

In yet another system, a laser beam directed by a computer produces a charged pattern on a plate or drum that will then pick up toner and transfer it to paper. The images on the plate or drum can be quickly erased and replaced by others. This system, like jet printing, has the capability for being the basis of a totally computerized image system, but it is still in the experimental stage.

Advantages and Uses

These electrostatic systems have the same advantages of other computer-controlled, impressionless systems. They have been used in computer printout machines to get super-high speeds as compared with strike-on machines, to print on such exotic surfaces as pills, eggs, and fruits and to serve as the basis for office copiers.

Duplicating and Copying Systems ⸺⸺⸺

Although they do not have the glamour of some of the major printing systems, smaller duplicating systems and devices are valuable tools for all kinds of communicators.

So-called "quick print" establishments, company reproduction centers, and graphics service centers keep the communication lifeblood circulating through corporate organizations, educational institutions, and government agencies, as well as serving media needs.

Used in its broad sense, printing as a term cannot be restricted to large commercial systems. A photographer who enters a darkroom and emerges with glossy photographs in hand has just completed a "printing" process, and the term is accurately used in that sense. A secretary who enters a duplicating room to "run off" 100 copies of an interdepartmental memo or to "copy" a typed letter a dozen times on a copying machine is also engaging in printing.

Most spectacular of the duplicating methods is a combination of electrostatic and offset systems that creates a totally automated duplicating system. Original copy—anything from a simple letter to photocomposed mechanical—is fed into the machine. An offset plate (usually a *paper master* rather than a metal plate) is created electrostatically. The image area formed by toner is grease (ink) receptive and the nonimage area is not. Paper is fed automatically and counted automatically, and when a run is completed, the plate is removed and a new one is automatically made and fastened in place. Most of these machines print directly from the master, thereby avoiding the necessity of cleaning a blanket after each run.

These totally automated "quick printing" systems became possible because of two developments in the 1960s: perfection of a direct-image paper plate by Kodak and a camera by Itek. Kodak's "project-a-lith" paper and Itek's camera eliminated the need for all the intermediate steps of negative, stripping, and burning a metal plate. Other companies have since produced competing materials and machines, and "quick-print" shops seem to be everywhere.

Even more common, however, are office copiers such as the Xerox copiers. A routine type of office copier usually functions by electrostatic attraction: nonimage areas on a drum or plate are formed when exposure to light cancels an electromagnetic charge, whereas image areas retain the charge and will pick up toner. The toner, in turn, is applied to the paper by electromagnetic charge. Some copiers require special paper, others do not; some can enlarge and reduce, copy colors, and put images on both sides of paper. For copying images already in print (e.g., pages of books or incoming letters) such copiers are indispensable.

In many cases, however, less sophisticated duplicating systems can do the job at much lower cost. Two such systems are *mimeographing* and *spirit duplicating*. Mimeographing uses a stencil just as screen printing does, but the stencils are wax coated and receive an image via a typewriter or by hand with a drawing instrument called a *stylus*. A spirit duplicator uses a typed or drawn master that picks up a resin-carbon substance from a backing sheet. A liquid spirit (like alcohol) is used to moisten the paper before it makes contact with the master, and the liquid causes the paper to pick off enough of the resin-carbon to form the image. For limited numbers of memos, instruction sheets, and many other forms of intraorganizational communications, these systems are effective. Assuming that the original copy must be typed or drawn, this can be done easily on a duplicator stencil or master at very low cost—usually at a lower cost per copy than with office copiers, especially if special paper must be used for the copier.

Getting the Job Done: In Office or at the Printer

Selection of the process to be used is one of the first steps in getting a printing job done. Other early steps are planning, scheduling, and selecting a printer. Planning involves selecting a *format* (size, shape, and style) for the *medium* (newspaper, bulletin, magazine, booklet, advertisement, and the like.), determining strategy, and executing that strategy through words and illustrations. Scheduling involves deadlines for all steps involved: writing, editing, typesetting, photographs, layouts, and the like). All of these steps are important and present complicated choices. None is more important, however, than the selection of a production partner, the printer.

Sometimes that choice of the printer is not difficult—the printer and the user may be one and the same. Computerized typesetting, electronic data transmission, and automated duplicating systems have revolutionized printing so that, in many cases, all of it can be done "in house," meaning within the editorial operation. This is especially true when the output of automated duplicating systems is adequate for the needs of the publisher. In most cases, however, there is a division of labor with editorial staffs responsible for all steps up to the preparation of mechanicals and the printer responsible for *photomechanics* (making negatives and plates from the mechanicals) and presswork, folding, binding, and any other finishing step that might be required.

Regardless of circumstances surrounding any particular situation, it is essential that the responsibilities for all parties concerned be firmly established. This understanding is usually best accomplished through the use of *specifications* and a *contract* based on the specifications, or an agreement based on common understanding.

In dealing with outside printers, for example, it is impossible to compare prices without extremely definite and complete specifications that form a basis for a binding contract. With inside printers, a mutual understanding of responsibilities without the formalities of a contract can be accomplished.

Checklist: Printer's Specifications

Specifications (called *specs*) must include every aspect of production, and their compilation actually serves as a review of the steps involved in the reproduction of words and pictures. These steps are

1. Format
    a. What will be the size and shape of the final product?
    b. What is the "type page size" (the dimensions of the page within margins)?
    c. What column arrangement is planned?
2. Type composition
    a. Who will set the type?

     b. What type sizes and designs will be used?

3. Number of copies

     a. How many copies are needed? Allowance should be made for the printing trade practice allowing a printer to deliver plus or minus 10 percent of copies ordered.

4. Number of pages, if appropriate. Is there a separate cover?

5. Frequency of issue, if applicable.

6. Papers

     a. What color, finish, and weight are desired?

7. Number of photographs or approximate percentage of surface expected to be occupied by photographs.

8. Page layout

     a. Who will prepare the mechanicals?

     b. Will mechanicals include screened photoprints (Veloxes) or must photographs be stripped into flats separately?

9. How many colors are to be used?

     a. Will full color (four-color process) separations be required? If so, how many and what size?

     b. How many pages will be in color?

10. Finishing operations

     a. How is the final product to be folded?

     b. What kind of binding is required?

11. Delivery or distribution

     a. Is printer to handle mailing or other distribution? If not, what delivery arrangements are required?

12. Proofs

     a. Proofs of all type should be provided for correction and approval when it is first set.

     b. Proofs of all pages should be provided so that placement of items can be corrected and approved before plates are put on the press.

     c. Are press proofs required?

Quality and Service

Detailed specifications can insure mutual understanding between printer and publisher, but they cannot ensure satisfactory quality and service. Careful investigation of a printer's record for quality and experience in producing the kind of material desired is essential. Selection of the best process and printer, if matched by effective content and graphic design, will result in effective communication in print.

4 Type and Typesetting

PHAN

4-1 Space between letters and in the counters (enclosed or encompassed areas of letters) can be printed, and the word is still recognizable.

Type

4-2 *Above:* Normal metal type spacing. *Below:* In phototypesetting, the *y* can be nestled under the arm of the *T* and intraletter spacing made to appear more even.

Type

Pictures are important in graphic communication, but it is primarily by means of words that the reader's thinking processes are guided to what is hoped will be comprehension of a message that matches the intention of the source. However, perception or recognition of words must precede comprehension. The reader's primary concern with words is with the information that they convey. And, although the reader may be unaware of it, the visual patterns formed by the black lines—curved and straight—and angles that comprise the characters influence his or her thinking. As already noted much perceptual thinking proceeds without our being aware of it. For example, when you see someone at a distance, is that person really less tall than when he or she is up close? Is the grass in the shade of a tree actually darker than that just beyond?

To the designer type is more than black marks on paper. These marks break the white of the paper into various shapes as shown in Figure 4-1. Thus the spaces between letters, words, and lines of type contribute to type recognition. In addition, when a large number of words are composed, in total they form shapes of texture and tone which, when incorporated into a layout, interact with other elements.

To utilize such subtleties to the greatest advantage, it becomes important that the designer have a knowledge of typefaces, the mechanics of composition, and the terminology involved in typography. This chapter involves a discussion of these matters.

As previously noted, phototypesetting is the most widely used composition method today, and it has been warmly welcomed by the designer and the typographer for a number of reasons. From a design standpoint, phototypesetting allows greater freedom of spacing. From the time of Gutenberg until the advent of phototypesetting, letterforms were locked into the constrictions of rigid metal. Extra space could be placed between letters and words or between lines of type, but there was no way to remove this space. Note in Figure 4-2 the normal spacing of the word "Type" as compared to the spacing accomplished by phototypesetting. Because the latter allows greater freedom in placing exposure of characters, the Renaissance set of symbols can be set aside.

Other benefits are inherent in phototypesetting. First, the typeface is sharper and more defined. The pressure of inked metal type on paper tends to cause irregularities on the edges of the characters.

Second, it is faster. For example, the use of VDTs (see Chapters 7 and 8 for further discussion) eliminates the need for typewriters and double keyboarding (first by the writer and second by the hot metal typecasting machine operator). In addition, phototypesetting machines operate at speeds many times that of metal machines. Finally, since photocomposition can be done on film as well as on paper, the film can be taken directly to the photomechanical to be combined with other components of the job prior to making the printing plates.

Typesetting Terminology

This section introduces the reader to the terminology involved in getting words into print. The terms for the most part cover both phototypesetting and the traditional metal typesetting; there are some exceptions and they are noted.

Typeface Terminology

"Typeface" refers to the visual symbol seen on the printed page. These symbols collectively are called *characters,* and they include letters, numerals, punctuation marks, and other assorted symbols such as dollar signs, cents signs, ampersands (&), fractions, and so on.

Capital letters are called *uppercase;* small letters are called *lowercase.* They are generally abbreviated to be *u.c.* or *caps* or *c* and *l.c.,* respectively. Normally text is composed as *c/lc* (*caps/lc*) or *u/lc.*

4-3 Type terms.

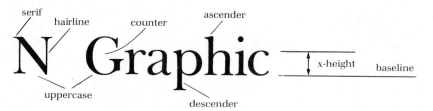

4-4 Not all typefaces have serifs and thick and thin strokes. This face is called *sans serif.*

Other terms refer to the "look" of characters in print:

x-height: The depth of lowercase center body letters such as *a, r, i, c,*
      and so on; actually based on the letter *x.*
ascender: The part of lowercase letters extending above the x-height.
descender: The part of lowercase letters extending below the x-height.
baseline: The line on which center body and capital letters rest.
counter: White space within a letter.
hairline: The thin stroke of a letter.
serif: The finishing stroke at the end of a main stroke of a letter.

Figure 4-3 shows a word and a letter with these terms identified.
Figure 4-4 shows a different typeface—one of the many typefaces that
do not have serifs and thick and thin (hairline) strokes.

Typeface Classification

For some time after the invention of printing, printers found one style
of typeface in one size sufficient for their purposes. With the passing of
time came an ever increasing demand for additional designs and sizes
to add variety to printed materials. As the expanding craft spread
across Europe, design changes reflecting the different cultures were
effected by a sort of natural evolution.

In Italy, for example, letterforms were designed and cast that resembled the graceful characters in manuscripts prepared by Italian
scribes. The basic Roman form has undergone so many mutations that
today there are literally hundreds of Roman style faces that have been
subtly individualized. The type face in Figure 4-3 falls within the category or set of Roman letterforms.

Other sets are composed of individualized letterforms. The face in
Figure 4-4 is an example. Literally thousands of faces are available in
the various sets. Often the differences are quite subtle and two or more
faces that closely resemble each other may have different names since
they are supplied by different producers.

Obviously the designer should be able to identify typefaces. But to
learn to recognize all, or any substantial number of them, would be a
monumental task. To facilitate recognition, the designer or typographer should learn how type is organized. Once the designer
understands the system, he or she will be better able to locate the face
that meets his or her needs.

Type is organized into (1) groups or races, (2) families, (3) fonts,
and (4) series.

Type groups

Type groups or races are based on two considerations: historical development of the various faces within each category or set and their
structural form.

Text faces   Type designs in this group resemble the calligraphy of German monks of Gutenberg's time. Many faces have evolved from this style; Figure 4-5 is an example. Faces from this group are difficult to

ABCDEFGHIJKLMNOPQRS

abcdefghijklmnopqrstuvwxyz

4-5   A Text face.

read when they are composed in several lines. These faces are appropriate for special occasions such as for announcements of weddings or graduation, for religious materials, and for documents and diplomas. They should always be set c/lc, since all-cap composition is difficult to read, as shown in Figure 4-6.

4-6   All-cap Text composition is difficult to read.

HARD TO READ

Roman faces   Faces within this group are the most numerous and most widely used. They are styled after the letterforms carved on Roman buildings, and this influence is most evident in the capitals; lowercase letters follow the handwritten style of Italian scribes who developed a variation of the capitals to enable them to copy faster and more easily.

Roman faces are characterized by contrasting light and heavy letter strokes and the use of serifs. These features offer two advantages: first, they make these faces easily read, and second, variations in positioning the thick and thin portions of the letters together with serif treatments make possible interesting textural appearance within the shape structured by a number of lines of type.

Although they are essentially similar in overall design, faces within the Roman group can be subdivided into two subgroups: (1) Old Style and (2) Modern.

Old Style faces   These faces are less formal than the Modern. Contrast of letter strokes is less pronounced, and serifs are bracketed or molded into the terminals of the strokes to which they are attached.

Modern Roman faces   The word "modern" suggests recency. Such is not the case; the first Modern Roman face was designed two centuries ago. The Moderns have a more mechanical and less "arty" or hand-drawn look than the Old Styles. The most distinguishing characteristic of Modern Roman is the straight, thin, and unbracketed serif. Figure 4-7 shows Caslon, an Old Style, and Bodoni, a Modern face.

ABCDEFGHIJKLMNOPQRSTUVWXYZ&
ABCDEFGHIJKLMNOPQRSTUVWXYZ&
abcdefghijklmnopqrstuvwxyz

4-7 *Above:* Caslon, an Old Style face. *Below:* Bodoni, a Modern face.

ABCDEFGHIJKLMNOPQRSTUVWXYZ&
ABCDEFGHIJKLMNOPQRSTUVWXYZ&
abcdefghijklmnopqrstuvwxyz

Gothic faces These faces, also called *sans serif,* are second only to Roman in number and frequency of use. They are monotonal and skeletal, with very little, if any, contrast in strokes, and they lack serifs (*sans serif* is French for "without serifs"). The inspiration for the use of Gothic faces first came with the Industrial Revolution, since they reflected a spirit of functionalism. Actually, the styling of the sans serifs was not new at the time of their introduction; they were patterned after ancient Greek characters, which bore strokes of uniform width.

4-8 Futura, a sans serif face.

ABCDEFGHIJKLMNOPQRSTUVWXYZ&
abcdefghijklmnopqrstuvwxyz

The spirit of functionalism was reinforced by the Bauhaus Institute. Established in Germany in 1918, this was a think tank of sorts dedicated to a revitalization of design in architecture, painting, sculpture, industrial design, and typography. Since that time the popularity of the Gothic faces has increased to the point that their use rivals that of the Roman faces. Figure 4-8 shows Futura, a sans serif.

Square serif faces A number of faces that might be termed Gothic with serifs added present a problem in classifying; we elect to consider them a subset of the Gothics. An example is shown in Figure 4-9. These faces are most often used for headings and less frequently for lengthy reading matter.

4-9 Stymie, a square serif face.

ABCDEFGHIJKLMNOPQRSTUVWXYZ&
abcdefghijklmnopqrstuvwxyz

Script and Cursive faces Members of this group emulate handwriting. Cursive letters are not joined, whereas Script letters appear to be joined. These faces are special purpose, used primarily for announcements, invitations, letterheads, and so on. They are not much used for composition of lengthy text. Examples are shown in Figure 4-10.

4-10 *Above:* Coronet. *Below:* Commercial Script. These are examples of Cursive and Script faces.

ABCDEFGHIJKLMNOPQRSTUVWXYZ&
abcdefghijklmnopqrstuvwxyz

ABCDEFGHIJKLMNOPQRSTUVWXYZ&
abcdefghijklmnopqrstuvwxyz

Decorative and Novelty faces This group cannot be so precisely defined that a face with specified features can be placed in it. It is a catchall for faces that are not Text, Roman, sans serif, or Script-Cursive.

Some faces might be termed "Mood," since they give a time period, place, or mood connotation. Examples appear in Figure 4-11.

ABCDEFGHIJKLMNOPQR STUVWXYZ
abcdefghijklmnopqrstuvwxyz

4-11 Legend, P. T. Barnum, Typewriter, examples of "Mood" faces.

ABCDEFGHIJKLMNOPQRSTUVWXYZ&
abcdefghijklmnopqrstuvwxyz

ABCDEFGHIJKLMNOPQRSTUVWXYZ&
abcdefghijklmnopqrstuvwxyz

The remaining faces must be termed Novelty, although perhaps *potpourri* would do, but who would be able to pronounce that? Examples are shown in Figure 4-12. These faces do not lend themselves to the composition of long copy.

ABCDEFGHIJKLMNOPQRSTUVWXYZ&
abcdefghijklmnopqrstuvwxyz

4-12 Lydian, Hobo, Cartoon, Neuland, Broadway, examples of Novelty faces.

ABCDEFGHIJKLMNOPQRSTUVWXYZ&
abcdefghijklmnopqrstuvwxyz

ABCDEFGHIJKLMNOPQRSTUVWXYZ&

ABCDEFGHIJKLMNOPQRSTUVWXYZ&

ABCDEFGHIJKLMNOPQR
STUVWXYZ&

Type families In our discussion of groups, we mentioned families—Caslon, Futura, Stymie, Commercial Script, Hobo, and so on. How the design elements or parts of the face are styled sets one family apart from another. Thus, an adequate definition of a family might be "a number of faces closely related in design, such as the Caslon family or the Bodoni family."

Family variations Within a given family there may be a number of variations, sometimes referred to as *typestyles*, involving width, weight, and posture. However, regardless of these typestyles, the basic family design characteristics may remain.

Width variations refer to the *condensing* of type, a sort of narrowing of the letterforms, and *expanding*, a sort of widening of them. Such treatments are referred to as *condensed* or *compact* and as *extended* or *expanded.*

Some typestyles are designed with thinner or thicker strokes than are found in the normal face. Such variations include *light*, *semibold* (or *demibold*), *bold* (or *medium*), and *extrabold.* Bold, or *boldface* often written *bf,* is the most common of the weight variations.

The normal typestyle is often referred to as *normal* or *fullface,* which means no variation in either weight or width. Typefaces that are slanted to the right are referred to as *italic* in contrast to the normal, upright posture, which is referred to as *roman.* Since the word "roman" (spelled with a capital *R*) also refers to a type group, this seems to be a sort of inconsistency, since there would be a roman Caslon as well as a roman Futura; the latter belongs to the sans serif and not the Roman group. Trade practice dictates that roman is the opposite of italic.

Some families are available with a number of variations, as shown in Figure 4-13. However, the majority come only as roman, italic, and

4-13 Variations in the Helvetica family. The word "Helvetica" alone refers to the normal or fullface version of the typeface.

Helvetica Light
Helvetica Light Italic
Helvetica
Helvetica Italic
Helvetica Bold
Helvetica Bold Italic
Helvetica Condensed
Helvetica Bold Condensed
Helvetica Bold Condensed Italic

bold. A few faces offer such variations as shaded, shadowed, and outlined letterforms. These typestyles are not usually thought of as family variations; instead, they may be classified as Decorative-Novelty.

Type fonts   A *font* consists of the letters, numerals, punctuation marks, and other symbols that constitute a branch of a family in one size. By *branch* we refer to a variation in the family. The different kinds and the total number of characters per font differ among the various phototypesetting machines as well as among metal composition machines. For example, some fonts may carry *ligatures*—combinations such as *fi, fl, ff, ffi;* others may have small caps, written *sc*, in addition to standard size uppercase letters. Such a font is shown in Figure 4-14.

ABCDEFGHIJKLMNOPQRSTUVWXYZ

ABCDEFGHIJKLMNOPQRSTUVWXYZ

abcdefghijklmnopqrstuvwxyz

ABCDEFGHIJKLMNOPQRSTUVWXYZ

abcdefghijklmnopqrstuvwxyz

4-14   A font of type (Baskerville), including small caps.

* © § ® † © ‡ ® ¶ ™ @ ¢ ☞ ⊗

○

● • ○ ■ □ ★

+ − × = ÷

4-15   A phototypesetting pi font.

Special characters   There are times when special characters not available in standard fonts are needed. Such symbols are called *pi characters* or *sorts* (usually a metal typesetting term) and may be available in special phototypesetting fonts called *pi fonts*. An example is shown in Figure 4-15. In metal composition, which involves casting type from molds, the machine operator will often hand-insert the molds for these pi characters in the line of assembled molds before casting the type.

In both phototypesetting and metal typesetting, most machines can compose from more than one font. Thus, it is possible to call for characters from two or more fonts, one of which might contain pi symbols.

Type series   The range in sizes in a family branch available for composition is called a *series*.

Type and Typesetting Measurements

Several units of measurement are unique to and are widely used in graphic communication. Principal among them are the *point, pica,* and *unit*. These units are discussed below in addition to two other terms: the *em* and the *agate line*. The inch is also used, but usually only for paper and page sizes and dimensions of pictures.

Type size is measured in points and line length is measured in picas. There are 6 picas in an inch and 12 points in a pica; thus there are 72 points per inch. Other uses of the point and the pica are referred to later. The unit is a measurement of the width of various letterforms and other characters and the space between characters and between words. The unit refers specifically to phototypesetting and is not generally used in the case of metal composition.

The Point   Type sizes generally range from 4-pt. (abbreviation for "point") to 72-pt., although some machines are capable of producing sizes ranging up to 144-point. Figure 4-16 shows the word "Type" set in 6-, 10-, 14-, 18-, 24-, 36-, 48-, and 72-point. Type sizes that range from 4-point through 12-point are usually referred to as *text* or *body* sizes and those above 12-point are referred to as *display* type sizes. The most frequently used text type sizes are 6 through 12 by one-point increments; most common display type sizes are 14-, 16-, 18-, 20-, 24-, 30-, 36-, 48-, 60-, and 72-point. Some body sizes are also available in half-point sizes, such as $5\frac{1}{2}$-, $6\frac{1}{2}$-, $8\frac{1}{2}$-point, and so on.

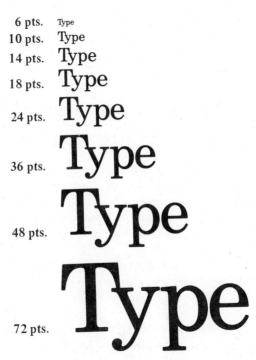

4-16   A word set in eight different sizes of one face.

6 pts.   Type
10 pts. Type
14 pts. Type
18 pts. Type
24 pts. Type
36 pts. Type
48 pts. Type
72 pts. Type

It is difficult to determine the size of type in print. If you look at Figure 4-17, one type appears to be larger, yet both are 18-point. One might measure the type with a *printer's rule* or *line gauge*, which is calibrated in points and picas, from the top of the ascender to the bot-

4-17   Both faces are the same size, yet one appears larger.

This type face

18 pt. Baskerville

This type face

18 pt. Century Schoolbook

tom of a descender and make a "guesstimate." But one would have to add a little extra space to allow for the fact that a small amount is added above ascenders and below descenders in the design of a face so that lines will not touch when they are composed one above another.

An alternative method would be to measure from one baseline to another. However, extra space may have been added between lines when the type was set, making an exact determination nearly impossible. It would be best to determine the identity of the face and compare it with samples in a *type specimen book*, a catalog of faces showing composition in different sizes.

Even then the exact size is difficult to determine, since it may have been altered photographically from its original setting. This is often done in making negatives of page pasteups before platemaking. Such negatives are often shot at sizes somewhat smaller than the pasteup.

The Pica   Line length or *measure* is referred to as so many picas or so many picas and points. Thus "15.6" would mean 15 picas, 6 points. This measurement would more likely be called "$15\frac{1}{2}$ picas."

The Em   The *em* is a square in the type size being set; thus a 10-point em is an area 10 points wide and 10 points high. In traditional metal typesetting an em quad was a square, blank body—that is, there was no printing character atop it. There were em quads for every font and they were used primarily for paragraph indention.

The Unit   The *unit* is a fraction of the width of an em. The number of units per em varies from one phototypesetting machine to another, although the 18-unit count is most common. Phototype faces are designed with each character being allotted a certain number of units. The character does not quite fill the width of its allotted units; the slight extra space is needed so that composed characters do not touch. The width of the various characters is called *set* or *set width*, and this dimension may vary from family to family. That is, an *x* may be 9 set or 9 units in one and 10 set or units in another.

Applying the unit system   A knowledge of the unit system and how to apply it in phototypesetting offers the designer a number of advantages that are not generally available in metal composition. The designer can call for either an increase or decrease of spacing between letters—called *letterspacing*—and for either an increase or decrease of spacing between words, called *wordspacing*. These advantages result:

1. The legibility of type can be improved.
2. The tone of a block of copy can be altered.

3. Tightening both letterspacing and wordspacing will permit getting more copy into a given space.

Type composed without intraword spacing alteration is said to have *normal letterspacing*. It is possible, however, to call for *loose letterspacing* (or *loose set*) or *tight letterspacing* (or *tight set*), or even very loose or very tight.

Such spacing is measured in units and half-units; loose and tight generally refer to $+\frac{1}{2}$ and $-\frac{1}{2}$; very loose and very tight refer to $+1$ and -1. These capabilities vary among machines, and the designer must be aware of such matters. Minus $\frac{1}{2}$ unit settings can allow about 5 percent more characters per line of type and minus 1 can allow about 10 percent more characters per line.

Wordspacing can also be referred to as normal, loose $(+\frac{1}{2})$, very loose $(+1)$, tight $(-\frac{1}{2})$, and very tight (-1). In most cases, if other than normal letterspacing is used, it should be combined with matching wordspacing—that is, $-\frac{1}{2}$ unit letterspacing with $-\frac{1}{2}$ unit wordspacing. Figure 4-18 shows the effects of various combinations. The first setting is with normal spacing, whereas the remaining four are with loose, very loose, tight, and very tight settings.

Most type is set with normal or with $-\frac{1}{2}$ unit spacing. The selection of the proper spacing is not a simple matter. These guidelines may prove helpful:

1. Type set all caps should be letterspaced, unless the letterstyle is condensed. Note the words that follow:

   NO LETTERSPACING   WITH LETTERSPACING

2. Display type can be composed with tighter set than text type.
3. Condensed type can be set tighter than wider type.
4. Faces with small center body (x-height) require little, if any, letterspacing.

Greater freedom can be exercised in the spacing of display type. A look through a number of magazines will prove very beneficial in terms of learning techniques used in between-lines spacing as well as word-and letterspacing.

On many machines, limited letterspacing can be used in special cases. Looking again at Figure 4-2, the placement of the *y* under the *T* is an example; this treatment is called *kerning*.

Some typographers decide on word spacing that best suits the typeface and apply it throughout the composition. When this is done, the composition must be *ragged right*—that is, the lines are of different lengths. They have a common starting point on the left, however, and are thus *flush left*, as shown in Figure 4-19. When all lines are even, right and left (as they are in this book), copy is said to be *justified*. The

Line length or measure is referred to as being so many picas or as so many picas and points long. Thus "15.6" would mean a measure of 15 picas and 6 points or 15½ picas. Lines of justified type are usually a whole number of picas long or a whole number and one-half.

Line length or measure is referred to as being so many picas or as so many picas and points long. Thus "15.6" would mean a measure of 15 picas and 6 points or 15½ picas. Lines of justified type are usually a whole number of picas long or a whole number and one-half.

Line length or measure is referred to as being so many picas or as so many picas and points long. Thus "15.6" would mean a measure of 15 picas and 6 points or 15½ picas. Lines of justified type are usually a whole number of picas long or a whole number and one-half.

Line length or measure is referred to as being so many picas or as so many picas and points long. Thus "15.6" would mean a measure of 15 picas and 6 points or 15½ picas. Lines of justified type are usually a whole number of picas long or a whole number and one-half.

Line length or measure is referred to as being so many picas or as so many picas and points long. Thus "15.6" would mean a measure of 15 picas and 6 points or 15½ picas. Lines of justified type are usually a whole number of picas long or a whole number and one-half.

Line length or measure is referred to as being so many picas or as so many picas and points long. Thus "15.6" would mean a measure of 15 picas and 6 points or 15½ picas. Lines of justified type are usually a whole number of picas long or a whole number and one-half.

Line length or measure is referred to as being so many picas or as so many picas and points long. Thus "15.6" would mean a measure of 15 picas and 6 points or 15½ picas. Lines of justified type are usually a whole number of picas long or a whole number and one-half.

Line length or measure is referred to as being so many picas or as so many picas and points long. Thus "15.6" would mean a measure of 15 picas and 6 points or 15½ picas. Lines of justified type are usually a whole number of picas long or a whole number and one-half.

Line length or measure is referred to as being so many picas or as so many picas and points long. Thus "15.6" would mean a measure of 15 picas and 6 points or 15½ picas. Lines of justified type are usually a whole number of picas long or a whole number and one-half.

Line length or measure is referred to as being so many picas or as so many picas and points long. Thus "15.6" would mean a measure of 15 picas and 6 points or 15½ picas. Lines of justified type are usually a whole number of picas long or a whole number and one-half.

spaces between words must often be varied in justifying composition (examine the spaces in a few lines here).

On the pages that follow, the
reorganization and its effect on various
banks are more fully explained in sections
which include the photographs of the
senior officers who are responsible for
individual areas.

4-19   Ragged right composition.

Composition with ragged right or the less common ragged left has a more even tonal appearance than justified composition since word spacing is the same in all lines. Such composition is thus very effective for narrow measures. (This is why ragged right and ragged left are used for the illustration captions in this book.)

Other uses of the pica   In addition to line length (a horizontal measurement) the pica is used to measure:

1. Width of columns (horizontal)
2. Depth of columns (a vertical measurement)
3. Size of margins between columns and also between type areas and the outsides of pages
4. Sizes of illustrations

Other uses of the em   In addition to being a unit of spacing, the em is also used as a measurement of quantity of type. One would calculate the amount of composition in a space 15 picas wide and $7\frac{1}{2}$ inches deep, if type were 10-point, as follows:

$15 \times 12 = 180$ points wide
$180 \div 10 = 18$ (10-point ems or set ems per line)
$7\frac{1}{2} \times 72$ (points per inch) $= 540$ points deep
$540 \div 10 = 54$ lines of 10-point type
$54 \times 18 = 972$ ems of composition

If the composition were 12-point type, there would be 15 set ems per line, 45 lines of type, and thus 675 set ems of composition.

Other uses of the point   The point is used for measuring interline spacing—that is, the extra space placed between lines of type. Such spacing is called *leading* (pronounced "ledding"). Type set without such extra spacing is said to be *set solid.* This terminology, though it was inherited from metal typesetting tradition, is in current use.

4-20 *Left column:*
This type is set in 10-point on a 14-pica measure. The face is Garamond, which has a relatively small x-height compared to Century, the face used in the right column. The paragraph at top is set solid, that is, without linespacing. In order below, it is set with the following leading: 1 point, 2 points, −1 point.

Several factors influence the selection of linespacing. The design of the type face is one. Faces with larger x-height require greater leading. The length of the measure is another. The longer the measure, in general, the greater the linespacing required. Finally, there is greater need to linespace the smaller text sizes, 5- to 8-point, to increase legibility.

Several factors influence the selection of linespacing. The design of the type face is one. Faces with larger x-height require greater leading. The length of the measure is another. The longer the measure, in general, the greater the linespacing required. Finally, there is greater need to linespace the smaller text sizes, 5- to 8-point, to increase legibility.

Several factors influence the selection of linespacing. The design of the type face is one. Faces with larger x-height require greater leading. The length of the measure is another. The longer the measure, in general, the greater the linespacing required. Finally, there is greater need to linespace the smaller text sizes, 5- to 8-point, to increase legibility.

Several factors influence the selection of linespacing. The design of the type face is one. Faces with larger x-height require greater leading. The length of the measure is another. The longer the measure, in general, the greater the linespacing required. Finally, there is greater need to linespace the smaller text sizes, 5- to 8-point, to increase legibility.

4-20 *Right column:*
This type is set in 10-point Century on a 14-pica measure. The paragraph at top is set solid. In order below, it is set with the following leading: 1 point, 2 points, −1 point.

Several factors influence the selection of linespacing. The design of the type face is one. Faces with larger x-height require greater leading. The length of the measure is another. The longer the measure, in general, the greater the linespacing required. Finally, there is greater need to linespace the smaller text sizes, 5- to 8-point, to increase legibility.

Several factors influence the selection of linespacing. The design of the type face is one. Faces with larger x-height require greater leading. The length of the measure is another. The longer the measure, in general, the greater the linespacing required. Finally, there is greater need to linespace the smaller text sizes, 5- to 8-point, to increase legibility.

Several factors influence the selection of linespacing. The design of the type face is one. Faces with larger x-height require greater leading. The length of the measure is another. The longer the measure, in general, the greater the linespacing required. Finally, there is greater need to linespace the smaller text sizes, 5- to 8-point, to increase legibility.

Several factors influence the selection of linespacing. The design of the type face is one. Faces with larger x-height require greater leading. The length of the measure is another. The longer the measure, in general, the greater the linespacing required. Finally, there is greater need to linespace the smaller text sizes, 5- to 8-point, to increase legibility.

Because many phototypesetting machines are capable not only of adding space but also of reducing space between lines, leading is also commonly called *linespacing,* the reduction of interline spacing being called *reverse leading, minus leading,* or *back leading.* In any event, leading and linespacing are measured in points (and $\frac{1}{2}$ points in phototypesetting).

If type is set 10-point with 1 point linespacing or leading, it is referred to as 10/11. If reverse leading of 1 point is done, the designation is 10/9. In Figure 4-20, the lines are set 10-point solid, leaded 1 point, leaded 2 points, and with -1 point leading.

Generally, text type is set with one or two points added; faces with small x-heights may require no leading. Display sizes can be linespaced with greater freedom. See Appendix B for the specifications for this book. Note that its text is 10/12; the captions are 9/10. The varying linespacings of the display type—the heads—are expressed as "points B/B," meaning number of points base to base, that is, baseline to baseline of the x-heights of specific lines. Very free treatments of display sizes of type can be seen in advertising headlines in national magazines, where there are fewer restrictions than in books.

Reverse leading also makes possible setting two or more columns of type on some phototypesetting machines. After one column is set, the paper or film can be backed up to allow another column to be set.

The point also measures rules and borders that are available from machine composition, metal as well as photo.

The Agate Line

Sometimes referred to as a *line,* the *agate line* is a measurement of advertising space. The cost of advertising is often quoted by the agate line, which can be defined as one column wide (horizontal) and $\frac{1}{14}$th of an inch deep (vertical). The agate line should not be confused with a line of type. Referring to an advertisement of 28 lines, can mean either an advertisement that is two inches deep and one column wide—written 28 $\times$ 1—or one that is one inch deep and two columns wide—14 $\times$ 2, spoken of as "fourteen on two."

The Metric System

Points, picas, units, and inches are terms common in the typographer's work-a-day jargon. Some day, it is believed, these terms will give way to metrication. Even today, many chemicals, paper, film, and other printing supplies bear labels showing metric equivalents. In Europe there is a definite trend to the metric system for measuring type sizes and spacing.

The table on the next page shows points and picas with equivalents in inches, centimeters, and millimeters. The figures, which are to the nearest ten-thousandths, are based on (1) the accepted U.S. standard

Metrication conversion

points	inches	cm	mm
½	.0069	.0175	.1753
1	.0138	.0351	.3505
2	.0277	.0704	.7036
3	.0415	.1054	1.0541
4	.0553	.1405	1.4046
5	.0692	.1758	1.7577
6	.0830	.2108	2.1082
7	.0969	.2461	2.4613
8	.1107	.2812	2.8118
9	.1245	.3162	3.1623
10	.1384	.3515	3.5154
11	.1522	.3866	3.8659
12	.1660	.4216	4.2164

picas			
2	.3320	.8433	8.4328
3	.4980	1.2649	12.6492
4	.6640	1.6866	16.8656
5	.8300	2.1082	21.0820
6	.9960	2.5298	25.2984
7	.1620	2.9515	29.5148
8	1.3280	3.3731	33.7312
9	1.4940	3.7948	37.9476
10	1.6600	4.2164	42.1640

that one inch = 2.54 centimeters (a metric yard = 39.37 inches), (2) one pica = .1660 inches, and (3) one point = .013837 inches. The latter two measurements were accepted by the printing industry in the United States in the late nineteenth century.

Type Composition

There are two basic methods of type composition: *cold type* and *hot type.* The latter refers to the traditional methods of composing symbols in metal type, whether by hand or by machine. For more than 400 years after Gutenberg, all composition was done by hand. Machine metal composition is relatively recent.

In this century, our knowledge has doubled every few decades and the need to communicate this knowledge has kept pace. The most modern typesetting methods—together called cold type—are capable of assembling as many as 10,000 characters per second (cps) and contrast sharply with hand-setting; highly skilled hand compositors could do little better than one cps. It has been forecast that cold type machines will reach a rate of up to 60,000 cps.

Cold Type Composition

Type composed by any means other than hot metal is referred to as *cold type.* Such composition is achieved by direct imaging of characters onto film or paper. There are several methods: (1) photo-typesetting, (2) photodisplay machines, (3) electronic composition, (4) direct impression or strike-on, and (5) transfer lettering.

Phototypesetting machines

These machines operate on a common principle. They print typefaces and other symbols onto paper or film by flashing a light through film negatives of the desired symbols. One such system is shown in Figure 4-21.

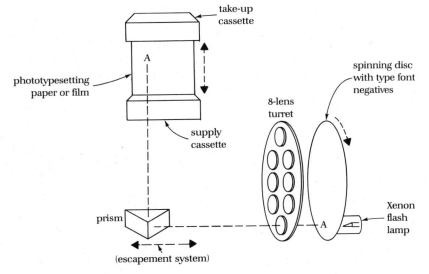

4-21 Optical system of a phototypesetter.

High-quality negatives of the various symbols in a font are contained in the type disk in the example. The disk spins at a high rate of speed. The Xenon lamp flashes a brief fraction of a second, just long enough to "stop" the desired character. The beam of light strikes the prism in the escapement system and is reflected toward the paper or film. En route, the light beam passes through the rotatable lenses for enlarging or reducing the image. The escapement system moves horizontally, which makes possible the composition of lines of type. In many machines the paper or film is capable of vertical movement, making possible reverse leading. In some machines the negative image carrier is stationary and the light moves.

The symbol negatives are not carried on discs in all machines. In some they are in the form of filmstrips that are affixed to drums; other machines use flat grids to which the negatives are attached. The film fonts are interchangeable. The various machines differ in many other ways, such as number of fonts on machine, type sizes available, speed of composition, paper or film widths, maximum line lengths, and flexibility in terms of spacing, tabbing, mixing of letterforms, reverse leading, and so on.

Two types of phototypesetters are in wide use today. The simpler type is called a *direct-entry* machine. In this application, the operator works at a keyboard that is part of the machine. The other type of phototypesetter is a *remote-entry* machine; access in this case is not direct but comes from different operators in locations remote from the machine.

Direct-entry machines These are the most widely used photocomposition machines today and may be found in printing plants, business offices, advertising agencies, and so on. Generally, they do not match the large, remote-entry machines in quantity of production.

Input comes from typewriterlike keyboards with additional keys to control word, letter, and line spacing, *quadding* left (setting ragged right), quadding right, centering, tabbing, kerning, reverse leading, and so on. On some machines the operator is signaled when nearing a line's full measure; the operator then decides on where to hyphenate the word, if necessary, or how to space out a line to justify it and thereby avoid hyphenation. Some machines offer the operator the option of using a computerlike processor for making the *h&j* decision. Such a processor is a part of the machine and contains basic logic rules for making these decisions. In some cases, small computers are used which store in memory an *exception dictionary* of words that cannot be accurately hyphenated by the logic rules.

Basically, type is set as it is keyboarded. Thus, speed of output is a function of the operator's typing skill. If the machine is not capable of h&j decisions, output is further limited, since such decisions require 30 percent of the operator's time.

Some of these machines display only a few characters—less than a measure—at a time and then cast the accumulated line before another can be started. Characters and spaces are stored in a buffer memory and are displayed much as numbers are displayed on an electronic calculator.

More recent direct-entry machines make possible the display of as many as 40 lines of characters on a *VDT* (*video display terminal*) before they are set in type. The operator, using special function keys on the keyboard, can edit the displayed copy before it is typeset. Some larger direct-entry machines can store beyond the 40 lines in a mini-computer memory until they are ready for composition. The VDT is further discussed in Chapters 7 and 8.

Some of the direct-entry machines are capable of storing copy for future use and also accepting input from keyboards that are off-line from the system.

Remote-entry machines   These phototypesetters are more adaptable to the requirements of larger printing plants and publishers of newspapers and magazines. They operate at higher output speeds, since they can accept a number of different inputs coming from remote locations. In general, these machines are capable of functioning with more different faces and sizes as well as more *formats* (typographic requirements for composition) than the direct-input machines. They are usually integrated into large computer-controlled typesetting systems such as those discussed in Chapters 7 and 8.

Photodisplay machines

These machines are used primarily for setting display size words. Phototypesetters (both direct-entry and remote-entry) are capable of enlarging smaller sizes to display, using special lenses, as shown in Figure 4-21. However, text and display sizes were traditionally separately designed. The smaller faces were slightly more extended and more space was allotted between characters. When enlarged appreciably, these characteristics were exaggerated.

Special machines are used for setting traditionally designed display sizes. Not only does their production have a more esthetic look but these machines offer other advantages. Spacing of headlines may be done visually, and the operator can place characters in positions other than "normal." Some equipment can apply special optical treatments, as shown in Figure 4-22.

The photodisplay machines are relatively slow and their operation requires manual selection of characters and exposure one at a time onto paper or film. Some are limited to setting single lines on narrow strips; others can compose several lines on sheets of paper or film.

Electronic composition

Because these typesetters compose type on a video screen, they are often termed *CRT (cathode ray tube) machines.* The generated images are focused by a lens onto paper or film; thus they are also referred to as *CRT phototypesetters.*

If the remote-entry phototypesetters are high-speed, the machines in this group are "super-speed," capable of composing 3,000 newspaper lines per minute. In one newspaper application, such a machine turns out full-size pages of classified reader advertisements, complete with rules, in approximately 70 seconds.

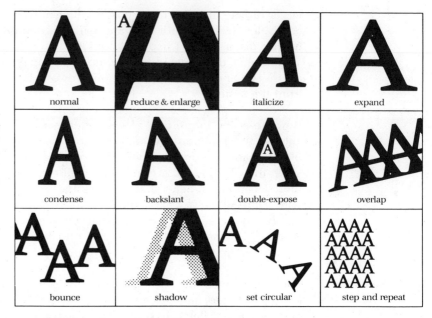

4-22 Optical treatments of photodisplay type. (*Photo Typositor® type reproduced by permission of Visual Graphics Corporation*)

The flexibility of the CRTs extends beyond that of the phototypesetters; in addition to the capacity to do larger areas, they are capable of broader computer control. Because characters are generated on a video screen, they can be electronically manipulated to appear as roman, italic, backslanted, condensed, expanded, or bold—even in combinations of such treatments. They can generate line art along with type, and it is also possible to scan continuous-tone art, such as photographs and drawings, and convert tones to dot form in the digital computer, later to be output as halftones.

Descriptive patterns for the generation of symbols are either stored in computer memory in digital form or matrix grids are scanned by a CRT (not the printout tube), which translates character descriptions into digital coding. In either case, the descriptive coding is utilized to direct the action of the printout CRT beam. This electronic beam "paints" the shapes of the characters on the screen much as the beam puts a picture on a home television screen. The shapes of the characters are formed by parallel, vertical lines, as many as 1,440 per inch. The greater the number of these lines the greater is the definition of the characters, but the slower is the composition rate. Some machines generate characters by means of closely grouped dots. The type sizes of these characters range 4- to 80-point. Figure 4-23 shows some examples of CRT composition.

Direct impression Also referred to as *strike-on*, the direct impression method of putting typefaces on paper involves the use of a special typewriter with inter-

4-23 **Examples of CRT composition.**

(Specimens produced on a Linotron 505 CRT phototypesetter, manufactured by Mergenthaler Linotype, an ELTRA Company)

SUMMER ARRIVES ON DOT WITH SOFT SWEATER DRESSING. *Easy designs for travel or town by Matti of Lynne in airy, carefree Celanese Arnel triacetate with nylon sweater ribbing. Tank Topped Cooler in white dots on yellow, with yellow ribbing; or navy dots on white with navy*

Electronically generated condensed and sloped (italic) composition.

Variable baseline composition for setting superior and inferior characters. (Phototypesetters are also capable of such composition; CRTs can perform the various formattings of phototypesetters.)

The following assumptions can be made: $\epsilon'_f \approx \epsilon_f$, and $\sigma'_f \approx \sigma_f$. (summaries of various methods of estimating ϵ_f and σ_f see [34].) Changes

$$\sum_{all\ i} 2N_f = \left(\frac{\sigma_f}{\sigma_a}\right)^{1+5n/n} = \left(\frac{108}{73}\right)^{14.1} = 260 \text{ reversals}$$

	4 WRC NBC
6 :00 :15 :30 :45	
7 :00 :15 :30 :45	7:45 Faith, Life News, Weather
8 :00 :15 :30 :45	Agriculture USA " " On Campus " "
9 :00 :15 :30 :45	Speaking Freely Ann Rand- Author, is Guest
10 :00 :15 :30 :45	Mass For Shut-Ins International Zone
11 :00 :15 :30 :45	Overview " " Issues " "
12 :00 :15 :30 :45	Dimension Washington Deena Clark's Moment With

CRT mixing: alignment of different sizes; also, generation of horizontal and vertical rules.

4-24 Electronically generated letter, enlarged. (*Courtesy ANPA Research Institute*)

changeable typefaces. Direct impression is limited to composition of text sizes only, but it serves well when low cost of composition is an overriding factor. Strike-on typefaces have low unit count values; thus finesse in letter-and word spacing is limited.

On some machines copy must be typed twice. At the first typing the amount of word spacing required for justifying is determined by the machine; on the second typing the line is spaced to full measure. The most widely used system records the copy on magnetic tape at first typing, which is done on a nontypesetting typewriter. The typist is unconcerned with typeface, line length, line spacing, and justifying. The tape is then fed to a processing unit that operates a typesetting typewriter. The latter justifies lines but cannot hyphenate. When hyphenation of a word is necessary, the operator must be on hand to make that decision. The operator must also stand by to change fonts, if the job calls for mixing of faces, as well as to set the composing typewriter for line length and leading.

Transfer type Transfer type is used for composing display faces. Such type fonts are carried on 10 × 14 transparent, thin acetate sheets. One kind of sheet requires cutting out the characters and adhering them to the working surface; the letters have an adhesive backing. A second kind of sheet requires positioning the letter and then burnishing the surface of the sheet; the letter is rubbed off the back of the sheet onto the working surface. Letters on both types of sheets are available in black or in white. Pi characters, rules, borders, tone patterns, and a wide variety of other symbols are also available.

Hot Type Composition Hot type is the setting of characters, rules, and borders cast in metal. Such type may be precast as individual symbols (*foundry type*) and assembled by hand. More commonly, composition is by machines that manufacture type as they are operated, either as a line of word symbols (raised faces) on a body of type called a *slug*, or as single letters. Three kinds of machines are used: linecasters, the Monotype, and the Ludlow.

Linecasting machines There are two *linecasters:* The Linotype and Intertype, both of which cast a line of characters on a slug. An operator at a keyboard assembles a line of brass molds, called *matrices* or *mats*, together with expandable spaces between words. When the assembled mats and space-bands approach full measure, the operator makes h&j decisions; occasionally the operator may drop extra word and letterspacing materials between mats and bands by hand; when the line is adjusted, the machine is directed to cast the line.

Composition is relatively slow; a skilled operator can cast perhaps four or five newspaper lines per minute (lpm). Some linecasters, operated by computer devices that calculate h&j, can set perhaps 12 lpm.

The range of type fonts on a linecasting machine is limited; most linecasters carry only two, generally the roman and either the boldface or italic typestyle; a few machines may carry four or more fonts but each is in only one size. Most linecasting machines are limited to setting 5- to 24-point and maximum line length of 30 picas. The faces available are not all aligned to a common baseline, as are phototypesetter faces, making the mixing of different families within one line more of a problem than in the case of photocomposition.

Extra spacing between lines can be accomplished by casting the leading area as a part of the slug. But linecasters do not offer the minus leading or tight letterspacing flexibility of phototypesetting.

The Monotype The Monotype machine casts lines of type from molds, but a letter at a time. Keyboard and caster are separate units. The operator at the keyboard perforates a paper tape, coded for letters and spacing. The operator makes all h&j decisions when the keyboard signals that composition is near the end of a line. Like the linecasters, the Monotype casts leading as a part of the type. Linespacing flexibility is therefore limited. Sizes 4-to 14-point can be set on the Monotype machine, but font-carrying flexibility is limited. Because it does not cast slugs, the Monotype is better adapted than the linecasters for setting tabular matter and scientific materials.

The Ludlow Like the linecasters, the Ludlow casts slugs. It is used primarily for casting display sizes. The operator of the Ludlow hand sets mats, which are then placed in a casting machine where the slugs are cast.

5 Elements of Good Typography

People pay a good deal of money to get visual symbols (words) into print because they want them to be seen and read. During the past century scientists, and primarily psychologists, have studied communication via the printed page. Their findings have tended to confirm the standards or rules that have been developed by typographers through their experience, especially in the area of selecting and using type.

Although the conclusions of the psychologist must be viewed as provisional, they have value either as suggestions for procedure or as a recall to standards established by practicing typographers. Most of the discussion in this chapter is directed to typographic practice in dealing with text type sizes through 12-point. Practices involving display are considered in later chapters.

Two aspects of the use of text composition are of particular interest to the typographer: (1) legibility and (2) appropriateness.

Legibility

The term "legibility" suggests a composition-reader interaction. It is, therefore, not enough to say that legibility means that the message is readily visible. The purpose of looking at composition is not simply to see it but to understand it—to grasp the meaning it carries. Comprehension is thus central to legibility.

Other aspects of legibility must also be considered. To be observed in the first place, type should be esthetically pleasing. That is, the face design should be consciously chosen, and letters, words, lines—in fact, the entire composition—should be so displayed as to invite and then sustain attention.

Comprehension comes as a result of processing information; thus it must be defined as units of understanding per unit of time. Comprehension determines the speed at which a reader's eyes move across the composition. If all other conditions—including comprehension—

under which reading is done are constant, the type that is read faster than another could be termed more legible.

A number of factors bear on legibility: face, size, boldness, leading, length of line, margins, even or uneven lines (justified or nonjustified), ink, paper, presswork, lighting, and the interest of the reader in the content.

The last factor is controlled by the selection of ideas, not by type, but is nonetheless important to the typographer. Tests indicate that reader interests are related to legibility and bear an effect on the use of type.

Testing Legibility Observations about the mechanics of reading are helpful to a discussion of legibility. Reading is done as the eyes make short jumps along a line. At each stop (fixation) several words are absorbed. Enough letters or words are perceived to fill in the gap between fixations.

Readers vary in proficiency. A skilled reader makes fewer fixations, has greater rhythm in eye movement, and rarely has to make regressions—retrace to a previous point to pick up something missed.

The legibility of words or idea groups is more important than that of individual letters. Effective reading requires recognition of whole words, usually more than one. The content of the words (their meanings), clarity of expression, and absence of unfamiliar words are aids to rapid reading.

The following are the major tests used in measuring legibility:

1. Tachistoscopic tests. These measure the subject's reading accuracy by presenting letters and words in brief exposures.
2. The measuring of a reader's ease in distinguishing letters and reading words by presenting them at varying distances.
3. Studies of eye movements, blinks, and indications of fatigue. Specially designed "eye cameras" record movements over a printed area. Either a light ray is reflected from the cornea or a white spot is affixed to it. A tracing is made of the movements and laid over the printed material to determine the path of the eye.
4. Focal variation tests, which present messages as blurs slowly brought toward focus. The threshold recognition is thus established. Such tests, like distance tests, might be applied, for example, to poster and package design testing.
5. Binocular rivalry tests, which present a different image to each eye. A device called a *haploscope*, which is somewhat like a stereoscope, is used. The viewer will see one image as dominant or will vacillate between the two with an effect similar to that in viewing a Necker cube (see Figure 2-2). If an image dominates, it is thought to be preferred.

6. Time-comprehension tests of prose reading followed by question-naires to reveal the extent to which the content was retained and errors made.

Researchers who are recognized as important contributors to this field have used the last method as their principal technique for measuring legibility. The results from various types of tests do not always agree. A face may be found more legible by one procedure than by another. But, in general, the findings have validated trade practices.

The student of typography should be on guard against confusing legibility testing with readability testing. The latter was developed by readability experts, most notably Rudolph Flesch, John McElroy, and Robert Gunning, who measure the relative difficulty of reading according to clarity of writing, ease of reading, and human interest. Briefly stated, these experts have found that a message is most readable when sentences are short and words are familiar and personal. Since these factors certainly influence reading efficiency, readability and legibility tests can easily be confused. Though both measure reader response, readability tests focus on content comprehension, and experts in this area have developed "readability formulas" to measure the level of difficulty in understanding written messages. Legibility tests, on the other hand, focus on the form of presentation of a written message.

The Typeface Typographers have long contended that legibility is maximized by the use of the standard Roman faces. Tests to date have neither confirmed nor refuted this contention, although researchers have been inclined to conclude that it is valid. Typographers believe that familiarity and design factors render legibility to such faces. They point out that we learn to read from books printed in Roman and that the majority of what we read thereafter in books, magazines, and other literature is also printed in Roman. Further, the more irregular design features of Roman faces help the reader grasp word forms more rapidly in the reading process than in Gothic. Contrasting strokes give a rhythmic structure to words and serifs assist horizontal eye movement.

On the other hand, the monotonous sameness of Gothic faces, they feel, impairs reading. Gothic is often used for text material, especially when the number of words is not great; its use for display is well established.

Earlier editions of this text pointed out the following: "Advertisers in the large national magazines, who seek the best possible typographical advice, prefer Roman faces for text matter, a fact the student can readily verify by browsing through the pages of well-known publications." Make this observation today; although Roman may still show an edge over other faces, the "fact" is not nearly so certain.

Burt has offered evidence that among the Roman faces the Modern designs seem less legible than the Old Style, especially for children and older persons.[1] He concluded that legibility is impaired in modern faces because the design emphasizes the similar parts of letters, whereas Old Style letter designs accentuate dissimilar letter characteristics. Contrast is the source of recognition, allowing the perception of defining features. Can this be applied to Roman compared to sans serif, where the contrast is even more pronounced? Binocular rivalry tests show that people have a preference for Roman.[2]

One study of the legibility of Roman as compared to Gothic was based on how the visual system is believed to function.[3] In this experiment, researchers developed a mathematical model of the way in which the neural components of the visual sytem are assumed to interact and abstract information to allow interpretation of what is seen. A testing of this model indicated that a computer, which processed information according to the model, misjudged geometric illusions (such as Figures 2-2 and 2-3) in the same way as humans do. Mathematical descriptions of these geometric figures were fed to the computer.

Information descriptive of Roman and Gothic typefaces was given the computer and it was then asked to print out what it "saw." The results indicated that Roman was more legible in reader sizes but there was no legibility difference in the case of display sizes.

In research completed in 1974 under the auspices of the American Newspaper Publishers Association, J. K. Hvistendahl of Iowa State University found that a sample of 200 newspaper readers showed a marked preference for Roman type over sans serif type for newspaper body copy. The typefaces compared were those in common use in American newspapers.

Further, Hvistendahl found that readers were able to read Roman type significantly faster in three out of four comparisons of type set in both $10\frac{1}{2}$ and 14 pica widths. In the fourth test the sans serif was read faster but the difference was not great. He concluded that newspapers should be ultracautious about changing from Roman to sans serif body copy.

What role does familiarity play in legibility? One noted authority, John R. Biggs, has indicated, "All the scientific experiments on legibil-

[1] Sir Cyril Burt, *A Psychological Study of Typography* (London: Cambridge University Press, 1959), p. 7.

[2] Bror Zachrisson, *Studies in Legibility of Printed Text* (Stockholm: Almqvist & Wiskel, 1965), pp. 128–131.

[3] David O. Robinson, Michael Abbamonte, and Selby H. Evans, "Why Serifs are Important: The Perception of Small Print," *Visible Language* 4 (1971): 353–359.

ity I have come across produced more or less the same results—that within obvious limits, people read most easily and with least fatigue those letter forms they are most familiar with."[4]

Two attempts at measuring familiarity have been reported by Zachrisson.[5] People were asked in one test to select from among various printed faces the one that most resembled the face in a book they had recently read and also the one that resembled the face in a printed piece they had seen earlier the same day. The results of this test led to the conclusion that typographers overestimate the impact of ordinary faces on the reader.

A second, two-part experiment compared the abilities of laymen (ordinary readers) and workers in the typographic field to recognize and reproduce the shapes of letters. The letters *a, f, g,* and *t* were used on both tests. In the recognition version, a proper form was given along with six to nine incorrect alternatives and the subjects were to indicate the correct form. In the reproduction part of the experiment the four lines that demark lowercase letters (to show the x-height, the ascenders and descenders) were presented with correct sample letters—other than *a, f, g, t*—in correct position. The subjects were to draw and position the test letters correctly. The results of the experiment indicated that both groups had a low level of ability to recognize and reproduce.

It would seem that, whereas people may perceive the total form, the structural detail is lost.

Typographers generally agree that, regardless of type faces, caps and lowercase are preferred to material set all caps. Paterson and Tinker have shown that text matter set in all caps caused a 12 percent loss in reading time.[6] This does not necessarily negate the use of all caps in display matter.

Like italics, the boldface variation of a typeface serves well for emphasis. The families designed to give a heavier appearance when compared to others have been suggested by Burt (1959, p. 10) as useful for the very young and the elderly.

Typographers recommend 10-, 11-, and 12-point types for text matter for the average reader, and tests have borne out their contention. Burt, however, believes those sizes may be too small for some individual readers. He asserts that larger sizes of type are often preferable for both younger and older-than-average readers.[7]

---

[4] John R. Biggs, *Basic Typography* (New York: Watson-Guptill Publications, 1968), p. 10.

[5] Zachrisson, op. cit., pp. 85 – 90.

[6] D. G. Paterson and M. A. Tinker, *How to Make Type Readable* (New York: Harper & Row, 1940), p. 23.

[7] Burt, op. cit., p. 12.

Logically, text matter presented in display sizes—as is occasionally done in promotional literature—risks a decline in legibility. It is likely to call attention to itself at the expense of the information it should be transmitting. Moreover, since few words fall within the eye span, more fixations are required of the reader with possibly the additional result of increased reading fatigue.

Leading   Printers and typographers use leading primarily to enhance legibility. These are the rules they follow:

1. For ordinary text sizes, one or two points of leading are adequate.
2. For faces that are small on the body, 1-point leading is sufficient.
3. As length of measure is increased, the need for leading is greater for any face.

Burt reported, "Little seems to be gained by 3-point leading; 4-point leading usually diminishes legibility; like excessive lettersize, it tends to increase the number of eye movements and fixation pauses."[8]

Length of line   The influence of the length measure on legibility has been substantiated by Burt's research.[9] Short measures in a large typeface require more frequent fixations, since the reader has more difficulty absorbing longer phrases. In addition, with short measures, the number of hyphenated words at the ends of lines increases. Both of these result in a decrease in reading comfort and an increase in the time required for perception.

Long lines, particularly in small type, also impair legibility, since the reader is slowed in picking up the succeeding line after swinging back from the end of the long line.

For many years charts expressing the limits for length of line relative to size of type have been available to printers and typographers. The limits have generally been expressed in picas or inch equivalents.

Burt has suggested that since set of type (width of individual letters) varies from face to face, limits of measure might better be expressed by lengths of alphabet. The term "length of alphabet" refers to the space required for composing lowercase letters *a* through *z*, with no extra space between letters. Burt has proposed that limits of two to three alphabets encompass maximum legibility and that alphabet length should correspond to body size. That is, if the type face is set 10 on 12, or 10-point leaded two points, the alphabet length of 12-point type should be used.

The usual book faces in 7-, 7½-, and 8-point are not considered satisfactory for newspaper editorial straight matter, partly because of

---

[8] Ibid., p. 13.

[9] Ibid., p. 14.

the narrow column width, which is generally 11 or 12 picas. Special news faces have been designed for use in what is becoming the standard width, 11 picas. Such faces are usually 9-point and are set with half-point leading. They have an x-height as large as possible and are at the same time condensed to allow 28 to 33 lowercase characters (counting spaces and punctuation characters) per line.

Although the number of alphabets per measure falls below Burt's minimum, his studies were primarily concerned with book printing. Moreover, one need but give a hasty check to realize that there are not an unreasonable number of hyphenations in the typical newspaper columns of straight matter.

A number of authorities maintain that the 11-pica newspaper column is too narrow for easy reading. One study conducted under the direction of Hvistendahl indicated an improved speed of reading with a 9-point news face on a 15-pica measure.[10] The wider columns also reduce the number of hyphenations and allow for more even spacing between words.

Many typographers find these rules of thumb for length of line useful: (1) minimum line lengths: one lowercase alphabet; optimum: one and one-half alphabets; maximum: two alphabets; (2) length of line in picas should not exceed twice the point size; thus 10-point type should not be set on a measure exceeding 20 picas; (3) lines should average 10 to 12 words.

These rules are not compatible. The words per line rule refers to average words, including such short ones as "the," "in," "on," "a," "by," as well as "Pennsylvania," "administration," "demonstration," and so on.

Printers generally consider the average word to be five characters plus one space. Lines averaging 10 words would thus accommodate 60 characters, somewhat in excess of two lowercase alphabets.

Margins   Research findings vary widely regarding the effect of book-page margins on legibility. Burt contends that excessively narrow margins may produce visual fatigue.[11] Paterson and Tinker, on the other hand, found that the reduction of normal margins had no effect on reading speed.[12]

Practitioners have long contended that ample margins invite reading, a belief that Burt seems to accept even though he suggests

---

[10] Roy Paul Nelson, *Publication Design* (Dubuque, Iowa: William C. Brown Company, 1972), p. 175.

[11] Burt, op. cit., pp. 14 – 15.

[12] Paterson and Tinker, op. cit., p. 109.

that reader preferences for margins are mostly a matter of esthetics. Margins comprising about 50 percent of a book are generally considered ample.

Progressive margins are most frequently used in book work; the narrowest margin is at the fold (inner margin), the next width is at the top of the page (head margin), next at the outside (outside margin), and the greatest is at the bottom (foot margin). These margins move clockwise on odd-numbered pages and counterclockwise on even-numbered pages. Thus, the odd- and even-numbered pages are held together by the narrow margins at the center.

The purpose of margins in all printing is to frame the type and other elements within a border of white space. Thus the amount of white space between elements within the printed area should be less than the white space of the margins in order to provide unity and coherence.

Even or Uneven Lines

Most body copy is composed in even lines. But today more text is composed with irregular line lengths, the so-called irregular right or ragged right. The left alignment remains even. The practice is often found in advertisements, but is appearing more frequently in book work and some newspapers are beginning to use the technique. Generally, if all lines are even, an occasional hyphenation at the end of a line is necessary. This is the most time-consuming operation in composition, and one purpose of the irregular right is to increase composition speed. Zachrisson has reported an experiment in which it was established that uneven lines have no adverse effect on legibility.[13]

Other Factors

The interaction between paper or printing surface and typeface has an effect on legibility. The principal factor involved relates to the contrast in brightness between print and paper.

Tinker and other researchers have concluded:

1. Black on white is superior to white print against a black background. When the message is short, white on black (so-called reverse printing) is useful for getting attention but text should be 10- or 12-point and preferably sans serif.
2. Black on tinted paper under ordinary conditions is probably an unimportant factor.
3. The legibility of different combinations of colored ink on colored backgrounds varies greatly. The best combinations have greater brightness contrast—e.g., dark ink on a light color.

---

[13] Zachrisson, op. cit., pp. 145–155.

4. Enamel paper should be carefully considered; glare may impair legibility.

Typographers follow several rules, which to our knowledge have not been researched. Old Style Roman faces were designed for letterpress printing on what was a relatively coarse stock in existence at the time of their creation. The combination of pressure printing on the coarse paper allowed the delicate hairlines to spread. Modern Roman faces with their fine lines print best on a smooth but uncoated paper. Highly polished paper tends to overemphasize the contrasts in such faces with a sacrifice in legibility.

There is no pressure in offset printing, for the image is transferred to the paper from a rubber surface. This printing method allows greater flexibility in selecting the type face.

The faces used in rotogravure printing must be able to withstand "screening," or breaking the image into a series of tiny dots. Typographers recommend avoiding hairline types, regardless of the nature of the paper. The density of the ink and the quality of the presswork are less under the control of the typographer than most of the previous factors. Their influence on legibility is obvious.

The typographer has no control over the lighting conditions under which the message is read, but, as suggested, he or she can control the background against which the type is seen.

Applying Legibility Factors

There are three major reasons why the typographer must exercise considerable judgment in applying the principles of legibility:

1. Since the testing has been primarily limited to book printing, adapting the principles to other areas requires care.
2. Researchers have noted a definite dependency of one factor on another. As Burt pointed out, "assessment obtained by varying just one characteristic in isolation may at times be highly misleading."[14]
3. Considerations other than legibility should enter the selection of type and its arrangement. If legibility were the sole criterion, all printed matter would tend toward a monotonous uniformity of appearance.

The typographer should thus look upon these principles as flexible aids to judgment rather than as an end in themselves, realizing that no one combination of the individual factors gives an absolute, maximum legibility.

---

[14] Burt, op. cit., p. 30.

Appropriateness of Type _____

Appropriateness, or fitness, is the second aspect to be observed in the use of type. In the process of communication the message from source to receiver should fall within a field of experience or knowledge common to both. In other words, the message must be stated in terms that can express the ideas the sender wishes to deliver and, at the same time, be comprehensible to the receiver.

The reader's response is conditioned by the overall effect of the complete printed message. The subject matter is embodied, of course, in the words. How they appear plays an important part in their delivery. The selection and arrangement of elements should combine into a unified communication that is appropriate to the message.

Appropriateness in this context has three meanings: it can be (1) the selection of faces according to the psychological impressions they bear; (2) the adaptation of legibility rules to fit the education and age levels of the reader; and (3) the use of faces harmonious with the other elements and the overall design of the printed message. "Compatibility" would be an appropriate synonym for "appropriateness."

Psychological Implications

The individual letters that comprise the upper- and lowercase alphabets of a given type face were designed to work together. The entire font is seen in infinite combinations within a block of type. From this comes a total visual impression that can be termed the "feel" of the face. It can suggest definite physical qualities in blocks of composition. For example, strength is conveyed by the Bodoni in the following paragraph. A touch of delicacy is suggested by the Caslon in the second paragraph. Both specimens are set in the same size type and leaded equally.

A block of copy set in Bodoni presents a "rough" texture somewhat like a corded material. This is caused by the vertical emphasis in the design of the face. Textural effect is due not only to the thickness of line but also to the amount of spacing between lines.

Copy composed in Caslon presents a "smooth" texture. The contrast between the vertical and the horizontal strokes is less pronounced than in Bodoni. The skilled typographer seeks a textural effect that is compatible with the nature of the message.

Touch or tactile experience plays a critical part in human behavior.[15] It is, as Frank has indicated, the primary means of infantile communication and is crucial to learning later in life, yet its impact on communication has largely been neglected. The infant learns early to enjoy tactual contact, especially with textures. As sensory awareness expands, the infant establishes visual images to reinforce his or her tactile experiences; signs and symbols become surrogates for tactile communication and arouse responses originally made to tactile stimuli.

The patterns of printing elements are such surrogates and deserve the typographer's careful attention. The face used and the leading between lines can change the textural tone of composition in interesting ways.

Some writers have suggested that the various typefaces, by reason of their design, can suggest different moods and feelings. Lists have been drawn giving a "personality" to each face, but these are no more than subjective evaluations. It will be far safer to depend on research to uncover the psychological associations with faces held by readers after more investigation has been done.

Using Legibility Rules The typographer can temper the application of legibility fundamentals to fit specific kinds of readers. Large bold faces seem desirable for the very young and the very old. Generous leading helps beginning readers to move from line to line. Where the degree of reader interest is higher, greater flexibility is possible, since reading will be done despite reduced legibility.

Harmony For the total printed piece to present a unified communication, the type and other elements must be in harmony. The tonal-textural feeling of the type should blend with the border, the illustrations, and other printing elements and should be compatible with the paper and printing process used.

Overriding all these conditions is, of course, the nature or "feel" the message is attempting to impart.

Checklist: **Typographical Rules**

To summarize, the real heart of a message is generally in its body copy. Headlines and illustrations serve to grasp attention; then, once the reader is caught, the body must be inviting to the eye and easy to stay with. Sound typography accomplishes this.

---

[15] Lawrence K. Frank, "Tactile Communication," The Journal Press: *Genet. Psychol. Monographs,* 56 (1957): 209 – 215.

A checklist of typographical rules follows. The student must remember that these rules have to be applied with judgment in every individual case:

1. Long copy should be broken for easy reading. There are several techniques: indent paragraphs, or, if they begin flush left, add extra space between paragraphs. Normal indentation is one em. Use subheads of contrasting face (different face) and/or contrasting weight; the bold face of the body type is good. Consider leaders and dashes, especially in advertisements. Relieve monotony by occasional italics and boldface at points of textual significance. Set copy in more than one column unless measures become so narrow as to impair legibility. Some paragraphs may be set on a narrower-than-text measure, centered in the column, especially in ads. Do not kill all widows (short line or a single word at the close of a paragraph) for they let in white space.

2. Set copy on the proper measure. One-and-a-half to two alphabets make a sound line length. As much as 60 characters and spaces (about 10 words) may also be safe, especially in book work.

3. Do not use too many different faces in one body. Harmony and unity result with a single face, with its italic and boldface, for body and display.

4. Avoid reverses for long body copy; this is especially true in newspapers where ink tends to fill in the letters because of low-grade paper quality.

5. Avoid text over illustrations or tint areas, unless you are certain there is sufficient contrast.

6. Ragged right seems safe; consider twice setting text in ragged left or ragged left and ragged right; the eye is accustomed to returning to a common point after reaching the end of a line.

7. Roman type is preferred in general for body copy, although the use of sans serif is becoming more popular.

8. Stay with 10-, 11-, and 12-point types for body copy. They are easier to read.

9. Consider leading as line length increases, or if the x-height is large. Don't overdo—3- and 4-point leading is seldom justified in text matter.

10. Margins should approach 50 percent of the page area and be progressive in book matter.

6 Using Type Creatively

In the last chapter we were concerned with the handling of body type. Visibility—more specifically, legibility—was our major concern. Now we turn to the fundamentals of using type in design.

Design is basic to almost everything we do. There is design in such common activities as shining shoes or scrubbing a floor; design also underlies the painting of a picture or the laying out of a printed piece. "A purposeful plan of action" is a satisfactory definition of design, except that for our purposes we should add the concept of "creativity."

Creativity suggests new and better ways of carrying out a purposeful action. When we need something—perhaps a machine to perform a certain function—if we are creative, we engage in purposeful action to invent it. But we need more than material things, such as machines. We also have spiritual or emotional needs—for joy, for happiness, for love.

Our museums contain many ancient artifacts the functional purposes of which we may not know; yet we find them a pleasure to look at simply because they express the joy, happiness, and satisfaction of those who designed them.

Any creative design is, therefore, both functional and expressive. To evaluate or judge a design we must know its purpose or function. If we do not know the purpose of an object, we can only value its design, as in the case of the ancient artifacts; that is, we can only say, "I like it" or "It seems to reflect the feelings of the person who designed it." In much of our everyday life we delude ourselves into believing that we are evaluating things, whereas we react only to likes and dislikes. This is one cause of our poor judgments. One might say that such judgments are "unreasoned."

Everything we have said so far directly involves the typographic designer. Since the designer's work is an integral part of the visual communication, he or she has an obligation to the source of the message and to the receiver. The designer must know the source's intentions—in other words, the function, and must also understand how the receiver will react not only to the content but to the form the message takes. Form is the means of expressiveness, and meaning exists not only in the content but in the form as well. For a message to be received with maximum effect, the two meanings must be compatible. It would never do for the typographer to use a design as a means toward expressing what he or she personally feels is "beautiful," at the same time ignoring the intent of the message.

Visual Syntax

Man communicates in print with verbal language and with visual form. Before we turn our attention to the latter, we should put both within the context of information processing.

Language is widely held by linguists to evolve naturally. Certain basic programs are "wired in," enabling man through exposure to a language to learn to use it. Stated another way, language is an innate structure in man. The languages of the world are similar in grammatical form, not in surface structure but in deep structure. This is because the enabling programs of language capacity are similar for all.[1]

One naturally associates organized structure, syntax, and technical grammatical rules with any verbal language. All this leads too easily to a tendency to see the visual or formal as an unorganized, nonintellectual mode of communication. Such is not the case.

Just as all human beings are endowed with language capacity, they also have a basic physical, visual perception system. What man looks at is structured by various constituent elements, just as verbal language is structured by spoken or printed words. And just as there are grammatical rules for composing effective verbal messages, there are rules for composing effective visual forms. Dondis refers to these rules as "visual syntax."[2]

Display Legibility

The body or text type is of little significance as impact value. Its purpose is not to attract the reader to a printed message. As a consequence, the typographer can concentrate his or her efforts on making the printed message as legible as possible. However, the typographer must give special attention to the treatment of type used for display purposes. Although legibility is also desirable for display, it is not so

---

[1] Noam Chomsky, "Language and the Mind," *Psychology Today*, no. 9 (1968).

[2] Donis A. Dondis, *A Primer of Visual Literacy* (Cambridge, Mass.: M.I.T. Press, 1973), p. 11.

imperative because it has a primary function before reading speed. The major use of display is to attract attention.

Although much literature is not illustrated, almost all of it has headlines or headings. In the remainder of this chapter we discuss the techniques for the imaginative use of type in display.

Although legibility may be secondary in display, it must not be overlooked. For example, heads in all-caps Script or Cursive (Figure 6-1)

6-1 Head in all-caps Cursive is difficult to read.

HARD TO READ

or set vertically and diagonally (Figure 6-2) become very difficult to read. In general, legibility of display is governed by the same principles as body type.

The New Typography ───────────

From the time of the early printers until the past century, type was displayed by centering each line on the measure. This style prevailed for some 350 years for several reasons. First, it presented a perfectly symmetrical effect. One's orientation toward space depends on one's sense of balance. Visual perception and this sense are closely related. Our need for balance has a major psychological effect on perception. Second, the avid desire of readers for the product kept the attention of printers focused on production rather than on design. Third, type can easily be composed this way by hand or by machine.

To understand the meaning of the ''New Typography,'' a term often applied to the present-day use of typographical materials, let us briefly look at a few historical high points in the development of printing design.

The cutting of display faces in the nineteenth century introduced a new kind of typography. Often blatant, sometimes bizarre, these faces were designed for use in the increasingly competitive world of commerce. Posters, publicity bills, and cards printed with these faces had a look quite apart from that of a book.

With the twentieth century came the development of what has been call *Modern* Art, bringing new ideas and forms. A number of styles came into being in Europe that had varying degrees of influence on typography there and later in the United States. Perhaps the most notable of these were Art Nouveau, Constructivism, and Dadaism.

Art Nouveau actually appeared in the last decade of the nineteenth century. In essence a style of decoration, its free-flowing lines and ornamentation were fashioned in wrought- and cast-iron furniture. Its effect on typography (see Figure 6-3) came with the free style

6-2 Heads set vertically and diagonally are difficult to read.

6-3 Art Nouveau influence on book design. Two pages from *The Canterbury Tales*, published by the Golden Cockerel Press in 1929; illustrated by Eric Gill. (*Reprinted from* The Art Nouveau Book in Britain *by J. R. Taylor, by permission of A. D. Peters & Co., Ltd.*)

of off-centered and counterbalanced lines and a more liberal use of white space.

Constructivism was an outgrowth of Cubism, the most controversial of the modern art styles. Cubism was based on analytical interpretation rather than on exact imitation of the subject. Decoration was eliminated and subjects were shown by means of geometric patterns involving cubes, squares, and rectangles.

The Constructivists continued the cubistic ideas of form and structure. The work of the Dutch painter Piet Mondrian is typical. He developed an asymmetrical style in which bold rectangular grid structures were counterbalanced. The Mondrian style has been somewhat subdued in the New Typography by the elimination of the rigid pattern of grids. However, the counterbalancing of rectangular elements is still a popular technique, as shown, for example, in Figure 6-4. The large dark areas represent photos; the smaller illustrations are drawings. The dark area on the left is a headline, and the remaining rectangles represent text type. (See also Figure 15-15.)

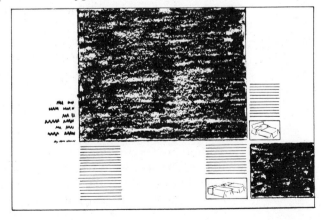

6-4 Modern layout is affected by Mondrian art style. Grid structure of a two-page spread in a magazine.

Dadaism contributed to the development of modern typography in a negative way. The very name of the movement—supposedly found by opening the dictionary at random—was a symbol of the confusion of the times. Dadaists worked directly in the typographic field. Their designs of printed messages were chaotic in appearance—lines of type using display and book faces running in various directions—even individual letters of words were positioned in a completely unorthodox manner.

In post-World War I Germany the Bauhaus, previously mentioned in Chapter 4, brought order to the chaotic movements preceding it. From this school have come these contributions, now evident in the New Typography:

1. Asymmetric design
2. Wide acceptance of sans serif type
3. Relaxation of traditional (progressive) margination
4. Bold placement of illustrations
5. More interesting division of space with contrasting shapes of elements placed in interesting juxtaposition
6. Simplification and release from extensive ornamentation
7. Greater concentration on a utilitarian use of typographic elements

Applications of the New Typography

Let us consider the applications of modern typography in two broad categories: (1) books and (2) ephemera. The divisions are based on the function of the material and reader attitudes toward the material.

Books

Books are generally intended for instructional or informational and entertainment purposes. Generally speaking, when a reader "settles down" with his book, his or her attention and interest are focused on its content. The designer must also remember that books are produced and bound for a more lasting impression. Convention and tradition have had a strong influence on book design.

Ephemera

All printing other than book production can be classified as ephemera. This material is less permanent and shorter than books. Included in this category would be newspapers, magazines, advertising matter, annual reports, and the like.

These categories may appear to be loosely structured, but a brief examination of the theory of communication provides the reason for the classification.

Although effective communication is a matter of learning, there are different situations in which learning occurs, and these situations demand different presentations. For example, in a classroom the audience is predisposed to learn; the level of attention is high. In a mass communication situation involving ephemera quite the opposite is true. Therefore, the designer considers different approaches to effective presentation when designing an advertisement or a magazine from those used when designing a book.

In mass communication the attention of readers is often low and their interest span short. Here the problem is to attract and to arouse attention. The message may be short and will be repeated in several contacts between the source and the receiver. Book design is often governed by convention and tradition, and the methods of presentation are more established, although this is changing. Thus, magazines, ads, and newspapers follow one set of design principles and books another.

Book design The generally accepted standard for the book format until the influence of the Bauhaus made its impression was that of the classical page with its progressive margins and Roman typefaces.

Figure 6-5, a spread of two pages, is typical of book margination. The page size illustrated is 6 by 9 inches, and the type page size is 26 by 42 picas. Margins are, progressively, $3\frac{1}{2}$, 4, $6\frac{1}{2}$, and 8 picas.

The spirit of the New Typography suggests that we might deviate from the rigidity of the classical book page. Deviation is a safe step if we bear in mind the Bauhaus principle that design must be functional. It must not infringe on effective communication.

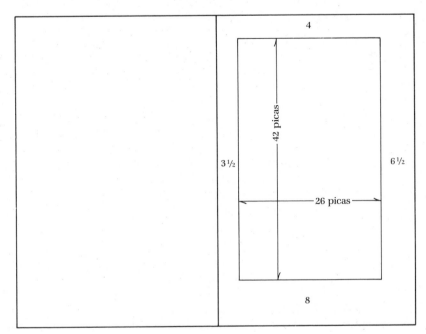

6-5 Traditional progressive margins on a book page.

A striking departure from the traditional is the use of sans serif for the entire text of a book. Traditionalists object to this, pointing out a loss in legibility. Those willing to experiment point out that a somewhat condensed Gothic set on a measure that allows eight to ten words per line would be quite legible. A few magazines use this technique and more books are being so composed.

Another major departure from traditional book designs is in the treatment of margins. Figure 6-6 shows a spread of $6\frac{1}{2}$ by $7\frac{3}{4}$-inch pages with most unconventional margins. The text was set on $17\frac{1}{2}$ picas; margin sizes are marked in picas. The book was profusely illustrated; the

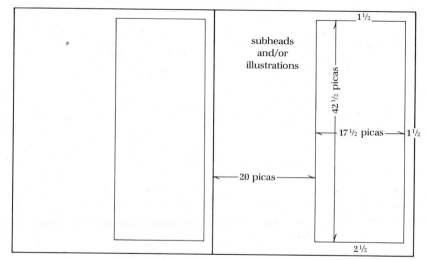

6-6 New Typography book margin treatment.

wide margins were used for the placement of illustrations and subhead lines. However, many pages carried only white space to the left of the copy blocks.

It is not possible to discuss here in detail the increasing number of nontraditional book-design techniques. It is suggested that the student become acquainted with them as they come to his or her attention. Illustrations, charts and diagrams, liberal use of white space, contrasting type styles, bleeds (running printed matter off the edges of the page), color, irregular type margins, and larger display faces are being applied more frequently.

Typographic design, like life itself, is an evolving process of change. It should not be changed for the sake of change but for improved function. The question becomes, "How interesting, typographically, should a book be?"

Design of ephemera It is in ephemera that the designer faces the fewest restrictions. This does not mean that wild experimentation is possible. The term "New Typography" does not imply bizarre design but rather orderly and logical treatment befitting the content of the message. Experimentation is justified if there is a logical reason for it.

For example, examine the full-page advertisement in Figure 6-7. The white space across the middle seems to divide the ad into two parts. The technique attracts, although it would seem to violate the principle that a message should have unity. In this case, the advertiser depends on reader curiosity to bridge the white space gap. Note the strong contrast in tone between top and bottom of the ad; provocative contrast also is in the content of the headline, urging the reader on.

23 million people could be fooled this year.

This year, 23 million people may think they're buying a pair of Fiskars scissors and end up with an imitation.

The reason is simple. Fiskars designed the original lightweight scissors. They perfected it. They introduced it. And then, 44 other companies started copying it. Most even went so far as to use orange handles. But that wasn't quite far enough. It takes much more to make a fine

pair of scissors. Like Swedish stainless steel blades that let you glide through yards of fabric without faltering. And comfort-molded handles that actually become an extension of you, offering a lifetime of effortless cutting.

So don't let the look-alikes fool you. If it doesn't say Fiskars on the blade, it's merely an imitation. And that doesn't say much for those other scissors.

FISKARS
Normark

If it doesn't say Fiskars on the blade, it doesn't say much for the scissors.

Normark, Minneapolis, Minnesota 55421. In Canada, Normark Limited, Winnipeg, Manitoba R3T1T4. Manufactured by OY Fiskars AB Finland. Normark Corporation is sole importer, marketer, and national distributor.

6-7 White space in the center of this advertisement provokes curiosity. (*Courtesy Normark Corporation*)

We deal with the use of pictorial elements in typographic design in Chapter 14. Let us now consider the use of type elements in design.

Symmetrical Design _____

The arrangement of type elements in a symmetrical pattern has its origin in classical book design. Although its applications today are limited, an understanding of the principles of symmetrical design is basic to an appreciation of the more widely applied asymmetrical design.

When we look at something we naturally perceive tone and shape. Manipulation of these two formal concepts arouses meanings in all of us. A single line of type parallel to the bottom of the page is seen as a pair of horizontal lines delineating the size of type:

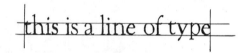

The tone of the type itself can be varied, for example, by using boldface, to give greater weight:

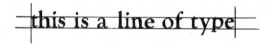

When several lines are composed in proximity, together they form a shape:

XXXXXXXXXXXX
XXXXXXXXXXX
XXXXXXXX

If at all possible, the major weight should be above the center of the shape. Alternating long and short lines should be avoided if possible, since this makes it more difficult to sense the shape and thus the meaning.

It is one thing to arrange the lines of type in a display that forms a shape. Often, however, the designer must compromise when the sense of the content will be broken between two lines.

What is the best way to display "The Art of Growing Old" in three lines, all centered in the symmetrical style? Would the following suffice?

THE ART
OF
GROWING OLD

First, it would be preferable to have the two top lines longer than the third. Second, as here set, the relatively unimportant word "of" is emphasized by being given a line alone. This would then seem preferable:

THE ART
OF GROWING
OLD

The word "of" belongs with the word "growing." Further, there is now a more discernible shape.

Consider the design of the announcement card:

BINGO PARTY AND
DANCE
OLD MAIN CENTER
TUESDAY
JANUARY 8, 1974
8:30 P.M.
YOU ARE MOST CORDIALLY
INVITED

Note that there is equal spacing between all lines. Imagine a monotonal recitation of the message with pauses of equal length after each line. In essence, this is the same thing in print. The following arrangement is an improvement. Now the thought units are grouped and the spacing better fits the content.

BINGO PARTY
AND DANCE

OLD MAIN CENTER

TUESDAY, JANUARY 8
1974

8:30 P.M.

YOU ARE MOST CORDIALLY
INVITED

Placing Emphasis Even though the spacing is improved in the preceding example, it seems to have too much of an overall gray tone. Certainly the simplicity and harmony satisfy the basic human urge for equilibrium and reduction of uncertainty. But one should not forget the equally important need for stimulation.

It is possible to improve this situation. One might place emphasis on certain words, composing them in all caps and a larger size if other words are caps and lowercase (Figure 6-8). If the other lines are all

Basic Considerations in
SYMMETRICAL DESIGN

caps, perhaps the emphasized words might be set in lowercase. In this example the lowercase letters should be larger than the caps in the other lines (Figure 6-9).

BASIC CONSIDERATIONS IN
symmetrical design

Other possibilities exist, of course. Variations can also be effected by using small caps, italic, boldface, and color. It is also possible to mix typefaces.

Remembering the designer's responsibility to meld the communication effect of the format with the content, one should be careful to place emphasis on the key verbal elements.

The Layout The designer arranges the elements to center on a vertical axis in the middle of the type page, that area remaining after margins are sub-

6-8 This hand-lettered head achieves emphasis by contrasting size and by contrasting caps and lower case with all caps.

6-9 This hand-lettered head achieves emphasis by contrasting large-size lower case with smaller all caps.

6-10 *Right:* Locating the optical center on a layout. The horizontal axis is about three-fifths up the page from the foot margin.

6-11 *Far right:* Formally balanced all-type layout. *(Copyright © 1968 by Holt, Rinehart and Winston. Reproduced by permission)*

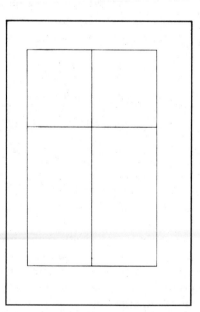

EDUCATIONAL
PSYCHOLOGY
A COGNITIVE VIEW

DAVID P. AUSUBEL
*Office of Research and Evaluation, Division of Teacher Education
The City University of New York*

HOLT, RINEHART AND WINSTON, INC.
*New York · Chicago · San Francisco · Atlanta · Dallas
Montreal · Toronto · London*

tracted from the page size. Generally, the designer lightly draws on layout paper the dimensions of page and type page together with the vertical axis. In addition, the designer draws a horizontal axis, approximately three-fifths up from the foot margin (Figure 6-10). The layout paper should be transparent enough to allow the designer to lay it over type specimens for tracing. The intersection of the axes marks the *optical center*, the position the eye prefers to the mathematical center.

In Figure 6-11 the major shape—major in content and form—falls over this point. Note that the lowest shape falls to the foot margin. In Figure 6-12 the number of lines required to follow the heading force it toward the top of the page.

Asymmetrical Design _____

There is a quiet dignity and elegance about a symmetrical display of type. Each line is centered with equal amounts of white space at either end of each line. The display is beautifully simple and logical.

One might suspect that "asymmetrical" means abandonment of simplicity, balance, and logical arrangement. This is not true; the asymmetrical design achieves balance in a different way, is equally logical, and is not more complicated.

Figure 6-13 shows an asymmetrical type design which should be compared with Figure 6-11. In symmetrical design the space on the page serves only as a background against which the type elements are displayed. The elements are more important than the space and the

he Use and Misuse of

LANGUAGE

edited, and with a foreword
by S. I. HAYAKAWA

selections from
ETC.: A Review of General Semantics
previously published in
LANGUAGE, MEANING AND MATURITY
and
OUR LANGUAGE AND OUR WORLD

illustrations by
William H. Schneider
and
Frank Lobdell

A Premier Book
CETT PUBLICATIONS, INC., GREENWICH, CONN.
Member of American Book Publishers Council, Inc.

6-12 Formally balanced all-type layout with major heading forced above optical center.

6-13 Asymmetrical all-type layout. (*Courtesy University of Illinois Press*)

THE MEASUREMENT OF MEANING

latter serves to frame the type display. In the asymmetrical situation space becomes an integral part of the design. This is more evident in Figure 6-14. Note how the left edge of the first four and the bottom three lines form a vertical axis as do the left edges of the three in the middle of the page. The left edge of the middle shape lines up with the "n" in "Edition." The groupings of lines form horizontal shapes that are placed on vertical axes. Figure 6-15 is a drawing depicting the various spaces established by the design.

6-14 *Right:* Asymmetrical layout with dynamic use of white space. (*Copyright* © *1964, 1968 by Holt, Rinehart and Winston. Reproduced by permission*)

6-15 *Far right:* Space division in the asymmetrical layout in Figure 6-14. The various relationships of the elements in the title page are immediately apparent in this drawing.

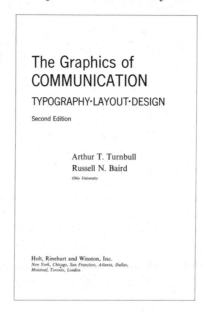

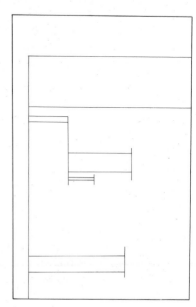

6-16 Symmetrical design and asymmetrical variations.

(a) Symmetrical layout. (b) Asymmetrical variation. (c) Asymmetrical variation. Note that two kinds of face design are used: "Type" is in italics of a Roman face; the other four words are in a sans serif face. (d) Asymmetrical variation.

<table>
<tr><td>(a)</td><td>(b)</td><td>(c)</td><td>(d)</td></tr>
</table>

Contrast is achieved within the type mass in symmetrical design by varying the features of the typeface. In asymmetrical design contrast is achieved through the placement of masses. There are fewer variations within sans serif alphabets than within Roman alphabets; consequently, the former are found widely used in asymmetrical design. This does not, however, preclude the use of Roman faces. In fact, a mixture of Roman and sans serif within asymmetrical design is not uncommon. This is demonstrated in the hand-drawn layouts in Figure 6-16.

Note the vertical axes in the three asymmetrical variations in Figure 6-16. In the first, the vertical axis falls along the stem of the *T* in the word "TYPE." In the second, because the *T* in "Type" is italic, the vertical axis is determined by a line that would be the center of gravity for the slanted letter. In the third, the axis is diagonal, established by the capitals *T* and *D*, and this axis establishes the placement of the two top lines.

Figure 6-17 shows an ad in which display and text are used in asymmetrical layout. Note that the left edge of the third display line establishes the margin for the text.

Automating the $8 billion newspaper industry

Some 63 million newspapers printed in the U.S. every day. $600 million spent for more productive equipment in the last three years.

Video typewriters. Electronic editing systems. Computerized phototypesetters. Automated offset presses. Automated inserting equipment. More.

Harris. Printing. Electronics. Joined.

Write for an annual report.

HARRIS
Harris-Intertype Corporation.
55 Public Square. Cleveland, Ohio 44113.
Communications and information handling.

6-17 Display and text in excellent asymmetrical treatment. (*Courtesy Harris Corporation*)

Headline Size

A number of considerations involving headline size are common to advertising and magazine editorial layouts. Many of these considerations apply to other forms of printing as well. The main heading should be sized large enough to stand out in competition with other elements of the page or ad and draw attention to the message. The main subhead should be large enough to attract attention to itself but not away from the main head. Beginning designers need to keep the function of the main head in mind, for they tend to undersize them.

Secondary subheads are often satisfactory if set in text size; it is important, however, that they contrast sufficiently with the body composition they accompany. This can be accomplished with boldface, italic, or a face of another type family.

These factors determine the size of the headline type:

1. Weights of other display elements.
2. Size of the space (page size or ad dimensions). Larger space calls for large sizes.
3. Amount of white space surrounding the head. A headline can be a smaller size when it is given emphasis with added white space.
4. Color printing of heads. Printing in color requires larger type sizes than printing in black.
5. Size of condensed type. A larger size is needed for condensed type than for standard width.
6. Length of the head. Longer headlines tend to force the designer to use a type size that is too small. The situation can be resolved by breaking the head into major and minor thought groups.

Some special headline considerations Two other aspects of handling headlines deserve mention: headline form and headline typographic style. Because the head is both a graphic and a verbal element, it can generate interest through its form as well as its content. People will read what interests them; the form in which it is presented will invite them to read.

The simplest and most direct form is a single line. When content is of a high degree of interest, a headline presentation in a single line can be very effective. Often headlines are too long to fit in one line. When heads are set in two or more lines, form becomes a more significant consideration. Two or more lines are often centered one above the other. This is perhaps the most conservative possible treatment.

The designer's task is to make the form compatible with other layout elements. At the same time the form should offer minimum interference with reader comprehension of the content. It frequently becomes necessary to deviate from the centering of lines to satisfy the need of compatibility. Flush-left or flush-right headlines are, therefore, another common form.

Additional techniques accent form. We cannot make a detailed inventory here, but we may take a brief look at some of them:

1. Use of color
2. Combining rules or ornaments with the head
3. Reverse blocks containing heads
4. All caps

5. Mixing typefaces
6. Printing the head on a tint block
7. Use of initial letters
8. Combining the head with art treatment
9. Use of hand lettering
10. Arranging the head in a special shape

Giving photographic treatment to headlines for unusual effects is also possible. Such a technique may be seen in Figure 6-18. A number of specialized businesses offer this service.

Many of these treatments can be applied to entire headlines or to portions of them—and they may be used in combinations. Knowing the importance of the headline, the designer is often tempted to call attention to it through emphasis on its form. Caution, however, is well advised. As mentioned before, form should never overshadow substance or the content of the message. In processing theory, STM can only handle so much information at a time.

Accent on form may be justified under such conditions as these:

1. The special treatment adds to the understanding of the substance. That is, the headline, through form accentuation, is made *self-descriptive.* Examples are shown in Figure 6-19.
2. The form treatment fits naturally with other layout elements. Photographic treatment of the head in Figure 6-18 slants letters to the left to build the head around the arm and hammer trademark. In

6-19 Self-descriptive headlines.

"There is nothing so powerful as an idea whose time has come."

If your NAILS BREAK OR SPLIT

* UNCERTAIN STOMACH

6-18 Photographic headline treatment. (*Courtesy Arm & Hammer Division, Church & Dwight Co., Inc.*)

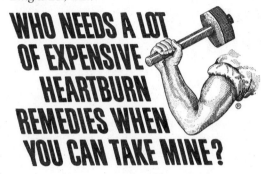

WHO NEEDS A LOT OF EXPENSIVE HEARTBURN REMEDIES WHEN YOU CAN TAKE MINE?

would
your tires
be
safe at
100 mph
?

The Dunlop Gold Seal is certified safe at 100 mph. So you're sure you're safe at 60, 70, or 80. And yet the full four-ply Gold Seal is still popularly priced.

And there's more safety to the Gold Seal. It has treads on the sides. Safety-Shoulders. They take the fight out of a tight turn, carry you smoothly up and over center lines or road shoulders without a lurch. They're patented*.

Then the Gold Seal has what tire men call a low profile. That means a 15% larger footprint area. More of the Gold Seal's wide tread is always on the road for better traction, greater safety, more miles of wear.

Doesn't the Gold Seal sound like a choice tire for a change? Drive carefully to your nearest Dunlop man. He's listed in the Yellow Pages.

Every new Dunlop tire meets or exceeds every official specification for safe performance.

*PAT. NO. 0.044.000

DUNLOP ... means quality in golf, tennis, and tires.

BUFFALO, NEW YORK

72

6-20 Head integrated into text.

Figure 6-20 the head is shaped to integrate it into the copy or text.

3. Among smaller ads, where competition for attention is especially keen, special head treatments are often effective. Such techniques as shown in 6-19, as well as reversing the heads (printing white against black), are often useful.

The typographic styling of heads primarily involves spacing, letter alignment, and punctuation. The need for spacing within all-cap lines of display has already been described in Chapter 4. Between-line spacing in headlines set cap and lowercase may often require visual adjustment, since ascenders and descenders may act to cause the lines to appear unevenly leaded.

The problem of letter alignment is shown in Figure 6-21. The example to the right is structured so that the letters at the left edges line up optically. The *W* is slightly to the left of the margin. For the most eye-pleasing appearance, *W*, *A*, *V*, *Y*, *X*, *C*, *O*, *G*, *Q*, and *S* should run past the margin, right or left.

WERLON   WERLON
by Wedley   by Wedley

6-21 *Left:* Normal letter alignment. *Right:* Appearance is improved through visual alignment on the left.

In Figure 6-22 the punctuation is placed outside the left margin. The same may be done on the opposite margin. Imagine the irregularity of the margin line if the quotes were set flush on the line. The *T* would appear significantly out-of-line. Such treatment is common in display-sized type.

6-22 Punctuation outside normal left margin: "hanging punctuation." Note the reverse treatment of the closing quotation marks: pulled in above the period to prevent them from seeming to hang too much.

JOSEPHINE, TV'S LADY PLUMBER, SAYS:

"Try this test and see Comet get out stains other cleansers leave behind."

Not all designers follow this form; it is obviously more expensive because the punctuation is outside the type measure being used. Yet it is in the best tradition of fine typography. Even today a few advertisers apply the treatment to body copy, as seen in Figure 6-23. But the style is seldom found in editorial columns, since its setting is time-consuming and hence costly.

6-23 Punctuation outside normal right margin. (*Courtesy Johnson & Johnson*)

Help heal the hurt with the new Johnson & Johnson First Aid Cream—the long-lasting antiseptic that helps fight infection, soothe the hurt, promote healing. Every minor skin break, from scrapes to scratches, from cuts to bites, needs Johnson & Johnson First Aid Cream.

6-24 Rising initial.

6-25 Set-in initial.

Initial Letters

We must mention the use of *initial letters* before leaving this chapter. These are display-sized letters integrated into body copy. They serve a dual function: first, to lend a spot of display to areas that are basically not display; and second, to bridge the gap between heads and text. There are two types: *rising initials* and *set-in initials*, shown in Figures 6-24 and 6-25, respectively. Note that with the former a word or two of the text is in all caps following the initial, which rests on the first line (small caps are often used after a rising initial). In the latter, caps generally do not follow and the initial rests on a lower line of the text.

Conclusion

Typography is not a free art. Elements and space are not arranged for purely expressive purposes. Rather, there is a logical basis. Typography is a means to an end. Its function is to aid in effective communication. The most prosaic typographic presentation is probably better received than typographic trickery and distortion. But there is always room for a freshness of style and presentation so long as it does not inhibit clear exchange of information and consequently meanings.

7 Electronic Copy Processing Systems

Computerization has been introduced into virtually every facet of contemporary American society, and the area of graphics of communication is no exception.

Words, on their way into print, are now almost certain to filter through a computer in one fashion or another. The blending of computers and electronics has created electronic copy processing systems that are marvels to behold. These systems have invaded every medium of communication, from the smallest newspaper to the largest metropolitan daily, and from the smallest specialized magazine to the circulation giants.

Advertising and public relations organizations have also been affected by the modern methods of getting words into print. Like it or not, even those who became involved in printed media because of their creative talents and instincts must have at least an elementary knowledge of how computers and electronics serve them, their masters.

Computers are indeed amazing machines, but they are based on some basic principles that are really fairly easy to understand. After all, the human hand is made up of digits (fingers), and many of us first learned to count and do simple computing by using our fingers. And we are also aware that we could, if necessary, *communicate* through our fingers provided we had a common code, for example, one finger meaning "yes," none meaning "no," and so on. It is the digitizing of information, the conversion of human communication symbols to a numeric code, that has made word processing systems possible. Some knowledge about digital computers is essential to an understanding of these word-processing systems.

A Little Bit About Bits

Basic to that knowledge is an understanding of the *binary digit* or *bit*, as it is called. Briefly defined, a bit is one piece of information derived by a *binary* (two-digit) code, a code that provides for only yes-no types of answers. If we want to know if it is raining outside, our caveman digital system can tell us the answer quickly if we know that one finger up means "yes," and no fingers up means "no." We could substitute a punched hole in tape to mean yes, and no holes to mean no; or a positive electrical charge to mean yes, and a negative one to mean no, and so on.

Computers operate on this basis. As they record and process information, circuits are either open or closed, switches are either on or off, transistors either conduct electricity or not, and current either passes through wires or not.

From Bits to Bytes

To see how such a digital system can actually work in getting words recorded and processed, let us look at a very common coding system used in automated printing equipment. This code is based on a perforated tape with a maximum of six punched holes in each row, thus making it what is called *six-level* tape and a six-level code. If we use only a two-level tape, we have only these four possibilities of punched arrangements:

0 0

X X

X 0

0 X

In order to deal in words and numbers, the arrangement of punched holes must be able to be different for 26 letters of the alphabet, plus numbers, spaces, capitals, and some other symbols. With six-level tape, 64 variations are possible, as Figure 7-1 shows (see next page). This is enough to take care of all letters plus typesetting commands and will suffice as an example here. Eight-level codes, which increase the variations from 64 to 256, are the ones most commonly used for computer operation.

Staying with the six-level example, let us decide that punching *only* the first hole out of the six possible ones represents the small letter *t*. The punch in the first hole is a *bit* of information for us, *but without knowing about the other five places, we are not helped.* Knowing that the first hole is punched and the second is not punched provides us with *two* bits of information, but we still do not know what character is represented by the full row of six bits. But when we know that all the other spaces have not been punched, we know that this is the letter *t*. This amount of information is called a *byte;* it comes from knowing all six bits of information from one row on the tape.

The six-level Teletypesetter code table (TS 729). Column headings read, SHIFT (top) / UNSHIFT (bottom):

SHIFT	UNSHIFT
Tape Feed	
T	t
Return	
O	o
Space Band	
N	n
H	h
M	m
Elevate	
I	i
R	r
C	c
L	l
P	p
G	g
V	v
E	e
A	a
S	s
U	u
D	d
J	j
F	f
K	k
Z	z
W	w
Y	y
Q	q
B	b
Shift	
X	x
Unshift	
Space	
Thin Space	3
¾	
PF or LM	$
!	
Add-Thin Space	
Em Space	8
⅞	7
-	✓
@	
½	4
*	
Bell	
Comma	
Quad Left	
En Space	5
Q R or UM	
⅝	)
(	
V Rule Em Sp	2
ff	
Em Leader	6
¾	0
lb	
fi	9
En Leader	
fl	:
Upper Rail	
&	
Lower Rail	
Period	
⅛	
ffi	
Quad Center	
Rub Out	

Row labels down the left side: 0, 1, 2, TAPE FEED, 3, 4, 5. The punched positions are indicated by filled dots (●) in rows 0–5 and by sprocket feed holes (○) across the TAPE FEED row.

7-1 The six-level Teletypesetter code used for perforating tape is adequate for a computerized word processing system; this code is used to operate many typesetters. Eight-level codes using magnetic tape or direct wire communication are now more common, however.

A better idea of how this works can be obtained by analyzing Figure 7-1. If you check the bottom horizontal row of holes only, you will find that 32 holes are punched. Knowing just the one bit of information, as in the previous example, we know that the *t* is represented by one of these 32 vertical columns, so we are halfway home in terms of getting our answer. If we then check the bottom two rows to find those that have the first one punched and the other one not punched, we will find 16 such combinations. So we are three-fourths of the way; we know the *t* is somewhere among these 16 combinations. When we check three rows, we will find that there are eight possibilities; with four rows there are only four, with five rows only two, and with all six rows there is only one. So with six-level tape all six bits are needed for one character (any letter, space, number, and so on).

If you check the tape in Figure 7-1 for letters and numbers, you will find that they are all there. There is also one set of holes for a *shift* (near the middle of the diagram); whenever this byte is read into a computerized typesetting system, the following letter or letters become capitals. So, in this case, two bytes really are needed for the character: one for the letter and the other to make it a capital.

Of the other bytes of information on the tape shown in Figure 7-1, those for punctuation should not engender questions, but there are other terms included that may or may not be familiar. Those, such as *em space*, *quad left*, and *em leader*, are typesetting terms, which are needed to communicate, in digital language, special typesetting instructions to automated typesetters.

Without belaboring the point further, we can conclude that it is possible to digitize human language—if one byte tells us a character, we can know an average eight-character word by knowing eight bytes. And this capability goes back to the *bit*—the result, for example, of a switch being on or off.

The details of this particular code are not of great consequence. The code was used as an example because it is the old TTS code that was used as the basis for automating old linecasting typesetting machines. It gets the name TTS (Teletypesetter) tape from that usage. Many newspaper electronic systems use this code as a base, but a more common one is called ASCII (askee), short for American Standard Code for Information Interchange. We mention codes again later.

The important point here is that, if information can be digitized, it can be stored and processed by a computer; sent over telephone lines, through the air or via any other means; and be received, stored, or processed by other devices at any other point.

A computer is thus a fast decision-making machine using a digital code and capable of a million or more operations per second. The logic to do these operations is *programmed* into the computer. The program might be fed into the computer by punched cards, punched tape, magnetic tape, magnetic disks—or a single program may have been wired into the computer, making it what is called a *hard-wired* machine.

For word processing, computer logic is used primarily for hyphenation of words and justification of lines of type, and in the role of "traffic cop" for a system—directing where and in what sequence the information is to go. A computer and its auxiliary devices can store information in great quantities (on punched tape, magnetic tape, magnetic disks like phonograph records, and others) that can be recalled when needed. The storage capacity of a computer data-storing device or memory is expressed in terms of K bytes. The K equals about 1,000 (1,024, to be exact). Thus, a 64K unit would have a capacity of about 64,000 bytes or characters.

Computerized Electronic Copy Processing Systems

The search for the most efficient method for getting words from the minds of their authors into type—and then onto a printing press—has gone on for centuries. For all practical purposes, this search has ended with the development of computerized electronic systems. Much modifying and amplifying of systems and their uses are to come, but electronic digital recording and transmitting of copy is the method of the future as well as the present.

Although varied in their detail, these electronic systems are all essentially formed with three types of equipment: *keyboard entry devices*, *computers*, and *output devices*. These components originate digital information, store and manipulate it, and output it in verbal form as type proof or printed pages.

In their maximum use, these system components provide means for authors to input their words and illustrations at the beginning of the system and for a machine to produce a plate for a printing press at the other end. Some systems totally eliminate the need for other human labor on the way, some require special attention to illustrations only, and others automate only some of the steps that are involved. There are so many different systems and so many different machines involved that none of them seem to be exactly alike. As we look at these systems, however, they can be understood if we keep in mind that all of them are intended to accomplish some simple steps of copy processing. These steps are:

1. Creating written matter by striking the keys on a machine.
2. Storing written material until it can be corrected.
3. Correcting the material.
4. Setting the material in type.
5. Fitting the material along with other elements into a page of a medium (magazine, brochure, newspaper, or the like).

These are all *prepress* steps that must be completed before a printing plate can be put on a press; consequently, the systems are often referred to as prepress or *front-end* systems. The operation of these systems begins with the authors' work at the input devices.

Input Devices: Video Display Terminals, Typewriters, Scanners

The primary input device for an electronic system is a *video display terminal* (VDT). VDTs are made by scores of manufacturers, each of whom provides some variation designed to make its unit superior to its competitors' or suitable for special purposes. VDTs are fundamentally alike, however, in that they provide (1) full alphanumeric keyboards like those on electric typewriters; (2) a set of keys for making editing changes; and (3) keys used to communicate with other hardware in the system, such as the computer or a typesetter. And each

7-2 A video display terminal, the most important piece of hardware for writers and editors. At the *Detroit News*, an editor corrects a story on a VDT. (*Courtesy* Detroit News)

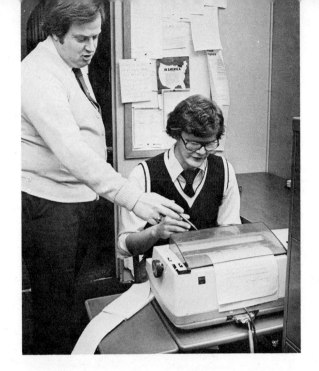

7-3 Training on the job. The managing editor of the *Troy* (Ohio) *Daily News* shows a reporter how to communicate with one of the paper's computers via a typewriter. The cable attached to the typewriter links it with the computer. (*Courtesy* Troy Daily News)

has a cathode ray tube (TV screen) display area. Their keyboards may be separate or attached to the tube unit.

VDTs differ in that they may be *slave, intelligent, or stand-alone* terminals. Slave terminals are nothing more than keyboards hooked to a computer. They are windows into the computer, able to do only what the computer can do for them, and contain no storage and processing capability of their own. Intelligent terminals have their own minicomputers so that they can be *programmed* with instructions that enable them to carry out some functions of their own without calling upon the computer for assistance. Stand-alones are what their name implies; they are independent units that carry on all necessary functions, such as correcting material and telling a typesetter how to set its type. Stand-alone terminals are not connected to a computer, but they may be directly connected to a typesetter.

VDTs are used for correcting as well as creating copy. After authors keyboard their stories at a terminal, the stories are stored somewhere, usually in a computer but possibly on tape or a disk storage unit. The stories can then be recalled to VDT screens and thoroughly edited by way of keyboard strokes.

With special modifications, some electric typewriters can serve as direct computer input devices. Modified so that they send computer signals (digital code) when the keys are struck, typewriters as computer terminals have a disadvantage in that corrections are difficult to make. When errors are detected immediately as they are made, the writer can signal the computer to delete the incorrect letters or words. In most cases, video display terminals are used to make corrections in

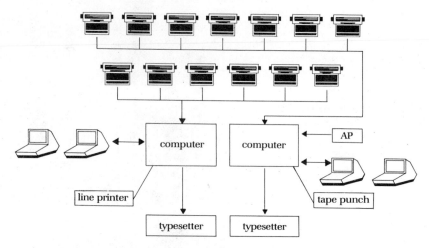

7-4 One of the earliest electronic copy systems is the one at the *Troy* (Ohio) *Daily News.* IBM Selectrics are used for input into the computers. VDTs are used for editing the copy before typesetting. Although due to be updated soon, the system has performed well for a number of years.

systems employing typewriters as entry devices. Figure 7-4 diagrams one such system in use by a community newspaper.

For most systems still relying on typewriters, an intermediate device, commonly called a *scanner,* is used to get typewritten material into computers and/or typesetters without further keyboarding.

In *Optical Character Recognition* (OCR) systems, copy that has been typed is fed into the scanner which reads each letter or other character and translates the letter into the code the computer will understand. The scanner, like other input devices, can be hooked to a computer by wire or via tape.

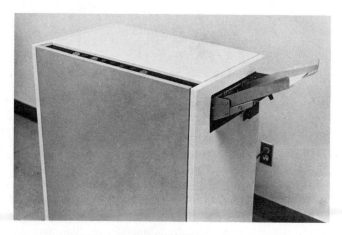

7-5 An Optical Character Recognition (OCR) device scans typed copy, digitizes it, and relays it via perforated tape, magnetic tape, or cable.

Scanner systems have the same inconveniences as those using only typewriters, but with video terminals for correcting, they are in wide use by newspapers and other media. The number of scanners in use by newspaper members of the American Newspaper Publishers

Association increased from 186 in 1973 to 738 in 1977. During the same period, the number of typewriters used with scanners increased from 6,107 to 23,538. The somewhat lower cost of equipping an electric typewriter with a special typeface that can be recognized by scanners, as compared with the cost of a VDT is the reason for the popularity of the modified electric typewriter.

Rigid typing requirements and the difficulty in correcting errors (see Chapter 8) are the major drawbacks of scanner systems.

Computers, Minicomputers, Microprocessors, Diskettes

After stories have been keyboarded at a VDT or typewriter, they must be stored, edited, and processed through the system and into type. In electronic systems, computers are the brains of the operation. They can be separate units or merely parts of a typesetter, VDT, or other device. Wherever they are located, computers have a good memory; they can store a lot of facts and they can remember how to do some functions better than humans can. Computers can keep a dictionary in their memory, as well as rules for hyphenating words. In a split second they can consult their dictionary and/or their rules and use that information to hyphenate words, for example.

Figure 7-6 represents the major functional units of a computer: the input, memory, controller, processor, and output. The input unit accepts instructions (programs) and information to be processed. The memory has two major purposes: storage of the program and the information to be processed. The control unit directs the execution of

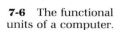

7-6 The functional units of a computer.

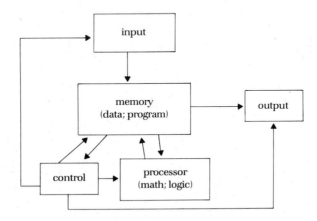

program commands in the proper sequence. For example, information may be called from memory and sent to the processor for manipulation; the processor contains the necessary arithmetic or logic circuits to do the manipulation.

Computers vary greatly in capacity and capability. The increased

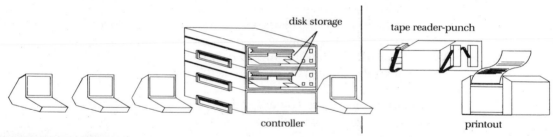

disk storage

tape reader-punch

controller

printout

7-7 *Above:* Front-end systems for small newspapers can be amazingly compact. This Newspaper Electronics Corporation system has four terminals, two disk storage units, one controller, one tape reader-punch, and a hard copy printout machine; this system can store and process wire and local copy and classified ads. Floppy disk storage and microprocessor technology make such systems possible. *Left:* A floppy disk is barely larger than the 45 rpm record shown lying on top of it, but it will hold a full day's news in digital form. It can store 250,000 or 500,000 characters, depending on whether it is a single or dual disk. Stories can be recorded on a disk and recalled for viewing as often as necessary. Eventually, disks can be erased and reused.

use of electronic systems can be traced directly to the development of less costly devices that substitute for large computers. These are *minicomputers*, which are small and technologically simple logic and storage devices. Many systems use *diskette* (disk) storage units to supplement minicomputers or microprocessors. Disks may be either hard or *floppy*; the latter are almost like 45-rpm phonograph records in appearance. A small floppy disk can store as many as half a million characters—plenty to fill a small newspaper. Figure 7-8 shows a system utilizing microprocessors and disk recording devices to form an inexpensive small newspaper front-end system.

Output Devices

The basic output devices in a front-end system are phototypesetters as described in a previous chapter. Typesetters often contain internal computers that perform the hyphenation and justification routines needed to produce columns of type. They may set only body type sizes, or both body and display. Typesetters may also provide area composition (i.e., body type in more than one column under a single headline), or even full pages. They may expose each character through film onto photo paper, or they may digitally form a whole page and expose it on photo paper by means of a cathode ray tube.

Many systems also have *printout* machines, such as a teletype. Although some of these machines produce typed copies at a normal typewriter rate, others are exceptionally fast. The copies that these machines produce are called *hard copies* to distinguish them from the *soft copies* that are developed on a terminal screen or stored in the computer. The reasons for desiring hard copies vary with the situa-

7-8 *Right:* The 10-terminal system at the *Hudson* (N.Y.) *Register-Star* (14,000 circulation) is typical of systems being installed at small to medium-sized newspapers. The two computer units (Microstors) are hooked together so any terminal can communicate with both of them; switching capabilities give good back-up provisions. Such a system fully automates a newspaper's front-end operations. *Below:* The electronic newsroom at the *Hudson Register-Star.* (*Both courtesy* Hudson Register-Star; *photo by Robert L. Ragaini*)

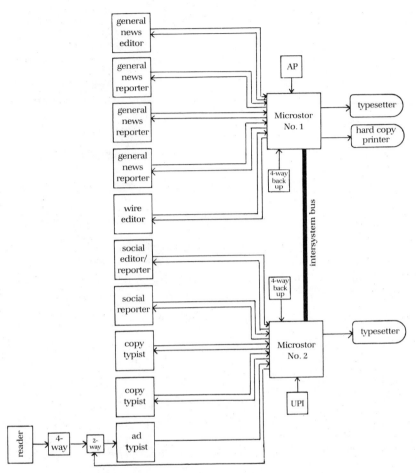

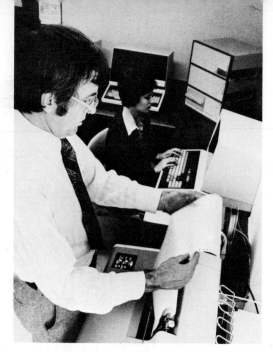

7-9 A hard copy printout device. Such machines are incorporated in most systems; many are extremely fast, like this one, which produces two typed lines per second.

tion, but they are rather obvious. Copies on perforated or magnetic tape may also be output from a system's computer or storage devices. The specific role of tape in an electronic system is described later.

Putting a System Together

To have input devices, computers, and output devices function as a system, they must all be able to communicate with each other. This means that they must have a common language and a means of transmitting that language.

The simplest and most efficient transmittal method is called *on-line*. Devices are said to be on line when they are hooked together by wire cable. With a video terminal on line with a typesetter, an editor merely sends the coded message through the wire and into the typesetter.

Another common method of transmitting the language from one machine to another is with tape, either magnetic or perforated. For example, many video display terminals are equipped with a tape perforator; when the screens are full and the writer wants to send a story into type, the writer "dumps" the story to tape. In other words, the characters that the writer has put on the screen are sent, in code, out of the terminal and into a perforator. The perforator puts a set of holes in the tape, one set for each character. The tape is then put into a reader on a typesetting machine, which takes each set of punched holes and exposes on paper a corresponding letter, thus forming lines of type.

Another method for communicating between devices in a system is with disks. Terminals may have disk units in them or the units may be separate. Bytes (characters) are originated at the keyboard and recorded magnetically on the disk. The disk is then inserted into a read-

7-10 A stand-alone video display terminal. This terminal has enough computer power for all editing functions, but when its screen is full, the words must be "dumped" into tape. The tape perforator at left is hooked by cable to the VDT. (*Photo by Ralph Kliesch*)

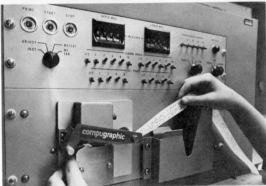

7-11 Six-level perforated tape is fed into a photocomposing machine. The machine reads the tape, exposes letters onto photopaper in lines, and does the necessary hyphenating and justifying.

ing attachment on a typesetter, which relays the disk information to the typesetter.

As long as characters are in binary form, they can go from device to device by any of these methods. They can also be sent through wire from point to point, from a computer in one city to one in another, or from an editorial office to some distant printer. Binary characters can also be sent by microwave relay stations or by satellite. As long as the sending device uses the same code and speed of transmission as the receiving devices do, the transmission possibilities for binary data are virtually limitless.

A system is formed when the various components are joined by wire, tape, or any other connecting device. Joining components by wire is called *interfacing*, and the machine that connects them is an *interface*. Interfaces sometimes must translate from one code to another. For example, a video display terminal using ASCII code often must have its message converted to TTS code before a perforator can produce TTS tape needed by many typesetters.

Figure 7-12 shows a mock system using all the peripheral devices we have mentioned. Actually, such a system would be rare because of its magnitude. Systems are designed to meet the needs of particular users, and, although some of them are somewhat standardized, many are unique. Cost, intended use, speed, and final output are factors that determine a system's configuration.

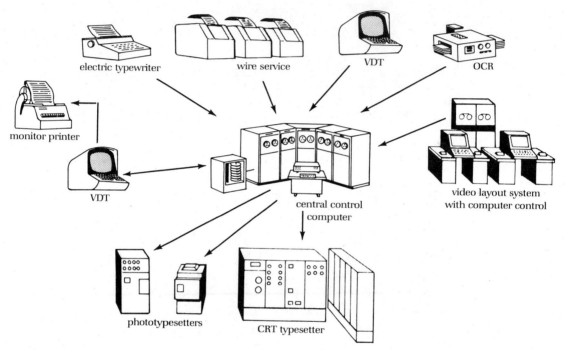

7-12 A theoretical system showing the many possible ways to input material for computer storage and processing. Systems are individually designed to use as many devices as each user requires. (*Adapted from material supplied by American Newspaper Publishers Association Research Institute*)

Some Typical Electronic Systems

Electronic copy processing systems are ideal for newspapers and magazines and they are widely used by both. These systems also are finding their way into advertising and public relations agencies, as well as countless corporate and governmental offices.

One of the many significant results of the introduction of electronic technology into type composition and printing has been the spreading of these areas of endeavor into rather strange places. "In-house" production is the term given to the phenomenon; what used to be the work of skilled artisans in a printer's plant is now done in the same building with editorial operations. In-house production has particularly spread rapidly in the magazine industry, but printing operations can also be found in advertising agencies, hospitals, universities, government bureaus, and corporate offices.

The electronic systems being used can range from one terminal plus typesetter to a system including hundreds of terminals, several computers, and several typesetters. These systems are often composed of segments for specialized functions, as in a newspaper office where there may be separate subsystems for classified ads, circulation, and news, although they jointly form one system.

A Large Daily Newspaper System

In recent years, electronic printing systems have been installed at the *New York Times, New York Daily News, Chicago Tribune, Detroit News, Washington Post,* and most other large and prestigious daily newspapers. Because of the vast demands on them, the systems used by these papers are massive and complex. Although the systems vary considerably from one large paper to another, one example should suffice to illustrate the principles involved.

The system installed at the *New York Daily News* is an ideal case in point because it is one of the few systems that include full page makeup at video terminals as part of the prepress system. At a cost of $6 million, the system was installed in 1977 and 1978 as "the largest and most advanced" prepress publishing system ever designed for a newspaper.

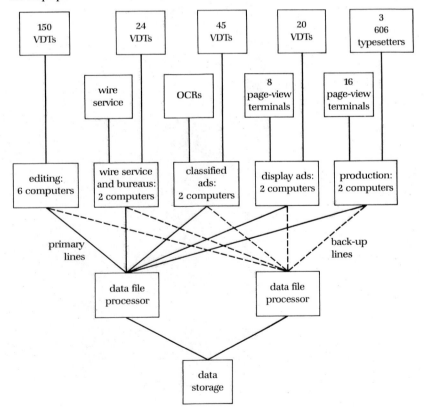

7-13 The system used at the *New York Daily News.* It includes 14 computers, many terminals, and OCR input.

As shown in the diagram (Figure 7-13), the system provides for entry of local copy via VDTs mainly but also includes two scanners for entry of classified advertising material; wire service copy goes directly into a computer. A total of 239 VDTs are clustered in groups to feed copy into one of 14 different computers for processing, including hyphenation and justification. There are also two central data base computers, one of which is for *backup*. For newspapers, the backup capabilities of a system are essential. The disaster term of electronic systems is *crash;* when a system malfunctions, it has *crashed.* Power outages, voltage surges, and equipment failure can cause systems to go down, and a newspaper cannot wait until the next day to get started again. Consequently, newspaper systems provide duplicate equipment, subdivisions of equipment, and full alternatives to provide emergency service.

Mergenthaler Page View Terminals (PVT) (see Figure 7-14) are used for *pagination* (electronic page makeup) at the *Daily News.* With these terminals, editors and advertising layout personnel can arrange material on a page and view their work at 95 percent of its actual page size. (A large, broadsheet size can be viewed at $\frac{2}{3}$ actual size.) Outlines of drawings, photographs, or other graphic material can be shown on the screen by drawing these outlines on a graphic tablet with an electronic stylus. All traditional pasteup functions are thereby done electronically.

For classified ads, the computer provides, via video terminal or OCR, for entering each ad, setting it in type, and placing it in a page, while also checking the credit of the advertiser and providing billing information.

7-14 A Mergenthaler Page View Terminal. This and similar terminals made by other manufacturers permit full-page layout. (*Courtesy Mergenthaler Linotype Company*)

The final production of editorial and advertising is handled by three cathode ray tube (CRT) full-page typesetters. The Linotron 606s set a full *Daily News* page, with windows for illustrations, in only 22 seconds (about 3,000 lines of type per minute). Linotron 606s are digital typesetters that store up to 2,000 fonts of type with sizes from $5\frac{1}{2}$ to 128 point.

A Large Magazine System

The magazine industry's model of copy processing efficiency has been in operation at the offices of *U.S. News and World Report* in Washington, D.C., for several years.

Designed to save precious time as well as cost, the *U.S. News* system was the first to put into operation devices that could convert photographs to digital information. Satellite transmission to remote printing locations is another glamorous aspect of this system.

Entry of words into the *U.S. News* system is effected through 80 VDTs that are on line to a sophisticated computer with a hyphenation dictionary of 125,000 words. In addition to doing h&j, the computer orders display and body typefaces at terminal command and stores both words and pictures. It also executes page placement commands for text and illustrations.

Pictures are entered into the system through a unique scanner that converts its reading into digital output on line to the computer.

With terminal keyboard commands, text and pictures in full page form are then sent on line to a CRT typesetter, which outputs full pages or magnetic tape ready for another CRT typesetter.

The *U.S. News* system includes a typesetter in the office at which full page proofs are produced for careful checking by the editorial staff. Actual production of the pages is accomplished in printing plants at three different locations: Los Angeles, Chicago, and Old Saybrook, Connecticut.

Pages, because they are in digital form on magnetic tape, can be transported to the printing plants by any means, but *U.S. News* uses Western Union's Westar satellite for transmission. The digital information is received on magnetic tape at the printing plants and is fed into CRT typesetters equipped with special recorders for the photographs.

Although satellite transmission of the pages of newspapers had been fairly commonplace, the *U.S. News* system was the first to permit transmission of pages *including photographs*. Recording photos digitally represented a major technological advancement for copy processing systems, which was accomplished by Information International, Inc., with a machine called a Model 3600 Illustration Scanner.

The Illustration Scanner contains a cathode ray tube that scans each photograph under the control of a minicomputer; as the tube scans, it records on magnetic tape, using tones of gray with a scale of

7-15 The *U.S. News & World Report* electronic copy processing system.

(*Courtesy* U.S. News & World Report)

photos

words

tape

full pages

The system as diagramed.

Editors at work at VDTs.

The computer control area.

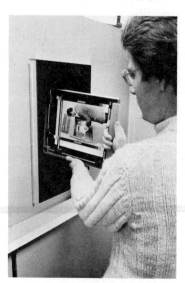

Insertion of a photograph into the scanner which will convert it to digital form. This digitizing of photos, a first at *U.S. News,* makes possible full-page layouts by computer.

The computer positions text and illustrations, and the typesetter delivers full-page proofs. Pages can be sent from the computer to receivers at remote printing plants for final reproduction.

256 shades. Each point in the scan is thus a piece of digital information that can be recorded and transmitted. From a teletype keyboard, the scanner can be set for size of the reproduction (as small as $\frac{1}{2}$ inch square and as large as 54 by 66 picas) and a screen value from 65 to 133 lines.

Total electronic copy processing—with words and pictures in page form—thus became a part of the present and not just a dream of the future.

Tailoring Systems to Individual Needs —————

The comprehensive systems used by the *New York Daily News* and the *U.S. News* would be out of place in other publishing offices, in some cases, like using a cannon to shoot a fly. Even other publishing giants have not taken the same approach.

For example, although the same systems firm (Atex) designed them, the systems at *Newsweek, Reader's Digest, Forbes,* and *National Geographic* are each distinctive. At the time of this writing, *Newsweek's* system provided for in-house pagination, but without the halftone recording feature, and pages were sent to printers by private wire rather than satellite. At *Reader's Digest,* the high cost of author's alterations brought about a desire for a different feature, a computer printout that was sophisticated enough to produce copies exactly as they would look in print. That capability has been provided. At *Forbes,* an IBM 360 computer with magnetic tape output that could feed into the Atex system was needed to provide a capability to set about 150 pages of complicated tabular matter for three special quarterly issues. And at *National Geographic,* emphasis was put on the typesetter because of the great volume of the society's other printing—about 175 million pieces a year. A Linotron 606 provided the capacity the management wanted.

How much can be done with a minimal amount of technical equipment can be seen in the example of Gordon Publications, a New Jersey firm that publishes 11 specialized business magazines. Just one machine, a versatile direct entry typesetter, was put into use to solve some common problems of cost and efficiency. With typesetting done at an outside printer, transporting of materials, such as copy delivered to the printer, proofs to the publications office, proofs back to the printer, and correct proofs to publications office, was time-consuming. Last-minute corrections are difficult and costly, and schedules must meet the printer's convenience. At Gordon Publications, in-house typesetting and page pasteup reduced the time from 21 days to 10 days for setting type for a complete magazine; the cost per page was reduced; and errors that formerly took two days to get corrected are now corrected in a few minutes.

7-16 An in-house typesetter in operation at Gordon Publications, part of an efficient system used to produce 11 business magazines. (*Courtesy Gordon Publications*)

Similar experiences have been reported by other magazine publishers. At *Hardware Retailing,* editor Robert Vereen reports similar advantages from similar equipment, and adds that it is now easier to meet deadlines for late news, which makes a publication's offerings much fresher. And at *Canadian Business Magazine,* a unit consisting of a video display terminal with direct keyboard entry to a typesetter that incorporates storage capability has resulted in greater efficiency and greatly reduced costs.

In-House Systems for Ad Agencies and PR Offices

Benefits from in-house copy processing systems are not limited to publishers of periodicals. Any organization involved with much typesetting (editor Vereen estimated the breakpoint at $500 per month) potentially could benefit from a system, and many are making the change.

For a quick review of possibilities in this area, let us look at an ad agency, the public relations department of a bank, an insurance company, and a state government, all of whom have benefited by the installation of copy processing systems.

Ad Agency For advertising agencies, in-house type composition systems have many advantages and cost savings is certainly one of them. Mandabach and Simms, an agency with offices in New York and Chicago, found that it paid for a magnetic-tape operated typesetter in about five months through savings derived from operating the equipment. Numerous other advantages were also realized: corrections were much easier to make when equipment was in-house, and pasteups were easier to do as were customized presentations for new business.

Bank Public Relations Department

Before purchasing their own equipment, the public relations department of Bankers Trust Company in New York used a shared-time computer terminal in its offices to set type. Copy was typed at the terminal and into the printer's computer; in a day or two type proofs would be delivered. Corrections were made in the same fashion, and in another day or two corrected proofs would be delivered. When this turnaround time was too great (such as in preparing quarterly reports that had to meet a date deadline) "rush" typesetting was ordered and a heavy cost penalty was paid for the service.

Using a VDT-typesetter combination unit like the one used by *Canadian Business Magazine* right in the office, the department was able to improve service and reduce costs. An employee newsletter and other publications are now typeset on the miniature system.

An Insurance Company

Travelers Insurance Company has had a printing center for a long time; the company's customized printing needs (it is required by law to print individualized policy forms) served to make such a center advantageous. And, relatively speaking, it was reasonably modern.

When equipment in the center started to become antiquated, a typical problem arose: How can the whole operation be updated while retaining some of the original equipment?

Computerized cold type photocomposition and perforated and magnetic tape were used in the system, but not efficiently. Computer time was shared; at one point in the system, copy had to be converted from one tape form to another, and type composition was limited in its variety. Old-fashioned tape perforating machines were used instead of video terminals or other modern data entry devices.

The company faced a problem typical of those faced by other firms with workable but inefficient equipment, and they solved it with a fast and efficient system using VDTs, a computer, disk storage, and a versatile typesetter. Gone is the need for a large room to store paper tapes, the necessity of converting from magnetic to paper tape, and the sharing of computer time. Now an operator at a VDT can call a policy form from the computer, enter the individual modifications as required, and return the individualized form to a "queue" (lineup) until the typesetter can output it.

Not only did the new equipment make the policy printing more efficient; it also opened up the opportunity to do a company newspaper and magazine in-house.

A State Government's Processing System

One of the most elaborate nonmedia copy processing systems is in use by the State of Wisconsin. The Wisconsin system uses VDTs, OCR, and strike-on entry units, a large computer, and a CRT typesetter for output.

Six IBM Selectrics equipped for copy to be scanned by a Compuscan scanner start copy on its way. The scanner reads the typed copy and sends it, in digital code, on line to a 128K computer. Four VDTs are used to edit and proofread the copy before the computer turns out magnetic tape. The magnetic tape then drives the CRT typesetter.

State offices generate enough typesetting to keep the system busy, and the system eventually is expected to save the state about a million dollars annually.

Other System Uses

Although all these systems have some unique functions or uses, they all are geared primarily to processing copy from author to type with one keyboarding. Other uses of computers and terminals may not be directly related to typesetting, though that may be the ultimate destination.

Wire Service Systems

The use of electronic systems by the wire services, Associated Press and United Press International, is a good example. These agencies provide words to newspapers and other clients, but they are not directly involved in preparing the words for a printing press.

These services do, however, initiate copy, store it, and transmit it from point to point. VDTs, computers, and digital transmission are fully used to perform these functions. In the wire service bureaus, reporters now work at video terminals, not typewriters. When they are finished with their stories, the reporters store them in a computer. Their editors draw their stories from the computer to a VDT screen, make any corrections they care to make, and then assign the story to its fate: statewide distribution, regional, national, or killed (sent to the electronic "wastebasket"). From the bureau, stories may be distributed in slow, standard teletype speed as they have been for years. But increasingly the stories are drawn from central computers by the client and are received there at digital speeds. AP calls its high speed system *Datastream;* UPI calls its system *Datanews.*

Through high-speed transmission, a full-day's news can be received in minutes rather than hours. Gone is the necessity of breaking stories into takes so that papers with different deadlines could be assured of getting at least a short version of each story. Processing of wire copy is greatly simplified because newspapers with electronic systems can receive and store the wire service copy much more rapidly and process it quicker.

Applications of Remote Terminals

Another aspect of copy processing that should not be overlooked is the use of remote terminals. Regional bureaus and sports coverage provide the best examples. Many newspapers have always relied heavily on regional or statewide coverage to serve their readers. Telephones and teletypes have been the traditional transmission devices. With computer-based systems, VDTs are playing an important role. VDTs in a remote bureau can "talk" to the home office computer and leave stories in the computer for further editing at a considerable time savings.

The use of portable terminals at sports events perhaps is the best example of remote terminal usage. By carrying terminals with them to press boxes, the sports reporters can save precious time and make their newspapers' coverage much more timely. One of the most time-consuming jobs is setting sports box scores, and stories of sports events are often those that come in closest to deadline. Via video terminal, the writers of sports stories can have their stories keyboarded at the press box, formatted by them (use the keyboard to tell the computer to set box scores as usual), and sent over a phone line to the home office computer in minutes. The time needed for editing and typesetting is also cut to a minimum.

Checklist: Electronic Copy Processing Systems

Although newcomers to newspaper, magazine, advertising, and other communications jobs do not have to be computer systems experts, they are certain to be involved with such systems eventually.

Remember that all systems are intended to produce type pages; they generally fall into one of these categories:

1. Direct entry (typing at the keyboard of a typesetter produces type directly).
2. Tape connected (typing at a keyboard produces a magnetic or perforated tape that operates a typesetter).

3. On-line (typing at a keyboard sends the bytes—characters—through a cable to the typesetter).

4. Typewriter to storage to VDT to typesetter. Material typed on a specially equipped electric typewriter is output as coded bytes to storage, called from storage for editing on a VDT, and then sent to typesetting.

5. Typewriter to OCR to storage to VDT to typesetter. Material typed on paper with an electric typewriter is scanned by an OCR device that converts the typewritten characters to coded bytes on a tape or sends them through a cable to a computer for storage and/or a VDT for editing and then typesetting.

6. VDT to storage to VDT to typesetter. Material typed on a VDT is stored, then edited on a VDT and sent to a typesetter via tape or cable.

7. Remote entry and transmission is possible for all systems; telephone lines and satellites can relay information keyboarded at one point to any other receiving point for storage and/or typesetting.

8. Computer arrangement of elements into desired formats (pagination) is included in some systems. Material in computer storage is positioned by VDT commands to form complete ads or pages and sent to a phototypesetter that produces the complete ad or page on photopaper, thus eliminating the pasteup operation.

The techniques of preparation of copy for entry into scanners, and the intricacies of a video display terminal keyboard are now musts, and an acquaintance with the fundamentals of systems and the terminology involved in them are also now essential.

Communication careers tend to be appealing to creative people who may view technology with suspicion. But each passing year reduces the possibility of finding a career slot that is totally removed from technology. Wise students will therefore prepare themselves to apply their creative instincts while using technology to its utmost. In any case, the technology of processing copy electronically is fascinating. Its ingenuity in itself presents a challenge to understand and master it. The next chapter will help you meet the challenge.

8 Processing Copy Electronically

Video display terminals and the other elements of computerized electronic copy processing systems are many things for many people. For publishers, they are the fastest and most economical methods ever devised for getting words into print. For the writers and editors who use them, they are essential tools of their trade. For students, they are an exciting part of their preparation for a professional career in mass communications.

Now not only must students be proficient on a typewriter so they can carry out their role as writers or editors; they must also be prepared to transfer their typing skills to other machines involved in getting words into print.

Unfortunately for everyone concerned, computerized systems are not all alike. As pointed out in Chapter 7, scores of manufacturers design and market systems, each of which has its own peculiar capabilities and features. But some basic elements are common to all systems, and students should know these common elements. Variations are too numerous to memorize, but at least it is beneficial for newcomers to know they exist and to know what questions to ask about them.

The approach here will be to try to delineate what should be common knowledge for anyone about to use an electronic copy processing system and also to point the way to questions that ordinarily must be asked. Where possible, answers are given for those questions.

Working with Electronic Systems: Some Basics

One of the most important things for a newcomer to understand while sitting down at a keyboard entry device (usually a video display terminal, a VDT) is that he or she is going to be involved in the operation of a system, and that the end goal of that system is to produce printed matter without additional human typesetting. Anything done at a keyboard (or, perhaps more commonly, anything that is *not* done at the keyboard) that hinders the flow of words through the system and out into type is defeating the purpose of the system.

Of equal importance is the knowledge that systems sometimes do *crash*, and precautions against these systems breakdowns are essential. Checking and double-checking the systems can avoid many disasters. If you think you have recorded your story in the system, check to be sure that it has been received there before clearing your terminal. Along this same line, you should know that anything written on a VDT screen must eventually come off the screen, but no one wants it to vanish unintentionally. Sometimes one accidental touch of a key results in the loss of a story, so beware of keys labeled "clear," "kill," or something similar. Although many processing systems provide safeguards against accidental clearing of screens and losing the results of hours of work, others, unfortunately, do not.

It is also important to remember that work at a VDT keyboard has two facets: (1) typing characters onto a screen, much like typing them on paper, and (2) using the keyboard to communicate with other elements in the system. The first of these presents very few difficulties; some slight variations in keyboards can be a nuisance, but these can be learned very quickly. It is the second of these facets that is new and different and consequently can be troublesome. It is helpful in this regard to remember that each key that is struck represents a digital piece of information. In talking to a computer or other element in a system, a small letter instead of a capital or one extra space in a command can totally change the meaning of that command. The figure 1 and the small letter *l* are totally different in digital code; the same is true of capital *O* and zero.

Accuracy in typing intrasystem commands is thus essential, but so is the mere typing of a story on the screen. In computerized electronic systems, the writers and editors at the keyboard are the final authorities regarding what gets into print; there no longer are printers to blame for errors in typesetting. Full control over accuracy rests with the writers and editors, and the pressure upon them to maintain a high level of accuracy is greater than ever before.

All of these cautions seem to make working with an electronic copy processing system a fearful prospect, but actually it is not. Writers and editors like the fact that they have total control over their product, and, once they are accustomed to the new machines that are involved, they are almost unanimous in their enthusiasm for them.

Learning the VDT Keyboard _____

The first thing to confront anyone sitting down to write into a computerized system is the keyboard—or perhaps we ought to say *keyboards*, because they usually are divided into segments. Although there is a

8-1 Keyboards on video display terminals vary considerably, but they all have the usual typewriter keys. This terminal also has a block of editing (cursor control) keys at right and a block of typesetting command keys at extreme right. Other special keys are the format keys and *word wrap* and *wire strip* keys in the top row and the scrolling keys below. This keyboard operates a Newspaper Electronics Corporation terminal. (*Photo by Ralph Kliesch*)

wide variation in detail among keyboards of various systems, there are some common traits. All of them have, for example, the *basic keyboard* containing the normal characters and numbers found on any typewriter. All of them also have, in one form or another, a set of *editing* keys to make changes on the screen and a set of *system* keys that are used to communicate with other parts of the system. Many keyboards also have a group of typesetting keys. The labels and locations of these keys vary, but for a system to operate, they must be there in some form.

The basic keyboards are "old hat" to anyone who has ever used an electric typewriter. The letter keys are there, and in the same place, and there are also shift and shift lock keys, but here is where the first variation will probably occur. As the shift lock key is depressed, the shift key does not depress, and the lock key pops right back. So there is no way to know that the shift is on unless, as some terminals provide, the key has a light bulb that comes on when the shift is locked.

You should also know of some other probable differences in basic keyboards. For example, keyboards will provide a different method for typing quotation marks. Typesetters set beginning quotation marks that are different from the ending marks, and, because VDT keyboards produce type, they provide for differentiating between beginning and ending marks. Terminals usually will have one key that will seem to be an apostrophe and/or comma that can be struck with the shift key down to get one half of the other quote mark. Striking the key twice in each instance provides for the double mark in type.

As pointed out earlier, an electronic copy processing system is based on digital information, and one byte on tape or in wire signals equals a character. By depressing the single open quote key, we provide one byte of information that will cause a typesetter to form one little black mark; a second depression of that key will produce the other byte and the other mark. Usually, striking one key (such as for a small letter) produces one byte and that byte will equal the desired character. That byte shows on the screen as a letter, and later will go through the computer as impulses, tape holes, or magnetic dots. For capital letters, two bytes are needed, one to specify a capital and the other to specify the letter; therefore, to form a capital letter we must hit two keys, the shift key and the character key.

There probably will be a *return* key somewhere on the board, but it will not return a typewriter carriage because there isn't one. The return key will, however, serve a similar purpose of moving the action on the screen from the end of the line to the beginning of a new line. In some systems, it is also used for the last key stroke in all commands that are given to a computer.

8-2 Extra typing speed is a bonus on VDTs because there is no carriage to be returned at the end on each line. This Hendrix terminal automatically ends each line at the end of the last full word in the line. Some terminals require a key stroke to produce this visual image. (*Courtesy* Detroit News)

Ending lines at the keyboard is not a problem for VDTs. Most systems permit endless typing, each line filling the maximum number of characters that the screen can accommodate with no hyphenation required. A *word wrap* feature is usually available; either automatically or at command of a keystroke, the system will end each line at the end of the last possible word. In some systems the keyboard operator may be able to dictate hyphenation at his or her keyboard, but hyphenation is usually the function of the computer. At any rate, it pays to be wary of putting hyphens at the ends of lines; striking the hyphen key creates a byte of information, too, and hyphens can then appear where they do not belong in typesetting. The hyphen key may also have some special functions.

There is thus nothing in the basic keyboard really to be concerned about; the few peculiarities that may appear are quickly and easily mastered.

The Cursor and Editing Keys

Any text change or correction that is usually made with pencil and paper can be carried out on a video screen with keys on the keyboard and something called a *cursor*. The cursor is a small block of light, usually about the size of a character, that can be moved to any position on the screen. Cursors usually blink so that they can be spotted quickly, and they can be in the form of a rectangular block or an underline. Regardless of their physical appearance, cursors all serve the same purpose; to locate, on the screen, the action that results from keys.

As one types at a VDT keyboard, the cursor moves just ahead of the character display, ready to position the next character at that spot. When an error has been made, the cursor can be moved to the spot of the error and the correction can be made with key strokes.

Most terminals will set aside a separate little block of keys for movement of the cursor and the making of corrections. The common keys in this cluster are directional arrows for moving the cursor, one each for the basic compass directions. Striking the up arrow will move the cursor up one space on the screen; holding that key down will move the cursor steadily and without interruption in that same direction. With these keys the cursor can be moved anywhere, but to speed the process keys are usually available to place the cursor instantly at the beginning position (upper left corner in most cases, lower left corner in others), and to move the cursor to the extreme left position on any line.

8-3 The cursor control keys, the most vital keys on a VDT keyboard. Speed in moving the cursor in four directions and back to *home* is essential for efficient editing. (*Photo by Ralph Kliesch*)

Some terminal manufacturers even provide cursor control through a rotating ball in a socket, thus permitting movement in all directions with fingertip guidance. Others provide additional directional movement beyond the four basic directions. In any event, the use of the cursor is the most important single difference between typewriters and terminals, a fact that causes one common error: the use of the space bar instead of cursor control keys.

When the space bar is touched, it creates a blank space on the screen; when that blank space travels through the system in a digital code, it is a byte of information. Striking the space bar will not move the cursor; it will simply place more blank spaces at the cursor location or eliminate letters at that location. The only way to move the cursor, and thus change the location of the characters called for by key strokes, is with the cursor control keys.

The speed of editing at a terminal is directly related to the speed of manipulation of the cursor, and it is wise to quickly learn all shortcuts that are available; precious time can be wasted while moving the cursor space by space when it can be positioned instantly.

After the cursor is in position, any necessary change can be made with the other editing keys. These include *insert*, *overstrike*, *delete*, and *move* any character, word, paragraph, or block of material.

One key stroke will usually place a terminal into either the insert or overstrike mode. Striking the insert key, for example, will set up the terminal to permit the insertion of as little as one letter to as much as several paragraphs just ahead of the cursor position. In what seems to be a magical manner, all the material, from the cursor on, just moves out of the way and allows room for each character as the key is struck. If, however, the terminal is in the overstrike mode, as each key is struck, the new character appears in place of the old character, which just vanishes from the screen. Thus terminals permit totally neat over-striking, not like typewriters that place one character over another with the usual result that no one knows which character is intended to be there.

Delete character, delete word, delete paragraph, and *delete block* are common editing keys. With many terminals, placing the cursor at a character and striking the *delete character* key removes the character; placing the cursor anywhere in a word and striking *delete word* elimi-nates the whole word, and so on with paragraph and any block of words. In others, a safety feature is provided: with the cursor at a character, striking the delete key will cause the character to blink as a warning that it is the one that will be deleted. A second touch of the delete key then eliminates the character, and so on for word, para-graph, and block.

Working with a block of words that do not constitute a single sen-tence or paragraph necessitates the identification of the block with the cursor. Place the cursor at the beginning of the block and a *define block* keystroke will mark the beginning, and the same procedure will mark the end. The material thus marked can then be deleted.

Words, paragraphs, and blocks can be moved in the same fashion: identified with the cursor and moved with appropriate keystrokes. The new location for elements to be moved is spotted by the cursor. Assuming that we want to move paragraph five ahead of paragraph two, we would place the cursor in paragraph five and identify it by striking the definition key, then move the cursor to the beginning spot of paragraph two. Striking the key *move to cursor* or perhaps merely *move* results in the opening up of the space between paragraph one and two and the insertion there of paragraph five.

Once proficiency with the movement of the cursor has been ob-tained, editing with cursor and keyboard can be done as rapidly as with pencil-paper methods, and often more rapidly.

System Function Keys

Most of the variations among systems occur in the use and labeling of keys involved in intrasystem communication: for video terminals to talk to computers and computers to talk to typesetters, and so on. Custom engineering of systems has caused this variation to be so great that they can be discussed here only in the most general terms.

Let us look at system keys fom the standpoint of the function they perform for the user, beginning with the writer and concluding with the editor.

From the standpoint of newspaper reporter or magazine writer, video terminals are tools for composing their thoughts into words that are then turned over to editors for further processing. The writers' involvement in the system is minimal; they want to put their stories where editors can find them and where, should the need arise, they can find them again and get them back for further work. In pencil-paper terms writers put their stories on a spindle or in an "in-basket" where they and their editors can find them.

In electronic system terms, the writers must put their stories in storage. In order for such storage to be useful, it must involve a fool-proof filing system so that stories can be located and recalled when needed. For this purpose, computers are better than humans, and in the filing process computers can prepare a list of every filed item instantly. If the humans using the system are careful, there is almost no chance of error.

Most systems are highly restrictive in the number of characters that are available for assigning file names, and this restriction must be known by all writers. If the limit is six digits, there is no way to "fudge" on that limit; in that sense computers are rigid and unyielding. Also,

8-4 Editors must be able at any time to get a listing of all stories that have been put into storage. This directory uses six-digit file names (slugs) and gives typefitting information in terms of the number of disk sectors filled by each story. (*Photo by Ralph Kliesch*)

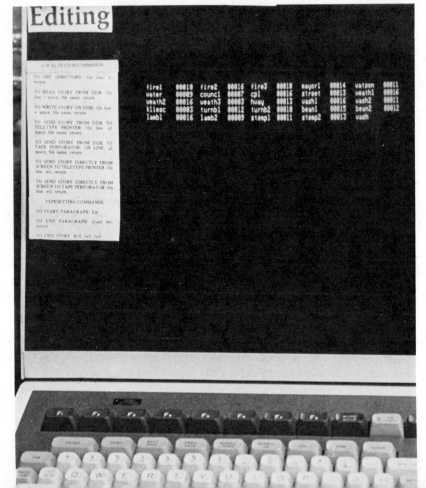

computers take file names absolutely literally: if a reporter enters "Fire" as a file name for a story and erroneously types "fiRe," the computer will accept it and record it in that fashion. Any listing (called directory or queue) of what is in storage will record it as "fiRe," and for recalling that story, the name must be exactly the same. Anything else (Fire, fire, FIre, FIRE) will not work.

In filing stories at large installations, such as the *New York Times* and *Washington Post*, it may be necessary for the writer to tell the computer in which queue or directory to put the work because departments may have their own listings as part of a larger directory. At smaller newspapers, there may be just one centralized storage area called either a *directory* or a *queue.*

The use of system commands for filing and the like may seem to be complicated and difficult to understand, but actually they become routine very rapidly. Even with multiple files, for example, a reporter usually writes into only one (e.g., sports) and is not concerned with the others. And in almost every instance, "crib sheets" are located at every terminal listing the keystrokes involved in all common commands. Such crutches help the newcomer but are soon forgotten after only a short time because they are no longer needed.

The first step in using any system command is to make sure that the receiving hardware can "hear" the command and thus receive it. In many systems this requires a key stroke, which can be compared to picking up a telephone receiver and dialing a number. The result of this operation is to hook the terminal into the system, to put it "on-line" with the other devices. For some systems it is important also to be sure that the terminal is "off-line" when it is functioning as a typewriter; for others, the "on" switch that gives the terminal power immediately puts it on-line with the computer.

Calling stories out of storage

Recalling stories from storage is usually carried out in one of two ways. The first of these is to call the directory to the screen and place the cursor next to the file name of the desired story. One key stroke will then bring that story to the screen. The other way is to use the keyboard to execute a command such as "Get" followed by the file name of the story. In this way you are telling the computer to "get" the story and bring it to the screen.

In either case, the entire story often does not appear in view; sometimes the system provides only the first few paragraphs, or there may not be room on the screen for the complete story. To take care of this problem, VDTs have *scrolling* capacity. Keys labeled *scroll up* enable the user to run the story upward across the VDT screen to bring lower parts of the story into view. *Scroll down* keys permit the opposite: running downward on the screen so that top paragraphs come into view. Most terminals also have *page* keys that simply permit block scrolling, jumping forward or downward in large segments rather than in a steady rolling fashion. In pencil-paper terms, this is like looking at the bottom page, then jumping page by page back to the beginning instead of looking at each line on the way back.

When dealing with filing, modifying, and retrieving stories in an electronic storage system it is important to give modified stories a new name if they are to be put back into storage. If we have improved our writer's "fiRe" story and want to put the improved story in storage until later, it must be given a different label: "Fire, fiRe 2," or what have you. Otherwise, our possibilities are only to "kill" the original version and list only the edited one, or we might have a separate department (a separate queue, perhaps) in the directory for edited stories. The point is that duplicate names in the same storage area are impossible.

Putting stories into type Besides correcting the work of writers, editors usually write the head-lines or titles and mark the story and the headline for typesetting. Systems engineers have designed terminals so that these same functions can be carried out with keystrokes.[1]

Most VDTs provide for quick, routine selection of boldface or italic type options because sometimes even the reporter would like to specify these options. Placement and terminology may vary, but one can usually find these keys easily. If not labeled *italic* or *bold*, they may be called *UR* (for upper rail) and *LR* (for lower rail) because of old line-casting machine terminology. Upper rail traditionally has meant the optional choice (either bold or italic), and lower rail was the normal choice. When using such keys at a terminal, you must remember to mark the beginning and ending of the option. If one word is to be in italic, the italic key (perhaps *upper rail*) must be struck before the word is typed, and another key (perhaps *lower rail*) must be struck to have the typesetter return to normal setting. Otherwise, large unwanted blocks of italic or bold can show up in proofs.

Other typesetting keys often found on VDT keyboards include *flush left*, *flush right*, and *centered*. Where traditional terminology is used (i.e., upper rail and lower rail) these keys are usually labeled *quad left*, *quad right*, and *quad center*. The result is the same self-explanatory positioning of type on lines. Type is normally justified, which means that each line is automatically made to be flush to both edges of a column.

Beginnings and endings of paragraphs are also important elements of information to convey to a computerized typesetter. Most systems have keys plainly labeled, and many have one *paragraph* key

8-5 A set of typical typesetting command keys.

---

[1] Writing and editing both involve copyfitting to space. Electronic processing greatly simplifies this procedure. See the brief discussion on page 175.

8-6 In most editorial offices, a list of the basic commands for the system is posted on each terminal. After using terminals for only a few days, most staff members find they no longer need to refer to the list. (*Courtesy Hudson Register-Star; photo by Robert L. Ragaini*)

that serves to start and end a paragraph. Other systems have traditional typesetting terminology: *em* for starting paragraphs and *quad left and return* to end paragraphs. TTS tapes for linecasting machines used those terms to tell the automated machine to indent one em to start a paragraph, and to put in quads at the right to make the last line be flush to the left.

Super Shifts and Pi Characters

Typesetters set many characters that do not appear on an ordinary typewriter keyboard, including such typographical miscellany as stars, bullets, check marks, and so on. These miscellaneous strange characters are called *pi* characters, a term that also comes from printing tradition: type pieces that were not in a proper bin (all mixed up and in disorder) used to be called *pi*.

In order to sort these characters out on a VDT, the keyboard provides for what is called a *super shift* or *double shift* function. When the regular shift key is pressed, the capital is called for instead of the lower case letter. When the super shift key is struck, followed by a normal character key, a specific pi character is called for. The pi characters available vary from system to system and are listed in system manuals where they may be consulted as needed.

A part of the problem in standardizing copy processing systems has been the need to have them serve a variety of typesetting machines, as described in Chapter 4. After copy has been corrected on a VDT and "marked" for typesetting on a VDT, it must be sent to a typesetter and it must be in a language understood by the typesetter. The methods of transmission vary, too, from perforated tape carried to the typesetter to magnetic tape, wire cable, telephone line, and satellites. But from the standpoint of the editor, transmission is a keyboard function that is easy to carry out. With a story on the editor's screen, a key stroke or two is usually sufficient to send the story from the screen and into the typesetter, whether it is nearby or not. If the story is in storage, it must be identified by keyboarding its file name as well as the command to send. Every effort is made by systems designers to make the transmission of copy to typesetters as simple as possible.

Formatting   VDTs usually have some provision for *formatting*, a simplified method for communicating complicated typesetting instructions. Format keys permit one key to communicate a list of typesetting instructions that are used frequently. Example: one key can tell a typesetter what kind of type to use for a by-line, how to position the words in the line, what column measure is to be set, and the leading that is required. The computer will have been programmed to follow these instructions when the appropriate key is struck. Formatting is especially helpful when headlines and body type are written together at a terminal and composed as area composition by the same typesetter. Small systems may only provide for a few special formats; the first portions of the *New York Times'* system installed in 1976 contained 180 formats that could be designated with a *uf* (use format) key plus the number of the desired format.

   Although some keyboards contain tabular keys like a typewriter, it is more common to use format keys for tabulated materials such as football scores, stock market reports, and the like.

Wire Service   The processing of wire copy (the stories that come to a newspaper
Copy   from organizations such as the Associated Press and United Press International) can be much easier in an electronic system than with traditional pencil-paper methods.

   With transmission being only from computer to computer (AP's computer to the newspaper's computer) stories can travel much more rapidly—a full day's news in a matter of minutes. Traditional teletype transmission is at a medium typewriting speed. Sending long stories in the slower speeds always has presented a problem for the wire services and their clients whose deadlines vary greatly. In order to make sure that a client with an early deadline can get at least a part of all the news, stories are sent in "takes," which must be put together at deadline time to form as complete a story as possible. New developments during a day's news cycle are handled with periodic new beginnings (new leads) that must be incorporated with earlier takes. The new data speed transmission from computer to computer cuts such piecing of stories to a minimum.

Whether a newspaper receives high-speed or traditional transmission, processing of wire copy is carried out in the same fashion as locally written copy. Wire news is recorded in storage as it arrives, each with a file name and each listed in a directory. Directories and files can be called forth to video terminals where the stories can be headlined and corrected before going into type.

Sometimes wire copy is received into storage in Teletypesetter form with all the hyphenation and justification codes already in it. To permit quick elimination of these commands, terminals are usually equipped with a *wire strip* key. Striking that key strips the copy of all the h&j commands, and displays the story on the screen in standard form.

Split-Screen Merging

Large metropolitan newspapers often get different variations of news coverage from more than one wire service and prefer to blend these versions into one more comprehensive story. This is one area in which paper-pencil editing has been simpler, but systems have been developed to make electronic merging of copy equally efficient.

To make story merging easier, systems provde for splitting the VDT screen so that two stories can be displayed side by side. With the ability to move words, paragraphs, and blocks from one column to the other, the editor can blend the stories without too much difficulty. As the editor works, he or she can also type in his or her own paraphrasing whenever desired. Without the split-screen feature, editors must work with one version on the screen and the other in typed form, and much more keyboarding is required.

Getting Hard-Copy Printouts

Especially in the handling of wire copy, editors may wish to look at *hard copies* of story segments with which they are working. Hard copies are paper copies as contrasted with *soft copies* as they exist in electronic form in computer storage or on a video screen. Reporters and writers also often want hard copies, and systems usually provide printout devices to deliver these copies. These printout devices can be nothing more than teletype devices operating at typewriter speed, but they often are high-speed computer printout devices that will give story copies in seconds.

The procedure for getting a printout is often very much like the procedure involved in sending copy to a typesetter because it is simply a matter of sending the copy to a different machine—in one case it is the typesetter and in the other case it is the printout machine (often also called the *line printer*).

8-7 Electronic equipment used at newspapers: its versatility and variety.

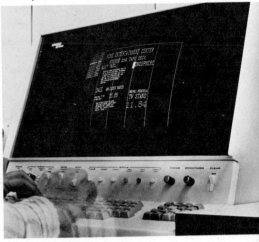

Many terminals provide split-screen capability for merging stories. This terminal with two full screens goes a step farther.

The Harris 2200 Layout Markup Terminal. With its computer, this terminal provides the capability to lay out an ad (even in full-page size) with key strokes, view all type in actual size and position, and then send the ad diretly to the typesetter. The typesetter outputs the ad, eliminating all pasteup.

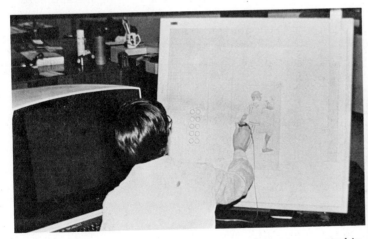

The type as set around the shape of the ball player

At the *Dallas-Fort Worth News-Texan,* an employee uses a graphic digitizer to position copy and set it via a Raycomp 100 full-page ad composition system. The digitizer makes fitting type around irregular shapes simple.

Typewriters and Optical Character Recognition As Entry Devices

Although VDTs have become the usual keyboard entry devices for computerized copy processing systems, typewriters alone and in combination with Optical Character Recognition (OCR) devices also serve the same purpose. Although these devices have shortcomings when compared with VDTs, their usage is continuing even in connection with some of the most elaborate newspaper and magazine systems.

In order to avoid the primary shortcomings of typewriters—a difficulty in editing (making changes)—they are usually used in conjunction with VDTs. The original entry by writers is by way of typewriter keyboard and final editing is on a VDT screen. The scanning of copy by an OCR device permits quick entry of features, columns, and other syndicated material that is typed at its source for such scanning.

To serve as entry devices without a scanner, typewriters must be retrofitted so that the characters struck on paper with keys are translated into digital code and sent through wire cable to a computer or tape output device.

To work with scanners, typewriters must be equipped with a typeface that the receiving scanner will recognize and they must be able to put an excellent image on paper for the scanner to read. Sometimes the typeface incorporates a bar code for the scanner to recognize. In any event, some code keys must be included on the keyboard. Typing for a scanner is also very restrictive in terms of margins, line beginnings, soiling, and crumpling of paper.

In either case, without cursors and editing keys to make corrections on video screens, typewriters as input devices complicate the editing process rather severely.

Errors discovered while copy is being typed can be corrected fairly easily by inserting a symbol after the error that tells the computer or scanner to ignore the erroneous material preceding the symbol. For example, if a word is typed including a transposition of letters, a delete word symbol plus the corrected word retyped immediately following will produce a corrected version. The code symbols for deleting words, characters, sentences, and paragraphs can be anything not ordinarily on a keyboard: bells, triangles, and the like. Such symbols in connection with letters or numbers can be used for paragraph openings and closings as well as other purposes.

Correction of errors after the paper has been removed from the typewriter is more cumbersome. For some scanners, deletions can be made with pen, but they must be made very carefully. Deletion lines that are just a little short or a little long can result in less or more being

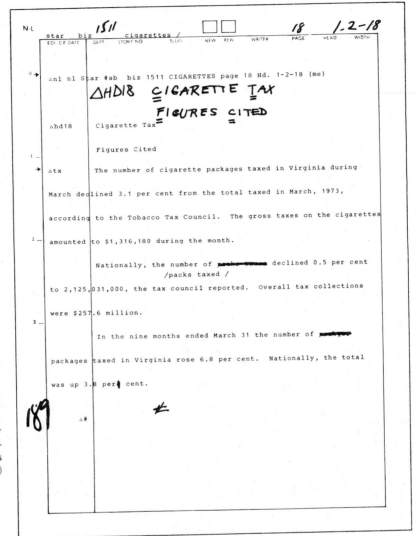

8-8 A sheet of copy ready for an Optical Character Recognition device. The headline and the traditional corrections in pen were written in a color not visible to the scanner. Then the headline and corrections were typed in place for reading by the scanner. (*Courtesy* Richmond Times-Dispatch and News Leader)

deleted than is intended. Handwritten insertions are not possible because a scanner could not be expected to recognize everyone's writing. Those corrections are made with a colored pen (often red for laser scanners and blue for others) that the scanner will not detect, and the typed story is returned to the typewriter for correcting. The typed-in substitute material must be carefully placed for it to be read properly. Some scanners require that these substitutions or insertions be placed in sequence at the left margin below the line to be corrected. Others require placement below the line, but directly beneath the

8-9 Some typical command codes for copy being fed into an OCR device. (*Courtesy* Pony-X-Press)

error. All insertions must be enclosed in *delimeters*, two slash marks that note the beginning and ending limit of the insertion.

Typesetting commands are also troublesome when editing scanner copy. They must, of course, be typed and placed properly. Some sample commands from two scanner systems are shown in Figure 8-9.

As one might imagine, typing proficiency is vital for anyone working in a system that uses typewriters as input devices. This necessity, plus the ease with which corrections can be made on VDTs, have made VDTs the much-preferred entry device. But even the most recent figures indicate that OCR machines continue to be on the increase in usage for newspapers, magazines, and commercial and in-house printers. In virtually every case, however, VDTs are used for final editing before copy is sent to typesetters.

Checklist: Electronic Copy Processing: Some Helpful Hints

The great variation among electronic systems makes it impossible for newcomers to prepare themselves in advance so they will be totally knowledgeable and proficient with the exact electronic devices they might face on their first job. Some things can be done, however, that will make working in an electronic copy processing system much easier.

1. Sharpen your typing skills. Although it is easy to correct copy on video terminals, a high level of accuracy eliminates many frustrations that can come from errors in typing commands. Computers are absolutely rigid in their language comprehension; one letter in the wrong place might be recognized as an obvious error by another human, but computers take everything literally. For working in OCR systems, accuracy in typing becomes even more essential.

2. Understand the basics of the system operation. This understanding helps you know which questions to ask. As a writer you must know how to put your material into storage; as an editor you must know how to get it out and correct it and then send it into type. In any system, there will be short, precise commands for accomplishing these tasks, and the right question can bring a quick solution to any problems. If crib sheets listing such commands are not available, make your own for handy reference until you get used to them. Preliminary reading of procedures manuals can be very helpful. Although it may not be possible to absorb everything a manual contains, reading a manual will usually eliminate many basic points of uncertainty and make adjustment to a system much easier.

3. Practice with any video display terminal. In spite of the wide differences among them, a little "hands-on" experience goes a long way in removing the fears that may slow down efficient operation when you start using a specific system.

4. Above all, remember that electronic systems put full responsibility for accuracy and quality of the final typesetting into the hands of the editorialist. In electronic systems, the compositor is you, not some handy scapegoat for unfortunate errors.

9 Preparing Words for Printing: Traditional Methods

Copy preparation and processing are primary factors in implementing effective printed material. The techniques involved when computer-related technology is used were explained in Chapter 8. Traditional methods for getting words ready for printing are still much used, however; they are discussed in this chapter.

For all printing, the words of an author are valuable raw material, but they must be thoroughly edited and processed before they can appear on the printed page. This editing is the last line of defense against error, against misunderstanding by the compositor and the readers, and against sloppy appearance. When the compositor receives copy, that copy must be accurate in every detail, or errors will certainly mar the final result. Furthermore, without specific and detailed instructions, its appearance in type may not even resemble what was desired. And, as every novice who has been sent in search of a "type squeezer" knows, copy must fit prescribed areas: lead type slugs or lines of phototype cannot be compressed after they have been set.

On the other hand, it takes only one instance of less copy than that needed to fill a space to show that too little copy is as bad as too much. There are two solutions to this problem: extra leading (white space) between lines or writing additional material. Either solution will require more work for the compositor and will increase costs.

Therefore, three important aspects of copy preparation must be understood: copy correction, copy marking (with typesetting specifications), and copyfitting.

Copy Correction

Fortunately for the student, the basic techniques of traditional copy correction are the same for all media—whether copy is being prepared for newspapers, magazines, books, promotion pieces, or advertising. A universally accepted set of symbols makes this task relatively fast and efficient. These symbols are easy to learn because they are functional and are based on common sense.

<u>Correction Desired</u>   Symbol

Change from:

    3 to three. . . . . ③

    three to 3. . . . . (three)

    St. to Street. . . . . (St.)

    Street to St. . . . . (Street)

Change capital to small letter . . . . ℓ

Change small letter to capital . . . . d̲

To put space between words. . . . . the time

To remove the space. . . . . news paper

To delete a letter and close up . . . . judgᵉment

To delete several letters or words . . . . shall ~~always~~ be

To delete several letters and close up . . . . . . superintendent

To delete one letter and substitute another. . . . receᎥve

To insert words or several letters . . . . of ^the time

To transpose letters or words, if adjacent . . . . recᎥeve

To insert punctuation, print correct mark
in proper place:

    comma   ⟩   parentheses (

    period   X   opening quote ⟨⟨

    question ?   closing quote ⟩⟩

    semicolon ⸮   dash —

    colon   ⸝   apostrophe ⌄

    exclamation !   hyphen =

To start a new paragraph. . . . . ¶ It has been

To center material. . . . .]Announcements[

To indent material. . . . . The first

    day's work

Set in boldface type . . . . The art of

Set in italic type . . . . The art of

To delete substantial amounts of copy, draw
an X over the area and box it in.

To set several lines in boldface type, bracket
the lines and mark <u>bf</u> in the margin.

9-1 Copyreading marks and symbols.

Copy to be set should be typed double- or triple-spaced. All corrections can then be made at the spot of error, either on the line or above the line. Figure 9-1 shows both the symbols for correcting errors in typewritten copy and those used for typesetting instructions; the latter are discussed in more detail later. Figure 9-2 shows a story that has been edited, using these symbols.

The correcting process does not end with typewritten copy, of course. When the copy has been set into type, galley proofs are read to detect and eliminate errors made by the typesetter. There is seldom enough space between the lines on a galley proof to enable a proof-

9-2 A copyeditor has corrected this story, using symbols, before giving it to the compositor for typesetting.

```
      Cross

      Clifton Fire


      CLIFTON, W.Va.--There will always be a question in the minds

of Clifton residents as to what their town might have been today

had it not been for a fateful day 73 years ago.

      Clifton on April 7, 1893, was Mason County's leading community.

With a population of about 2500, it was larger than the county seat,

Point Pleasant, and it boasted several thriving industries and

coal mines.

      By Sundown that day, Clifton's present and future had gone up

in smoke in what is possibly the worst fire in the county's his-

tory.

      The "day of the fire" is a poignant part of clifton history,

and the 73 intervening years have been marred by repeated specula-

tion as to just what the town might have been today had not most

of it been levelled by fire.

      Filson Lockett, retired miner and new York Central employe,

recalls vividly the day fire cut a zig-zag path through the bustling

river village. He was just nine, but the excitement and suffer-

ing made a deep impression on him

      He remembers that the day was exceptionally windy. Without that

wind, and the fact practicaly all the buildings were frame, Clifton

probably wouldn't have suffered so much.
```

reader to use any of the symbols shown in Figure 9-1 at the point of error. Even with enough room to do so, the typesetter would have to read through complete proofs to find the symbols instead of being able to see each correction at a glance. Therefore, special *proofreading* symbols are used *in the margin* to correct material that has been set in type. A mark may also be made at the point of error. Many proofreaders for newspapers and magazines draw a line from the point of error to the correction in the margin; most readers for book publishing firms do not. When guidelines are drawn, care must be taken to avoid obliterating the remainder of the line to be corrected. The symbols for

---

Page 2

Cross

Clifton Fire

The fire broke out about noon in a structure around a salt well, near the bank of the Ohio river. It spread quickly to a salt storage shed. The blustering wind fanned flames and embers into the furnace section of the salt works, and across the road where a small plant was destroyed.

Townspeople quickly rallied to shrieks of plant whistles and church bells, but they were pitiful with their bucket brigade as fire roared through the timbers.

A call for help was sent to Middleport, across the river. Middleport possessed one of the few fire engines in the area. ~~It was modern for its day, but inadequate for a blaze raging with the intensity of the Clifton fire.~~ The fire engine was loaded on to a ferry boat and started toward Clifton. Winds raised such high waves on the Ohio that water broke over the deck of the ferry.

Middleport's fire engine did some good. Stationed at the corner of Mason and olive (Sts.), the Middleport firemen managed to save the Woodrum home, which stands today.

~~At that point~~ *then* the flames veered eastward a long Olive (st.) to Columbia and High and out Columbia. At one point *they* burned all the homes between a saloon and church, causing one wag to remark "she burned from hell to heaven."

30

marginal marks (Figure 9-3) are basically the same for either system. A marked proof is shown in Figure 9-4.

Many errors creep into printed material because someone fails to follow through after the galleys have been corrected. If errors are detected at the first reading, revised proofs with corrections should be checked, for a compositor can err when setting a correction in a line or when substituting corrected lines. Instead of pulling the line containing an error, the compositor may take out another one and replace it with the one corrected. The result is double-talk that can destroy all meaning for the material.

There is usually another opportunity for corrections to be made even if revised galley proofs are not called for, but this final reading should not be used for detecting errors in typesetting. These last proofs are made in the form of pages or, in the case of advertising, of the completed ad. These proofs provide a chance to check if the material is positioned properly, headlines are with the right story, if the captions are with the correct picture, and so on. To delay typesetting corrections to this point is wasteful because it takes more time to unlock a form or alter a pasteup to exchange lines than it does to make the change when the type is still in galleys.

Compositors accept responsibility for their errors, but charge for the time spent correcting errors that were not detected in original copy or remaking lines for an editor or author who has merely changed his or her mind. These revisions become more expensive as the material moves into the advanced production stages.

Publications with their own mechanical departments can hide the cost of author's alterations or other laxities because there is no bill that must be paid by the editorial department. But the cost remains nevertheless.

Some publications require duplicate sets of galley proofs, one for marking corrections and the other to be cut apart and pasted on layout sheets. The set to be corrected is usually on white paper; the other is often on colored stock. Proofs for pasteup bear markings across the type area to identify the storage location of the type or film negatives. For offset printing, this helps the compositor's makeup person find the proper type if the compositor is to do the camera-ready pasteup; or it helps the makeup person find the proper negatives for stripping into page positions. For letterpress printing, the proof markings help the compositor locate the actual type for making up pages.

Press proofs are also obtainable, and in some cases this additional safeguard may be warranted. But if the person who must check the proofs is not on hand when the material first goes on the press, expensive press time can be wasted, since the time the job is on the press must be paid for whether the press runs or not.

∧ Make correction indicated in margin.

Stet Retain crossed-out word or letter; let it stand.

. . . . Retain words under which dots appear; write "Stet" in margin.

X Appears battered; examine.

Straighten lines.

✓✓✓ Unevenly spaced; correct spacing.

// Line up; i.e., make lines even with other matter.

run in Make no break in the reading; no ¶

no ¶ No paragraph; sometimes written "run in."

¶ Make a paragraph here.

tr Transpose words or letters as indicated.

ℛ Take out matter indicated; delete.

ℛ Take out character indicated and close up.

¢ Line drawn through a cap means lower case.

9 Upside down; reverse.

⌒ Close up; no space.

Insert a space here.

☐ Indent line one em.

[Move this to the left.

] Move this to the right.

sp Spell out.

⌐ Raise to proper position.

⌊⌋ Lower to proper position.

w.f. Wrong font; change to proper font.

Qu? Is this right?

l.c. Put in lower case (small letters).

s.c. Put in small capitals.

caps Put in capitals.

c.+s.c. Put in caps and small caps.

rom. Change to roman.

ital. Change to italic.

Under letter or word means caps.

Under letter or word, small caps.

Under letter or word means italic.

Under letter or word, boldface.

⌃ Insert comma.

;/ Insert semicolon.

:/ Insert colon.

⊙ Insert period.

/?/ Insert interrogation mark.

(!) Insert exclamation mark.

/=/ Insert hyphen.

ᵛ Insert apostrophe.

❝❞ Insert quotation marks.

ℓ Insert superior letter or figure.

∧ Insert inferior letter or figure.

[/] Insert brackets.

(/) Insert parentheses.

$\frac{}{M}$ One-em dash.

$\frac{2}{M}$ Two-em parallel dash.

bf Boldface type.

Set *s* as subscript.

Set *s* as exponent.

9-3 Proofreading marks and symbols.

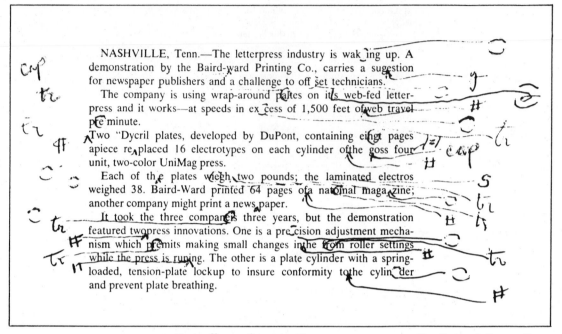

NASHVILLE, Tenn.—The letterpress industry is waking up. A demonstration by the Baird-ward Printing Co., carries a suggestion for newspaper publishers and a challenge to off set technicians.

The company is using wrap-around plates on its web-fed letterpress and it works—at speeds in excess of 1,500 feet of web travel pre minute.

Two "Dycril plates, developed by DuPont, containing eight pages apiece replaced 16 electrotypes on each cylinder of the goss four unit, two-color UniMag press.

Each of the plates weigh two pounds; the laminated electros weighed 38. Baird-Ward printed 64 pages of a national magazine; another company might print a news paper.

It took the three companys three years, but the demonstration featured two press innovations. One is a precision adjustment mechanism which permits making small changes in the from roller settings while the press is runing. The other is a plate cylinder with a spring-loaded, tension-plate lockup to insure conformity to the cylinder and prevent plate breathing.

9-4 A specimen galley proof as corrected. The number of errors has been intentionally exaggerated here to show a wide variety of symbols. Actual proofs have very few errors.

Regardless of precautions, errors occur. Absolute vigilance from the beginning of the typed copy to the final production steps keeps them to a minimum. Nothing can be taken for granted; it is amazing how easily errors seem to occur in such obvious places as headlines and titles in large display type.

Marking Typesetting Specifications

Before a compositor can set a single line of type, at least 10 basic points of information, the specifications (or specs), must be supplied:

1. Type size (expressed in points)
2. Type family (Century, Cheltenham, . . .)
3. Family branch (bold, condensed, extended, . . .)
4. Letter posture (italic or roman)
5. Letter composition (caps, lowercase, . . .)
6. Leading
7. Line length (expressed in picas)
8. Appointment of space (flush, centered, . . .)
9. Wordspacing
10. Letterspacing

Theoretically, then, the instructions for setting the type for this book would read: "10-point Zapf Book Light roman, caps and lowercase, leaded 2 points, set by 26 picas, flush left and right, normal word-spacing and letterspacing." However, much of this information does not have to be written on every piece of copy. Depending on the circumstances, it can be taken for granted that some of the instructions are understood by the compositor.

In body copy, for example, it is assumed that the appointment of space is to be flush left and right. Only exceptions must be marked. Letter composition is considered to be as shown in the copy; that is, typed capitals are to be set as capitals, lowercase letters are to be set as lowercase. Compositors also set copy with roman letter posture and with no leading and only normal word-and letterspacing unless there are indications to the contrary.

The marking of copy for titles and headlines is also simplified because of the following assumptions that are mutual to editor and compositor: (1) posture is roman unless marked; (2) machine leading is not needed unless marked; (3) line length is to be "line for line"; (4) letter composition is to be as shown in the copy; and (5) word-and letterspacing are to be normal.

But whether by mutual understanding or by specific copy marking, a line of type cannot be set unless the compositor has the 10 points of information. This is especially true of "transient" material, as distinguished from periodical copy. The procedure for periodicals differs because the regularity of issue permits considerable uniformity.

See the specifications for this book in Appendix B.

Newspaper Procedure

Marking copy for the mechanical department of a newspaper is simplified by several factors. The selection of type sizes, style, and leading is a decision of management and is seldom subject to change. Column widths (line lengths) are standard, although there may be some variation on the editorial page for by-line columns or special features. Speed in processing copy is essential and time is at a premium. Because headlines have such a direct effect on the character of a newspaper, they are standardized as much as possible.

Copy is channeled through one central (universal) copy desk, a number of departmental desks, or both. These desks are directed by people who are expert in the English language and versed in the newspaper's style and its composing and pressroom procedures; they prepare copy quickly and efficiently for the mechanical department.

Because body type specifications do not change, much of the copy is sent to the composing room with no marked instructions other than those for exceptions (multicolumn leads, special treatment for editorials or columns, and so on). Standardization applies to headlines too. A comprehensive schedule that visualizes all possible headlines and gives all the information a headline writer may need is prepared by the editorial department for the composing room. Each headline is keyed by a number or letter; to give the composing room all necessary information about the final appearance of a headline, the writer simply labels the headline with any agreed-upon designation, such as "#1" or "AA," and this immediately refers the compositor to the type size, face, and so on, similarly marked on the comprehensive schedule.

9-5 A typical newspaper page dummy.

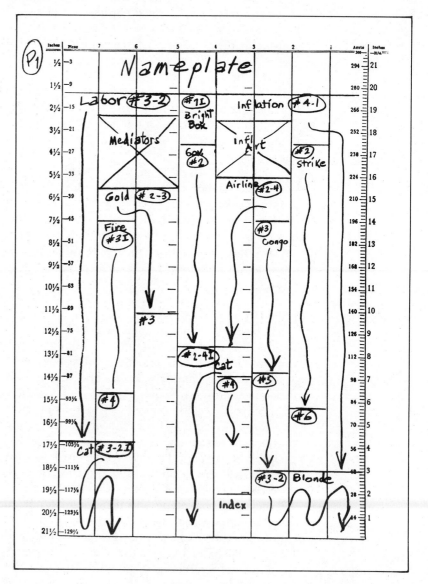

To place a headline over the proper story when pages are made up, a "slugging" system is used. The body copy is slugged with a word or two to identify the story—most newspapers use the first two words of the headline. As the text type is put in place, the slug line is replaced by the headline it identifies.

Other special problems for the newspaper are handled with equal efficiency. Continuing stories (which are set in type in intervals as they develop during the day), stories that must be changed slightly between editions, and stories that must be set before a headline has been written require special markings. These vary from newspaper to newspaper, but are always conveyed by techniques that simplify the communication of instructions from the editorial department to the composing room.

Body and headline copy are usually sent to the composing room on separate sheets. Traditionally, the display sizes are set on different machines than those used for straight matter (the usual body type), and if headlines and body copy are on the same sheet, the compositors cannot set both at the same time.

Newspaper makeup instructions

A newspaper must be put together in a hurry. Virtually every step of the makeup process is based on approximation, rather than on exact calculation. As stories are processed, their length is estimated and each is recorded with pertinent data on an inventory sheet usually called a *copy schedule.*

This information is used for page dummies. As the makeup person prepares the dummy, he or she writes the slug for each story in the position on the page that the story seems to merit. The makeup person indicates the probable length of the story with an arrow and shows the placement of illustrations by drawing an X through the space. The dummy then serves as a pattern as the stories and headlines are put in a form prior to stereotyping or printing. Figure 9-5 shows a typical newspaper page dummy marked up.

Advertising and Brochure Procedure

The marking of copy for advertisements is quite different. In most cases a full *markup* (Figure 9-6) is used for communicating instructions about typesetting and makeup to the printer. It is best described as a drawing of how the ad is to look when printed. All display lines are lettered in exact position, illustrations are sketched in, and body type areas are indicated by drawn lines. Instructions for type sizes and style are written with colored pencil and circled next to each bit of display type or in the margin. The body type areas are identified by letter—A, B, C, and so on.

Body copy is provided in typewritten form, is marked with typesetting instructions, and is slugged with the corresponding letter from

9-6 A typical markup: an ad layout marked with instructions for the printer. It serves the same function as a dummy.

the markup. By following these instructions and checking with the markup, the mechanical department or printer can create an exact replica of the ad as designed by the advertiser or the agency. The same procedure is followed for flyers, handbills, direct-mailing pieces, and other brochures.

Magazine Procedure

The preparation of magazine material is usually a cross between those used for newspapers and for advertisements. Sometimes articles are prepared with full markups by an art department; or the editor may follow a fast course like his or her newspaper counterpart. But in most cases a middle ground is followed.

Often there is no headline schedule; titles follow no set typographical pattern. They are lettered in position on a dummy, with typesetting instructions entered as in advertising markups. The relative stability of column measure and the other aspects of body copy permits the use of minimum marking for such material.

Because there is usually sufficient time between issues, a magazine dummy is made by pasting galley proofs of text material or specimen copy of body and caption type in position, with the titles lettered in by hand (Figure 9-7). Rough layout sketches in miniature or full size often precede the completion of this dummy. Also, if the magazine is

9-7 *Right:* A magazine dummy with galley proofs pasted in position and the display type lettered in position and marked for the compositor. *Below:* The printed pages show how accurate the dummy was. (*Courtesy Aramco World*)

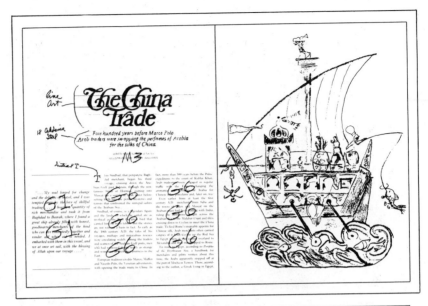

to be printed by any of the photomechanical printing processes (offset and rotogravure), camera-ready pasteups may be required. Making these pasteups, called *mechanicals*, is discussed in Chapter 12.

Perhaps the best example of care and precision in processing copy is in book publishing. Books must be more carefully edited and produced than any other printed product. More permanent in nature than newspapers and magazines, they are relied on by readers for au-

9-8   Steps in the dummying of two pages of a book.

(Photos by John King)

Materials used. From lower left, clockwise: photographs, T-square, scaling wheel, manuscript of caption copy, galleys, line gauge-pica rule, blank dummy sheet.

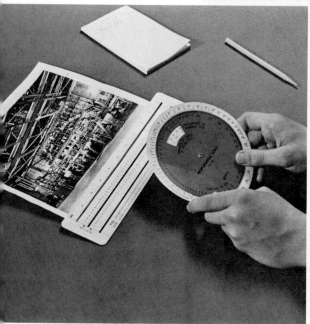

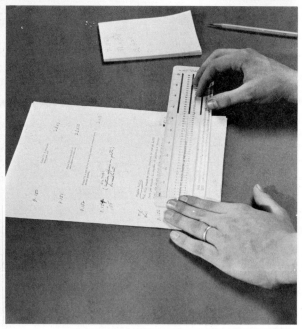

First step: size the illustrations. Decide on placement of photographs and text. Assess each photo and decide whether or not to crop. Reduce (or enlarge) each photo with all these factors in mind, with the aid of the scaling wheel (see page 207).

Determine caption width and depth. As with the illustrations, decide on best dimensions and position for caption copy. Measure the original copy and calculate the typeset size from the number of characters.

Wax the backs of all galleys, in preparation for pasting. Also, number each one all along its face. Then, as here, trim galley margins.

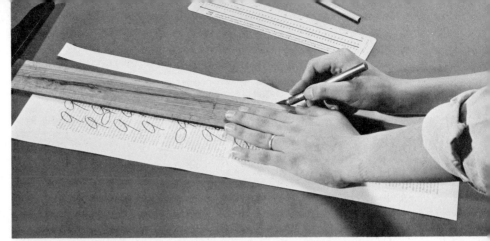

Place the waxed galley in position on the dummy page. Though skill in the graphic arts is of primary importance in dummying, a dummyer must also remember such makeup necessities as alignment of facing pages and prevention of widows.

Finished dummy pages. Note outlines of sized photos at upper left (bleeds) and caption boxes. The line illustrations are reduced photocopies of the art for position guidance. Galley sections are in place and about to be pressed down. The dummy will now go to the compositor, who will follow it carefully in making up pages.

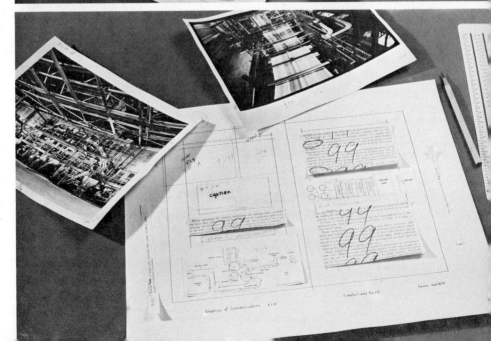

thoritative and accurate material presented in legible fashion. Also, there usually is more time for more meticulous attention to detail than with other media.

This attention to detail starts with the raw manuscript and proceeds to the final dummying stage. The photographs in Figure 9-8 show that, with design specifications already established, each set of facing pages is carefully crafted after all type is set. This pasteup dummy is the blueprint for mechanicals prepared later or for the stripping of film negatives of type and illustrations into exact page positions for making offset printing plates (or for preparing page forms for letterpress printing).

Copyfitting

The planner of any kind of graphic communication is vitally concerned with copyfitting. It is important to the editors of newspapers and magazines, the advertising designer, and the public relations person who puts together booklets and brochures. Without copyfitting, unnecessary costs are incurred or attractive layouts are destroyed, or both may occur. If more type than needed is set, the payment for the *overset* is wasted cost. Titles that cannot fit a given space must be rewritten and reset with unnecessary loss of time and money. Areas of text type that fail to fill their allotted space can jeopardize the effect of a good design.

Depending upon the circumstance, copyfitting may be rough or extremely accurate. There are several methods for copyfitting, each suitable to its purpose. Newspapers, for example, have no time for complicated copyfitting methods. Stories are written so that they can be cut from the bottom up without destroying meaning. If the stories are too short, filler material is used. Consequently, estimation is based on the number of words in a column inch. Depending upon point size, column width, and leading, this figure usually ranges from 30 to 40 words per column inch. When reporters use uniform setting for line lengths on their typewriters, this figure can be converted into lines; that is, four typewritten lines equal 1 inch.

Estimating body type space needs on a "words per column inch" basis may be adequate for many newspapers when column widths and type size are standard, but it is not accurate enough for any other purpose. In figuring space requirements for display type, even newspapers require an extremely accurate system—one that takes into account the varying widths of letters as well as the differences inherent to various typestyles. This system, called *unit counting*, is discussed in detail later in this chapter.

The most accurate and most commonly used method for estimating space needs for body copy is based on the counting of characters, a character being any letter, number, space, or piece of punctuation. Although it does not make allowance for varying widths of letters, the character count method is sufficiently accurate for the precise work of preparing copy for advertisements, promotion pieces, and magazine pages. Type designs—even those considered standard and not condensed or expanded—vary considerably in the number of characters that will fit into a line, and the character count method compensates for these variations.

Character Count Copyfitting

The first step in estimating space by way of the character count method is to obtain information about the specific type size and face from a printer or type manufacturer. Accurately compiled tables showing the number of characters that will fit in various line lengths or the number of characters in each pica of line length are readily available from these sources. The table below shows the characters per line for two typefaces. The table on page 170 shows the characters per pica of 26 selected typefaces in various sizes. These tables are based on normal typesetting; if special tight or loose spacing is going to be used, information relating to that spacing has to be obtained.

Copyfitting problems are in only two forms: finding the depth of space needed for a manuscript on a layout that is being made, or finding the amount of copy to write to fill a space on a layout that is already completed.

In either case, copyfitting boils down to the two basic steps of determining how many lines of type will be involved; and how many characters fit into a line. Some changing of units of measure (points to picas and vice versa) is also often involved, but essentially there are only two major steps.

Characters per line of two typefaces

10-point Kennerly

Line length in picas	12	14	16	18	20	22	24	26	28	30
Character count	27	34	39	45	51	57	62	68	74	79

10-point Vogue

Line length in picas	12	14	16	18	20	22	24	26	28	30
Character count	28	34	40	46	52	57	62	68	73	79

Courtesy Lawhead Press, Inc., Athens, Ohio.

Characters per pica of selected typefaces

Characters per pica of a number of selected typefaces are presented here as a tool for practice in copyfitting. Copyfitting can be accurate only when the characteristics of the individual type design are taken into account, since types of the same size use different amounts of space according to the design of their faces. In addition, the space required by many typefaces varies slightly according to the manufacturer (e.g., the Baskervilles of two type makers may differ) or according to the method of composition (e.g., Linotype Palatino differs from Linofilm Palatino). And if special tight or open spacing is specified, the space variations must be taken into account during copyfitting.

Face	Point sizes							
	8	9	10	11	12	14	18	24
Bernhard Modern Roman	3.59		2.99		2.54	2.15	1.74	1.31
Bodoni with Italic	3.13		2.6		2.36	2.11	1.64	1.28
Bookman	3.11	2.88	2.6	2.37	2.21	1.84		
Caledonia	3.12	2.87	2.63	2.44	2.26	2.00		
Caslon 540	3.39		2.91	2.56	2.21	1.86	1.49	1.06
Cheltenham	3.56	3.2	2.99	2.72	2.53	2.15		1.42
Clarendon	2.6	2.4	2.3		2.0			
Cloister	3.56		3.11	2.97	2.75	2.45	1.93	1.46
Cooper Black	2.6		2.03		1.75	1.42	1.09	.83
Dominante	2.6	2.5	2.3		2.0			
Egmont Light	3.4		2.7		2.3	2.2		
Electra	3.2	2.88	2.68	2.5	2.4			
Franklin Gothic	2.66		2.1		1.89	1.63	1.26	.98
Futura Medium	3.6		2.87		2.42	2.11	1.61	
Garamond with Italic	3.37	3.18	2.95	2.7	2.59	2.3	1.77	1.38
Goudy Old Style with Italic	3.36		2.74		2.42	2.01		
Helvetica	3.03	2.68	2.45		2.10	1.97	1.53	1.17
Kaufmann Script			3.12		2.84	2.54	1.94	1.5
Melior	3.08	2.75	2.48		2.14			
Optima	3.28	2.95	2.67		2.29	1.97	1.53	1.17
Palatino	3.08	2.75	2.48		2.14	1.87	1.44	1.11
Park Avenue					2.83	2.54	2.07	1.64
Scotch Roman	3.18		2.85	2.7	2.26	1.87	1.45	1.12
Stymie Bold	2.92		2.29		2.02	1.67	1.31	1.03
Weiss Roman	3.76		3.16	2.93	2.58	2.27	1.7	1.37
Weiss Italic	4.54		3.51	3.38	2.92	2.66	2.09	1.69

Finding the amount of space needed on a layout

The first step in finding out how much space is needed is to find out how long the copy is in terms of characters. The simplest way to find this out is to count an average line of the typewritten material and multiply it by the number of lines in the typing. When doing this, all lines should be counted as full lines, including those that end paragraphs. Next, the number of characters that will fit into a line of type (from our table) is divided into the total number of characters in the article to find the number of lines of type that will be involved.

With this accomplished, we have an answer of sorts, but usually we want to convert the number of lines of type into picas so that we can proceed with drawing the layout with a line gauge marked off in picas. We convert lines to picas by first multiplying the number of lines times the line thickness in points and get an answer in points. To convert points to picas, we divide by 12.

As an example, let us use the two-page manuscript in Figure 9-2 and compute the space we would need to have this set in lines that are 18 picas long if the type is to be 10-point Kennerly leaded one point (10-point type on an 11-point line).

Step 1   Find out how many characters there are in the manuscript. To complete this step, count an average line in the manuscript (we will use the second line) and find that there are 64 characters in that line. Then count the number of lines, short ones included, to find that there are 41 lines, 21 on the first page and 20 on the second. By multiplying 41 times 64 we find that the article contains 2,624 characters.

Step 2   How many characters will be in each line of type? By looking at the table we find that 45 characters will be set in each 18-pica line of 10-pt. Kennerly.

Step 3   By dividing the 45 characters in each line of type into the total number of characters to be set (2,624), we find that the typesetter will have to produce 58 lines and then still have 14 characters left over, so it will have to set 59 lines of type. (When this answer produces a fraction, always round up to the next *highest* number of lines, because the typesetter will have to set another line, short though it may be.)

Step 4   Convert from the number of lines (59) to points by multiplying by line thickness (11 points); 59 times 11 equals 649 points. Note here that line thickness includes leading.

Step 5   Convert from points (649) to picas by dividing by 12 points in a pica; we find that we will have to allow 54 and $\frac{1}{12}$ picas of depth on our layout.

Finding the number of characters to write to fill a space

In many situations, the amount of space for copy is already definitely fixed on a layout, and only enough characters to fill that space must be written. The first step in these situations is to measure the width of the copy area to determine how many picas will be in each line of type. Then we use a scale to find the number of characters to write for each line of type. Then we measure the depth and convert it to points so that we can divide by the thickness of a line to find the number of lines that will fit into the area. When we know the number of lines and the number of characters in a line, we simply multiply the two to get the total number of characters.

As an example, let us assume that we have an advertisement in which a copy block is to be filled with 9-point Baskerville type with one extra point of white space for each line (9-point Baskerville on a 10-point line).

Step 1　We measure the width of the block and find that it is 15 picas.

Step 2　We look in the scale and find that the typesetter will set 2.96 characters in each of those 15 picas, so we multiply the two to find that there will be 44.4 characters in each line of type, which we will round off to the closest full character, 44. Use of the decimal would give us a slightly more accurate answer, but it is not worth the effort.

Step 3　We measure the depth and find that it is 18 picas, which is 216 points (18 picas times 12 points in a pica).

Step 4　We divide the line thickness (10 points) into the depth (216 points) and find that 21.6 lines will fit. Here we round off to the *lowest* whole line; 22 lines will not fit into the depth, and in terms of depth there is no such thing as a fraction of a line. If we can enlarge the block by 4 points, then we could fit 22 lines into the block. Assuming we have no authority to change the layout, we stay with 21 lines, and go ahead and write 21 lines each with 44 characters in it for a total of 924 characters. Extra white space between paragraphs would fill out the type to 216 points.

Making Copyfitting As Simple As Possible

Editors and graphic designers detest copyfitting; working with figures is not appealing to verbal and artistic types of individuals. But the job must be done. To simplify copyfitting we can use some shortcuts. For example, on a magazine or other publication with standard column measurements, copy paper can be printed with vertical lines to mark the beginning and ending for each line of typing. By spacing these lines so that the number of characters that can be typed between them is the same as the number of characters that the typesetter will produce in the columns, we can avoid a lot of counting. Each typewritten line is the equivalent of a line of type. Or at least, we can force manuscripts to be typed with standard line settings so that we know how many characters are in a line without counting an average line.

In any instance involving standardized typeface and line length, copyfitting can be made extremely simple; it is really not a serious problem for magazines. For ads and other variable work, little can be done except to follow the steps outlined previously. The results are worth the effort.

For general estimating—judging the number of pages involved in a booklet—a *word count* system can be used for copyfitting, but the results are not very accurate. In one of these systems, a table showing the number of words per square inch is used (see Appendix C). Another system uses an estimation of 3 ems per word if type is 10 point or smaller, and 2.5 ems per word if type is 11, 12, or 13 point. Words vary so much in length that either of these systems can be effective only for preliminary work; they also do not take into account the different space requirements of different typefaces.

Fitting Display Type to Space _____

Even the character count method is inadequate for computing the space requirements of headlines, titles, or other lines of display type. For ads, brochures, and magazine pages, it is usually best to hand-letter display type to exact size for layouts, thus guaranteeing precise fitting. Tracing letters from type examples is helpful in getting size and spacing just right while lettering. Pastedown or transfer type can also provide for accurate fitting of display type.

Since newspapers have to process scores of headlines in each issue, a system of counting is commonly used that takes into account the variation in width among letters.

Unit Count for Headlines

For near-perfect copyfitting of newspaper headlines, varying unit values are assigned to characters according to their widths. Characters are assumed to fall into four categories: thin, normal, wide, and extra wide. Normal letters are assigned one unit, thins are assigned one-half, wides are one-and-one-half, and extra wides are two. Although characters vary considerably more than these four categories allow for, the slight inaccuracy is tolerated in the interest of simplicity of counting.

For newspapers with headlines containing only capitals, as well as headlines containing capitals and lowercase letters, the assignment of units is made as simple as possible in each case.

For capitals and lowercase headlines, the following allotments are made:

all lowercase letters and numbers 1 unit

     except

m and w	$1\frac{1}{2}$ units
f, l, i, t, and 1	$\frac{1}{2}$ unit
all capital letters	$1\frac{1}{2}$ units

     except

M and W	2 units
I	$\frac{1}{2}$ unit
spaces	1 unit
punctuation	$\frac{1}{2}$ unit

Depending upon the design of the type, occasionally *j* and *r* are assigned only a half unit. Other variations can be made, but these assignments meet most situations.

The unit count for headlines of *all capitals* is different from that of both capitals and lowercase. For simplicity in counting, the basic capital letters are assigned one unit in all-cap heads. The unit allotments in all-capital display lines are

all letters 1 unit

     except

M and W	$1\frac{1}{2}$ units
I	$\frac{1}{2}$ unit
spaces	$\frac{1}{2}$ unit
punctuation	$\frac{1}{2}$ unit

Note how the two headlines in Figure 9-9 are counted.

9-9 Unit count for headlines. Note the differing values for caps and lowercase and all capitals. (The fact that each first line totals 7 units is coincidence.)

Virtually all the work connected with display types involves writing lines to fit a given space. It is therefore a matter of ascertaining the maximum number of units for the line, and then writing within that limitation. In newspaper offices these maximums are shown on a headline schedule. Originally, they are derived by setting lines composed of a normal assortment of letters and spaces and counting the units in these lines. Character counts shown for display type in printer's type specimen books may also be used as line maximums.

Whatever the source, the maximum count per line has to be observed. The temptation to squeeze an extra half unit may be strong if the wording of the title or headline seems especially good—and occasionally such fudging on the count pays. But when it fails, the waste of time for the writer to rewrite and for the compositor to reset the line is inexcusable. The gamble is not worth the effort and expenditure.

Electronics: A Boon for Copyfitting _____

As already noted, the traditional copy-processing methods described in this chapter are steadily being replaced by electronic devices and procedures. Video display terminals and computers as described in Chapter 8 are splendid devices for many aspects of copy preparation, but in none of their functions are they appreciated more than for copyfitting. Video terminals that show a running total of characters in the story being typed save the chore of counting a line and multiplying the characters by the number of lines. Other terminals that are fully programmed for copyfitting can give the depth in picas exactly at any time and with virtually no effort on the part of the terminal operator.

Headlines can be typed onto a terminal screen and the units that do not fit into a line are dropped to a second line, showing at a glance what the count problem is, without the necessity of any human counting. Until there is no traditional copy processing, however, there is no way to avoid the tedium of character counting and unit counting for accurate typefitting.

10 Illustrations in Graphic Communication

Although the hackneyed adage "One picture is worth a thousand words" defies proof and begs argument, the basic value of illustrations in graphic communication is beyond dispute.

Without attempting to put a relative value on illustration as compared with words, we can still be aware of the special effectiveness of images in accomplishing communication goals. The pervasiveness of images in our communication system is without question; we start to learn our verbal language from picture books and move on to maturity in a world of television, motion pictures, illustrated magazines and books, and newspapers.

Indeed, television seems to have launched us into an age of images, made us a nation of viewers rather than readers. All print media have responded to television's impact with more, bigger, and better illustrations. And an orator without "visual aids" to supplement his or her verbal presentation is swimming against the stream of imagery that seems to be flooding communication today. Even highway signs have been evolving from verbal to visual images to achieve instantaneous communication with motorists and to surmount the language barrier.

This increased emphasis on images for communication is not surprising. It comes merely as the result of technological innovations that have made the use of illustrations easier and more effective. The inventions of photography, photoengraving, motion pictures, and then television have each taken us one step farther toward our reliance on illustrations for communication. And if we look back to the early attempts of human beings to communicate graphically, we can see that pictures were the first message form. The caveman's pictograph demonstrated an appreciation of the communicative potential of illustrations at the earliest stages of graphic communication development.

With our communication system now in an advanced stage of development, we seem to be completing a cycle that places pictorial images again in a position of primary importance.

The Many Functions and Forms of Illustrations

Much of the effectiveness of illustrations comes from the variety of communication functions they can perform and the many physical forms they can take. Although a discussion of illustrations cannot totally separate function from form, we can at least place emphasis on their functions as we also discuss their forms.

As explained in more detail in later chapters, one of the basic functions of illustrations is to *attract and get attention*. Magazine editors, advertising designers, and other media users have long realized that a striking illustration is perhaps the best means for attracting a reader's eyes to a page or design. Although all forms of illustrations can accomplish this function, the *photograph* has been the primary choice. Photographs, because they are true-to-life duplicates of images that the human eyes see in the world about them, can compel attention quickly and forcefully. The emotions or reactions that are aroused as we view life about us can be aroused and catered to by photographs better than by any other means. The impact of television and motion pictures stems from this capability of reproducing true-to-life images, and the creators of print media are merely showing their understanding of this impact as they use photographs as attention getters.

Photographs are also primary tools for the communicator who wants *to inform* readers precisely of what took place at an event or happening. Auto accidents, sports action, parades, and other such

10-1 *Below:* A photograph often can appeal to emotions far more effectively than words. (*Photo by Mac Shaffer*)

10-2 *Below, right:* A photograph often can effectively transmit information. Without the photograph, many words would be needed to describe this tornado damage. (*Courtesy Patricia A. Beck*)

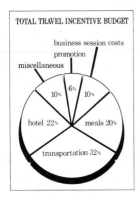

TOTAL TRAVEL INCENTIVE BUDGET

business session costs
promotion
miscellaneous

10%   6%   10%

hotel 22%   meals 20%

transportation 32%

10-3   Pie charts are old standbys for presenting information showing relative amounts used or allocated. (*Courtesy* Advertising Age)

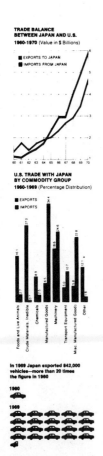

TRADE BALANCE
BETWEEN JAPAN AND U.S.
1960-1970 (Value in $ Billions)

■ EXPORTS TO JAPAN
■ IMPORTS FROM JAPAN

U.S. TRADE WITH JAPAN
BY COMMODITY GROUP
1960-1969 (Percentage Distribution)

■ EXPORTS
■ IMPORTS

In 1969 Japan exported $42,000
vehicles—more than 20 times
the figure in 1960

1960

1969

DATA FOR CHARTS COURTESY
UNITED STATES-JAPAN TRADE COUNCIL

news events can be shown to readers through photographs more effectively than with other kinds of illustrations.

The graphic communicator who wants to *instruct* readers how to do something, however, will often find a *drawing* to be more effective. The editors of *Popular Science,* for example, often find it necessary to present step-by-step drawings to show readers how to assemble complicated objects. As pointed out later, drawings can take many forms, ranging from simple stick figures to works of art containing a full range of tones and colors. It will suffice here to emphasize the point that drawings often are as vital or more vital than words in giving instructions to readers.

When the primary goal is *to explain,* illustrations can again be a primary tool. The understanding of complicated subjects can often be lost in a deluge of words but be clarified if explanatory illustrations come to the assistance of verbal elements. The presentation of virtually all statistical data can be aided by illustration. Consider, for example, budget figures—a *pie chart* showing basic allocations can clarify relations much more efficiently than the statistics alone, as can *pictographs,* so called because relationships are shown by pictures. *Bar graphs* can serve the same function as pie charts; and *line graphs* can show trends (such as the ups and downs of Dow Jones Industrials for a year). On the other hand, *schematic diagrams* can explain the operation of printing presses and other machines better than photographs, words, or charts. And if the goal is to explain to readers how to get from place to place or the nationwide weather outlook, a *map* can be indispensable.

As comic strips attest, illustrations can also be used *to entertain* the reader. Political cartoons, such as those drawn by Thomas Nast for *Harper's Weekly* a century ago and those created by Bill Mauldin for today's newspapers, have shown the effectiveness of illustrations when the objective is *to influence.*

It may be necessary to combine types of illustrations for maximum effectiveness. For example, the line illustration used as a diagram of a football play and superimposed on a photograph can be the only truly effective way to show how the action developed.

In thinking of the functions of illustrations—and types of illustrations as they relate to functions—we must keep in mind that illustra-

10-4   Here, from bottom, a pictograph, bar graph, and line graph are used to convey information. Pictographs give dual information at a glance: what the items being compared are and what the relative amounts are. Bar graphs present statistical information showing the realtionship of amounts. Line graphs show statistical trends over time periods. (*Copyright 1979 by* American Way, *inflight magazine of American Airlines; reprinted by permission*)

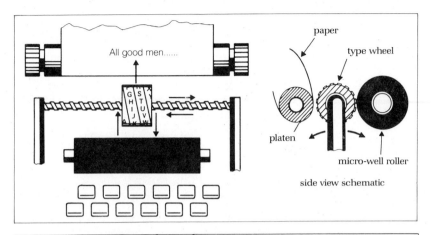

10-5 Want readers to understand a complicated device? A schematic diagram is usually the best supplement to words. *(Reprinted from* Product Engineering; *copyright Morgan-Grampian, Inc., 1970)*

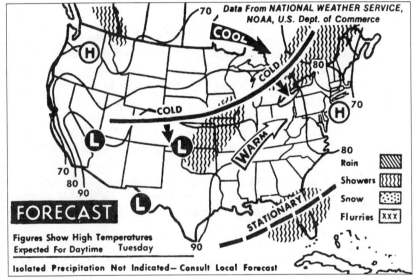

10-6 A map can eliminate the communication confusion that often accompanies verbal directions. Imagine the difficulty in trying to convey verbally what this weather map shows visually.

tions work best in combination with words. The marriage of words and illustrations that makes them equal partners usually provides the most efficient communication.

The Production Aspects of Illustrations

So far we have looked at illustrations from the standpoint of the original form of the illustration as created by an artist or photographer. Before illustrations can be viewed by masses of readers, however, they must be produced in quantity by a printing process. As we consider illustrations from the production standpoint, different terminology, different categories, and different concepts emerge.

As explained in Chapter 3, many printing processes are available for the mass reproduction of words and illustrations. Some of the technicalities of the production of illustrations vary among these different processes. But for the two primary printing processes most production terminology and procedures are the same; these similar procedures are discussed here and the technical differences are explained in later chapters.

Basic Types of Reproductions of Illustrations

From the standpoint of their mechanical reproduction, there are two basic types of illustration each of which contains some subtypes. These two kinds of reproductions, *line* and *halftone*, are best explained by briefly tracing their production steps.

Line reproductions

Some drawings, such as pen-and-ink renditions, are composed of only solid tones, black lines on a white background, called *line drawings*. When printed, they are called *line reproductions*. Figure 10-7 shows a basic line reproduction. In order to reproduce Figure 10-7, the printer followed a relatively simple photographic procedure. The original artwork, done with pen and black ink on a white background, is first photographed in order to get a production negative. During this photographing, the image may be enlarged or reduced, with reduction being most common. Line illustrations are usually drawn larger than the reproduction in order to minimize flaws that might be present in the original drawing. The negative that is created is then used to transfer the image to a metal surface for use on a printing press. This image transfer is possible because of the light sensitivity of the films and metals that are used.

For example, when the line illustration is mounted in front of the lens of a large camera (called an *engraver's camera*), light is beamed toward the illustration. That light reflects from the white background and strikes the film in the camera, making it black in the background. The dark lines of the illustrations reflect no light, thus letting the film

10-7 A drawing that contains only lights and darks and no middle tones is called, when printed, a *line reproduction*. (For letterpress printing, it is called a line cut, line engraving, or line etching.)

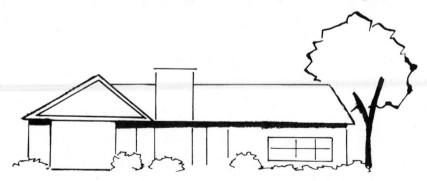

remain clear in the image areas. The developed negative, therefore, is dark (opaque) in the nonprinting area and clear in the printing area. The image it contains is a reverse image of the original drawing. This image is transferred to a light-sensitive metal sheet by beaming light through the negative to the metal. Light thus exposes the metal sheet where it is to carry ink but leaves the nonprinting area unexposed. The metal sheet can then be chemically developed or etched with acid for printing, depending on the printing process to be used. In either case, the light-exposed portion of the plate carries ink and the nonexposed area does not.

Halftone reproductions

The reproduction of illustrations that contain tones between the extremes of white and black is more complicated and puzzling. These reproductions, called *halftones,* are necessary for all photographs, wash drawings, oil paintings, water colors, or any other original illustration containing *continuous tones.* The continuous tones that lie between white and black in a photograph cannot really be carried to paper from a printing plate—either black ink is deposited on the paper or it is not. In order to create the impression of continuous tones in printed reproductions, an optical illusion is employed. The illusion of middle tones is created by breaking the printing image into tiny dots, each of which will carry ink from plate to paper; if the dots are small and widely spaced the area will appear to be light, and if they are large and closely spaced they will create a darker image. Figure 10-8 was made with a coarse screen to make the dots readily visible.

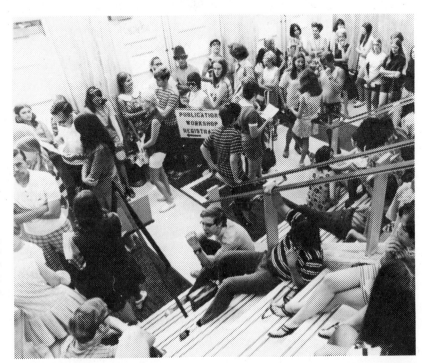

10-8 This halftone, made with a coarser screen than the paper permits, contains a dot structure visible to the naked eye.

10-9 The dot pattern is submerged in this fine-screen halftone. This is an example of a basic reproduction of a photograph, oil painting, or other continuous-tone illustration that is called a *square-finish* halftone.

The dot pattern for halftones is created through the use of a screen in front of the film in the engraver's camera. The screen, either on glass or film, is composed of parallel lines that intersect at right angles. Although these lines are usually too fine to be seen by the naked eye, under a magnifying glass the screen pattern they create looks much like the screen used for a household door or window. The coarseness of the screen is dictated by the number of lines per linear inch, and the designation of the screen desired for halftone reproductions is of considerable importance. Figure 10-9 shows how a fine screen submerges the dot pattern in a halftone.

Screen coarseness varies usually from 55 lines to 175 lines per linear inch. Traditionally, the coarser screens have been used by newspapers and other media being printed on rough paper. Newspapers still using the traditional printing method are restricted to about 55 to 85 line screens. Media using other printing processes or finer paper (i.e., magazines) can employ the finer screens. Generally speaking, the finer the screen, the better is the reproduction. Consequently, in specifying the desired screen, one must consider the printing process to be used, the smoothness of paper, and the quality level desired.

How halftone reproductions are made With the specified screen in the camera, the photoengraver places the copy on a copy board in front of the lens, puts the film behind the screen in the camera, and proceeds to make one or more exposures.

Halftone negatives may be made with only one exposure, like line negatives, but photoengravers usually take a series of short exposures in order to get greater tone control and to retain detail in the extreme light and dark areas of the copy.

As the light is beamed to the copy, it reflects back through the lens opening and the screen to the film. Because the light that goes through the lens is reflected from the copy, it varies in intensity directly according to the lightness or darkness of the various areas of the copy. A photograph of a man with a white shirt and dark suit, for example, will reflect light strongly from the shirt and weakly from the suit. Note in Figure 10-9 the variation between the light dome and the dark trees.

When the light pierces the thousands of tiny holes in the screen, it is broken into thousands of small beams. The intense light spreads, as it goes through these apertures, breaking the screen lines into clear dots on the negative. The dots vary in size and shape and are connected or separated, depending upon the amount of light reflecting from the copy. Because of this variation in the dot structure all the tones in a photograph or other such illustration can be captured on film, transferred to a plate, and finally produced in the printing process.

The developed halftone negative looks to the naked eye like a standard photographic negative. With a magnifying glass, however, the thousands of dots created by the lines of the screen can be clearly seen. The image is composed completely of dots, both clear and opaque. One can readily realize how tiny the dots are by understanding that the number per square inch is always the square of the screen size: a 50-line screen produces 2,500, a 100-line screen produces 10,000, and so on.

Halftone negatives are transferred to a plate surface by the exposure of light through the negative to the light-sensitized metal. On the finished plate, each of the dots that was clear on the negative becomes a tiny printing surface; the metal surrounding these areas has either been treated to repel ink or has been etched away so that it cannot receive ink. Areas that were dark in the original copy will have many relatively large and closely grouped dots to carry ink to the paper. Consequently, as the plate is printed, most of the paper will be covered with ink in these areas, and these areas will be dark to the eye. Light areas of the copy will contain relatively small dots widely spaced and will be light when printed.

The magic of the dots   One point about halftone reproductions should be emphasized. The dot pattern of a standard halftone, though it varies considerably, is present over all portions of the negative and consequently will be present over all portions of the finished plate. Therefore, there are no pure black or pure white areas in a standard halftone. In areas that seem to be pure white in the original, some dots will stand to carry ink to paper. Areas that were pure black are marred

 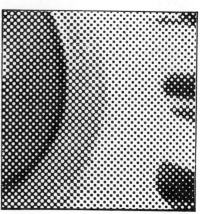

10-10 *Right:* A small portion of the silhouette halftone of the cogwheel at left has been enlarged to show how the dot structure produces shades of tone. (*Courtesy S. D. Warren Company*)

by the presence of tiny clear dots. Figure 10-10 shows the picture of a cogwheel seemingly containing blacks, whites, and grays. However, the enlargement on the right reveals the presence of dots throughout.

In spite of the fact that halftones rely on dots to create the illusion of tones, when the proper screen has been selected the reproduction can be excellent. To the viewer, unaided by a magnifying glass, the dots on a halftone reproduction blend with the background to form a faithful reproduction of the original, as Figure 10-9 shows.

The principle of blending dots with the background can be easily illustrated by any student. By holding a newspaper at normal reading distance, all the letters and characters can be seen clearly. These represent the dots of a halftone. By pinning the newspaper to a wall and stepping back several paces, the letters and characters appear as masses of gray; the difference in tone created by columns of standard type matter as compared with areas of boldface type is the best illustration of how the dots make tones vary in halftones.

Tint (tone) blocks   It is possible, because of the dot magic of the halftone process, to reproduce areas of any given size in a uniform tint, or tone, of the color being used in a printing job. These tints can be produced in any percentage of the full density of the color.

For example, when black is being used, a 50 percent gray (just half the density of solid black) can be printed from a plate made to that specification. Other desired percentages, such as 20, 30, or 80, can also be obtained (Figure 10-11).

These "tint blocks," as they are called, are prepared through the halftone process. Instead of photographing an illustration, a white board is put in front of the camera and the desired tone is achieved by controlling the amount of light going through the screen to the film. Any screen, 55-line, 133-line, and so on, can be used.

Solid tints (100 percent of the tone) are made by exposing the plate area through a clear, unscreened film.

10-11 Screen tints provide panels of color or tone, sometimes as background for type. *Above:* 10, 20, 30, 40, 50 percent tone values. *Below:* 60, 70, 80, 90, 100 percent tone values.

The impression that an additional color was used in printing is often created by screened tint blocks. When red ink is used, for example, a tint appears as pink; when brown is used, tan results. Tint blocks behind type areas of another color are effective in drawing attention to areas that would otherwise be weak in display.

Creating special effects for line reproductions

Reversing tones When it is desired, the values in a line drawing can be reversed for reproduction; that is, the black areas in the drawing can be made to print as white and the white areas as black. Figure 10-12 shows the effect created by a *reverse line* reproduction. Figure 10-7 showed the same illustration reproduced in standard fashion.

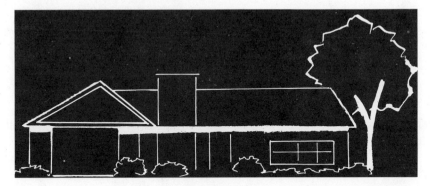

10-12 The tone values of a line drawing are reversed when the drawing is reproduced as a *reverse line* illustration.

To obtain a reverse line reproduction, a normal line negative must first be made. Then, by placing the line negative over another sheet of film and exposing it to light, a negative can be produced on which the values are the same as the original copy. The lines that were black on the original drawing are black on the negative; the other areas are clear.

When the second negative is transferred to the printing plate, the areas that were white on the original will be exposed on the plate surface and thus be made to carry ink to paper.

Common uses for reverse line illustrations are for signatures of advertisers or in other cases when an especially bold, black area is desired. Words in type can be line illustrations and treated as such for production, as shown by the reverse line reproduction in Figure 10-13. (See also Figure 15-24: *Friends.*)

10-13 Type can be treated as a line drawing and reproduced with reversed tones.

OHIO UNIVERSITY

Creating middle tones Line reproductions can be used only for illustrations that contain no middle tones—only the extremes. However, artists can produce illustrations that appear to have middle tones but in fact do not and are reproducible as line illustrations. Drawings done with a pen, as shown in Figure 10-14 can be produced as line illustrations when the shading is composed of hatch marks or

10-15 A drawing made on a textured board, such as coquille board, gives the impression of tones because the ink adheres only to the raised parts of the texture. Such drawings are usually reproduced as line illustrations, but this one, done in pencil and charcoal, is a *highlight* halftone.

10-14 When middle tones are created by hatch marks or other lines, a pen-and-ink drawing can be reproduced as a line illustration.

other lines. Brush-and-ink drawings are also acceptable for line reproductions. They have a somewhat different flavor from those made with pen and ink, especially when the *dry-brush* technique is used. To create such drawings, the artist uses a brush that is virtually dry. To get ink coverage, the artist rubs the ink on the paper instead of flowing it on. By using rough illustration board for the surface, the artist introduces grays into the drawing because the ink does not seep between the high spots of the illustration board (Figure 10-15).

Coquille board, for example, has a surface composed of scores of small raised dots. By drawing on it with crayon or ink, the artist coats only the peaks of these dots. The dots then provide an illustration that looks like a halftone although no screen is used in its reproduction. Pencils used on a special velvety paper and charcoal on a rough paper expressly made for that purpose also create interesting effects without being reproduced as halftones, as shown in Figure 10-15. But pencil, crayon, and charcoal drawings on smooth paper usually must be reproduced as halftones, or the grays and softness of tone that characterize these drawings will be lost in the reproduction.

Applying shading mechanically The most common method for adding shading to line illustrations is a mechanical one called *Benday*. The method gets its name from the inventor of the original system used by engravers as they artificially added shading to the relief line plates needed in traditional printing. The term Benday now more commonly refers to the shading sheets used by artists for adding tones to line illustrations. These shading sheets are available at most art supply stores in a wide variety of patterns; common trade names are Craftint and Zip-a-tone. They usually are adhesive-backed clear acetate sheets on which the patterns of dots, hatch marks, and the like have been printed. The artist applies the piece of patterned acetate over the desired area and then trims and peels away the excess, leaving the pattern precisely where desired. Benday shading has been added to our line illustration in Figure 10-16.

Another system employs drawing board (i.e., Craftone or Doubletone) that has been preprinted with shading patterns that are invisible to a camera until developed. The artist draws a line illustration on the board, then paints the areas to be shaded with a developer that brings out the preprinted pattern. With one kind of board

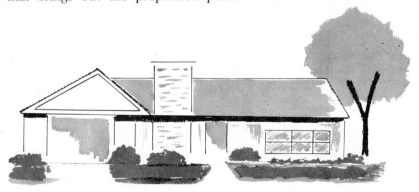

10-16 When shading is added by the Benday process, a line drawing can still be reproduced as a line illustration.

(Doubletone) a second developer can be used to bring out a second, deeper shade of tone, thus providing the drawing with four tones: black, white, and the two added shades.

Line conversions An interesting technique that came into vogue in the early 1970s is the use of a line reproduction for a photograph or other continuous tone illustration. To achieve this special effect, the original illustration is photographed as a line illustration would be—

10-17 A *line conversion* reproduction of the photograph in Figure 10-9. When the subject is clearly recognizable, a line conversion gives the interesting artistic effect shown.

without a screen in the camera. All the middle tones are then lost and a highly contrasty representation (Figure 10-17) results. When the subject of the illustration is clearly recognizable without the middle tones, this treatment creates the impression of an artist's line drawing of the subject (see also Figure 10-23).

Types of halftone finishes

In addition to the wide variety of line reproductions available, the designer of modern pieces of graphic communication also has at hand an equally varied assortment of halftone treatments.

A basic halftone reproduction is called a *square-finish* halftone because it is a common rectangle (as in Figure 10-9). Any variation from a square finish requires special effort and time during production. This extra time and effort results in some added cost, the amount of which depends on the printing process that is involved as well as the amount of time and effort. In spite of extra cost, however, the use of a multitude of special finishes is common among all print media.

Special geometric shapes The simplest variations from the norm of a square finish halftone are special geometric shapes ranging from *circles*, *ovals*, and *triangles* to the most elaborate geometric designs.

The oval shape is used to create on "old time" impression for a photo, because photos often were framed as ovals in the early days of photography. Other irregular shapes can provide a directional emphasis in a design; some are given rather bizarre dimensions to add to their attention-getting value.

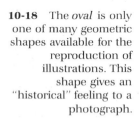

10-18 The *oval* is only one of many geometric shapes available for the reproduction of illustrations. This shape gives an "historical" feeling to a photograph.

Vignette This finish provides a soft edge for a photo; instead of sharply delineated dimensions, the reproduction has an edge that fades into the background. The general shape of the vignette edge may be quite irregular or it may be more standardized as it is with the oval impression created in Figure 10-19. A feeling of age or beauty is often being sought when the vignette finish is ordered. The removal of the dot pattern gradually from the edges creates the vignette; this work is accomplished partially by an artist but requires careful, detailed attention in production also.

Silhouette Also called *outline*, this finish is as the name implies; the background of the photo is completely eliminated so that the central subject stands in sharp outline or silhouette against a blank background. The dot pattern that ordinarily is present in the background is completely removed from the halftone negative before it is exposed on metal for printing. This treatment serves to avoid distraction from the

10-19 Softening the edges of a halftone creates a *vignette* reproduction.

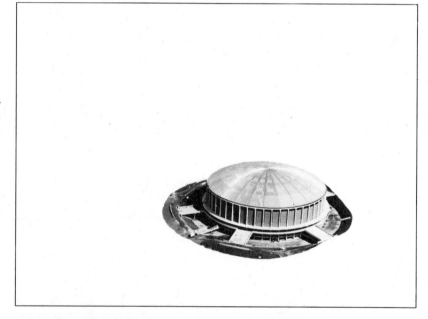

10-20 Outlining or silhouetting the central subject can help emphasize it because competing background details are eliminated.

10-21 A *mortise* halftone contains an interior cutout.

background and to give emphasis to the central subject by the sharp contrast between the subject and surrounding area.

Mortise A *mortise* halftone is one containing a cutout (Figure 10-21). If the cutout is from the outside it may be called a *notch* halftone (Figure 10-22). Notches or mortises are usually rectangular cutouts; the most common is a rectangle cut from one corner of a square-finish halftone. In traditional printing, irregular mortises were difficult to saw from the metal engravings that were used; modern printing systems have afforded the opportunity for greater versatility in this re-

10-22 A *notch* halftone contains a cutout from the outside.

gard. For some printing systems any irregular shape can now be masked out of a halftone negative with little difficulty.

Mortises are usually made to provide for the insertion, within the halftone area, of type messages or other illustrations.

Highlight (dropout) halftone Special care and handling of a halftone negative can give a reproduction that is devoid of dots (Figure 10-15) in some areas. A model's teeth in a toothpaste ad, for example, can be made pure white by painting out the few dots that ordinarily would carry ink to paper. Special attention given to exposure and development during the making of a halftone negative can virtually eliminate the dots in a highlight (light gray) area, but hand painting with an opaque fluid is usually required.

Veloxes   The use of a screened, continuous-tone photo called a *Velox* provides an efficient, versatile method for highlighting halftones and producing other special effects. The making of a Velox is identical to the making of a halftone printing plate except that it is made on photographic paper; this screened print, therefore, contains the usual dot pattern needed to reproduce the various tones. If a highlight effect is desired, the dots can be painted out with white paint on the photoprint. A Velox print can be photographed as a line illustration because each dot is copied just as if it were part of a Benday pattern.

Advertisers use Veloxes a great deal because they often want to highlight portions of an illustration in order to focus attention on particular features of their products; the Velox also makes it possible to paste all elements of an advertisement together to form a single line illustration ready for an engraver's camera. Any possibility of error in the arrangement of material in the advertisement is thus eliminated.

Special screens for special halftone effects   Special halftone screens that will produce tonal variations while adding mood effects to reproductions have become a common tool for the designer of graphic communications.

Screens are made up of concentric circles, parallel lines, parallel wavy lines, thin irregular lines resembling old steel engravings, mezzotints, wood grains, and patterns of various materials such as twill and burlap. Each special screen pattern produces continuous tone reproductions with a special flavor (see Figure 10-23). Especially good for giving variety to subjects that must be shown repeatedly, these mood screens, along with line conversions (Figure 10-17) and posterization, became especially popular with designers in the 1970s. Because these special screens often are used to make Veloxes which are then photographed as line illustrations, the special-effect illustrations are also called line conversions even though they reproduce continuous tones and screens are used in making them.

Also in vogue in recent years has been the enlargement of the dot pattern in a halftone reproduction to such a magnitude that the reproduction resembles a line illustration made with dots (see Figure 10-24, a small part of Figure 10-22).

Posterization   Posterization, another mood device, is especially effective when two colors can be used but it can also be effective without an added color (Figure 10-23). To achieve posterization, the wide range of tones between black and white is reduced to a single middle tone. This middle tone often is reproduced with one of the special screens and/or in a second color.

All the special screen effects for halftones tend to have one thing in common: they seem to convert standard photographs into artistic

10-23 Artistic effects for photographs: special line screens.

(Photo by David Vine. Line conversions by Joel A. Levirne/Graphic Images, Ltd.)

Concentric circle (bull's-eye) screen.

Straight-line screen.

Etching screen.

Mezzotint screen.

Linen-texture screen.

Three-tone posterization.

10-24 Deliberately enlarging the dot pattern of a halftone is sometimes useful to produce a special effect.

renderings. Effectively used, they add a desired dimension to a piece of graphic communication.

Combining line and halftone in one illustration

It is possible for an artist to use a pen to create a line drawing on the face of a photograph thus combining a line illustration and a continuous tone illustration. This procedure, however, would result in a reproduction containing a screened line illustration because the drawing would be broken into a dot pattern by the screen used in the engraver's camera. (Remember: there are no pure whites or pure blacks in a halftone.) Letters (such as type in a headline) can be handled in the same way but with the same shoddy results.

To get sharp, clear line illustrations on the face of halftones, separate negatives are made for the line and halftone portions of the illustrations; these negatives are then exposed together on the printing plate to form what is called a *combination* illustration.

There are two kinds of combinations, one in which the line illustration appears in dark lines and the other in which the illustration appears in white lines (Figure 10-25). The first of these is a *surprint combination,* also known as an *overprint, overburn,* or *double burn.* To produce it, the halftone negative and the line negative are separately made as they ordinarily would be. The line negative is then exposed on the metal sheet, followed by the exposure of the halftone negative in the same position. Its many names come from the fact that these two photo printings or "burnings" are necessary. The plate produced in this fashion will reproduce the line illustration in pure blacks while the halftone takes care of the continuous tones. The other combination is called a *reverse combination* because it produces a reverse line illustration on the face of the halftone. To prepare a reverse combination, the halftone negative, the line negative, plus a reverse line negative (film positive) must be made. The two of these negatives that are needed (halftone and reverse line) can be placed together in position on a printing plate for a single exposure. The single exposure is possible because the background of a reverse line negative is completely clear and does not hold back any light.

A common use for surprints and reverse combinations is to get words across the face of a halftone. Figure 10-25 shows both types of combinations, plus some other treatments. Any and all of the special finishes can be used in concert in order to achieve a special communication goal.

10-25 *Left:* A surprint combination. *Right:* A reverse combination that also has an outline finish at top and a vignette finish at bottom.

Adding Color to Illustrations

Simply stated, color is added to printing by running a printing press with the desired color of ink in the press; for each color desired the paper must go through the press an additional time. The same thing can be said of illustrations, with the addition that a separate illustration must be reproduced on a printing plate for each color. Therefore, line illustrations can be printed in as many colors as one might desire. Sunday comics are good examples of line illustrations in full color (the three primary colors plus black). Line illustrations in only two or three colors are also common. The preparation of artwork for multicolor reproductions is described in Chapter 13.

Halftones can also be reproduced in color, and it is even possible to reproduce a black-and-white photo in more than one color. Take, for example, the situation in which an editor has a black and white snow scene to be used on a page that will also be printed in blue ink. The editor can order the work necessary for a *duotone* reproduction that will appear in blue and black, a combination that would add a special chilly feeling to the reproduction. The editor will require two halftone negatives specially made to avoid the clashing of halftone screens that occurs unless the screen angle is changed as the two negatives are made. This clashing produces an undesirable *moiré* effect (Figure 10-26); because of this moiré one cannot use clippings from printed material to serve as the original for halftone reproductions.

When two halftone negatives of the same subject have been properly made (one is usually toned down also) they can be used with excellent two-color results. Brown with black for desert scenes and green with black for forests and meadows are especially effective.

10-26 The "screen door" look of this halftone is caused by the clashing of two halftone screens. It is because of this moiré effect that a picture clipped from a publication usually cannot be original copy for a second reproduction.

Sometimes a color is added to a halftone area by printing a tint block with the halftone, thus adding a flat color uniformly across the surface. This method is easier and cheaper but produces less spectacular results.

Also, original artwork (i.e., paintings) done in two colors can be faithfully reproduced, but in a different manner. To reproduce original illustrations composed of blendings of more than one color, a color separation process is involved. The preliminary camera work is the same for the two basic printing systems. The following discussion, though it relates directly to the making of acid-etched plates for traditional printing, incorporates the principles of color separation that are common to both systems.

Process Plates for Full-Color Reproduction

Originals for color reproduction include all copy in which the subject is rendered in full continuous-tone color, such as oil, watercolor, or tempera painting; the color transparency; and the photoprint in full color, such as carbo, chromotone, dye transfer, imbibition, and wash-off relief.

Under discussion here are full-color originals where facsimile reproduction can only be achieved through the blending of the three primary colors plus black. Where an original is to be reproduced in one color only, the line etching or halftone is printed in that color; when a two-color original is to be reproduced, duotone halftones are employed, but, for full, four-color reproduction, it is necessary to make process color plates, one for each of the primary colors and one for black. Should the black plate be eliminated, the reproduction becomes a three-color process, still achieving the full blending of the primary colors but lacking the emphasis of black and its shades.

All full-color originals drawn or painted upon a material such as paper or canvas are reproduced by the light reflected from the original, whereas color transparencies are reproduced by transmitting light through the transparency. The color transparency is preferred over color photoprints because some loss of detail and color value occurs in prints or copies made from transparencies. Hand-colored photographs are inferior in reproduction because the underlying photographic image is recorded in the negatives and interferes with correct color separation.

The Color Process   In pigment, such as printing inks, the primary colors are yellow, red, and blue. By mixing these colors in correct proportions, any desired color can be obtained. In the same manner, superimposed printing of the process color plates in precise register causes a color-blended image with all the colors and values of the original. An artist can paint a picture using pigments of a score of different colors and hues, and a perfect reproduction can be achieved on the printing press using three halftone plates, each printing one of the three primary colors. In four-color process, a black plate is added to obtain strength in detail and to produce neutral shades of grays, which are difficult to make with the primary colors. The addition of the black plate also makes possible the use of red and blue printing inks in purer tones than those used in straight three-color process.

Color Separation Negatives

Although the color principle of light differs from that of pigments, it is not essential to consider this distinction here. Photographic color separation takes a simple knowledge of the pigment primary colors and their complementary relationships.

In photographing a color original, the photoengraver first analyzes it for yellow, red, and blue color content. He or she then separates and records each of these colors on film. A color separation is accomplished by photographing through a color filter that absorbs or quenches those colors of which it is composed and permits the remaining color to be recorded.

To separate the yellow color in the original, a violet filter that prevents the photography of its component colors, red and blue, is used, and and only the yellow is recorded. Similarly, to separate the red, a green filter deters yellow and blue and permits the red to be recorded; to separate the blue, an orange filter blots out the yellow and red and permits the blue to be recorded. To make the black separation, a specially modified filter is employed that limits color absorption and produces the required negative, eliminating the primary colors.

In the indirect method of color photography, the resultant negatives are in continuous tone (no halftone screen) and are called *continuous-tone separation negatives.* They are an accurate record of each of the primary colors in all their gradations of tones, plus black.

Color correction—that is, improvement of color rendition—is usually done at the time separation negatives are made, by a process of applying photographic masks to the art or introducing them in the camera.

The negatives are then placed before the camera and rephotographed to produce positives; or they are placed in contact with photo film and a photoprint (positive) is made. Further correction is possible on both the separation negatives and positives by retouching. It is necessary to make the positives so they can be photographed through a halftone screen.

It is also possible to employ a direct method of color photography to separate the primary colors and produce screened halftone negatives in one operation. Correction masks are either registered over the copy or placed over the screen in the camera. The copy is scaled (enlarged or reduced), screened, and corrected directly.

Once halftone separation negatives have been prepared, either indirectly or directly, further correction can be done by chemically reducing the size of the dots on the negatives—a process called *dot etching;* in the case of letterpress and gravure platemaking, dots can be even further reduced on the metal printing surfaces chemically—a process called *re-etching*.

Color Halftone Negatives

In order to print continuous-tone color, the metal plate must have printing surfaces capable of reproducing color gradations. This is accomplished with the halftone screen, which breaks up the image into minute dots varying in size, shape, and proximity.

In making halftone color negatives, each color positive is photographed through the same desired screen, but, for each color, the screen is placed at an angle 30 degrees apart from the other colors. This is done so that in the printing no color dots will interfere with proper blending. Experience has determined that this angle will also keep a moiré pattern from forming.

This is the standard procedure for three-color process negatives. With the introduction of the fourth color, black, the screens for the black, red, and blue negatives are placed 30 degrees apart, and the screen for the yellow negative is placed between the black and red positions at an angle of 15 degrees from each. The yellow dot being the least visible, the moiré is not offensive.

Decisions Facing the Designer

Major responsibility for high-quality reproduction rests with the platemaker and the printer. However, the designer can also contribute much to an effective end-product. Decisions must be made concerning (1) the kind of original copy, (2) the method of separation to be employed, and (3) changes to be made in the original copy.

Original copy

Full color illustrations are of two types: (1) color transparencies, often called *chromes;* (2) reflection copy, such as paintings, and full-color photoprints, such as dye transfers and the widely used Type C prints.

Since platemakers generally prefer to work with transparencies, if photographs are to be taken for the job, they should generally be of this type. Whenever possible, they should be larger than 35 mm (approximately $1\frac{3}{8}$ inch by 1 inch). Satisfactory enlargements may be possible with this "slide size," but often the film grain becomes obtrusive, and imperfections such as scratches begin to be emphasized. Transparencies of 8 by 10 inches are highly desirable.

Separation methods

The designer can select any one of three methods for making separations: (1) direct photographic, (2) indirect photographic, or (3) electronic scanning. The first method is least expensive and widely available. The second offers greater flexibility in terms of color correction.

The electronic scanner is the ultimate separation technique. Color correction is automatic, under computer control. Originals— transparencies or flexible reflection copy—are affixed to a rotating drum and scanned by a light beam. The latter is then split into the three primary colors, and each of these components is transformed into digital information and fed to a computer. Here corrections are made according to information programmed into the computer concerning inks, paper, required alterations, and other printing requirements. The altered digital information then activates exposing lights that generate separation films on another rotating drum. The computer also calculates exposure for a black negative.

The scanner is capable of fast production of direct and indirect separation negatives in varying sizes. The highest quality negatives are produced by laser exposing lights. Since separation information is in digital form, it may be stored or transmitted to other locations.

Altering original colors

Within a fairly broad range, the platemaker can alter original colors. They may be subdued or intensified, and contrast can likewise be altered. When such changes are required, they should be written on a photostat of the original. However, color changes are best made on the original copy. This may even require reshooting photographs or returning paintings to the artist.

There are times when exact color matches cannot be achieved through separations, as, for example, in the case of product illustrations. In such cases an extra press run may be required, beyond the normal four, to lay down an exact match. The platemaker should be given a color swatch along with the artwork and specific instructions about where the color is to fall.

It is also necessary to tell the platemaker whether the black used in printing type can also be used for printing process color. At times an extra black press run is justified in order to print the exact black required for high-fidelity process reproduction.

Normally the designer sees separation proofs before the job is printed. These may be printed on specified paper with specified inks by special proof presses or be in the form of overlay transparent sheets, each carrying a separation color. When they fall on each other in register, the final result is visible. Proofs should be studied under lights that match those used by the platemaker when viewing the proofs. Satisfactory proofs of reflection originals (C prints, paintings, and so on) should be a close match. However, proofs of chrome originals may fall somewhat short: these proofs are reflectives, but made from originals that must be viewed by transmitted light.

11 Preparing Illustrations for Production

Photographs and other illustrations are copy to the photoengraver and lithographer, just as text and titles are copy for any printer. As copy, they require the same careful editing and preparation that is taken for granted while working with words for printing, but is too often neglected while processing illustrations.

Essentially, the processing steps for illustrations are the same as those for verbal copy. Drawings and pictures can and do contain errors, both mechanical (smudges, creases, chemical spots) and qualitative (poor tones, faulty backgrounds). Such errors should be corrected, or the work should be redone. With regard to the marking of instructions, it should be obvious that information about size and shape must be given. And a picture that is too large or too small for its space causes as many problems as overset or underset type.

Processing illustrations is essentially the same for both traditional printing and offset lithography. The slight differences that are present are pointed out in the following discussion.

Cropping Photographs

Photographs, like news stories or magazine articles, are sometimes verbose, poorly constructed, too large, or too small. They must be edited to tell only what they are supposed to tell, reconstructed to give emphasis where it is needed, and reduced or enlarged to fit space.

The basic part of picture editing, called *cropping*, is the figurative cutting of the original photograph to eliminate these faults when it is in plate form on a printing press.

Cropping is "figurative" cutting because portions of a photo will rarely be cut away with scissors or blade; marks made with a grease pencil are used to indicate the finished dimensions. These are usually placed in the white border around the photograph, or on the mounting board used for backing.

Every photograph that enters production should contain four crop marks. These marks set the dimension of the photograph; two of

11-1 The four crop marks were put in the margins with a grease pencil. The marks indicate the new dimensions of the photograph; only the area inside them will be included in the reproduction. How does the photo look when cropped? See Figure 1-5 on page 10. Percentages of original size: Figure 11-1, 57 percent; Figure 1-5, 72 percent. (*Courtesy* Detroit News)

them mark off the width and two mark off the depth. Although some production people assume that the lack of crop marks means that the full dimensions of the original are to be used, it is not wise to count on that assumption. A photograph is not completely edited and marked if it does not contain the four crop marks shown in Figure 11-1.

Cropping for Content

As photographic prints come from a photographer, they often contain shortcomings that should be corrected. Unnecessary or disturbing detail should be removed, attention may need to be shifted to the important feature, and composition may need improvement.

In most cases, judicious cropping can eliminate these weak points. To decide what should be cropped, it is helpful to use two L-shaped pieces of cardboard that can be moved over the face of the photograph until they frame the most desirable portion. Crop marks corresponding to the inside corners of this frame, but drawn on the white margins of the photograph, later direct the platemaker to use only the portion of the photograph that is enclosed in the frame.

Reductions and Enlargements

Photographs for publication in printed media are usually provided in one or two standard sizes (8 by 10 or 5 by 7 inches), but any original of any size can be used for reproduction. In most cases, the reproduction size must be different from the original size, thus requiring an enlargement or reduction by the lithographer or photoengraver.

11-2 The shape of a rectangle is determined by the relationship of its two dimensions. Equal dimensions: square. Width greater than depth: horizontal rectangle. Width less than depth: vertical rectangle. Any photographic reduction or enlargement has the same shape as the original.

Enlargements and reductions are no problem for either the lithographer or engraver; their cameras are capable of enlarging or reducing to any desired percentage of the original, such as an enlargement to 110 percent or a reduction to 50 percent. But enlargements and reductions made in a camera will always have the same *shape* as the original: a square will reproduce as a smaller or larger square, a vertical rectangle will reproduce as a verticle rectangle, and a horizontal will reproduce as a horizontal.

An appreciation of shapes is very helpful in understanding some of the basics of processing illustrations for reproduction. Shapes are formed by the relationship of their width to their depth. In Figure 11-2, the first shape is a square because its width and depth are equal, that is, they are in a ratio of 1 to 1. The second shape is a horizontal rectangle because its width is longer than its depth. In this instance, the width is twice as long as the depth, so that they are in a ratio of 2 to 1. The reverse is true for the vertical; its width to depth ratio is 1 to 2.

Enlargements or reductions of these shapes provide different *dimensions*, but the relationship of width to depth remains the same;

cameras cannot magically change shapes. If they did, they would produce reproductions that would look like the distortions one sees in a funhouse.

Cropping to Fit Space

Editors are sometimes forced to reproduce illustrations in a predetermined shape and size, but the original illustrations made for them are not of that shape and size. In other words, a layout has already been completed and the space for the illustration has already been allotted. In such cases, *cropping for shape* is required. By figuratively removing some portion of the overly long dimension with crop marks, the editor makes it possible for a reduction or enlargement to be made. If this cropping removes vital parts from the original illustration, the situation is impossible; a new illustration must be made or a new layout must be made.

If a horizontal illustration is to be reproduced as a vertical, the need to crop something from the width is apparent; the width must be cropped to be less than the depth if a vertical shape is to result. The change from vertical shapes to horizontals by cropping from the depth of the original is also easy to recognize. Changing a horizontal illustration so that it will be either less or more horizontal to conform to a layout is not so easy to recognize, however.

In any case—those modifications involving enlargement or reduction without change in shape or those also requiring a shape change—there is some figuring that must be done in order to make the dummies and layouts produce the required results.

Proportioning or Scaling Illustrations

This figuring called *proportioning* or *scaling* is the equivalent of copyfitting for words. We may start with one dimension on a layout and figure what the other dimension of the reproduction must be so we can complete the layout, or we may start with a completed layout and determine what dimensions we must give to the original so it can conform to the space allowed for it.

To provide examples of this figuring, let us start with obvious shapes and think in terms of these proportions or shapes. If we start with a photograph that is to be reproduced to fit a certain width, and we place our crop marks so that the original is a square, we can know in advance that the depth of the reproduction will be the same as the width. For example, the reproduction must fit a column 15 picas wide; we have cropped the photo to be 6 inches wide and 6 inches deep. As a ratio, we show the original as 6 over 6. For the moment, disregard whether these are inches, feet, picas, or whatever, The reproduction ratio would be expressed as 15 over 15. We can look at these ratios as equals, therefore:

$$\frac{6}{6} = \frac{15}{15}$$

They are equals because they are of the same shape: note that the product of the means (6 × 15) equals the product of the extremes (6 × 15). Although this shape is so obvious that we did not have to do the computation, we could find our missing dimension in this fashion:

$$\frac{6}{6} = \frac{15}{x}$$

and multiply 6 times x to get 6x, and 15 times 6 to get 90.

We then know that 6x equals 90 because the product of the means equals the product of the extremes. Then, if we divide both sides by 6, we can find that x would have to be 15. Our 6-inch by 6-inch photo would reduce to a 15-pica by 15-pica reproduction. There is no need to convert from one unit of measure to another if only two different units are involved and we are aware of their places in the ratios.

Another example: The original photograph is 6 inches wide and 12 inches deep and must reduce to fit a column 15 picas wide. How deep will the reproduction be if

$$\frac{6}{12} = \frac{15}{x}?$$

Although the answer of 30 picas should again be obvious because the shape is obvious (the depth is twice the width), we could compute the answer in this fashion:

$$6 \text{ times } x = 6x;\ 12 \text{ times } 15 = 180$$

If we now know that 6x = 180, then we can divide both sides by 6 and find that the reproduction depth would have to be 30 picas.

If a crutch is needed to compute for an unknown dimension, you can use this set of ratios: Original width (OW) over original depth (OD) must equal the reproduction width (RW) over the reproduction depth (RD):

$$\frac{OW}{OD} = \frac{RW}{RD}$$

Let us use this crutch to solve the problem that seems to be most difficult for those just learning to proportion illustrations. In this example, we have a layout completed, and the reproduction must be 12 picas wide and 14 picas deep. We have a photo that is, before cropping, 10 inches wide and 8 inches deep. The problem is to determine how to crop the photograph so it will be in the proper shape to reproduce as 12 by 14 picas, and 10 inches by 8 inches obviously will not do that:

$$\frac{12}{14} \text{ does not equal } \frac{10}{8}$$

We must reproduce as a vertical rectangle an original photo that starts out as a horizontal; therefore, the width must be cropped to be less than the depth, 8 inches. We must take into account the content of the photo as we work, but the minimum of cropping is involved in this case if we change only the width of the photo. Why not change the depth? We cannot stretch the photo to make the depth greater, and to cut off part of the depth makes the cropping problem more severe. So we use these figures:

$$\frac{12}{14} = \frac{x}{8}$$

Looking at these figures, you should know that x will have to be less than 8, but we find the exact answer by multiplying 14 times x for $14x$, and 12 times 8 for 96. Dividing 96 by 14, we find that x must be $6\frac{6}{7}$ inches. We would then go ahead and place crop marks to make the width $6\frac{6}{7}$ inches and the depth 8 inches. The original is thus in proportion to reduce to 12 by 14 picas.

As long as we know three of the four dimensions that are involved, we can solve any proportioning problem as shown in these examples. We can use the same figures, however, and approach them differently —thinking in terms of reducing originals to scale and not being concerned about the ratios expressing shapes.

Returning to the original example of reducing a 6-inch by 6-inch photograph to a width of 15 picas, we can look at it in this way: As the 6 changes to 15, the other dimension (6) must change to exactly the same degree if the result is to be a scaled version. Therefore:

$$\frac{OW}{RW} = \frac{OD}{RD} \text{ or } \frac{6}{15} = \frac{6}{x}$$

As we solve this problem just as we did the earlier one, we find that $6x$ equals 90 and x therefore equals 15, so we arrive at the same answer from a different approach. If we want to change the figures so that they are in the same units of measure (change inches to picas, for example) we can use percentages to get an answer here. Going from 6 inches (36 picas) to 15 picas, is a reduction of the original to almost 42 percent of its original size and the other dimension (66 picas) must be reduced to the same percentage, or $27\frac{1}{2}$ picas. The percentage of enlargement or reduction is determined by dividing an original dimension into the equivalent reproduction dimension.

The cameras that are used to make reproduction negatives are set according to percentages, so that many printers would prefer that their customers determine the percentage of enlargement or reduction and order the reproduction on that basis. There is something to be said, however, for ordering by dimensions instead of percentage of reduction because some errors can be avoided by doing this. For one thing, the customer need not convert units of measure. Also, if a printer makes an error in determining percentage, it is the printer's responsibility. If a customer makes an error and gets a reproduction of incorrect size as a result, it is the customer's responsibility. Customer errors that occur in figuring dimensions usually are caught before the reproductions are made; their errors in figuring percentages are usually not caught.

Use of Circular Scaler or Slide Rule

Most of the danger of human error can be eliminated by using mechanical devices called *proportion wheels, slide rules,* or *scalers.* These devices (see Figures 11-3 and 11-4) are a blessing for anyone who must do much processing of illustrations. No one likes to do all the figuring involved if a mechanical device will do this task. Pocket calculators are also helpful, but they are not as convenient as these devices.

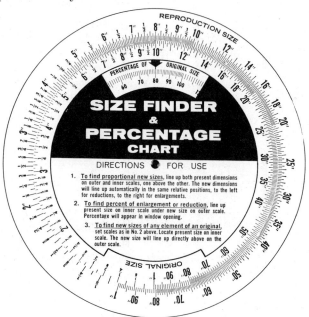

11-3 A proportion wheel. Rotate the inner wheel until a known present dimension is opposite a known reduced dimension on the outer wheel. Then the unknown dimension is opposite the other known present dimension. As set here, the wheel shows that if an 8 × 10 photo is reduced so the long dimension is 8 inches, the other dimension will be 6⅜ inches. It also shows that this is a reduction to 80 percent.

11-4 A slide rule works in the same way as a circular scaler. Slide the inner part until two dimensions are opposite each other; the unknown dimension is then found lined up with the third known dimension. The slide rule is also set to show 8 × 10 to 4 × 5.

Whether in circular or slide rule form, both of these computing devices simply provide for automatic alignment of equal ratios. If you line up 2 with 2, all other ratios around the wheel or along the slide are equal, 4 to 4, 1 to 1, and so on. Thus, if you know the three dimensions, you can find the fourth by looking for it in the right place on the device. Although instructions are usually provided, scalers can be easily used just as you would set up the ratios in the previous examples. If you are accustomed to using OW over OD equals RW over RD, spin the wheel or slide the slide so that the upper (outer) figure is the width and the bottom (inner) figure is the depth. As an example, for the original width 6 over depth 6, the required reproduction depth (15) can be found just under the reproduction width (15). (You can work with either inches or picas when using one of these devices, of course.)

Proportion wheels usually also provide a means for determining percentages, as shown in Figure 11-3.

Use of a Diagonal   Another method, somewhat inaccurate but usable in most instances, employs a diagonal line to find any unknown dimension in picture scaling. No mathematics are involved; the work is done entirely by drawing and measuring lines on an overlay sheet, not on the photograph. Care must be taken so that the pencil does not press a line into the emulsion of the photo, for such lines show in the finished engraving or plate.

The diagonal method, illustrated in Figure 11-5, starts with the bisection of a rectangle by a line drawn diagonally from one corner to another. Any smaller rectangle formed by right-angle lines drawn from adjacent sides of the large rectangle to the diagonal line is proportionate to the large rectangle.

Figure 11-6 shows how the diagonal is used to solve a typical problem. The larger rectangle represents a photo cropped to be 8 inches wide and 10 inches deep. The reproduction width must be 2 inches and is measured across the top. A perpendicular from that

11-5 Diagonal system of photograph scaling.

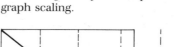
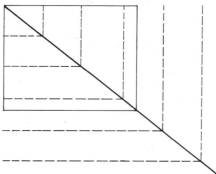

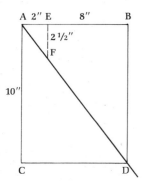

A 2″ E   8″   B

2½″

F

10″

C   D

11-6 Finding depth when width is known. Measure width A-E, 2 inches, along width A-B. Measure perpendicular E-F to the diagonal to find the unknown depth of the reproduction.

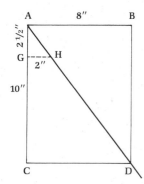

A   8″   B

2½″

G ---- H
2″

10″

C   D

11-7 Finding width when depth is known. Measure depth A-G, 2½ inches, along depth A-C. Measure perpendicular G-H to the diagonal to find the unknown width of the reproduction.

point to the diagonal (line E-F) is the depth the reproduction will be, 2½ inches.

All inaccuracies in drawing lines affect the accuracy of the answer when using the diagonal method. If the perpendicular is not exactly at 90 degrees, or if the diagonal slightly misses a corner, the answer will be slightly inaccurate.

Figure 11-7 shows the use of the diagonal to find the width when the depth is known. The procedure is identical to that used in Figure 11-6, except that the perpendicular is drawn from the side (because the depth is known) to the diagonal.

The use of the diagonal method to solve a problem when both dimensions of a reproduction are known and information about how much to crop the original is needed is shown in Figure 11-8. In this example, the diagonal bisects the rectangle formed by the reproduction dimensions, and not the original picture. The amount to be cropped is found by measuring the distance between the intersection of the diagonal with the line B-D and the corner D.

11-8 Finding amount to crop. Lightly draw a rectangle with the reproduction dimensions. Draw a diagonal for that rectangle. Measure the distance from the intersection of the diagonal with original dimension B-D to corner D. This is the amount to be cropped.

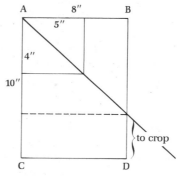

A   8″   B

5″

4″

10″

to crop

C   D

Choosing a Scaling Method

The scaling or proportioning method used is relatively immaterial; whatever is easiest for the user will ordinarily suffice. Most editors and graphic artists prefer to use mechanical devices, such as proportion wheels. For beginners, however, an understanding of the simple mathematics involved is essential if they are going to be able to successfully use a mechanical aid. Beginners must also understand the purposes behind the figuring; that they are either trying to find a missing dimension so that they can complete a layout, or trying to find what cropping must be done so that an original will have the correct proportions to fit a layout that has already been executed.

Other Methods of Altering Photo Content

Cropping is not the only method by which the content of a photo can be changed. An artist can *airbrush* photographs to remove disturbing background or to emphasize certain portions of the subject (Figure 11-9). The platemaker can also do this and can manipulate the camera settings to *highlight* (make white) some sections of the picture subject that might otherwise be gray and dull.

Through the use of special plate finishes as described in Chapter 10 (silhouette, partial silhouette, vignette, geometrical shapes), the appearance and shape of photographs can be changed when they appear in print.

Although airbrushing and retouching require special skills, the journalist can get special plate finishes without an artist's assistance. Through the use of overlay sheets the journalist can adequately communicate his desires to the platemaker who creates the special effect as the platemaker makes the plates. To order silhouettes, for example, an overlay sheet is fastened snugly to the photo and then the subject to be silhouetted is lightly outlined with a soft pencil. To avoid misunderstanding, "outline" or "silhouette" should be written in the area surrounding the line.

Vignettes can be indicated in similar fashion. The beginning and ending of the fade-out area can be drawn on an overlay. Mortises, notches, and geometric shapes (circles, ovals, irregulars) can also be shown on an overlay. The change in size brought on by enlargement or reduction in platemaking *must always be considered* when working with overlays.

An overlay sheet is also used to show desired highlight areas for highlight halftones and to locate line work on combination plates, both reverse and surprint. For letterpress printing, combination plates are expensive, but on many occasions they are especially effective. If

11-9 An airbrush can be used to eliminate disturbing background in a photograph.

type matter or line illustrations must appear over a halftone (in white or in the color of the halftone) a combination plate is required. Along with the halftone copy, reproduction proofs of type matter or sharp black-on-white line drawings must be provided to the engraver so that he can make good combination plates. These techniques are also used in offset lithography, but they do not involve special *plates.* The special treatment needed in each case centers around the *negative* preparation in lithography.

For any method of printing, a size allowance must be made if illustrations are to run off the edge of the page. These *bleeds*, as they are called, must be given an extra $\frac{1}{8}$-inch for each edge that goes off an outside edge of the paper. This allowance is necessary so that the illustration will still bleed after the printed piece is trimmed; otherwise, a thin white streak may appear on what were meant to be bleed edges.

Photomontages (composite pictures made by combining several photos into one) are usually made by pasting the photos together on mounting board. They can also be made by the photographer, in which case the negatives are used to print several subjects on one sheet of photographic paper. The edges of the component photos can be sharp or blended into each other by an airbrush or by retouching. The component photos require no special instructions for reproduction.

Processing Line Drawings

Although they are the simplest and cheapest of illustrations, pen-and-ink drawings are highly versatile and effective. In letterpress printing, the required line etching is simple to make and is the least expensive kind of photoengraving. In offset, there usually is no special treatment and no extra charge is required for line drawings. If the drawings are created in the same size as desired for reproduction, they can be pasted in position with type matter and processed with no special treatment or added cost. If they must be reduced or enlarged separately, a slight charge is usually involved.

For best reproduction, these drawings are done on white bristol board with black ink; the primary production demand is for sharp, clear, black lines on a contrasting background. Although a pen is most commonly used, brushes can produce good line illustrations also, as described in Chapter 10. The quality of reproduction is often enhanced when original drawings are reduced for reproduction; any drawing that can be reduced to 50 percent of its original size will lose many minor flaws that might have been present in the original art.

Line drawings and other artwork must be crop marked, just as photographs are, as they are being processed for publication. Although crop marking is usually not needed to change the shape or content of a line illustration because the illustration usually was drawn to specifications, crop marks are needed to set the dimensions to be followed. As with photos, four marks are needed: two to set the horizontal dimension and two for the vertical.

Any drawing that contains only pure darks and pure whites is reproducible as a line drawing. This includes those that will appear to have middle tones because of Benday shading or drawn dots or lines; it is important to recognize the wide variety of artwork included in the line-drawing category. Cartoons, bar graphs, charts, diagrams, and maps are usually prepared for line reproduction.

Color in Illustrations

The preparation of copy for color reproduction is explained in Chapter 13. As mentioned there, both line and halftone copy can be reproduced in color. Full-color photographs or film transparencies, oil paintings, water colors, and other original full-color continuous-tone materials are reproduced by the halftone process through color separation. It is wise to determine the preferences of individual engravers or lithographers before submitting copy for separation negatives and plates. For color in line illustrations, separate drawings keyed for exact positioning must be provided for each color. Enlargements and reductions are possible for color reproductions just as they are for black and white.

Marking Illustrations for Reproduction

All original illustrations require some marking of instructions if they are to be reproduced as desired. This marking includes crop marks, size of reproduction, a specification of the screen if needed, and any special finishing to be used in the reproduction.

Crop Marks Every original illustration must contain four crop marks. Although the lack of crop marks may be assumed to mean that full dimensions of the original should be used, it is not wise to rely on this assumption. Production people have no certain way of determining whether missing crop marks resulted from forgetfulness or intent. The use of only two crop marks for each dimension is preferable to the use of four marks for each dimension. When marking the width, for example, with two crop marks across the top and two on the bottom, inaccuracy is almost certain to result and a production person will not know which set of two crop marks would produce the best results.

Care must be exercised so that crop marks do not inadvertently appear in reproductions; the marks should be placed in the white margin for photographs, and outside the reproduction area for line drawings and other illustrations.

Specifying Size

Either a percentage of enlargement or reduction or the reproduction width and depth must be clearly specified for all illustrations; if dimensions are provided, the best location for this information for photographs is on the back. Ordinarily the width is given first, in either picas or in inches. The dimensions must be lightly written so that the pressure of the writing point does not make an impression in the emulsion of the photograph. For drawings, there is usually ample marginal space on the front for all instructions.

Specifying Screen and/or Metal

For continuous-tone reproductions, the screen to be used must be specified. As pointed out in the previous chapter, the fineness of the screen determines the quality of reproduction—the finer the screen the better is the reproduction. In letterpress printing, however, this statement is true only insofar as the fineness of the screen and the smoothness of the paper are properly matched. Fine screens require smooth papers in letterpress; in offset lithography good reproduction of fine screens can be obtained on rough papers.

Other chapters on illustrations and paper provide information on the proper matching of screen and paper, but generally speaking, screens with under 100 lines per inch are used with rough papers in letterpress, and finer screens require the smoother calendered or coated papers. The common screen for high-quality work is 133-line.

For letterpress engravings, the metal to be used must also be specified as either zinc (rougher screens) or copper (finer screens and longer runs).

Specifying Special Finishes

The standard reproduction of any illustration is as a rectangle, called a *square finish*. Any other reproduction may require some special treatment.

These special treatments include vignettes, silhouettes, highlighted, combination plates, and special shapes, such as circles or ovals. As explained earlier, overlays are usually used to show the location of special treatments, but verbal instructions are also needed.

A typical marked photo might, therefore, have a tissue overlay showing the portion to be outlined, four crop marks to show the dimensions to be used, and these verbal instructions on the back:

$3'' \times 5''$, 133 line silhouette halftone

Such complete instructions eliminate most misunderstandings; the original illustration should be kept free of all other markings. Such things as the original dimensions of the photo or other numbers on the original can only cause confusion and error.

Checklist: **Reading Proofs of Illustrations**

Although the errors in illustrations differ from the misspellings, wrong fonts, transposed lines, and the like, that creep into type matter, they nevertheless demand careful attention. Engravers and lithographers provide proofs of their work with illustrations, just as printers do with type, and these proofs should be checked in time for necessary corrections to be made before deadlines.

It is difficult to discern some illustration errors; others are easy to spot. With a little care and practice, anyone can detect the common failings. Some of these errors result from poor work by the engraver or lithographer, but many are the result of improper preparation. Wherever the fault lies, it is essential to detect and correct all flaws before the final printing.

Here are some common failings:

1. Wrong dimensions. This error often can be traced to the person who marked the original copy, but occasionally a production person will err in figuring the percentage of reduction, or a camera operator may shoot the copy incorrectly. But whether an editor placed a crop mark incorrectly or an operator set the camera improperly, the negatives or plates must be remade to fit their space. The only debate is about who pays the extra cost.

2. Imperfections on the edges. Photo reproductions with jagged edges need not be tolerated. Engravers can smooth plate edges, and lithographers can recut mask openings to eliminate such blemishes.

3. Content not as desired because plate dimensions do not follow the crop marks. Sometimes an illustration will be reproduced in the desired size, but material that was to be cropped out may be included in the reproduction. If the original was correctly marked, the illustration is redone at no charge.

4. Scratches. Engravers and lithographers try to handle negatives and plates with care, but unsightly scratches sometimes do appear. Circle them on the proof so that the cause of the flaw can be located and corrected.

5. Spots. These should also be circled on the proof. Although spots often are only the result of a bad proof, it is possible that they are actually in the reproduction. If they are merely proof flaws, a new

proof will prove the fact; otherwise the error must be corrected in the negative or plate.

6. Proof too gray or too contrasty. A good halftone requires accuracy in the determining and making of several camera exposures. Bad camera work or etching can cause a halftone to be a poor reproduction of the original. Mark the proof "too gray" or "too contrasty," and the engraver will deliver a better plate if the evaluation was reasonable.

7. Some faint handwriting on surface. Poor editing can be the cause of this problem. Any handwriting done on the back of a photo may show in a reproduction. If this shows up on a proof, the reproduction must be redone at the cost of publisher or supplier, whichever caused the flaw.

8. Paper clip marks on edge. This is also usually the fault of the editorial staff, not of the engraver or printer. Paper clips should not be used on photos; they often scratch or dent the emulsion. Such scratches or dents will appear in any reproduction.

9. Hairline cracks. These usually result from improper handling of the photo. Photos should not be rolled or folded, otherwise emulsion cracks will result.

10. Dark line on part of an edge. Improper cropping can cause this failing. Lines should not be drawn to indicate a dimension of a photo; only marginal crop marks are needed. Any line drawn to show cropping will appear in a reproduction if it is slightly off angle.

Some imperfections in illustration reproductions can be seen only with a magnifying glass; others may only show up when the plate is put on a press. But most shortcomings that can cause serious difficulties can be detected by careful inspection of proofs. Time so spent is certainly worthwhile.

12 Preparation of Pasteups (Mechanicals)

After type has been set on photocomposing machines and illustrations have been scaled for reproduction, the next step in the preparation of copy for modern printing methods is the creation of what is called a *pasteup* or *mechanical.*

As its name indicates, a pasteup is a pasted version of a printing job ready to be photographed and made into a plate. The use of the term *mechanical* stems from the fact that the pasteup is to be "camera ready"—ready to enter the photomechanical steps of printing as a precise entity.

If there is more than one color, a separate pasteup is usually required for each color; in these cases, one of these pasteups is the *key* (or *base*), and all others must be matched precisely to it. (In special cases, such as overprinting a headline across a picture, two separate pasteups may be required for only one color.) The additional pasteups are made on transparent or translucent film; they are called *overlays.* Marks resembling gunsights, called *register marks,* are used to match up the pasteups. More is said later about this *register* or *registration* (precise positioning) of elements so that they match other colors or other elements.

To understand the whys and hows of pasteup preparation, the basic differences between line illustrations and halftones discussed in Chapter 11 must be recalled here. Line illustrations contain only pure tones and whites, and none of the tones in between. Phototype fits this category, as well as any pen-and-ink drawing, and thus is included in what we call *line work.* Original illustrations containing various shades of tones, such as photographs, are *continuous tone* illustrations and must be separately photographed through a screen before platemaking. For this reason, they often are not included on pasteups. In addition, each pasteup must be separately photographed, and the resultant negative is stripped into a mask for platemaking as described in Chapter 3. Hence a pasteup is also a piece of communication to the stripper who will guide it through the platemaking steps.

Who Does Pasteups and Why

Pasteups may be done by either the printer or by the customer, but there is a definite trend toward having the customer prepare them. Most in-house printing operations now involve pasteups. It has always been common practice for advertising agency art departments to prepare mechanicals, and the development of cold type composing systems has now made it a frequent chore for magazine and public relations personnel as well. In newspaper shops, pasteups are usually the responsibility of union personnel, but in some nonunion situations editorial personnel are also involved in preparing pasteups.

What Makes a Good Pasteup?

When properly done, a one-color pasteup contains all line work, so that only one camera exposure is needed to reproduce it. The primary role of the pasteup is to avoid tedious working with film during platemaking; it is much easier to paste each piece of display type and body type into position than it is to cut holes in a mask and strip pieces of film into position.

A good pasteup will also have all elements positioned *exactly*, with all elements of an even tone so that they will photograph well. A good pasteup will also be without blemishes and will have all instructions needed by a stripper clearly shown. Incorrect positioning, uneven type proofs, dirt and fingerprints, vague or missing instructions, and missing elements result in poor pasteups.

Some pasteup flaws can be corrected after the negatives are made by *opaquing* the negatives (painting them), but this should be avoided as much as possible. It makes no sense to do pasteups to lower costs and then add to costs by forcing someone else to paint out thumbprints or other blemishes that show as clear spots on a film negative. A good pasteup keeps opaquing to a minimum.

The photographs in Figure 12-1 show some of the tools and procedures involved in making mechanicals.

Tools Needed for Preparing Camera-Ready Mechanicals

A Complete Preliminary Layout Is Essential

In order to prepare mechanicals well and efficiently, pasteup artists must start with an accurate and detailed plan for the job—a *layout*, or *dummy*, as it may be called. Without the complete plan at their disposal, pasteup artists have to expect many false starts and errors resulting from changes that must be made. Accurate copyfitting and photoscaling are essential parts of any such layout. No one can put a jigsaw puzzle together if the parts do not match or if pieces are missing.

A Suitable Surface Is Needed

The surface on which type proofs and other elements are to be pasted is extremely important for a number of reasons. First, the surface must accept the adhesive well and it must permit drawing with ruling pens without causing lines to spread and become fuzzy. The surface also must be dimensionally stable if any precision work is required; shrinking or other distortion cannot be tolerated for close-register printing.

In advertising agencies where mechanicals are prepared, not only to be photographed for platemaking but also to show clients in an impressive, neat, and exact fashion what the finished product will look like, heavy and expensive illustration board is usually used for the key. In printers' art departments the preferred surface for the key, if *tight* register (also called *hairline* or *close* register) is required, is usually a polyester (plastic) material. The printers' preference is based on the need to have the surfaces for all parts of a mechanical of the same material—so that they all react the same way to moisture, heat, and other conditions. A set of color pasteups with the key (black) pasteup on board and the overlays for colors on film cannot be expected to stay in exact register; yet overlays must be transparent or translucent, so they obviously cannot be on boards. For newspaper and other periodical work where precision is not required, key pasteups are usually done on paper sheets that are preprinted, gridded, and tailored to the publication's format.

Grids, Jigs, Underlays

Preprinted forms for mechanicals can be extremely helpful, especially in periodical work. With a *grid* that has been precision-printed (do not try to make your own) with lines that are very close together, pasteups can be done quickly and with reasonable accuracy. Grids can be set off in picas, half-picas, fractions of an inch, or millimeters depending on their intended use. The grids may have heavier lines at regular intervals (perhaps at every sixth pica) if these lines can be useful. A center line from each dimension and crossing at the exact center can also be helpful.

A *jig* is a customized grid sheet (also called a *pasteup dummy sheet* or *dummy sheet*) that clearly shows placement dimensions for all standard elements: column lines, margins, trim edges, page numbers, running heads, and so on. Any repetitive work, such as that involved in magazine, book, and newspaper pages, can be made simpler with jigs. All printing on grids or jigs is in light blue, a color the camera does not "see."

Good tools are needed for good mechanicals. Some of them are shown: drawing board, T-square, triangles, pens, X-Acto knife, calipers, rulers, scaling wheel, light box, white paint, brush.

12-1   Some procedures in preparing a mechanical.

(*Photos by Neil Sapienza*)

This mechanical is nearing completion. Most of the waxed type proofs are in position. Use tweezers to handle small pieces, as here. Note the completed overlay for a second color, flipped back onto the table while final work is done on the key pasteup.

For precision trimming of proofs, use a T-square.

For precision align-
ment of proofs, use a
T-square and triangle.

Preparation of a second
overlay begins.

Register marks are placed on the new overlay to
insure precise alignment with the first overlay
and the key.

In order to avoid or reduce the cost of preprinted jigs or grids, an *underlay* printed in black can be prepared and used on a light table. Sometimes paper underlays will work, but they often are made as film positives because the lines are blacker and the background is clear.

Light Tables, Drawing Boards, T-Squares, Triangles

Grids and jigs are invaluable aids for any pasteup artist, but "eyeballing" with the aid of grid lines is not accurate enough for close work. A number of devices are used to increase precision.

A light source under the work surface is extremely helpful if the pasteup sheets are translucent. Tables with built-in fluorescent tubes under a glass top or what could be called lighted drawing boards are widely used.

Wooden drawing boards with metal edges, metal T-squares, and clear plastic triangles are also useful aids. These devices should be constantly checked for accuracy by drawing a line first with the T-square guided at the left and then drawing another with the T-square on the other side; these lines must be absolutely parallel or something is out of square. Flipping the triangle for a second line can serve as a check on its accuracy.

If a large amount of precision pasteup is to be done, mechanical substitutes for T-squares are often used. These *drafting machines*, as they are called, have a geared head containing horizontal and vertical straight edges; the head moves about on an arm that can be pivoted into any position. The edge guides are always at right angles and prevent the misalignment that often comes when T-squares are not quite tight against a board edge.

The great advantage of using pasteup composition of pages is lost when the elements are not squarely positioned; off-angle work is the curse of printing processes requiring photomechanical prepress steps and must be avoided. Extreme care is essential at all times during the pasteup process.

Adhesives

Type proofs and other elements are fixed in position on a mechanical with a variety of materials or methods. Among these are wax, rubber cement, both single- and double-faced Scotch brand or similar adhesive tapes, and spray adhesives.

The most efficient and most common adhesive is hot-melt adhesive wax. Wax requires special applying devices, either hand-held or table-top models, to permit the wax to be melted and applied evenly. These devices usually apply the wax in parallel strips; sometimes double coating by running a proof through twice and in opposite directions is required.

The outstanding feature of adhesive wax is that it allows elements to be moved from one position to another; an element can easily be lifted and repositioned without losing its adhesive properties. It is important to use the right wax for the machine and for the paper it must adhere to, as well as the right temperature for melting. If these are correct, waxing is the cleanest, fastest, and most convenient method of fixing proofs to the pasteup surface.

Rubber cement is the old standard. It can be used wet, in which case only the back of the element is coated and the element can be moved about somewhat as it is being pressed on a board or paper surface. Or it can be applied to both the element and the board, and then permitted to dry before being positioned. The latter provides better bonding but requires extreme care in placement because the bonding is instantaneous and no sliding is possible. The main disadvantages of rubber cement are general messiness, the fact that it will form a yellow stain, and its tendency to draw dirt around edges. It also tends to slow down pasteup work. Nevertheless, it is still in common use.

When pasteups are to go before a camera quickly and there is no need to retain them for any length of time, adhesive tapes are adequate. Double-faced tape at strategic places can hold elements in position if the camera operator is careful not to let edges get turned over when the mechanical is placed under the glass cover of the copyboard. Single-faced tape can be used if it can be kept clear of any image area; it can show in reproduction, especially of continuous tone.

Spray adhesives can be used, but they have the obvious disadvantage of settling on unwanted places even when great care is taken.

Getting the Job Done: Commercial Register Work _____

The purpose for which a mechanical is being prepared dictates the best procedure to follow in its preparation. Because pasteups for some periodicals are simpler and require less care than for some others, let us first assume that we are to complete a pasteup of that kind, with tight register of colors not being required. This kind of noncritical register is called *commercial* register.

All type proofs should first be gathered. It is poor practice to start without all proofs, but obviously this may sometimes have to be done in newspapers and other periodicals if deadlines dictate it. At any rate, the type proofs must be carefully checked for imperfections. White specks in type can quickly be corrected with a pen; uneven development usually requires resetting, but it cannot be tolerated. Along with off-angle work, another curse of printing systems using photographic prepress steps is a variation in tone for type. To have the body type of one story darker than for all the others is not acceptable; even worse

12-2 For most newspaper work, screened prints (Veloxes) are fixed to the mechanical along with type and line illustrations. The mechanical is then photographed as if it contained only line copy.

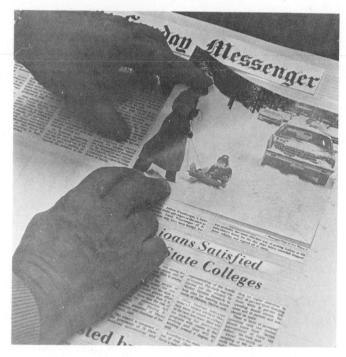

are the correction lines that are of a different tone. Good pasteup personnel carefully check all type proofs before sticking them down; it is much more difficult to make substitutions at a later stage.

Next, illustrations should be checked. Usually any line illustrations are drawn directly on the pasteup surface or prepared separately in exact size ready to be pasted in position.

Periodicals vary in their handling of continuous-tone illustrations. Often these illustrations are scaled to size and screened in a process camera to produce a screened photoprint. These screened prints (Veloxes) can be pasted in position and then treated as line work (see Figure 12-2). They are, in effect, the same as Benday line illustrations — they are composed of screen-created dots that can be captured by a camera along with type or line drawings.

For finest quality, Veloxes are not used, because there is a limitation to the fineness of the screen that can be used; therefore the dots created are large enough to be visible in reproduction. Also, in printing, every step involved in camera reproduction tends to decrease quality slightly, and the rephotographing of Velox dots is an added step.

Use of photomechanical transfer (PMT)

Veloxes are often prepared on a *photomechanical transfer machine* (PMT) that automatically develops the screened print after it has been exposed through a screen in a process camera. Newspapers, particularly, make much use of this process. Use of the process camera and PMT for enlargement and reduction of both type and line illustrations is also common. (The treatment of continuous-tone reproductions for maximum quality is discussed in the next section.)

After type and artwork are gathered, they should be separated for color. For our example, we will assume that everything is black and white except a headline which is to be printed in red. We will therefore set aside the headline and work only with the remainder.

For maximum efficiency, all proofs should be coated with adhesive first, before cutting out each piece. The waxed proofs can then be placed face up on waxed paper for cutting and trimming; even small pieces will stay in place and stay free of dirt until they are positioned.

This is the time—before proofs are positioned—to draw or position borders and lines that are to print. Borders and *rules*, as they are called, are available as pressure-sensitive tape and in various thicknesses and styles. If these are used, they can be pressed into place. If rules are to be drawn, good ruling pens and undercut line guides (T-squares, triangles and rulers) must be used. Pens of mechanical drawing quality should be used and tested to make sure that the ink does not spread and fuzz out on the particular surface. The T-squares, triangles, and rulers used as guidelines should be undercut so that lines will not smear when they are drawn; without the undercutting, ink runs under the edge. Although special ruling guides can be bought, they can also be "rigged up." The only requirement is that the edge be slightly raised off the paper when it is positioned for drawing; a strip of masking tape can do the trick.

What Lines Mean

So there is no doubt about which lines are to print and which are not, it is wise to coordinate their color with their purpose. Blue lines, because they have the same effect on film as if they were white, are for guidelines and instructions. They must be light blue, as mentioned; blues are dark only because they contain some black, and they can contain enough to be reproduced. (A nonreproducing blue pencil is essential in preparing mechanicals.) Black lines should be reserved for material that is to be reproduced. Red lines reproduce as well as black; their use should be restricted to placement lines that must show in a negative but will be removed before a plate is made.

Working with Type Proofs

With rules in place, trim all proofs, including illustrations. Type proofs should be cut, if possible, with an edge of at least $\frac{1}{8}$ inch around them; the raised plane of the proof can cast a shadow. If the edge is far enough from the image, it will be covered by the mask when the negative made later is stripped into position, and shadows will be no problem.

Corrections in type are always a problem when they must be made at this point. Pasting them over the proof adds still another layer to the pasteup that creates shadow problems in photographing. It is best to cut out the errors, if possible, and replace them with the corrected material. Patching in lines, and especially words, is often done, but it can lead to imperfections and lost corrections when the pieces fall off.

One tip for getting type proofs lined up: make two short vertical cuts in the proof in line with the left vertical edge of the type, one just above the type, the other just below. Then by lifting the two corners

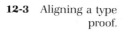
12-3 Aligning a type proof.

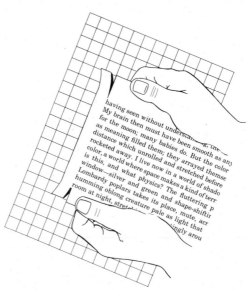

you can align the type itself with a grid line or straight edge under the proof. In other words, the border on the proof is thus prevented from being an obstacle to lining up the type (see Figure 12-3). A light blue line along the edge of the type from top to bottom edge of the proof can serve the same purpose as the cuts.

To get Veloxes sized and positioned accurately, they should be roughly trimmed only before they are pasted in position. The final cutting, following crop marks or a guideline, can be much more precise if it is done with the proof pasted in position rather than before it is placed.

Preparing Color Overlays

With type proofs, rules, and illustrations in position, we are ready to turn to the preparation of a mechanical for the red plate. Although the example we are using does not require close register, we should still use register marks to ensure proper positioning of the color image.

Marks are available on adhesive-backed, pressure-sensitive clear tape or sheets, or they can be drawn, if necessary. Register marks (crossed lines about $\frac{3}{4}$ inch long) should be put in two places outside (but relatively close to) the image area on the key mechanical. The lines should be horizontal and vertical, not at some other orientation.

The second pasteup, for the red, must be on a transparent base because it will be laid over the key mechanical and integrated with it by sight. The first step here is to fasten the overlay securely to the base mechanical; the second is to place matching register marks exactly over those that can be seen on the key. Then, following the location

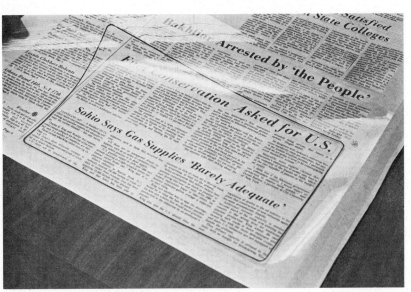

12-4 A transparent second-color overlay. The copy to be printed in red—in this case, a box border—is laid over the key mechanical and positioned with register marks. Note these marks near upper right and lower left corners of the box. (Register marks are opaqued from the negative before platemaking.)

shown on the layout pattern, paste the headline in position on the overlay (see Figure 12-4).

The mechanicals are then ready for the steps involved in platemaking. Each one will be separately photographed, and their negatives will be stripped into two separate masks. They will then be positioned in the masks by using the register marks, which will then be covered up before the light is beamed through the masks separately to form the two plates.

Preparation of Mechanicals: Tight Register Work

Some changes in technique are involved in preparing mechanicals that involve tight register and maximum quality for the best possible reproduction of photographs, maps, and other exacting artwork.

As already noted, most printers find that maximum accuracy is possible only if the key and the overlays are made of the same material; thus a transparent or translucent stable material such as polyester is used for all. Many printers, however, use illustration board for the key.

Most printers also say that really accurate register is only possible with a pin and punch system similar to the one they use to register the negatives into flats. This system requires that holes be punched in each mechanical so that, when these holes are used to fasten the mechanicals to properly positioned pins, the mechanicals will not move. However, many use only the register marks, relying on pasteup personnel to make sure that the crosslines stay lined up as they work. In any case, the register marks are essential.

Many printers also prefer to "break for color" when they are working with negatives, rather than work with two or more mechanicals. They can ensure absolute hairline register if, working from one mechanical, they make duplicate negatives and then block out those elements that do not belong in the color run that is involved. Many problems, including different degrees of stability in the pasteup surfaces and inaccuracies in register marks, can be eliminated because the negatives are identical. Many customers, however, still prefer to avoid a printer's charges for this work by preparing a separate mechanical for each color.

In some cases where positioning is tight (for example, a cutline that must be extremely close to a photo) or when line work is to be combined with continuous tone, separate pasteups may be required. The pasteups are then masked separately and exposed in sequence on a plate. This process is called *double burning:* the halftone is burned (exposed) onto the plate through one mask, and the line work is burned through the other mask. Separate pasteups to get tight positioning are necessary because the stripper cannot place two negatives (one a halftone and the other line) very close together; a fairly sizable strip of the mask is needed between the two or it will tear, bend, and slide out of position. Veloxes eliminate some of these double burns, but they are not used when top-quality reproduction is required.

Placement of Illustrations

To process continuous-tone elements separately, mechanicals must make provision for their accurate placement through the use of what are called "windows" because they end up as areas of clear film when the negatives are made. These areas on the pasteup must be totally devoid of light-reflecting capability. Red tone sheets that are pressure sensitive (will stick when pressed) are usually used. The tone sheet is put down just as if it were a Velox and is trimmed to the exact dimensions to be occupied by the photo. Black ink can also be used to color in these areas, but there is always a possibility of some reflection if small areas are missed or the ink is not black enough.

An advantage of using red sheets is that they can be seen through, but still not reflect light. This permits the use of photostats under them to identify the illustrations and show how they are to be positioned. It also makes trimming easier, because guidelines can show through.

The placement of illustrations can also be shown on a mechanical with a red outline. The identification of the illustration comes from a blue line drawing in sufficient detail to avoid any possible confusion about the identity of the illustration. A device called a *camera lucida* can be used to project artwork at the desired scale so this drawing can be quickly and easily done. The blue lines must be light enough so they will photograph as white. Or, the red keyline area might be labeled with a letter or number that will correspond with a letter or number on the original artwork. This last method is easiest for the pasteup person, but it has the greatest potential for error and is an inconvenience for a printer. For the printer, this means that the stripper must have the original copy of illustrations at hand in order to identify each negative.

Use of Photostats   Although it is perhaps the most expensive method of handling line work, the use of photostatic enlargements or reductions on the pasteup is foolproof and has many advantages. Photostats (often called *stats*) are reproducible and become an integral part of the mechanical. Many type display problems are solved with photostatic enlargements and reductions; reverses (white lines on a black background) are efficiently handled with photostats.

A photostat machine is useful because it makes enlargements and reductions directly on paper. A lens in the machine keeps the original image right-reading on the negative, but the image is reversed: blacks are whites, and whites are blacks. In order to get a positive image, the negative print must be reexposed in the machine. Therefore, reverses for logotypes and other uses are cheaper than positives.

Photostat paper has a minimum size, $8\frac{1}{2} \times 11$; thus "ganging" of illustrations can keep photostat charges to a minimum. This necessitates grouping illustrations that have the same percentage of enlargement or reduction, but the effort is worthwhile.

Care must be taken in ordering photostats so that there is no misunderstanding about whether the reversed negative print or the positive print is desired. Since the negative means one exposure and the positive two, the best way to make an order clear to the photostat operator is to express it in those terms: first print or second print.

Newer types of photostat machines (two trade names are Duostat and Statmaster) make stats in a process that requires only one exposure. In this case the lens produces a wrong-reading image on the negative. This image is directly transferred to the positive sheet during development, to form the right-reading positive stat. A reverse stat is made in the same way, but with specially treated negative paper. Thus the order to the operator of one of these machines need only specify a positive stat (often called a direct positive) or a reverse stat.

When ordering a photostat, size must be carefully specified, just as it would be for a printer's camera, and the type of paper (glossy or matte finish) must be designated. The less expensive matte finish is adequate for prints not to be used for reproduction, but only glossy prints give enough blackness for reproduction.

In publication offices with access to a production plant, a PMT machine is often used instead of a photostat machine. The PMT provides enlarging-reducing capability by means of a process camera; it produces photoprints mechanically. As mentioned earlier, the PMT can also produce screened prints (Veloxes) of photographs and other continuous-tone illustrations that can then be treated as line work.

Screen Tints and Special Treatments for Illustrations

The screen tints discussed in the chapter on illustrations can be applied directly to a mechanical or they can merely be located on the mechanical and specified for insertion in the mask at the stripping stage. Any line illustration that is on a mechanical may also have some of its components screened in order to create some middle tones.

If screens are on a mechanical, they should be checked for flaws and replaced if necessary. It has been assumed in our discussion of mechanicals that they will all be reproduced without enlargement or reduction. They can be reduced, of course, and if they are, the effect of the reduction on any screen used on the mechanical must be considered.

Although it involves a stripping charge, it is sometimes advantageous to let the printer strip in a film screen rather than put one on the mechanical. Accuracy of reproduction is thus assured. It is possible, for example, to get distortion in a screen if it is applied to the mechanical over an irregular area of a pasteup caused by the edge of a type proof. The surface under a screen must be clean and smooth. If a printer is to apply a screen panel, the area should be precisely bordered by a red line on the pasteup.

Line work can be reproduced on a screen background by applying a positive photostat within a blue border on a pasteup; a negative photostat with a red border will result in a reversed line image on the screen. For the printer, the surprinting of the black line requires a double burn; the reverse image does not. Both require additional negatives and stripping. If the line image is to surprint (be in black) the tint must be light (a low percentage), and vice versa for a reverse.

Line work, including type, can also be reproduced over halftone reproductions to form surprint and reverse combinations as described in the chapter on illustrations. The procedure is the same as with tint screens.

Outlines and irregular shapes can be expedited by using red tone sheets cut to form the outline and placed in register on an overlay. The red "knocks out" the image wherever it is used.

Multipage Mechanicals If more than one page is to be on a press plate, the work of the printer can be minimized by putting all the pages on a single mechanical. In order to do this, the way in which the pages must fall on the press plate must be known before the mechanical is prepared. The different ways in which pages can be arranged (imposition) depend on folding and binding and are fairly complicated. These subjects are discussed in Chapter 18. It should suffice here to point out that the imposition is critical, and no multipage mechanical should be attempted without full knowledge of it.

Guidelines and Dimension Marks ⸺

Guidelines, dimension marks, and instructions are an important part of mechanical preparation. They are more complicated for multipage mechanicals, but some such marking is essential to any mechanical, both as an aid during its preparation and for the printer during later processing.

Actual finished size for any mechanical must be clearly marked, usually with blue lines forming the outline, and black corner marks emphasizing the corners. These marks show the *trim size*, the finished size of the printed paper after it has been trimmed. Corner marks are in black because they may be retained by the printer as trim guides; printers may also prefer to opaque them from the negative and use their own marks.

A *bleed* dimension, $\frac{1}{8}$ inch additional on all trim sides, is also marked if any portion of the image area is to go off a trim edge. The bleed edges should be shown with a red line.

Fold lines are shown with a short, dotted black line that is outside the trim line; it is a helpful guide during the preparation of the mechanical and may also be used as a guide by the printer.

Any guidelines used merely to determine accurate placement of elements, whether part of the preprinted grid form or drawn in place, must be light blue to assure that they will not be photographed by the camera and thus appear on the negative.

What are called *call-outs* (instructions written at the end of a line drawn from the point of reference) should be beyond bleed lines in marginal space or on a special tissue overlay.

Checklist: Mechanicals: Some Helpful Hints

1. Remember that anything black, red, or gray on a mechanical may end up in print; do not rely on a printer to remove all errors by opaquing.

2. Read all proofs carefully before starting; correction of type errors after a mechanical has been begun is inconvenient, to say the least.

3. Use full-page electronic "pagination" if it is available. The extra planning and markup is worth it; pasteups are only a poor substitute for full-page photoproofs from a computerized typesetter.

4. If full-page typesetting is not possible, at least use area composition to its fullest capability. The fewer the pieces involved in preparation of a mechanical, the fewer are the chances for error.

5. Keep cutting tools sharp, pens and brushes clean, and work area tidy and well lighted.

6. Keep checking T-square and the alignment of elements to catch any flaws as quickly as possible.

7. Use red film sheets instead of painting in black areas. Results are more certain and it takes less time.

8. Watch edges of individual pieces of proofs or illustrations. Dirty edges will appear as lines on negatives and require opaquing. For reverse solid areas, paint the edges black so that they will not reflect light and appear on the negative.

9. Use pastedown and transfer letters when unusual, "this time only" typefaces are required, but be especially careful with alignment and spacing.

10. When ruling lines, to get a good beginning and ending, place a piece of tape at each end before starting with the ruling pen. Then start the line over the beginning tape and run it beyond the ending tape. Line ends are then exact and free of flaws.

11. Keep a nonreproducing blue pencil on hand for writing instructions on mechanicals.

13 Color in Graphic Communication

What we see in the "real world" is in color. Yet, when we look at visual images of the real world (photographs or drawings or their printed reproductions), we recognize what is represented, and this is true whether the photographs or drawings are printed in color or in black and white.

Contrast is the source of all meaning. Recall the "offs" and "ons," the yes and no answers, and the elimination of alternatives in computer operation. It is believed that our brains function in a similar manner. Nerve synapses function in some fashion analogous to the computer when we process information. Concept formation is looking for similarities and differences—defining features are either present or not present. Decision making and comprehension result from reducing alternatives. We learn to recognize shapes because of tonal contrasts in space. Shapes are delineated by lines, but there are no lines in nature. We "see" them because of juxtapositioned tones. We only see something because of the presence of light.

There must be something about the interaction between the visual system and light that allows us to accept black and white as a representation of reality. The two dimensions of light—brightness (wave amplitude) and hue (wavelength)—are of significance here.

We are sensitive to all the hues (colors) in the color spectrum. When all our hue sensitivities are equally stimulated by light, we see white light. When the light primaries are equally mixed they give white light, called *achromatic* light (light without color). When all our sensitivities react, but some more than others, we sense both the achromatic and the *chromatic* (light with color). Both red and pink light are chromatic, but the red is a heavy color saturation and the pink is a light saturation. Hue may be thought of as white light with color added.

In summary, when we perceive light we sense differences in tone. The tones may be chromatic or achromatic. The differences in tone are the result of the relative brightness of the light reflected by what we look at. One can remove the color from a color TV picture, yet the tonal contrasts remain.

It is tempting to conclude from this that whereas color is useful, it is not necessary in printed communication and in a way this is so. In fact, much printing is done in black and white. However, color is an important tool in graphic communication. We consider some of its applications later.

The scientific aspects of color have been largely developed by physicists through their study of light. Their findings are of little *direct* help to most people involved in graphic communication, but inasmuch as they foster an understanding of the psychological effects of color, these findings are important and are summarized here.

The Nature of Color

The source of all color is light. When we look at a red rose, we see it only because light reflects from it into our eyes, making the rose and its color discernible. But why are the rose and its surroundings, seen through the same source of artificial or natural light, not all the same color?

Light is visible radiant energy made up of various wavelengths. It is one of several electromagnetic waves listed in order of their frequency and length: long electric, radio, television, radar, infrared, visible light, X rays, cosmic rays, and gamma rays. The longest waves are invisible. As waves shorten and their frequencies increase, they are felt as heat—infrared, for example—then reach visibility in a varying range we know as color. Magenta red is first as the longest; as the waves shorten they move from oranges, yellows, into greens, blues, indigo, and violet. Beyond violet, at the shortest lengths and highest frequencies, are the invisible ultraviolet rays.

As the several wavelengths of light are separated—by raindrops, as in the rainbow, or by a glass prism—the colors appear. The white light of the sun contains all wavelengths of light. When light falls on a surface that reflects all the white light, the surface appears white to our eyes. When it falls on a surface that absorbs all the white light, we see the object as black. When some of the light rays are reflected and some absorbed, color is evident. The red rose reflects only red rays; in a like manner, the color of everything depends upon which color rays are absorbed and which are reflected.

Color, then, is a property of the light waves reaching our eyes, not of the object seen. The latter has the property of absorbing some wavelengths while allowing others to reflect.

The Primary Colors Three colors in light and three in pigment are called *primary colors.* The familiar pigment primaries are red (actually magenta), yellow, and blue (actually a blue-green referred to as *cyan*). The light primaries are green, red-orange, and blue-violet. All pigment colors are derived from mixtures of the pigment primaries; all light colors are derived from mixtures of the light primaries. But the primaries themselves can be derived only one from the other. A pigment primary is caused by the reflection of two light primaries; a light primary is caused by the reflection of two pigment primaries. This means that a pigment primary is a secondary color of light, and vice versa, since secondary colors are the result of a mixture of two primaries.

Color Dimensions in Pigment

In order to apply color effectively, the typographer, artist, engraver, and printer need a basic understanding of the various dimensions of color—hue, value, and chroma.

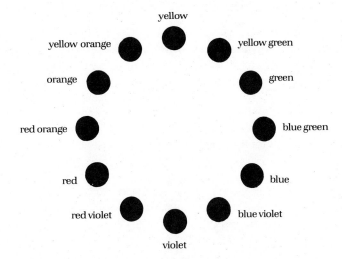

13-1 The color wheel.

Hue *Hue* is a synonym for color. We distinguish one color from another because of the quality of hue. For purposes of identification, hues are classified by arrangement in a circular scale (Figure 13-1).

The three secondary colors, orange, green, and violet, can be obtained by mixing the primaries to either side; for example, green is made by mixing blue and yellow.

The intermediate colors result from mixing a primary with a secondary. For example, yellow and green make yellow-green. Intermediate colors can also be made by mixing adjoining colors; for example, yellow and yellow-green.

Value *Value* refers to the lightness or darkness of a hue. A color can be lightened by being mixed with a lighter hue of the same color or by the addition of white. Lightening a color produces a *tint*. The printer can lighten a color by mixing the color ink with white ink or by screening the printing plate with a tint block.

A darker value, called a *shade*, is achieved by adding either a darker hue of the same color or black. The printer can reduce the value by mixing a color ink with black or by overprinting the color ink with a screened black.

Chroma

Chroma refers to the purity or strength of a color. *Intensity* is a similar term. To alter chroma is to change the *tone* or to weaken, dull, or neutralize a color. This can be accomplished by adding the complementary color or gray. Gray is actually a color without hue and can be developed by an equal mixture of black and white.

Psychological Aspects of Color _____

The use of color is justified only to the extent that it contributes to the realization of three major objectives of graphic communication: (1) to attract and gain attention; (2) to be legible and comprehensible; and (3) to make an impression.

Form and color are basic elements of visual stimulation. They have a vital share in man's emotional life. An object familiar in the daylight can seem to have a different form at night and becomes capable of arousing negative feelings.

The psychological impact of color has been researched primarily through several means of testing: (1) observation; (2) instrument; (3) memory; (4) sales and inquiry; and (5) unconscious-level. These tests also have been useful in developing many workable principles of advertising layout.

Observation tests study the reactions to color of subjects who are unaware that their behavior is being viewed and evaluated. The testers are often hidden behind one-way glass.

Instrument tests employ eye cameras, the tachistoscope, and lie-detector equipment. The psychogalvanometer, which is the best known of the latter, measures reactions to color as revealed by somatic variations, such as pulse, blood pressure, and sweat-gland activity.

Memory tests involve questioning persons to determine how much and what they recall of items in print. These tests might show for example, that advertisements using color rate higher than advertisements in black and white.

Sales and inquiry tests measure the effect of color on merchandise sales or on offers of such things as booklets or samples to the readers of advertisements. A common technique is to advertise items for sale through the mail, running some ads in black and white and some in color. Not only can color versus no color be tested but so can one color versus another or one color versus two, and so on. Sales or numbers of inquiries are considered to be indicative of the effectiveness of the different applications of color.

Unconscious-level, or indirect, testing uncovers attitudes that subjects cannot or will not reveal. People are not generally conscious of the effects of color. This is why the value of opinion testing—asking people directly how they react to colors—is questioned by most experts. Indirect testing, on the other hand, attempts to reveal unconscious reactions by depth interviews and projective techniques, such as word association.

Often the decision to use color is based on the assumption that it is better than black and white. The decision is never that simple. Many factors should be given careful consideration before the right color or colors can be selected. Once determined and properly applied, color can contribute substantially to effective communication. In some contexts, of course, it is essential.

The artist's knowledge and skill in the use of color are valuable aids in planning color printing. But it should be remembered that the end result of the planning should be the scientific application of color to the communications task and not a form of abstract expression in color.

Functions of Color

The functions of color in printing are

1. To attract attention
2. To produce psychological effects
3. To develop associations
4. To build retention
5. To create an esthetically pleasing atmosphere.

Let us consider each function in turn, bearing in mind that they are interrelated and that they contribute to the three goals of graphic communication.

To Attract Attention This is the major use of color. Contrast is the basis of attention. Thus, the addition of a bright color to a piece printed in black increases the attention-getting value of the piece.[1] Tests have shown conclusively that the number of people noting a printed communication is increased by the use of color.

---

[1] In printing terminology, anything printed in black plus a color is called a two-color job. Black is considered a color in the printing field.

When we say "attract attention," we refer to two separate responses from readers. First they are attracted; then they pay attention if what attracted them holds meaning or interest.

Color should be applied to the elements of greatest significance. Since emphasis results from contrast, color should be placed with discretion. One color plus black offers the greatest contrast, for a color is always its most intense when used with black.

To effect contrast without black, several color schemes are possible. They are, in order of descending contrast: complementary, split-complementary, analogous, and monochromatic.

The *complementary scheme* uses colors that are opposite each other on the color wheel. Colors can be divided into two groups according to psychological suggestion—warm and cool. One complementary is warm, the other cool. Cool colors are blue, or predominantly blue. They are relaxing and recede on the page. Warm colors are red, or red and yellow. They are stimulating and advance to the foreground. Green and red-purple lie between the warms and cools and are thus relatively neutral.

Selecting colors takes care. Full-value complementaries can be disturbingly vibrant. A rampant hue can be controlled by changing its value or chroma, or by its selective use in a limited area.

The *split-complementary scheme* contrasts three colors. A color is used in contrast with the colors adjoining its complementary on either side. For example, the split complements of red are yellow-green and blue-green.

The *analogous scheme* uses colors that are adjacent to one another on the wheel—green, blue-green, and blue; or red-orange, orange, and yellow-orange. Related colors are either warm or cool. Analogous colors are less exciting than complementaries since contrast is missing.

The *monochromatic scheme* calls for the use of different values and strengths of a single hue. Generally in this arrangement weak, dull areas of the hue are the largest; small, bright areas provide the contrast.

Four helpful hints for planning color contrast are

1. The tint of a hue is stronger on a middle gray than on a full strength of the hue.
2. Warm colors are higher in visibility than are cool colors.
3. Contrast in values—light versus dark—is greater than contrast in hues—blue versus yellow.
4. The darker the background, the lighter a color appears against it.

To Produce Psychological Effects The colors that predominate in an ad or other printed piece should fit the overall mood of the message. The color suggestions of coolness and warmth, in turn, suggest formality and informality. Red implies life and many moods and ideas associated with life, such as action, passion, and gaiety. Blue connotes distinction, reserve, serenity. Green is nature; purple is splendor and pomp; white is purity.

To Develop Associations

It is natural for people to associate certain colors with different products. Red is happily associated with cherries, whereas the thought of green with fresh meats is not pleasant. But many associations are not so obvious and research may be called for before a color selection is made. Personal judgment cannot always be trusted: although one might suspect that pink is preferable to blue for a face-powder message, an error could be made without a more tangible basis for the choice.

To Build Retention

In describing something we are likely to refer to its color. This is because color has high memory value, a feature that the communicator can capitalize upon. A color should predominate because it helps readers remember what they saw. Advertisers are particularly interested in reader recall of the message and repeat certain colors in their campaigns in order to establish product identification.

To Create a Pleasing Atmosphere

The misuse of color in a message is worse, from the viewpoint of the communicator, than the use of no color at all. Color may get the initial attention, but unless this is sustained and developed into interest, the reader will not spend time to absorb the message. Poor choice and application of colors can repel readers immediately after their attention has been aroused.

Colors, including black, gray, and white, in the printed piece should be arranged in accordance with the same basic principles of layout: balance, contrast, proportion, rhythm, unity, harmony, and movement.

Balance comes from the judicious placement of the elements by weight. Color adds further weight to the elements. Bright colors appear lighter; dark colors appear heavier. When used with black for a two-color job, the color should be given a relatively light weight so that it will not draw undue attention from the black. Normally, it should be run in large areas at a 30, 40, or 50 percent level; that is, screened to that amount. Solids of the color should be reserved for emphasis.

Contrast is necessary for legibility. Contrast in values is more significant than contrast in colors. For this reason, where color serves as a background, care should be given to its treatment so that it will not detract from other elements. If the latter are dark, the background should be light, and vice versa.

Proportion refers to the relationships between colors. Proportional arrangement calls for a pleasing balance of (1) dark colors and light colors, and (2) dull or weak colors and bright colors.

Rhythmic use of color is achieved through repetition at various points in the printed piece. Spots of a second color can be used effectively in this way to guide the reader's eye through the message.

Color, as well as form, can contribute to the unity of a printed piece. Misplaced, it can disintegrate the total effect, even cause the message to seem divided.

Harmony in its broadest sense results from abiding by the other principles of color use—balance, contrast, proportion, and so on. More specifically, harmony applies to the so-called color schemes. Thus, one speaks of monochromatic, complementary, split-complementary, or analogous color harmony. Complementary colors are not automatically harmonious together, however, unless some consideration is given to their use.

Psychological tests have uncovered personal color preferences. Blue is highly popular, being *the* color preferred by men and second only to red by women. Tests also show that women are more color conscious than men and tend more to prefer tints and softer colors. Color preferences vary according to age, education, and geographic location of those tested. Bright colors appeal to young people, soft colors to older persons and to those with high levels of education.

Preference tests are of some value to the designer if he or she knows the specific group to which the message will be directed. But the value of general tests is questionable in view of the fact that researchers have also found that "favorite" colors can be unattractive in certain uses.

Types of Color Printing

Color printing can be divided into two types: spot color and process color. Process, meaning the various ways to reproduce color copy—photographs, drawings, or paintings—was discussed in Chapter 10 on photoengraving.

Full-color copy is usually reproduced with four inks by the *four-color process*. Occasionally, *three-color process* is used for full-color copy by eliminating the black plate. This effects a substantial savings, but not all copy lends itself to this treatment. Subjects in a light key, such as outdoor scenes, are adaptable, but portraits, people, and indoor scenes are better reproduced by four-color process, since the black gives the definition and detail needed for a more realistic effect.

Paintings or other copy done in two colors are subjected to camera separation and *two-color process printing*.

Spot color refers to multicolor printing (two or more colors), by methods other than process. The simplest form is *flat-color printing*. A message with text in black and headlines in red is an example. In this form, colors do not overlap to form new colors—red is red, blue is blue, black is black, and so on.

Flat tones can be used with solids. In addition to headlines in red, red tints can be placed behind certain portions of the type or perhaps behind halftones of photos printed in black.[2] If the flat-color spots do not touch, the entire piece can be prepared as if it were all one color. A pasteup or mechanical is made up with all elements properly positioned. The platemaker (litho, gravure, or letterpress) can *break for color* by making separate plates from a single photomechanical negative made from the pasteup. Only the elements to print in black are exposed to the plate to carry black ink; only those elements to print in a second color are exposed to that plate, and so on. There are two ways to indicate to the printer what is required. A layout drawn in the proper colors can accompany the mechanical or an overlay of thin paper can be affixed to it to indicate the colors for the different elements.

For letterpress, printing direct from type and engravings, the printer breaks for color by separating the elements to run in red, for example, into one form and the elements for black into another form.

Much spot-color work calls for laying one color over another to form additional color. Tints and solids can be used in this way. The Sunday color comics are an excellent example.

Often *color register* is significant. The term "register" refers to the positioning of the impression on the sheet. For example, when a book page is viewed against a light, both sides should be aligned. If so, they are registered, or properly lined up. Color register refers to the alignment of one color with another.

If the colors do not touch and are not closely interrelated, the printer can break for color. This is called *loose register*.

When colors touch or overprint, the register is described as *tight*, *hairline*, or *close*. Modern printing equipment is capable of maintaining the position of impression at a tolerance of $\frac{1}{1000}$ of an inch. An almost imperceptible lap can be given where spot colors come together.

There are several ways to indicate color register to a printer. One technique of copy preparation (described in detail in Chapter 12) requires the use of a clear acetate *overlay*. This is fastened over the *key drawing* of the copy to which other colors will be registered. The key drawing is the copy for the black plate. Art for an additional color is drawn on or pasted to the overlay, a separate overlay being used for each color. Register marks are added to the key drawing and overlay art and must coincide exactly when the overlay is positioned over the

---

[2] To say that the color tint is "printed behind" the type does not mean that the color is necessarily printed first. Often the black is laid on the sheet, and the color is then printed. The one requirement is that the colored ink be transparent.

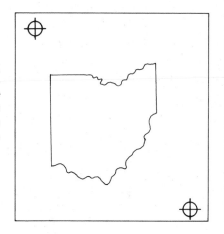

13-2 *Left:* Key art. *Right:* Overlay for second color. The register marks exactly coincide when the overlay is in place.

key. These marks bring about the proper positioning of copy on the printing plates. Figure 13-2 shows key art, left, and an overlay for second color with register marks, right.

Another common method of copy preparation is the *keyline* technique. Black and color art are drawn on a single board or paper. Separation between colors is indicated by a keyline. The areas to appear in color and in black are painted with black ink to within $\frac{1}{4}$ to $\frac{1}{8}$ of an inch of the keyline. For example, assume Figure 13-3 is a keyline drawing for a circle, the left side of which will be blue, the other side black. Two negatives are made from the drawing. On each negative the area of the other color is blocked out and the space up to the thin, center line filled in. The keyline thus becomes the overlap.

13-3 Keyline drawing for color register.

The Cost Factor in Color Printing

The added cost factor is usually an important consideration in the decision about whether or not to use multicolor printing. Expense piles up because the paper has to go through a single-color press as many times as there are colors. Between impressions, time must be taken for press washups, changes of ink, and additional makeready. Extra designing, camera, and plate charges are also often involved.

Multicolor jobs can be run through two-, four-, and six-color presses. This can mean some savings, but such equipment is used only for long runs. The manner in which color is used adds little to the cost. A small spot or a more expansive spread of a second color applied to a sheet affects the total expense very little.

Designers and buyers of printing frequently hesitate to spend the extra money required for two-color or full-color printing. Yet there is abundant evidence of the significance of color in modern life. The marketplace is alive with the use of color to sell products. The practical business world is under the influence of color now, as bright, warm reception rooms replace the austere, walnut-paneled ones of the past.

Color acts as a warning: do not park, stop, or go. Color also promotes efficiency and safety through scientific application to work areas, and used in modern architecture to an extent undreamed of a generation ago.

These are signs that the communicator cannot well ignore. There are evidently advantages to be gained from the use of color, but the communicator needs to know as precisely as possible what is gained from the extra cost.

Memory tests have shown that, on the average, the number of readers increases with the addition of color. However, since there is no conclusive evidence that the ratio of increase is greater than the increase in cost, this may not justify the added cost. Other functions must account for the difference, but the dollar value of pleasing atmosphere, psychological effect, esthetics, and other intangibles cannot be appraised.

The communicator can solve the added cost problem only by resolving to apply the color allowable under the budget in the way that most efficiently accomplishes its particular functions.

Fidelity in Process Color

There are certain basic weaknesses in process color printing that mean that the purchaser cannot expect exact reproduction or fidelity. These weaknesses occur because of (1) differences between colors in light and in inks; (2) ink deficiencies; (3) the nature of halftone dots; and (4) the quality of paper.

Physical Colors and Pigment Colors

The colors that enter the engraver's or lithographer's camera at the time of color separation behave according to the physical properties of light. The printer, on the other hand, must use pigmental or surface colors in the reproduction. To understand the difficulties this leads to, let us review the separation process. As explained in Chapter 10, a violet filter is used in preparing the yellow plate. As shown in Figure 13-4, this filter allows the red and the blue light to pass and record on the negative. Areas on the negative where these rays strike are dense. Yellow, the complement of the color in the filter, is held back. Thus, the

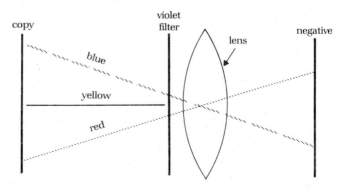

13-4 Use of violet filter for making a yellow negative.

yellow areas become the most transparent on the negative. When the plate is made, a reversal of values occurs—yellows are the darkest; reds and blues are lighter.

The orange filter passes reds and yellows and holds back blue; the green filter passes yellows and blues and holds back red. These filters are used respectively for the blue and red plates.

The filters are analogous to the primaries of light in absorption and transmission, and they are complementary to the printing colors.

If artwork could be submitted in standardized colors, the printer's chores would be much simpler. There is, however, no standardization, and countless colors are available from many different sources. For example, the violet filter is used for all of the many yellows.

The printer's surface colors represent white light minus a color primary, since the three color primaries together represent white. Thus yellow is white minus blue, reflecting red and green. Cyan is white minus red, and magenta is white minus green. If a color in the artwork, a certain yellow, for example, does not absorb all the blue light, the result on the plate is a distortion, a weakening, of the true value of that color. Similar distortions of other colors result in the separation process.

Ink Characteristics

The process inks used by the printer give rise to similar difficulties. Cyan is farthest from perfection, reflecting some red, which it should absorb completely, and absorbing much of the blues and greens, which it should reflect completely. For this reason colors requiring blues, notably purples and greens, suffer in reproduction. Magenta absorbs some of the blues and reds and reflects a high percentage of green. Yellow is the most effective of the process inks, since it absorbs nearly all blue and reflects green and red very effectively. True red, which should be effected by using magenta and yellow, also suffers in reproduction.

Halftone Dots

The nature of the halftone process is a further obstacle to full fidelity of reproduction. Color photographs are reproduced with three layers of superimposed, continuous-tone primary colors. In an area of a halftone print where orange is being reproduced, for example, some of the magenta and yellow dots fall side by side, and others overlap. The result is a variation in hue from the original.

Effect of Paper

Paper for process reproduction should absorb all colors equally—at least as nearly as possible. A pure white, perhaps with an enamel surface, which reflects all colors with a minimum of absorption, is preferred. Reflecting more light from its surface through the inks, the white paper adds a brilliance to the reproduction.

Research, however, has led to the development of coordinated inks and papers to make process printing possible on pastel-colored stock with noteworthy results.

Color Correction Despite these deficiencies, it should not be assumed that process printing is ineffective. If straightforward separations were made, reproductions *would* fall far short of the original. However, the photoengraver's color-correction methods minimize the deficiencies by special treatments of negatives and plates.

Checklist: **Practical Pointers in the Use of Color**

A number of practical pointers help the designer plan printed pieces with color. By no means an exhaustive list, the following cover many frequently overlooked considerations that are applicable both to monochromatic *and* multicolor printing:

1. When using more than one color, reserve the darkest for the basic message, using the additional color or colors for emphasis or for setting a mood.
2. Color used behind type should be light to ensure easy legibility. In general, the smaller the type, the lighter the color should be. This is accomplished, of course, by having the color screened.
3. Running type in color demands care. Some colors are too light ever to be so used on white stock—yellow, for example. If the type size is large, color has a better chance of supporting legibility. It is safest, however, to use color on type to emphasize a few words in a headline.
4. If four-color process and black-and-white halftones appear in the same form, the printer should be consulted before planning the layout or ordering engravings. If the black-and-white halftones are large and dark, they may require such heavy inking for satisfactory printing that, as a result, the black process plates will have to carry excess also, thereby muddying the color reproductions. Consultation with the printer and engraver in the planning stage can often solve this problem.
5. Care is required when running type in color (other than black) on a sheet on which process printing appears. Let us assume that a red or an orange is desired. This necessitates printing type from two plates—magenta and yellow—in exact register. A satisfactory result is possible if the type is large. If it is small or light in weight, even the slightest imperfection in register will show.

6. Likewise, when printing in reverse is to appear on a color formed by overprinting two or more plates—for example, on a dark green formed by printing a screened black on a light green, the reverse printing must be on both plates. Unless they are printed in very close register, the type will not appear as a clean white. Naturally, the smaller the type, the more critical is the problem.

7. Type printed in reverse should be within a fairly dark area to preserve legibility. As a general rule, it is best to avoid reverses in a tone below 40 percent. If type is to appear in one color against a background of another—red on a black panel—the color on the type should be bright.

8. Often the artist prepares art for reproduction by overprinting one screened color on another and applies the screens to the artwork, using screen tones on self-adhering acetate sheets. Improper angling of the screens must be avoided, for it results in an undesirable moiré pattern.

9. Several halftones printed on a page with a second color occupying the remainder of the space except for an even, narrow white border around each photo will mean that even the slightest variation in register will be discernible, since the white borders become uneven.

10. It is sometimes possible to get full-color effect from two-color process plates made from full-color photos. This technique is not a substitute for full-color process, but startling results can be obtained under controlled conditions. The color photos should be composed of hues that are predominantly the same as those of the inks to be used in printing. For example, a color photo of a pair of dark brown shoes worn by a model dressed in a brown suit, posed against a red background might be effectively reproduced with process red and black.

11. Restraint must be exercised in the use of additional color. Because of cost, there is often a feeling that color ought to be applied lavishly to get one's money's worth. But an overuse of color can defeat the reason for the extra expense. Often a single spot of color is sufficient; or two spots can be utilized, one to contrast with the other, and the two together to contrast with the basic color. Too much color, however, can create a weak communication.

14 Design: Combining Pictures and Words

In this chapter we return to the design of the printed message. A few basic things about the subject were said in Chapter 6; now let us look at it in greater detail.

All design has structure. The human IPS (information-processing system) automatically seeks to impose structure on uncertainty. With this comes order and meaning, enabling man to cope with his environment. This is as true of typography and the other applied arts as it is of music, speech, writing, dance, or any of the fine arts.

Design can be effected in two ways, either intuitively or through a logical and detailed plan. By either process it may emerge as an effective creation. This implies that there are standards for evaluation. To discover these standards requires conscious effort. Once discovered these standards can be transposed into rules to follow in building an effective design.

Meaning in Design

The objective of the source of the printed message is the transfer of meaning from the source's mind to that of the reader. To this end, the source selects the elements, verbal and graphic, and arranges them in a structure.

Before we proceed further in this discussion, we need a clear understanding of "meaning." As Garner points out, two types of meaning exist in a structure.[1] *By signification,* meaning exists in the elements. For example, by *association,* we find meaning in the words and illustrations. A separate kind of meaning exists in the structure—the relationships among the separate elements. As Garner puts it, in information measurement terms, one can distinguish one set of symbols as being better structure than another. That which is more meaningful is better structured.

---

[1] Wendell R. Garner, *Understanding Structure in Psychological Concepts* (New York: John Wiley & Sons, 1962), pp. 142 – 143.

An example of a self-embedded sentence is: "The man who said that a thief shot the housewife is a policeman." One sentence, "A thief shot the housewife," is embedded within another of the same grammatical form. This embedding follows a perfectly good structural rule in English. We do it all the time, perhaps intuitively, and without realizing it is a sound transformational rule.

There is no stated limit on embedding. It is possible to add a second embedding, a third, and so on; that such sentences are grammatically correct is indicated by the fact that they can be diagrammed just as any other sentence can be.

Let us embed "the watchdog chased" after "thief"; "the family borrowed" after "watchdog"; and wrap the entire bit inside the sentence, "It seems more certain than not." This is the interesting result: "It seems more certain that the man that said that a thief that the watchdog that the family borrowed chased shot the housewife is a policeman than not."

Signification meaning can be attached to each word, but there is a crumbling of the overall meaning when the reader comes to the string of verbs. Obviously the structure is at fault. One could find a better way to get across the information.

In information-processing terms, the structure puts too much of a strain on STM (short-term memory). One is forced, when one reaches the verb string, to attempt to fit each verb with the proper preceding information.

Structural Meaning

To get a better understanding of structural meaning in the typographic design we can profitably continue our typographic design-verbal language analogy. Let us consider the matter of syntax. Here are four words and their paraphrased dictionary meanings:

1. anesthetizes—renders insensible to pain, touch, and so on
2. doctor—a person licensed to practice medicine
3. patient—a person under a doctor's care
4. frightened—filled with fright; afraid

These words can be arranged in 24 different orders. Some make little or no sense, even though we understand the meaning of each word individually. Consider three possible orders:

frightened patient anesthetizes doctor
doctor anesthetizes frightened patient
patient anesthetizes frightened doctor

Meanings are changed according to the ordering of the words. The way in which words combine in various structurings to give meanings is called *syntax*. Words come from the vocabulary of the user of the verbal language.

14-1   Imaginary line suggests movement. Actual size: 10 inches high. (*Courtesy Red Carpet Inns of America*)

In Chapter 6 we spoke of visual syntax. The typography designer also has a vocabulary, from which he or she draws the various elements and arranges them syntactically to convey various meanings. Because we have grown up with it and are well experienced in the use of our verbal language, we can speak or write it with a high degree of competency in syntactical effect. To become effective in communicating graphically the typography designer must first become acquainted with the vocabulary of design. After that he or she should learn the principles involved in its use. Then it's a matter of practice, practice, and more practice.

Design Vocabulary

We have been drawing parallels between verbal language and visual language. Let us not forget, as pointed out in Chapter 6, that the visual cannot make conditional or logical statements. Its major function is to arouse the reader—to "tune him or her up" physiologically. But the visual form *is* a language, although primarily an "emotional" one. As a language it has a vocabulary, which consists of the elements of: point, line, shape, tone, and texture. Selection from these elements and the arrangement of them lead to the visual statement.

The Point   This structural element is both imaginary and real. Either way it is a reference to a position in space and holds a strong attraction for the eye. The optical center is an example of the imaginary point. Initial letters act as points. Leaders are actual points; so are large dots used to attract the eye.

The Line   The line, too, can be real as well as imaginary. It is real enough when it is used to delineate shape, as in a line drawing or in figures or the letters of the alphabet. Words and sentences in themselves form lines. The line, real or imagined, shows direction and movement. It does not exist in nature. We "see" it as a demarcation between adjoining tones.

The imaginary line is vital in planning the position of the elements in typographic design. Look at Figure 14-1. An imaginary line is "seen" that begins at the left end of the names of the couple and falls vertically past the woman's face to the edge of the line reading "Call Toll Free" and is actually seen in the post holding the "Master Hosts Inn" sign. This direction of the eye to positions where important verbal information can be found is purposeful and controllable within the syntax of visual communication.

14-2 Real lines suggest movement. (*Courtesy Dancer-Fitzgerald-Sample, Inc.*)

Real lines can accomplish the same mission. Note the purposeful direction of lines in the male model's clothing in Figure 14-2. The lines take the eye to the verbal areas at the bottom.

In the reference to Piet Mondrian in Chapter 6, we referred to his use of the line in the composition of visual elements. In Figure 14-3 is an example of an ad that shows the Mondrian effect with visible lines dividing the space.

This would suggest that the design space could be "gridded" with horizontal and vertical lines. Then, taking advantage of the fact that the eye moves left to right and top to bottom, the various elements could be so placed as to be seen in a certain order (syntax). This is done in Figure 14-3, in which the grid lines are visible. The ad in Figure 14-4 follows a grid structure but here the lines are only suggested. The grid structure is a common pattern in book and periodical design. You will see it in the magazine and newspaper design chapters.

14-3 Visible grid lines divide the space. (*Courtesy Pitney Bowes*)

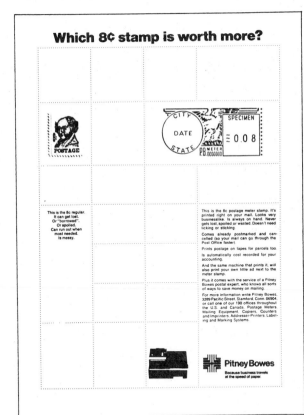

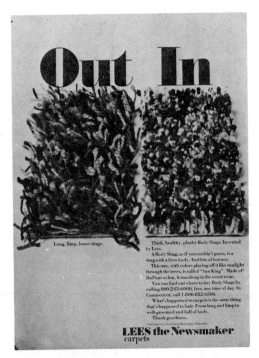

14-4 Imaginary grid lines dividing the space are strongly suggested. (*Courtesy Lees Carpets; agency: Doyle-Dane-Bernbach*)

The brain-computer naturally processes information in horizontal-vertical terms. We sense our "feet-on-the-ground" stability in this manner without always being conscious of the fact. We are upright (vertical), feet on the ground (horizontal). The use of lines capitalizes on this basic fact.

Shape   Lines articulate shapes. Shapes may also be defined as tone, texture, edges (regular-irregular), and size. Groups of words can form shapes. The block of small type at the bottom in Figure 14-2 is a rectangle. Squint at it so that the words are indistinguishable; you can then better sense its shape, weight, tone, and texture.

We impose on what we look at three basic shapes: square, circle, and triangle. There are endless variations of and combinations of these shapes and each shape psychologically suggests its own meaning. We call certain "dull" people (as we see them) "squares." We speak of the "love triangle." The circle suggests peace, protection, and safety.

Tone (or Value)   If it were not for tone, we would see nothing in the first place. The word "tone" refers to relative lightness or darkness. Only by this contrast do we visually sense points, lines, weight, and texture.

Our visual systems are set up to sense color, and that is what we see in nature. However, a black-and-white symbolization or representation—e.g., a black-and-white photograph—is perfectly acceptable and interpretable. One can change a color TV picture to black and white for instant and dramatic proof of this significant fact. Such a switch demonstrates the basic importance of tone to perception and consequently the acquiring of information. Relative lightness is called "value" whether one is speaking of chromatic (color) or achromatic (white) light. Thus, value is synonymous with tone in this discussion.

Texture   Any surface structure can be sensed visually as having texture. Thus we visually "feel." It is as natural to want to touch as it is to want to look. We referred to this in Chapter 6; texture is sensed not only in a block of type composition but in the surface of all shapes. An example: Figure 14-2. Why the man wears a corduroy coat is obvious.

Putting It All Together

Now that we know the elements of the designer's vocabulary, let us see how the designer puts them together to make a composition. If the finished work is to be an ad, the composition the designer draws will be called a *layout;* if it is a page in a newspaper or magazine, it is termed a *page dummy.* The complete compilation of all pages is referred to as a *dummy.*

In the following discussion of composition, we concentrate on layouts. Advertisers have been more active in researching the effects of composition than have printers or publishers. This is probably the result of the high cost of advertising space and the rough competition for attention the advertisers face. We use examples of magazine layout where they are particularly applicable. However, more treatment in detail is found in Chapter 15.

Basically, the design task starts with arrangement of the four components of printed communication: (1) text type; (2) display type; (3) illustrations; (4) white space. The end result must be a unified entity, reflecting the principles of sound design.

White space can be, like silence, golden when properly used. Its interplay with the more "tangible" components can be counterpart to the pause for effect. White space should be moved to the outside; if allowed to appear in the center of a layout, like a tornado, it scatters the "tangibles" in all directions and the reader cannot sense the unity and simplicity of the presentation.

Kinds of Layout   The laying-out or ordering process puts the elements of vocabulary into a composition that, through syntax, delivers an effective message (transfer of meanings). Therefore, it must be carefully planned. The first step, *visualization,* is a thinking process from which come such decisions as

1. The ideas (content) the symbols (verbal and graphic) represent.
2. The number of elements to be used.
3. The relative importance of the information-bearing elements.
4. The order of presentation; this is what syntax is all about.

These decisions are influenced by the kind of product being advertised, the nature of the consumer, and the degree of the consumer's interest in and relationship to the product. The designer must know these things, for they affect the composition.

There are three kinds of layout, classified according to the care used in drawing them. This care is directly related to the purpose of each of the three kinds. They are: the *miniature* or *thumbnail sketch,* often made to aid in visualization; the *rough;* and the *comprehensive.*

The miniature   This simplest of designs can be any size. It is generally smaller than the full-size, printed image, but it is usually proportional to it.

Miniatures have three advantages:

1. They are an economical way of testing the visual syntax.
2. Because they can be done quickly, the designer is free to try several approaches, discarding those he or she does not like. Working full-scale would expend precious time and energy, perhaps leading to a hesitancy to discard a bad try.
3. The working of miniatures begets new ideas. The first and second sketches may miss the mark, but they warm up the creative, problem-solving process, leading to a flow of more productive ideas.

There is a strong parallel between editing verbal copy and visual copy. Experimenting with miniatures is really editing—defining and redefining the syntax and grammar of the visual statement.

In Figure 14-5 are minatures of the ad seen in Figure 14-1. There are definite means of indicating the various elements in a miniature. Comparing the three figures you can see how the elements are represented. Note the treatment of headlines, illustrations, body type, and the logotype or signature. Note that the weights of the units are roughly equivalent. The weight of the elements is influenced by relative size, shape, and tone. Miniatures can be prepared with any degree of finish. The first example is drawn roughly. Figure 14-5 also shows the next stage: a miniature done with reasonable care.

The rough layout   The miniature selected as best is redrawn as a rough, which is a full-size layout (Figure 14-6). This is more utilitarian than experimental. Several drafts of a rough may be called for to take care of revisions and changes. The final rough bears a close resemblance to the printed ad. Headlines are lettered in to approximate their printed form. Illustrations are often hastily sketched. The position of the elements is precise enough to allow the compositor to work from a rough in composing

14-5 *Left:* Rough miniature of the ad in Figure 14-1. *Right:* More precise miniature of the same ad.

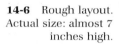
14-6 Rough layout. Actual size: almost 7 inches high.

and making up the ad. In effect, the rough could be a "blueprint" for construction.

Designing layouts is simplified by the proper equipment. The best paper is a transparent bond known as *layout* paper, although a tough tracing paper will also do nicely. A drawing board is a desirable work surface; a T-square and triangle facilitate accuracy. Also needed are at least three black pencils—a 2H for light lines, a 2B for heavier lines, and a 6B for broader, heavier strokes. An Ebony pencil is also handy. A sandpaper pad is useful for shaping the leads to fit the kind of stroke you are using. Colored pencils are useful in rendering color roughs. You may want to use the colored, wide felt pens for laying down colors in larger areas.

The beginner should learn early in the game to draw type faces in display sizes. Rule three light guidelines to indicate the x-height and the top of caps. Then lay the paper over printed specimens and trace. Be sure you make heavy enough strokes to suggest the proper density of letters in print. You will be surprised how quickly you can get the "feel" of display lettering. And (would you believe?) it won't be long before you can draw guides and simulate letters without the specimen crutch. All it takes is practice. Music students practice. Typographers should, too. Your practice will reward you with unexpected proficiency.

The comprehensive layout

The so-called *comp* is very exact, rendered to show how the layout will look in print. Illustrations imitate their finished look and heads are precisely lettered in. Body type is usually ruled in. A type comp is drawn with proofs of type pasted in position so that the sponsor can get a still better representation of how the ad will look than is afforded by a rough.

The comp should not be confused with the mechanical. The latter is copy to be "looked at" by a camera, while the comp is viewed by the person responsible for approving the final appearance of the printed material.

Design Principles

The term "style" as applied to the use of language, refers to how one puts thoughts into words. If we say of a writer, "He has no style," we mean we do not like how the writer says it. The writer's thoughts are not distinctive, and are expressed poorly. "Style," however, can be more broadly applied. According to the dictionary, it refers to distinction and excellence in any artistic or literary expression. So here it refers to design principles.

There are standards of style in layout as well as in writing. In this section we examine these standards—design principles—in turn: contrast, balance, proportion, rhythm, harmony, movement, and unity. It would be convenient to say that these standards are listed here in order of importance. This can hardly be done, however, because they are interactive, as you will understand when we discuss them.

The nervous excitation that takes place in the brain becomes a part of the visual design when we look at it. A simple do-it-yourself experiment will make this clear. Draw two parallel lines on a piece of paper, $\frac{3}{4}$ inch apart and $2\frac{1}{2}$ inches long. Put a dot midway of their length and their distance apart. Draw straight lines fanning out from the dot as in Figure 14-7. Be sure these lines extend an inch or so beyond your parallel lines.

Now look at your drawing as you would look at railroad tracks below you. Your parallel lines no longer look straight but bowed. Are they, really?

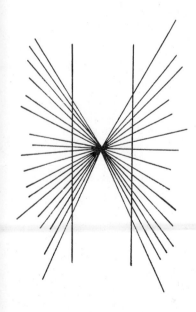

14-7 What the eyes see excites the brain.

Look at Figure 14-8. The two dark rectangles are $\frac{3}{8}$ inch apart. They seem to belong together. Now look at the right part of the same figure. The two rectangles are repeated, still $\frac{3}{8}$ inch apart. But next to each at a distance of $\frac{1}{8}$ inch is another, same sized, dark rectangle. The original two rectangles no longer seem to belong together. What happened?

14-8 *Left:* The two rectangles belong together. *Right:* The two rectangles pulled apart.

The various layout elements interact. We feel these changes and call them *attractions*. Attraction refers to the "pull" resulting from these energy effects we project into the image. It is thus possible to attract the eye. But attention differs from attraction. This is more than a matter of semantics or verbal nit-picking.

Attention comes after attraction—maybe only a few milliseconds after, but *after*. This idea is compatible with processing theory. Attention involves assigning meaning to what attracts. Perhaps an ad is merely intended to remind. The product is shown in large size, the verbal message is minimal, and meaning is quickly attached. This is the typical task of a poster or billboard. Simple ads of this nature in periodicals are often called *poster ads.*

On the other hand, some ads must do more of a selling job. Do you recall the discourse about concept formation? Before the reader can develop a sound brand concept—that is, discover its meaning—he or she must learn its positive instances or defining features, as we labeled them in Chapter 2. Such an ad attempts to do this. More points of attraction must be placed in the ad. More attention is necessary, and the reader must be held longer to learn the concept(s) involved.

Contrast In any form of communication some materials (ideas) must be stressed more than others. The selection of these is a part of planning or visualization.

Contrast is the source of all meaning. Where is the understanding of "high" without the concept of "not high" or "low"? Contrast is, in fact, the only reason we see at all and explains why "see" may serve as a synonym for "understand."

In Figure 14-9 there is masterful use of contrast, the designer's most potent tool for bringing meaning into sharp focus. Read the headline. There is a subtle contrast in meaning. The two steaks have been broiled, yet they still have their price tags—contrast because it is unexpected. The one on the left is a more expensive cut; the one on the right is less expensive, according to the tags—contrast again,

IF YOU DON'T MIND PAYING LESS, YOU CAN GET A BETTER STEAK.

Some people still judge things by their price tags. If it costs more, they reason, it must be worth more.

To which Adolph's says, "Nonsense!"

Especially when it comes to steaks. Because the less-expensive cuts, like round steak, flank steak and sirloin tip steak are just as nutritious as the costly ones. They have a richer, beefier flavor. They have less fat, usually less bone. More protein, fewer calories. Pound-for-pound, they're a better value for your money.

In fact, the only thing they lack is natural tenderness.

And that's where Adolph's Instant Meat Tenderizer comes in. Use Adolph's on those less-expensive cuts and you can broil or barbecue a round steak to taste as tender and juicy as a porterhouse. You can barbecue a flank or sirloin tip steak deliciously tender enough to serve company.

And if you'd like to vary your menu, use Adolph's 15-Minute Meat Marinade instead. Then you can have the deep-down flavor and juicy tenderness of a delicious gourmet meal. And have it quickly too. Because Adolph's has taken the time and trouble out of marinating. It works in just 15 minutes!

So, next barbecue time, remember: If you don't mind paying less, you can get a better steak.

14-9 Contrast skillfully manipulated. (*Courtesy Chesebrough-Pond's Inc.*)

through a subtle visual treatment. Who would not read the text after this invitation? The copy continues the contrast—less expensive cuts are as nutritious and have fewer calories and less bone; all they lack is tenderness and the product takes care of this problem.

Contrast can be achieved by applying polarities of size, shape, tone, texture, and direction. We use the term "polarity" advisedly. Hot-cold, high-low, and so on, represent polarities in meaning. In physical science, the term refers to contrary powers, and we are speaking in terms of physiological energy.

Contrast in size On the left of Figure 14-10 is a layout showing illustration and text of approximately equal size. On the right, the presentation is livelier because a dominant illustration supplies contrast.

14-10 *Left:* Monotony of sizes. *Right:* Liveliness increased by dominating illustration.

14-11 *Left:* Monotony of shapes. *Right:* Attraction enhanced by one irregular shape.

Contrast in shape Although sizes contrast satisfactorily in Figure 14-11, a monotony of shapes exists. Attraction is enhanced on the right by the irregular shape. Note we speak of attraction, not attention.

14-12 *Left:* Monotony of tones. *Right:* Attention assured by contrast.

Contrast in tone

The dullness on the left in Figure 14-12 is brightened by tonal accent on the right. The headline at the top has greater attraction. The package has greater attraction. If the reader already knows what it is, it will have greater attention because of his or her earlier experience with it.

Tone is also associated with color. Look at Figure 14-13. The first pin on the left was blue in the original ad. So were the pin that is tipped forward and the ball on the left. The eye follows these tones, first pin to fifth pin, then back to the ball, which lines up with the copy below. It is also interesting to note that these three items form an inverted triangle pointing at the copy. An accidental arrangement? Hardly!

14-13 Color tones can be used to direct eye movement. (*Courtesy Fisher-Price Toys*)

Fisher-Price Bowling

Here's bowling—simplified, speeded up and very satisfying for young children. No instructions, either. When a ball hits the center pin, all the pins tip over.

And it's a strike! And because all five are permanently attached to the central axis, there are no loose pins to pick up.

Sliding counters from 1 to 10 let them keep score their own way. Two plastic balls store in ball rack.

©1973 Fisher-Price Toys, East Aurora, New York 14052. Division of The Quaker Oats Company.

Contrast in texture Look again at Figure 14-2. The contrast of the textures of his coat and her blouse serves an obvious purpose.

Contrast in direction The major aim in contrasting direction is to guide the reader's eye through the message. Figure 14-2 shows this. The horizontal headline is in contrast to the vertical models, backed up by the vertical lines in the man's garb.

Balance Balance exists when the elements are placed with a sense of equipoise or equilibrium. That is, the weights of the elements counteract so that they seem settled where they are placed. The weight of an element is the result of its size, shape, and tone. Large elements, the other factors being equal, appear heavier. Irregular shapes bear greater weight than regular shapes. Dark elements outweigh light ones, though a small, dark element can appear heavier than a larger but lighter mass.

We have already discussed the two kinds of balance: symmetrical and asymmetrical, mainly with respect to the placement of type elements. Let us consider again the asymmetrical, but now involving the placement of graphic as well as type elements.

To hold a seesaw in balance, the heavier of two children must sit nearer the fulcrum than the lighter child. Weight times distance on

14-14 Two ways to place two units in balance.

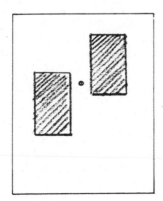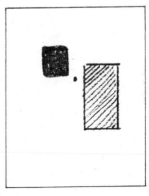

14-15 Proper placement of more than two units.

one side must equal weight times distance on the other side to achieve balance.

The same principle is at work in layouts. The optical center becomes the fulcrum. Figure 14-14 shows two similar weight units as elements in asymmetrical balance and Figure 14-15 demonstrates the proper placement of more than two elements. Figures 14-1 and 14-2 show asymmetrical balance in actual ads.

A major difference between the two kinds of balance lies in the use of white space. It is passive in the symmetrically balanced design. In the asymmetric, on the other hand, this space becomes an active part of the visual presentation. Thus, the layout becomes more exciting and dynamic, offering various points of attraction.

Symmetric balance—or perhaps balance with only minor variations—is found oftener than you might think. Skim through several national women's magazines. The standard content of large illustration, headline, copy block, and signature is not uncommon. Why should this be so in this highly competitive age? As you recall, the reader can process information in only limited amounts. If the ad is too complex, a stimulus overload could result. It is better, such advertisers reason, to subdue form and concentrate on getting across a few major points. Context is an aid to processing. The reader in the women's magazine is within a context compatible with the message in such an ad.

Proportion   The range of visual stimulation approaches 180 degrees. However, one can focus on details only within about 3 degrees. Thus the eye moves in jumps over a layout. The calculating brain is constantly comparing the new information with the old in STM. Since contrast is the source of meaning, there is a constant measuring process going on. Compositional forces are being measured. This is larger than that; that is darker than this; that texture is smoother than this; and so on.

Proportion represents the results of the reader's decision making. It refers to the relationship of one element to another or to the design as a whole in ratios reflecting size and strength.

Certain proportions are more attractive to the eye than others. The first task in layout is to select the size of the ad or its dimensions. A similar task exists in book work except that page or sheet size is predetermined.

Attractive dimensions are those in which the relationship of width to height is not obvious to the eye. Thus, a square layout, with dimensions of 1 to 1, is less attractive. Proportions of 2 to 1 are too easily detected and are to be avoided. Proportions close to 1 to 1 or 2 to 1 are weak because of their proximity to those just mentioned. Because they are less obvious, 3 to 1 dimensions are better. This applies to element relationships involving tones, weight, size, and so on, as well as to ad dimensions.

Among the more interesting ratios are those evolving from the golden mean summation series: 2 :3 :5 :8 :13 :21 and so on. Can you determine what number would follow 21? These suggest continuing ratios—2 :3 ::3 :5; 3 :5 ::5 :8; and so on. As you learned in high school algebra, "The product of the means equals the product of the extremes?" Thus 2×5 should equal 3×3. However, there is an error of 1 and it continues through the series, probably the result of Greek mathematicians' dislike of fractions.

Several things are of interest here. The 2:3 ratio is common in nature. For example, spirals in one direction on pineapples are in this ratio to spirals running in the opposite direction. The same ratio is found in flower petal arrays. To mathematicians these are known as logarithmic spirals, which evolve through growth and development in nature. As the summation series expands it exhibits a rhythmic pattern, suggesting the subtle interrelationship between proportion and rhythm. It is also interesting that the eye finds a point in blank space, the optical center, three-fifths from the bottom.

We suggest these things only to indicate that there is a beautiful logic in the design of the printed message, just as there is in all nature. Art is, after all, a reflection of order in the universe, a means of "telling it like it is."

There is an elegant contrast between a square and a so-called golden mean rectangle, the proportions of which are approximately 3:2. This contrast was common in Greek architecture. It is seen in an application in Figure 14-16 to the design of an annual report. The rectangular notch is approximately a 3:2 shape in contrast to the near-square shape of the large halftone. The eye calculatingly finds a match to the small shape on the right-hand page.

14-16 The approximate 3:2 notch contrasts with the near square shape of the large halftone. The notch-size halftone on the right-hand page strongly attracts attention. (*Courtesy Columbia Gas System*)

participated in the drilling of 27 exploration and 48 development wells. Fifty-three of the wells are considered to be commercial.

Columbia owns 102 billion cubic feet of proven Canadian gas reserves. In addition, Columbia has a call (subject to Canadian export approval) on 2,125 billion cubic feet of additional reserves primarily in the Arctic Islands. The company holds an interest in approximately 37 million gross acres and 4 million net acres of oil and gas leases in Canada.

The new Kotaneelee gas field discovered last year in the Yukon Territory is expected to begin production early in 1979. Initial gas sales will be on an annual basis to Westcoast Transmission Company, Ltd. Columbia is the operator and has a 22% ownership interest in the field.

During 1978, Columbia and Chevron Standard Limited entered into a joint exploratory agreement involving an expenditure of $30 million (Canadian), primarily in Canadian frontier lands. The first well under this program was drilled offshore Labrador last summer and resulted in a gas discovery. Additional drilling will be required to evaluate the discovery. The second exploratory venture under the Chevron agreement is the drilling of a well at Northeast Banks Island in the Canadian Arctic Islands.

Gas Distribution Operations

As noted earlier, Columbia's seven affiliated retail distribution companies are preparing to take on new customers for the first time in more than six years. Early in 1979, applications will be filed with individual state regulatory agencies to end the sales moratoriums necessitated by declining gas supplies in the early 1970's.

During the year, the distribution companies strengthened their communications programs. A high level of conservation information activity was maintained, including a special program in the fall to focus the attention of customers on the energy efficient qualities of modern gas appliances.

Efforts were continued to aid customers in dealing with the impact of heating bills during the winter, utilizing a budget payment plan and direct consultation with individual customers when appropriate. The budget payment plan is used by more than 660,000 customers to spread gas costs evenly over a 12-month period.

Propane Marketing

Propane service provided by Columbia Hydrocarbon Corporation (Hydrocarbon) was extended in 1978 to secure more potential customers for the Columbia distribution companies when those units are able to take on new customers. A special promotional program was directed toward new residential developments and about 1,200 homes in twenty different areas were equipped to use propane instead of other fuels. These developments are all piped with distribution systems sized for natural gas and served with propane provided from a central storage system. This will facilitate their ultimate conversion to natural gas.

Hydrocarbon also added about two hundred additional propane commercial accounts with an annual requirement equivalent to 180 million cubic feet of natural gas. It continues to provide propane to industries to supplement their available natural gas or to fuel processes in plants where natural gas is unavailable.

Propane sales in 1978 totaled 78 million gallons, providing the heating equivalent of seven billion cubic feet of natural gas.

Research And Development

Columbia maintained a broad research and development program in 1978, both through support of projects being conducted by outside organizations and by its own activities directed from System laboratories in Columbus, Ohio. Emphasis continues to be placed on better ways to locate and develop new gas supplies.

Gas Research Institute: The Gas Research Institute (GRI) became fully operational in 1978 as a cooperative industry research funding organiza-

Left: New residential gas customers are supplied with propane from a remote central storage facility until natural gas service is available.

9

Rhythm   Rhythm is achieved through the orderly repetition of any element—line, shape, tone, texture. The eye will spot rhythm and follow its pattern. Rhythm is thus a vital force in movement. That was seen in Figure 14-16 where the blue tones carried the eye to the apex of the triangle pointing to the copy block.

Rhythm interacts with proportion, as noted earlier. It is, like proportion, a manifestation of growth and development in nature. Look in a dictionary or encyclopedia for illustrations of snowflakes. Here you will find rhythm and proportion beautifully expressed. You will also find the other standards for judging effective design: contrast, balance, harmony, movement, and unity.

Note the rhythm of the six rectangles in Figure 14-17. The ad, printed in full color, carried skin tones and dark brown backgrounds

14-17 Contrasting shapes and rhythm in color and tones skillfully matched to message intent. (*Reproduced by permission of The Procter & Gamble Company*)

in all six rectangles. Note the subtle juxtapositioning of the numerals 1 and 2 in the squares versus the numerals in the bottom two rectangles.

Harmony

It was previously stated that meaning lies in polarity—hot vs. cold; high vs. low; and so on. Harmony and contrast are bipolar. This would seem to be a contradiction, for how can both be standards for evaluating a layout? The answer comes from processing theory. To find order and reduce uncertainty seems to be a basic force in human nature. Human beings are programmed to seek understanding. What would we be, where would we be if we were in a perfect state of balance, if all sensations were harmonious, and if we understood everything? Impossible, for contrast is the source of understanding.

Harmony exists in the mutual characteristics of the elements' tone, shape, size, texture. A book page printed in one face—with variations in sizes and weights, the use of italic for folios and headings, and borders and decorative devices matching the weight and design of the type—is a good example. The principle is clearly evident in the design of this text. Only one type, Zapf Book, is used throughout (see Appendix B).

Complete harmony is passive. Contrast, on the other hand, is active and vigorous. It produces emphasis and dynamic movement. It relieves monotony.

Movement

The very act of reading produces a sense of movement, even in the most prosaic, formally balanced presentation. The eye moves from left to right and from top to bottom. In other types of design, the control of eye movement becomes more of a problem. Inasmuch as the entire message is present at the same time (not true of TV or radio), the reader is free to look at any given point at any time. If the message is to be a cohesive whole, this must be discouraged. Manipulation of the elements—the syntax and grammar of design—is the means of eye movement control. The basic question in applying this standard is: "Does the movement that exists in the design carry the eye in the directions required by the content?"

Unity

It has been shown in a number of tests that although the gist of a well-presented visual message may be remembered, the details of the message may not easily be recalled. Establishing the theme is the plus that unity should give to the message. The Adolph's ad, Figure 14-11, did an excellent job of establishing the theme: Tenderize less expensive cuts and they will equal the costly cuts.

The individual elements of the message must relate to each other and to the total design so that they effect coherence. Without this unity an ad cannot register a single, overall impression. In the left of

Figure 14-18 five rectangles are placed at random. In contrast to this confusion is the orderliness in the right-hand sketch in which the five rectangles are divided into two groups, one of three units, the other of two. A layout that lacks unity is likely to "fly apart." The beginner should remember to relegate white space to the outside rather than to allow liberal amounts to fall among the elements of the ad.

14-18 *Left:* Lack of unity. *Right:* Orderliness achieved through grouping.

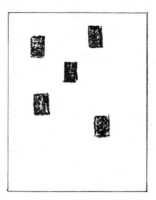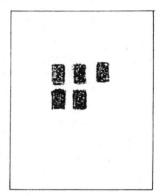

Making Design Articulate

Structural relationships among elements in the layout should be accommodated to (1) the sequence of eye movements and (2) the order of absorbing the information the source hopes to impart. The latter is the prime function of form.

What we are considering here is organizing the elements. Organization presupposes a process of indicating to the reader (1) how some elements are related; (2) how others are different in their functions; and (3) which elements are most important in their function.

Eye Movement The designer may devote considerable time to individual parts of his or her effort, but the reader tends to scan the total layout for an overall impression. After that, assuming that points of attraction engender attention, the designer may devote some time to details.

Thus it becomes important to consider the eye-movement tendencies of the reader as he or she scans a page, a spread of pages, or an ad. These tendencies have been revealed through laboratory experiments using the eye camera, with the following conclusions:

1. The eye tends, after leaving the initial fixation, to move to the left and upward.
2. The exploratory coverage of the space is from this point in a clockwise direction.
3. The eye prefers horizontal movement.

4. The left position is preferred to the right and the top position is preferred to the bottom. Thus the four quadrants of a space might be given communication values from 1 to 4 in descending order as shown in Figure 14-19.

Figure 14-20 illustrates what we have said about eye-movement tendencies. Point 1 represents the initial fixation, *usually* at the optical center. The clockwise path from 2 through 3 is exploratory. Conceivably the eye may leave the space at 4(?) and move out of it.

14-19 *Right:* Communicative value of layout space decreases from quadrant 1 to quadrant 4.

14-20 *Far right:* Eye movement tendencies, beginning at point 1.

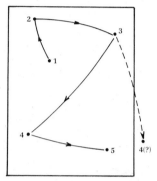

The fact that these have been labeled "tendencies" means that this is not necessarily the path the eye will follow. The designer can influence the direction by the proper placement of elements. But if the eye is to be drawn to points 4 and 5 it is important that they involve content of interest to the reader.

If you will analyze a number of ads in several different printed media, you will notice that some are primarily illustrative with little verbal copy, whereas others are structured to highlight copy.

Copy should tend to be longer when the product is of exceptional interest because it is new or offers new features, when the need is more immediate, or when the product is technical in nature. An advertiser who is trying to solicit orders or convince nonusers of the product's merit is also likely to use longer copy. Copy is often shorter if the ad is a reminder, primarily reaffirming favorable attitudes, or if the product is of low inherent interest.

Admittedly these ideas are oversimplified. Their purpose is to point up the fact that the designer must consider the nature of the proposition and reader interests before he or she begins to work.

Indicating Element Relationships

We have already indicated how elements can be associated by means of real and imaginary lines. Several other techniques are available, including (1) similar shapes, (2) similar tones, (3) similar size, (4) similar texture, and (5) enclosure in a portion of the ad by the use of borders, tints, reverses, and so on.

In Figure 14-17, most of these techniques are used. The question asked in the headline is the "hook" for getting reader interest. The four large rectangles emphasize the question. The answer is in the small rectangles. Sizes in the "question rectangles" are similar; sizes in the "answer rectangles" are similar. Tones and texture are similar in all six. All are interrelated through logical alignment. Note the subtle matching of numbers and ages in the answer rectangles in a sort of counterpoint. The reader can readily find examples of the fifth technique in the list.

Indicating Element Differentiation

If the need for relating elements exists, then means are needed for disassociating them. This is necessary in the interest of function. Differences can be made through shape, tone, size, texture, and by separating similar elements and differentiated elements with two enclosure techniques.

In Figure 14-17 the small rectangles were similar to the large ones and at the same time differentiated. It is through such subtle interplay that the designer manipulates visual forces for maximum effort.

Controlling Amount of Information

Consider the following facts: the eye quickly scans the entire presentation, searching for points of interest; the capacity of STM, where points of interest are stored until they can be brought together in the total "visual image" is low; the output (decision-making) capacity of the IPS is relatively slow. Moreover, readers have only a limited amount of time available for looking in this day of vast competition for their attention.

Here is a rationale for clean-cut simplicity. The number of visual elements should be held to a bare minimum. The way in which these elements are handled should lead to the tightest possible organization.

Look through ads in national magazines. Photographs of products are so treated that extraneous, distracting information is controlled. Perhaps the product is outlined—that is, it is shown alone. Not only does this focus interest but it offers the designer an irregular shape (nonrectangular) with which to work. Perhaps the product is shown in a square-finish illustration, but the background is plain, and either light or dark, thereby eliminating distraction; or the background may contain detail, but it is subdued or in softer focus than the product.

Newspapers offer numerous examples of techniques that are useful in presenting large numbers of elements, particularly in large department and discount store ads. The grid method or the enclosure of individual items to effect a sectionalizing of the total ad are the only feasible means.

There are occasions when reproductions of photographs do not give enough information. Perhaps vital details cannot be clearly seen

14-21 A few basic lines can deliver a message.

and are ambiguous. In such cases the photograph, before printing, is specially treated by an artist who *retouches* it—paints it with the necessary colors and values to bring out the details.

There are even occasions when photographs give too much information. The answer may well lie in the use of line drawings, which function in much the same way that poetry does verbally. Both involve the use of highly abstracted information and state a message much more indirectly. The same message, if stated in full detail or directly, would lose its simplicity and thereby its effectiveness. Figure 14-21, with a few simple lines, is capable of conveying a feeling of puzzlement and concern. The nose is only suggested and the eyes are missing. The viewer "sees" them, however, and knows from experience they are there.

In Figure 14-22 simple line drawings detail construction features that become much easier to visualize.

14-22 Simple line drawings make construction features easy to visualize. (*Courtesy E. H. Titchener and Company*)

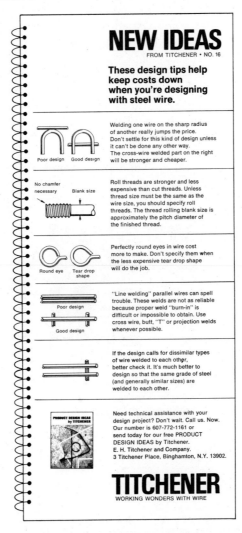

Pie charts, bar graphs, and line charts, as mentioned in Chapter 10, are effective means of summarizing information into visual form. Often their visual effectiveness can be enhanced by adding simple illustration to them, in effect creating *pictographs.* For example, rising prices might be indicated by high flying kites, with dollar signs on them. The pie chart might become a silver dollar or a bill cut into sections.

Handling Illustrations

The design of the printed piece starts with decisions concerning the handling of illustrations and headlines. This is in large degree the result of the effects of newspaper, magazine, and television practice. Newspapers, in an effort to communicate quickly and efficiently, have developed the technique of giving the gist of the story in the headline, picture, and first few paragraphs. Magazines, reaching more selective readers and being produced under less pressure of time, have refined the basic newspaper formula and applied it to full pages and spreads. In a short span, using the picture as the basic component, supplemented by a concise verbal message, the TV commercial develops a basic concept with strong impact and dynamic movement.

It is usually best to begin the arrangement of the elements within a given space by the placing of illustrations. This is not necessarily because they are more important, but because the designer has greater latitude in placing headlines and subheads. Furthermore, through contrast with other visual elements, illustrations play a major role in attraction.

If only one illustration is used, it can carry strong visual impact if it dominates the page. Additional emphasis can be given through

14-23 *Right:* One large illustration dominates.

14-24 *Far right:* Several illustrations treated as one large irregular shape.

bleeding one or more of its edges. A smaller illustration can be given added impact by surrounding it with extensive white space. Two illustrations can be sized equally and placed together and treated as a unit. Or they can be sized and shaped differently and placed in balance.

The problem of arranging several illustrations is somewhat more complex. One technique in solving the problem is to size illustrations equally and treat them as a unit. Another is to organize them into two or three groups and place them in balance. Both methods can be seen in Figure 14-17. A third technique calls for sizing one illustration much larger than others and using it as the focal point of interest. The illustration selected should emphasize the message and the interests of the reader. This is shown in Figure 14-23. It is also sometimes possible to gather several illustrations of unequal sizes into a group so that they appear as one single, irregular shape, as shown in Figure 14-24.

Handling Headlines The headline is the most important of all printed elements that vie for the reader's attention. But even when a headline is not used—for example, in books or newspaper classified ads—chapter headings and classification titles serve a similar function by attracting the reader to the text of the message.

Nor are headlines always used in competitive reading matter, such as display ads, but when they are not used in such cases, the interest of the reader must be sufficient to bridge the gap and carry the reader from illustration to message.

In a broad sense headlines serve two functions: (1) they summarize or directly suggest the content of the message, or (2) they appeal primarily to a basic reader interest after which an attempt is made to present the source's message. The two headline categories can be classified as *direct* and *indirect*.

Direct heads are found on newspaper and magazine editorial pages. They are also found in advertisements when the reader's interest in the product or proposition is considered sufficient to carry him or her on to the message after the reader receives his cue from the headline.

Often the designer considers the indirect head more effective, as in Figure 14-25. Note that the illustration involves the product but the head does not. In many ads neither head nor illustration relates to the proposition.

The headline is considered the most important element in competitive matter because seldom can the illustration alone complete the contact with the reader's interests. Illustrations may attract but they may be individually interpreted. Words are more consensual in meaning and are therefore more effective in completing the attraction-attention function.

14-25 Indirect head-line. (*Courtesy Dow Chemical Company*)

A number of headline treatments were discussed in Chapter 6 and are pertinent within the context of this section. One matter remains for consideration here—positioning the headline.

The word "headline" suggests that this element should appear at the top of an editorial page or an advertisement. At one time this placement was common, but today more imaginative treatments are used. Even so, top placement is still widely used.

The student would do well to examine as many publications and ads as possible to analyze headline placement. For example, the main reason for varying the placement on editorial pages in magazines is to relieve the monotony that develops as the reader finds page after page with the headline at the top. How does the designer achieve this variation? The range of possibilities is limited only by his or her imagination. A wide search will reveal many interesting treatments.

Head placement in ads is somewhat more complex. Variation cannot be introduced simply to relieve monotony. Other considerations are involved. The importance of the head relative to the body copy will have a great deal to do with its placement. If the effectiveness of the ad depends on the readership of the text, the head must be so worded and placed as to carry the reader's eye from the initial point of attraction to the copy.

A common presentation to this end uses a dominant illustration with head immediately below, followed by the text. It is a format to which readers are accustomed. Placement of the head above a large illustration is also common. However, in this case, the head must be of sufficient type size to capture the reader's eye and compete effectively with the attraction power of the illustration. This can be seen in Figure 14-17.

Often the designer's task is to see to it that the headline, the major illustration, and the signature or a picture of the product be seen at a glance. When this is the objective, the text is very short or may not exist at all. This is true with reminder ads. Under these conditions the position of the head relative to the text becomes less significant than its relationship to the major attraction-attention illustration. Often head and package are combined with the major illustration to assure that the reader can grasp all the vital points of the message with minimum effort.

In Figure 14-9 we saw an ad that is of a completely opposite nature. The headline is integrated into the relatively long text to achieve that desired unity. The text—and its persuasive power—is considered more important than in the case of a reminder ad.

An advertisement is a single thing—a single communication—a transfer of meaning or a concept. The ad must thus present a unified impression. It can do so via large illustration and headline, or it may invite the reader to delve into the text.

15 Principles of Magazine Layout

From the standpoint of both design and content, magazines are a hybrid form of periodical. They have some of the characteristics of newspapers, and in some cases actually are purveyors of news. But on the other hand they have a quality and a lasting value that would make them more closely akin to books. In fact, the common term for magazines among the professionals who design and produce them is *book*. Then, too, magazines resemble advertising in that great attention is given to their visual appeal, and they can, as in the case of house organs (public-relations magazines), go so far as to have basic goals resembling those of advertising.

This multicharacter aspect of magazines is illustrated in Figures 15-1 to 15-4: the newsmagazine employs standardized headlines in newspaper fashion; the scholarly magazine is in traditional book format; the public relations and consumer magazines have a flair that comes only from the application of special attention and artistic design principles that are characteristic of advertising. These differences point to a first principle for magazine design: A magazine's appearance should be functionally suitable to its basic editorial goals.

15-1 Newsmagazines often use basic newspaper headlines to attract readers to articles or departments. (*Courtesy* Editor & Publisher)

15-2 Scholarly magazines often look just like books. (*Courtesy* Journalism Quarterly)

15-3 Some of the best magazine design is done for public relations magazines. (*Courtesy* Texaco Star)

15-4 Consumer magazines usually are designed with obvious flair and sophistication; they attract some of the most talented art directors. (*Reprinted by permission of* Travel/Holiday; © *1973* Travel Magazine, Inc.)

The magazine that deals in spot news should look different from the one that is concerned only with abstract concepts, and the one that is headed for a scholar's bookshelf can be radically different from a magazine headed for a homemaker's coffee table.

But even within each of the many categories of magazines there are and should be substantial differences. Each individual magazine develops a character of its own, and physical appearance is a primary factor of that character. Magazines tend to take on human characteristics in the minds of their preparers and their readers. Editors become very sentimental about their books; one would think to hear them talk that their subject is their own child rather than a magazine. And many readers look forward to their favorite magazine as if it were a friend stopping in for a weekly or monthly visit for coffee and conversation. The layout of a magazine must, therefore, take into account the specific personality and character that its readers perceive it to have. The principle that magazine design must relate to a magazine's basic editorial role and to its own individual character serves as a foundation pillar for our discussion of magazine layout.

One other point relating to the impact of graphics on magazines must be made here. Visual appearance has been extremely important to magazines throughout most of their history. In the years since the advent of television, however, design has become increasingly valuable. Experimentation, some of it wild and bizarre, characterized some of the general consumer magazines as they entered their death throes in the 1960s and early 1970s. In these cases, it seemed that publishers were calling on graphics to be the life preserver for their drowning magazines. Although the rescue attempts didn't work, the effort did put still more emphasis on magazine design.

The importance of layout for magazines is reflected in their staffing. Immediately following the editor, the first person listed in the masthead is usually the art director whose responsibility is the design and layout of a magazine. For many magazines, the art director and editor work as virtually coequal partners. The art director creates the physical external personality of the magazine, whereas the editor molds the "spiritual," internal character of the magazine. Obviously, both must work with full mutual knowledge and cooperation.

Volumes have been written about magazine layout and design, and this one chapter cannot present a depth discussion of that subject. In the space we have here we can, however, give some basic principles and relate the essentials of communication theory and basic design to magazine layout so that journalism students, whether future newspaper reporters or magazine designers, can understand the "why" behind the skilled output of professionals.

The First Step: Break-of-the-Book _____

The layout of a magazine actually begins with an editorial job called *breaking the book.* This task involves the allocation of the total amount of space among the ads, articles, departments, and other editorial material that is planned for the issue.

Because advertising determines the existence of a magazine, it is usually placed first, with consideration allowed for editorial-department needs. Although advertisers may request, pay for, and get special position, they are vitally concerned with the success of the editorial portions. As a matter of fact, their requests are often in connection with placement at or near certain portions of a magazine. Cooperation between business and editorial offices negates difficulties arising from advertising placement. It is common practice for the ads to be located front and back with the center reserved for the main editorial section.

One of the minor layout problems associated with this practice is to alert the reader to the beginning of the content. The reproduction of the name plate is often used on the first editorial page to signal the reader.

Several studies have shown that a large percentage of readers peruse a magazine backwards. (This can be checked in a classroom survey.) Some magazines have, therefore, found it expedient to place some strong features as complete single-page units at the end of the editorial section. These serve as a starting point for the "backward" readers.

As the main editorial section developes, the pace should change frequently. Long articles should not be lumped together but should be relieved by single or fractional page articles.

Although the ads are placed first, the breaking of the book is primarily the responsibility of an editor; he or she is the one to make space decisions for editorial content.

But as the editor decides which articles get only one page and which get more, or which pages will get special color treatment and which will not, he must be aware of some basic production requirements.

These requirements stem from the fact that magazines are printed on large sheets of paper, usually big enough for 8 or 16 pages, and these sheets are folded into sections of the magazine. Each of these sections is called a *signature.* In order to let the printer work efficiently, the editor must complete pages in units corresponding to those that will be on the press at any one time. And, if the editor is to use color economically, he or she must plan color to fit in those same units of pages. This planning to meet production requirements is explained in detail in Chapter 18.

Magazine layout, therefore, is often the result of a team effort involving the advertising manager who places the ads, the editor who allocates space, the production manager who keeps printing costs in check, and the art director who designs the pages.

The Dimensions of the Stage: Format

As pointed out in the chapter on design principles, all graphic communications are restricted by certain visual limits just as an actor is confined to the limits of the stage. Every page designed must fit the proportions that have been set for it.

The graphics equivalent of the actor's stage is the *format*, the shape, size, and style of the publication.

The *format* of a magazine is a basic factor in its layout and is not subject to artistic whims. Magazines vary considerably in shape and size, ranging from small enough to tuck into a pocket to dimensions that equal the tabloid newspaper (Figure 15-5). Format is the result of one or more of three practical considerations: (1) ease of handling, (2) adaptability of content to format, and (3) mechanical limitations of printing-press sizes.

Ease of handling is the chief advantage of the pocket size of the *Reader's Digest* and many other small magazines. Easy to hold and to store, the small-size magazine is particularly suited to its contents, which consist mainly of text, with the illustrations secondary. The large sizes are best for emphasis on pictures, because the larger the photographs, the greater is their impact. However, postage and paper costs have almost eliminated the larger "picture magazine" size.

Most magazines present text and illustrations on a relatively equal basis and use a format adequate for both—$8\frac{1}{2}$ by 11 inches or about that size. Since this is the same size as standard typing paper, filing these pages is simple; also, the dimensions are familiar and comfortable for the reader.

Most magazines are vertical rectangles, a traditional shape substantiated by the difficulty of handling horizontal formats.

Some Theoretical Bases for Magazine Design

The design principles discussed in Chapter 14 and based on communication theory apply just as strongly to magazine pages as they do to advertisements. The end goal of magazine pages is to get information

15-5 Magazine formats range from pocket size through the relatively standard 8½ by 11 to the large-format picture magazines.

into the mind of the reader—to have the reader get meaning from the pages. Because magazines are usually more concerned with concepts than with straight transferral of specific facts, the role of graphics is especially important; more so than for the newspaper, for example.

The transferral of concepts requires the utmost in sophistication of visual presentation. Visual syntax must be clear and correct; the order and simplicity that are characteristic of any good design are especially important if magazine pages are to accomplish their communication goals.

Achieving Meaning Through Orderly Presentation

The orderly design of magazine pages starts with the margins that are used to frame the content of the page. Margins are important for two reasons. First, they are either the ending or the beginning marker (or both) for verbal copy. Try cutting the margin from both sides of a magazine page and note the reading difficulty incurred without the frame of white to set off the line endings. Second, they help make pages and spreads attractive and unified by wrapping the elements on a page into one package with a border of white margins. In this respect margins act like the frame around a picture.

Margins are usually considered mandatory for type matter because of their contribution to legibility. But exactly what size they must be varies widely.

Many magazines follow traditional book margins because they are being designed in traditional fashion; most early magazines differed in appearance from the books of their day only because they had no hard covers. The scholarly magazine shown in Figure 15-2 is typical of book-like magazines.

Traditional book margins are progressive, with the bottom margin being the largest and the inside margin the smallest. The area inside the margins is called the *type page* because all type is required to be within that area. Type pages ride slightly high on a page because they are centered on the optical center which is slightly higher than the geometric center.

It is generally most important that the inside (*gutter*) margin be the smallest—ordinarily no more than half the size of the bottom margin. Gutter margins that are too wide destroy the order and unity of two facing magazine pages, and in most instances it is desirable to design facing pages as one unit. If each page is to stand separately, then extra white space at the gutter may be desirable.

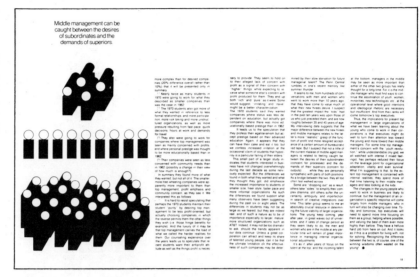

15-6 The panel of white at the top gives a directional movement to the design and helps tie the pages together. (*Courtesy* Long Lines, *AT&T Long Lines Department*)

As several of the illustrations in this chapter show, modern designers take great liberty with margins on magazine pages. Certainly no effort is made to have type fill out the full dimensions of the type page. But when there is extra white space available, most designers move it to the outside of the design, thus maintaining a white frame, however irregular it may be. Another common technique is the use of large panels of white to create movement in a design (Figure 15-6).

If a magazine's policy is to give special emphasis to pictures, *bleeds* can be especially effective. A photo is said to bleed if it runs off the edge of the page. Bleeds are a good device for any magazine because:

1. They provide a change of pace in comparison with the pages with unbroken margins.
2. They give more room on a page by adding the marginal space to the content area.
3. Most importantly, they offer extra magnitude for pictures; without frames, photos seem to go on and on.

Balance and Simplicity Help Create Order

Probably the most important contributor to order in magazine design is *balance,* the feeling of equipoise that results from a relatively equal distribution of weights with respect to the optical center of a design area.

15-7 Symmetrical balance can be achieved by centering the illustration and title on the vertical axis. (*Courtesy Long Lines, AT&T Long Lines Department*)

15-8 *Below, left:* Symmetrical balance can be achieved by placing like elements on both sides of the vertical axis. (*Courtesy Seventy-Six, Union Oil Company of California*)

15-9 *Below, right:* Informal balance can be achieved by placing lighter elements farther from the fulcrum and larger elements closer to it. (*Courtesy NCR World*)

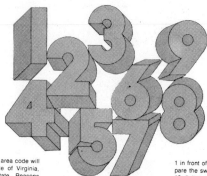

AN AREA CODE IS A NUMBER OF THINGS

ON JUNE 24, 1973 a second area code will be introduced in the state of Virginia, making it a two-code state. Reasons given: tremendous statewide growth of both telephones and central offices in the past 20 years. While 22 states still don't have the traffic to warrant more than one area code, many others — with New York in the lead with seven — require several.

Developing and assigning these codes, which speed calls accurately throughout the North American dial network, is a numbers game that has nothing to do with chance. It's been going on since the late 1940s, when area codes (also referred to as Numbering Plan Areas or NPAs) were introduced.

Two underlying philosophies governed the original distribution of area codes: one-code states would have 0 in the second digit position; and high population density areas would be given the lowest numbers for fast dialing (this was the pre-Touch Tone® calling era). So it remains even today that one-code areas such as Utah, North Dakota and some of the Canadian provinces have area codes such as 801, 701, 604, and 603. Cities with a lot of incoming and outgoing calls have low dial pull numbers: New York, 212; Chicago, 312; and Los Angeles, 213.

There are 160 possible area code combinations in the North American dial network. Virginia's new code brings the total assigned to 132. Of the 28 remaining, eight are reserved for service codes such as 411 (directory assistance), and 611 (local repair service). Stringent central office conservation efforts are in effect to prolong the life of the remaining 20. It's expected that supply and demand can be matched until about the year 2000.

"After that—or whenever NPA codes run out—we'll start using central office codes (the first three digits of a local number) as NPA codes," explains Ray Cooper, a supervisor in the operations-traffic planning department, AT&T. "This will entail some equipment modifications and most likely a change in dialing procedures. Customers may be asked to dial 1 in front of a long distance call to prepare the switching system to process a 10 digit number."

In order to understand how an area code functions, give each digit in the New York code a letter. In the following example, the letter appears above its corresponding number.

EXAMPLE: ABC
212

It was decided very early that the A digit of any code would never be either 0 or 1. The equipment recognizes 0 as a call to the operator and the prefix 1 as an access code to toll switching equipment. In addition, three-digit codes starting with 0 and 1 are used for specialized routing, such as inter-city operator-to-operator calls.

On the other hand, digit B of the code *must* be either a 0 or a 1. This allows the equipment to recognize whether a seven or 10 digit number is coming. If a machine receives an 0 or a 1 in the B digit, it prepares itself to accept eight more numbers. If it records a number between 2 and 9, it gets set for only five more digits.

The final digit in the code — the C digit — may be any number from 0 to 9. Currently there are no area codes assigned which use 0 in the last place, other than specialized services such as inward WATS (800).

As you can see, area codes are no simple little numbers. They have a piece of geography that's theirs and, much like a flock of geese, rely on a built in homing sense to get them to it. ✥

19

Groundbreaking

"May It Be A Constant Reminder To Our People Of The Patriotic Sacrifice And The High Price Of Freedom"

Symmetrical design is readily recognized, easy to obtain, and widely used for single pages or two-page spreads in magazines. Most commonly, symmetry is created by so placing a dominant illustration that it encompasses and rests on the optical center; the caption, title and text that complete the page are also centered, thus assuring perfect balance (Figure 15-7).

Placing duplicate weights on each side of the vertical axis will also achieve symmetry (Figure 15-8); in magazines, however, there is usually a strong element that is centered on the axis.

For informal balance, weights are distributed at various distances from the vertical axis, with the lighter elements being put farther from the fulcrum in order to balance the heavier weights that are closer (Figure 15-9). Remember that weight comes from shape and tone as well as size.

For magazines, a page-to-page balance for spreads is also important. Readers, as they view a magazine, are almost always seeing two pages together. Except when they look at the front or back cover, the magazine is opened so that the eye can scan the two pages spread before them. These two pages thus form a design unit. Weights should be so distributed that balance exists between the two pages as well as on them (Figure 15-10). Also, the white space in the spread should be so assigned that the two pages hold together; the combined space of the two gutter margins must be overcome with any device that is available. Techniques for binding two facing pages into one design are discussed later.

15-10 Two-page spreads should be so designed that there is a feeling of equilibrium, even if balance is not obvious. (*Courtesy* NCR World)

The handmaiden for balance in achieving the order in design that is so vital to communication is simplicity. We have long known from readability studies that simplicity in verbal language is essential for efficient communication; the same is true for visual presentation. Simple, straightforward visual syntax is important for magazines because of the conceptual nature of most magazine content.

Of first importance in visual syntax is a starting point that dominates all other components of the page or spread. In Figure 15-11 a large photo has been used for this purpose; the reader can be expected to start there and then move to the title and the text. Pages with two or more equally prominent elements can create confusion because the reader may be misled into starting at a point in the design that would be equivalent to the middle of a sentence.

Special care should be taken to be certain that a reader knows where the text of an article begins on a magazine page. One common typographical device for accomplishing this goal is the large initial letter, as shown in Figure 15-12. In the earliest days of printing, long before modern communication research, the value of special initial letters was realized, and they have not lost their value. Many magazine designers also have learned the value of what we might call an "end-of-design" graphic period. They place check marks, logotypes, star dashes, or some other typographical dingbat at the end of the text of

15-11 A large photo in the upper left of this spread gives the reader a strong visual starting point. (*Courtesy Monsanto Company*)

At this rustic ski chalet near Vail, Colorado, insulation plays a significant role in winter fuel savings.

Blanketing The Energy Crunch

When it comes to easing the present "energy crunch," every American, starting with the President himself, has an important role to play—namely, the conservation of fuel resources through more efficient use of energy supplies.

President Nixon started the ball rolling with his 1971 Energy Message to Congress, when he called for ". . . better thermal insulation in a home or office building." Such insulation, the President explained, "may save the consumer large sums in the long run—and conserve energy as well."

"I am directing the Secretary of Housing and Urban Development," Mr. Nixon told Congress, "to issue revised standards for insulation in new federally insured homes. The new Federal Housing Administration standards will require sufficient insulation to reduce the maximum permissible heat loss by about one-third for a typical 1,280-square-foot home —and by even more for larger homes. It is estimated that the fuel savings which result each year from the application of these new standards will, in an average climate, equal the cost of the additional insulation required."

The FHA quickly complied with the White House request. The new regulations the agency issued for new homes financed through FHA or Veteran's Administration mortgages call, in general, for a doubling of the minimum amount of ceiling insulation to six inches and adding at least another inch to the two and a half inches of wall insulation previously required.

The fact that conservation of energy through insulation was included in a Presidential message underscores both the seriousness of the current fuel situation and the importance the government places on better insulating practices.

But what does this all mean to the new homeowner?

On average, it means that the building costs for new single- and double-family dwellings will go up about $100 per structure. However, the extra cost—and this statistic should be enough to send the owners of older homes up to their attics with more insulation—will be recovered in less than two years through reduced fuel consumption!

And this means continued long-range savings, as well as an impressive conservation of our nation's hard-pressed energy supplies.

To get a better idea of just what this could mean nationwide, consider some of the following facts:

—In the 1960s, a Ford Foundation study revealed that only 10 per cent of the some 60 million homes in the *(Continued)*

Easy-to-install attic insulation can cut heat loss by 40 per cent and hot-air infiltration by 25 per cent, saving both energy and fuel costs.

an article. These dingbats emphasize the end of a magazine article just as the period signifies the end of a sentence. Otherwise readers may be inclined to turn a page or move to a facing page, falsely expecting the continuation of an article.

Grouping, Gridding, Alignment

Simplicity becomes increasingly difficult to accomplish as the number of elements to be placed on a page is increased. This problem is solved primarily through the grouping of related elements. Note in Figure 15-13 how design elements, especially photos, are grouped to achieve simplicity. Note, too, how captions are handled to be essentially part of the photos they accompany. Captions, if placed too far from their

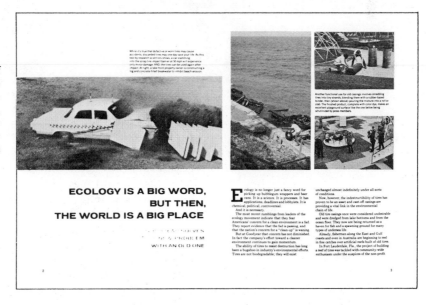

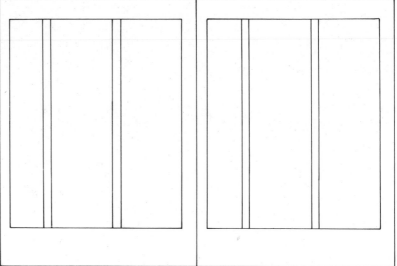

15-14 Under the grid system, the page is divided into rectangles that become guidelines for the placement of elements on the page. (*Courtesy Columbia Gas System*)

photos, become design elements in and of themselves and can contribute to clutter and disorder. The same thing can be said about subtitles; they ought to be close to and part of their main title.

Another way to bring order to magazine pages in spite of the large number of elements to be displayed is by the *grid* method, in which the page is first divided into equal basic segments, halves, thirds, or quarters. Each segment is further divided into equal squares (Figure

15-14). Titles, photos, and copy are then forced to conform to these squares, or multiples of the squares. The rigidity of the grid system forces order and at least a relative simplicity to what otherwise might be chaotic pages. The grid system requires careful preliminary planning and extreme accuracy in copyfitting and photocropping because if elements slop over any of the grid divisions the orderliness is lost. Figure 15-15 shows magazine pages in another grid pattern.

Alignment, which is a characteristic of gridding, is also helpful in creating order on magazine pages. Elements should be aligned as they are grouped so that the number of directions, as well as the number of elements involved on a page, is kept to a minimum. Analyze the accompanying illustrations to note how the photos are aligned with each other and with titles; how lines of titles are aligned with each

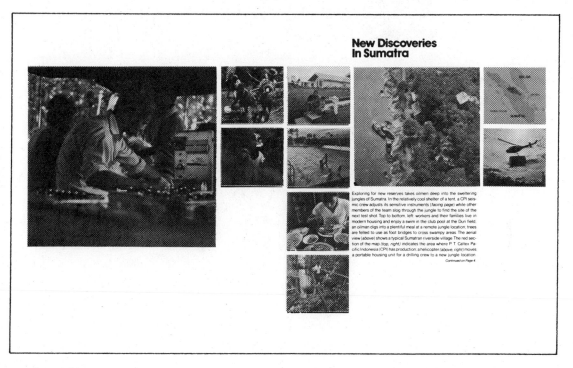

New Discoveries In Sumatra

Exploring for new reserves takes oilmen deep into the sweltering jungles of Sumatra. In the relatively cool shelter of a tent, a CPI seismic crew adjusts its sensitive instruments (facing page) while other members of the team slog through the jungle to find the site of the next test shot. Top to bottom, left: workers and their families live in modern housing and enjoy a swim in the club pool at the Duri field; an oilman digs into a plentiful meal at a remote jungle location; trees are felled to use as foot bridges to cross swampy areas. The aerial view (above) shows a typical Sumatran riverside village. The red section of the map (top, right) indicates the area where P. T. Caltex Pacific Indonesia (CPI) has production; a helicopter (above, right) moves a portable housing unit for a drilling crew to a new jungle location.

Continued on Page 4

15-15 Gridding produces a semblance of Mondrian design. (*Courtesy* Texaco Star)

other; how captions are aligned with the edges of photos or the edges of a column of type. Even alignment of an element within a photograph is considered by skillful designers (Figure 15-16).

Before a beginner places any element on a magazine page he or she should ask, "What should this line up with?" because the odds are that it should be in alignment with at least one other element. Brief study will usually show which one.

15-16 Here the designer has aligned the caption with an element within the photograph itself. (*Courtesy Texaco Star*)

A drilling rig provides a striking background as two oil field workers use some of their off hours to catch up on their fishing at the Pass a Loutre State Game Preserve. Other photos appear on Pages 12 and 13.

11

Controlling Direction

Once a reader has been directed to a starting point, he or she must be guided through the remainder of a magazine article until he or she has received the entire message. This guidance involves the use and placement of elements that create visual motion in desired directions. As pointed out in Chapter 14, this eye movement comes from reader habits but it can also be directed by lines, both implicit and explicit.

With horizontal flow generally preferred to vertical, magazines have an advantage because of their two-page spreads. The proportion of the 17-by-11-inch area formed by two facing pages of the standard magazine format is ideal for the display of visual material. In order to get linkage between the two pages, however, the vertical gutter formed by the two interior margins must be overcome. An obvious line, created by a series of dots or an uninterrupted line, either full-tone or shaded, can produce horizontal movement between pages very easily (Figure 15-17).

Photographs that have been grouped to form a horizontal line can also give horizontal direction (Figure 15-18). A regularity in the place-

15-17 Horizontal direction and eye movement can be achieved with obvious lines. (*Courtesy* NCR World)

15-18 Horizontal direction can be achieved by linear placement of illustrations or other elements. (*Reprinted from* DuPont Context, *the DuPont Company*)

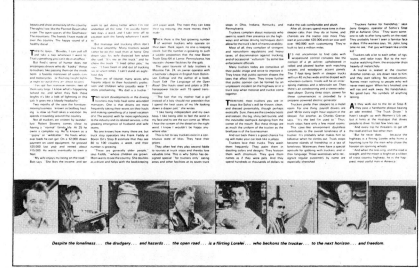

15-19 Horizontal direction and rhythmic pattern can be achieved by regularity of placement of layout elements. (*Courtesy* The Sohioan)

Despite the loneliness... the drudgery... and hazards... the open road... is a flirting Lorelei... who beckons the trucker... to the next horizon... and freedom.

ment of illustrations can produce a sense of rhythm as well as directional movement (Figure 15-19).

Pages or spreads must always be designed with the realization that North Americans have been doing their reading in a left-to-right fashion since the first day their first-grade teacher unveiled the magic of reading to them. The visual syntax must take this custom into account, and the starting point should ordinarily be in the upper left. Other elements should follow movement to the right and/or down. In most of the illustrations in this chapter, it can be noted that the starting point is in the upper left and normal reader eye movement is followed from that point.

Deviations from that pattern should be looked upon in much the same fashion as a writer looks upon incomplete sentences and other grammatical variations from the norm: they should be used only for desired special effects, and they should make the overall communication more efficient.

Controlling Contrast to Achieve Harmony and Unity

To give the reader a starting point on a magazine page, one element is made to stand out from all others and is placed in a reasonable location, usually the upper left. To get the reader to move along at the end of the message, we provide other "stand out" elements at intervals. In these and other instances we are employing *contrast* to get our communication job done.

Contrast, as explained in Chapter 14, comes from differences: differences in size, shape, tone, textures, or direction. Contrast is essential in magazine layout as it is for all layout because contrast makes each element discernible as an individual entity. Contrast can, however, be overdone. Too many elements shrieking for attention pre-

15-20 Type selection and page design can reflect the content of an article. (*Reprinted from* House Beautiful; *copyright 1972, 1973 The Hearst Corporation; all rights reserved*)

vent or delay the reader's getting meaning from a message. All shrieks and no whispers can obviously mean that nothing will be heard. And, in the final analysis, it is hoped that each magazine article will be related in a single voice, not a multitude of shouts.

Therefore, contrast must be controlled. On each spread or page contrast must be controlled so that the overall message will be communicated in harmony and with unity.

Harmony results from controlled contrast, and from using types and other elements that are different enough to be seen but similar enough to blend well with each other. Harmony also comes from the selection of visual elements that are in keeping with the subject or readers of the message that is being communicated.

With regard to magazines, harmony between the subject and its presentation is of primary importance. Considerable effort is invested in trying to have title type and design reflect an article's subject. Figures 15-20 and 15-21 show how type selection and basic page design can reflect an article's content.

15-21 Type, illustration, and white space are used together in an effective design that reflects content. (*Courtesy* Long Lines, *AT&T Long Lines Department*)

Once a design mood is set for an article on its opening page, it should carry that mood through to its conclusion. A six-page article that starts out with old-fashioned type dress and 1890 layout style should carry that dress and style throughout all six pages.

It is not necessary, however, for any magazine to carry the same typographical or design mood from cover to cover. There should be

15-22 Both these spreads are from the same magazine. Each spread was designed to be appropriate to its subject matter. (*Courtesy Gulf* Orange Disc)

some standardization throughout all its pages, but each article can take on its own personality, especially in a magazine that is trying to present highly varied content. The two parts of Figure 15-22 are from the same magazine; each spread is in harmony with its subject, and they differ from each other quite substantially.

A Word About Special Pages and Problem Pages

Front covers and table-of-contents pages require special layout attention—covers because they are so important; contents pages because they tend to be dull and uninspiring.

The Front Cover   A magazine's front cover is like a store's display window, a building's entrance, or an automobile's exterior styling. It should encourage attention and create the desire to go inside.

The functions suggested by these comparisons are vital, and there is the additional need for the instant identification of the magazine from its competitors and of its issue, as distinct from its previous issues.

Covers consist of type display alone or of type and illustration combined. The latter is employed most frequently today. The principal identifying characteristic is usually a distinctive name plate, but design or color or both may be used for the same purpose. A name plate must be unique and large enough to merit quick recognition.

15-23   Magazine covers vary widely in design and approach. Some are all type, some emphasize a drawing, and others are photographic.

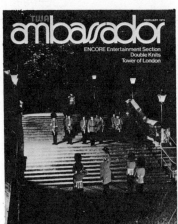

Design, as an aid to recognition, should be flexible so that necessary variations in the shapes of illustrations can be accommodated from issue to issue. Cover illustrations selected from the interior content can entice a reader into the magazine, but type is needed as well to direct the reader to specific articles inside. Reference to page numbers is an added lure.

Issues may be set apart from each other by changes in color, design, and the use of volume and issue numbers. No cover is complete without the latter, but such information is usually so subordinate that instant issue identification must be aided in other ways.

Because some magazines sell their front covers to advertisers at a premium price, the editorial department is compelled to create covers that are so valuable in maintaining readership that the business office will not appropriate this vital part of a magazine to add to income. This pressure, plus the cover's important functions, makes cover designing especially important.

The Contents Page

Any magazine that is large enough for the reader to have logical difficulty in locating material should have a table of contents. Its information may consume only a portion of a page but must have sufficient

15-24 Designers try in many different ways to add interest to magazine contents pages. (*Courtesy* Seventy-Six, *Union Oil Company of California;* Friends, *Ceco Publishing Company;* Tempo, *B. F. Goodrich Company*)

display to be found instantly, which usually necessitates its placement well forward in the magazine.

Paid-circulation magazines using second-class mail distribution are required to include certain basic information regarding entry as second-class matter, office of publication, and so on, somewhere within the first five pages. Since such masthead data is commonly on the table-of-contents page, the position of the latter is more or less predetermined.

The combination of masthead information and a long list of titles can mean a dull page. Therefore, many magazines now (1) make an effort to use illustrations on the page, (2) give special typographical display to some listings in the contents, and (3) bury the mailing and masthead information where it can be found when necessary but where it does not represent a major element on the page.

Small photographs, taken from important articles in the issue and used adjacent to the listing in the contents table, can help spruce up the layout, point out significant features, and inspire readers to want to turn to certain articles.

Checks, bullets, and other typographical dingbats can be used (perhaps in color) to give variety to the listing of titles and tempt the

eye. Whatever the device, monotony caused by a long list of items equal in display should be avoided.

Special display should be reserved for what is new in each issue; material that appears regularly, such as mailing information and titles of content departments, should not be emphasized.

Problem Pages Advertising on split or fractional pages creates layout difficulty for magazines as well as for newspapers. These pages are not a serious problem if their editorial portions are treated as separate design areas. They can be made attractive and functional by realizing that their shapes may be quite different from the ordinary page shape.

The extreme vertical often left after ads have been placed cannot be laid out like a two-page spread, but its dimensions can be exploited. Titles, illustrations, or other layout elements must simply be made to conform to the area. Two facing verticals can be brought together in the center of a spread by ads located on the outsides. Or, with ads spread across the bottom, the upper portions of two pages can be linked for a horizontal layout field. In such cases, the techniques used for spreads are applicable.

Many fractional pages are used for carryover material, but continuations are being avoided more and more. Most magazine articles can be confined to full pages up front, by adjusting the space for display (titles, and so on) to make the text fit. Fractional pages can then be used attractively for short items of various kinds that have adequate reader interest.

16 Newspaper Design and Layout

Of all the printed media of communication, the one that has placed the least emphasis on form throughout history has been the newspaper. The result has been predictable: the development of a medium whose appearance has paled in comparison with magazines, books, and other printed literature. Designers of printed media for years have pointed to newspapers as the most awkward, least attractive, and least readable of these media.

To place this shortcoming in proper perspective, two points must immediately be understood. The first is that there have been good reasons for the lack of attention to design by newspapers during their history in this country. The second is that current developments have been eliminating these reasons for many newspapers and have consequently been forcing a change in approach to the appearance of newspapers.

Why Newspapers Have Been "Made Up" and Not Designed

Problems of Format

The 1,750 daily newspapers and about 8,000 weeklies in the United States are divided between two basic formats: awkward and less awkward, with only a minority in the latter group. Most newspapers are of a size called *broadsheet,* about 15 inches wide and 23 inches deep. These newspapers are also of considerable bulk, scores of pages and several sections being common. Americans have wrestled with this overly large format and formidable bulk for years. Whether sitting in their comfortable living room chairs or on crowded public transit seats, readers of newspapers have been forced to try to fold their papers by hand into a manageable size. Fortunately for the subway rider, there is a less awkward format, the *tabloid,* which is exactly one half of the broadsheet. This size, although it is much more convenient and has gained particular favor for magazine supplements in Sunday editions and for special sections, remains the exception rather than the rule.

These large sizes seem to be the result of historical accidents, and they are still with us because of investment in equipment and tradition. The first several newspapers published in the American colonies were scarcely larger than this book, and not quite as large as typing paper. Later, when British newspapers adopted the broadsheet page size to circumvent a tax based on the number of pages, American newspapers followed suit. The development of the Penny Press in America just before the Civil War resurrected a smaller page size for the papers trying to attract a new audience of factory laborers with their penny price and human interest journalism. At the same time, however, some business or politically oriented newspapers went to extremely large formats. Some of these—in order to brag that they were the biggest papers in town—had page sizes as large as 3 feet by 5 feet and were called *blanket* papers. However, most steam-powered presses and related machines such as folders that were introduced at that time were designed to accommodate the "standard" broadsheet. The heavy investment that was then required for these new machines made further size experimentation almost impossible.

The tabloid, because it is half the size of the broadsheet, fitted the standard equipment, with one additional fold being the only special requirement for production. Unfortunately for newspaper readers, the use of the tabloid has been limited because it was tarred with a label of sensationalism when it first came into use in this country. The first tabloids of the 1920s sought mass audiences with an editorial product emphasizing sensational news coverage and appearance. Consequently, for many newspaper readers and publishers alike, "tabs" and sensationalism are synonymous. Although there has been some movement toward tabloid format by conservative and respected newspapers (e.g., the *Christian Science Monitor*) the broadsheet size remains a fact of newspaper life that designers must continue to face.

The charge that newspapers have not only been awkward but also least attractive (or even unattractive) is another aspect of newspaper design that must be understood and accepted. There are several reasons why this is also a fact of life.

For example, the mere size of the broadsheet makes functional, attractive arrangement of elements difficult. And if news coverage policies mandate the display of a score or more stories on a page, the task becomes still more difficult. The result has been some extreme but necessary design restrictions. In order to maintain a constant personality and give some order to a large design area that includes a score or more elements, *monotypographic* (all from the same family) headlines are often specified. Stringent *headline schedules*, which prescribe limited typographical patterns (e.g. flush left lines only and no more than two lines), have also been the norm. These restrictions, undesirable as they may be from a designer's standpoint, have been accepted as essential by most newspapers. With only a few minutes available for the layout of pages before deadlines, editors are forced to "go with what they have" and, without headline schedules and other aids, their job would become impossible.

Narrow newspaper columns and the resultant *vertical* flow of design elements that have been a characteristic of newspapers for years have also not been the result of mere whim. Primary newspaper financial support comes from advertising, and *column inches* and *agate lines* have been the basis for space rates to advertisers. Thus practical economics has favored narrow columns: narrowing columns results in more agate lines and column inches per page, and widening produces fewer agate lines and column inches per page. A recent tendency to widen columns for editorial matter to get better readability and to narrow them for ads to increase revenues or to save newsprint has added to what has always been a design problem.

With all of these factors at work, it is no wonder that newspapers have been made up and not designed. But perhaps the most important reason that newspaper designs have tended to be so unimaginative is that newspaper designers have not been forced to do any better. As pointed out earlier, the importance of graphic design varies inversely with the interest of the reader: the greater the interest, the less important the graphics. Football fans wading through scores of large pages to a sports section and from there to a column of scores presented in agate type obviously are not being stopped by a lack of graphic niceties. They are, in fact, pushing aside really formidable graphic obstacles to get information they desperately desire. The desire of readers for the news they offer has kept newspapers in an enviable position: form of presentation has been almost immaterial. However, current developments would seem to be forcing newspapers to give greater attention to their appearance.

In terms of having their products functional—that they be easily read—newspapers have also been behind other media. Type size, because newspapers have always tried to squeeze as much information into their columns as possible, has always tended to be too small. The same pressure has also kept adequate leading from helping the reader, and the long, narrow vertical columns have made readers struggle through unusually short lines as they have sought out their news. Display type has been crowded into position without adequate white space for it to do its work effectively.

All of these shortcomings are now getting increased attention because of changes both inside and outside the newspaper industry. These changes will force many newspapers to be less awkward, more attractive, and more functional in the future.

Times Are Changing— And So Are Newspapers _____

The impact of television on American society has been felt in every part of life—social, economic, political, and cultural. For newspapers, the impact has been especially forceful, both directly and indirectly.

Effects of Television

A direct effect of television is that newspapers have lost some of the national advertising that formerly filled their pages and formed a solid financial base for them. Television has been very efficient in selling cereals, cars, toothpastes, and other national brand items with the result that advertisers have bought more TV time and less newspaper space. Some reader time has been lost, too, and in the precious evening time period. A decline in the evening newspaper in contrast to its morning counterpart has been caused, in part, by this loss of reader time to television. Another change has been an increasing passiveness toward media—the development of watchers rather than readers. Reading is work; viewing pictures is not. The challenge of luring readers to the printed page and getting them to read what is printed there has become greater then ever before. But perhaps the most important development has been television's capture of a major role of the newspaper: being the first with the news. Not only can television reveal major details of news events before newspapers can, it often can be on the scene showing details of the event as it occurs.

To reduce television's time advantage in presenting spot news, many newspapers have been responding with greater depth of treatment and additional analysis for appropriate subjects, as well as more specialization and departmentalization. The end result for such changes has been to make these newspapers more like a daily magazine than a traditional newspaper. The more a newspaper tends to resemble a magazine in its content, the more it must consider the magazine as a primary competitor.

Effects of Magazine Competition

A resurgence of magazines, including the revival of some general consumer greats of the past but especially among the specialized and regional types, also is affecting newspaper design. Magazines have been joining suburban newspapers and free-circulation "shoppers" in competing with metropolitan dailies for local, state, and regional advertising dollars. If newspapers are to meet such competition successfully, their appearance must match the high quality of magazines.

Effects of New Production Technology

Another development, the radical change in the technology of newspaper production, has also been providing impetus for change. Offset printing, for example, is the most commonly used reproduction system for all media. For newspapers, offset makes possible a much more attractive product. With offset printing, illustrations can be handled more economically, more efficiently, and with much better results. Arrangement of elements on a page is no longer limited by the unbending right angles of metal type engravings. Cold type, area composition, and, perhaps most spectacularly, pagination by computer and cathode ray tube typesetters have forced total rethinking of newspaper design and makeup. In developing computer-assisted page layout systems, *templates* (patterns) are evolved. Since rectangles are much simpler to deal with than more complicated shapes, these templates use simple rectangles in building up full pages. One of the templates developed at Massachusetts Institute of Technology in a project funded by the American Newspaper Publishers Association is shown in Figure 16-1.

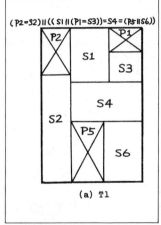

16-1   Experiments in computer-assisted page layout conducted at M.I.T. have involved formulation of computer-stored templates (patterns). *Above left:* A page of the *Boston Globe* as laid out by the staff. *Above right:* A template used to arrange the same page elements by computer. *Right:* The page produced from the template. (*Reprinted by permission from* Computer-Assisted Layout of Newspapers, *J. Francis Reintjes, Donald R. Knudson, and Hsin-Kuo Kan; Massachusetts Institute of Technology, December 1977; under a grant from the American Newspaper Publishers Association*)

Early attempts at page layout on video terminal screens also tended to force a similar approach to page design because the terminal screens could not show a full page at once. Even when full-page terminal display is possible, the rectangular building-block approach is used; see Figure 16-2.

16-2 A page produced for *Newsday* by means of x-y coordinates. The typesetter followed keyboarded instructions to set the headline and the first column of type, then moved the photopaper to set the caption, the next headline and the second column under it, and so on. A Velox print of the photograph was then pasted in place. Rectangular modules evolve naturally from electronic pagination systems. (*Courtesy* Newsday)

Changes in Approach to Newspaper Page Design

The impact of television, magazines, and new technology has brought about, for many contemporary North American newspapers, a new approach to the packaging of their product. Essentially, the change involves the acceptance of the proposition that newspapers must give more attention to their appearance, and the making of a strong commitment to accept the changes that would be involved.

For many papers, the first step has been the hiring of a designer to establish the typographic and layout practices that would result in an appearance that is both pleasing and functional. The second step has been to provide the staff and equipment necessary to produce a more attractive product under the pressure of deadlines.

Results of such redesigning efforts have varied according to the personality the paper's appearance is expected to reveal, policy restraints kept in force by publishers, the talents of the designers involved, and the usual constraints of equipment and deadlines. However, three broad categories of newspapers seem to have prevailed. These are (1) those that have gone to a totally "magazinelike" approach; (2) those that have accepted the principles that relate directly to a functional approach to news presentation but have re-

16-3 The *St. Petersburg Times* is one of the foremost advocates of contemporary design for newspapers. A design style book, as detailed and complete as the usual usage book, is a constant guide that helps keep this one of the most attractive papers in the country. (*Courtesy* St. Petersburg Times)

16-4 The *Morning Call* of Allentown, Pennsylvania, serving a medium-sized community, presents a very attractive "face" to its readers. Executive policy encourages attention to design, and an excellent art director carries out the policy. (*Courtesy* Morning Call)

tained some traditional approaches to news display and headlines; and (3) those that have made a minimum of changes because they want to retain a traditional personality. The first of these categories is designated *contemporary*, whereas the other two are termed *traditional*.

To call either of these categories better than the other is not the purpose of this discussion. For a newspaper, the most valuable asset is a personality that readers like and believe in, and appearance is an essential part, but only a part, of that personality. In the end, content must take precedence in the design of a newspaper. In every instance the goal is to present the news in the most effective fashion. From a study of examples of each category, it will be seen that great newspapers come in many different packages.

Contemporary (Modular) Design

The basic change that has been accepted by newspapers in the contemporary group as necessary to improve their appearance has been a willingness to break the large page format into *modules* (mods), each containing various graphic elements that can be independently ar-

16-5 The *Chicago Tribune*, serving a large city, has been a leader in the increased emphasis on graphic presentation. (*Courtesy* Chicago Tribune)

16-6 Measurable value for improved appearance: the 50,000-circulation *San Angelo Times* in Texas increased its circulation after changing to this lively contemporary design. (*Courtesy* San Angelo Times)

16-7 The 40,000-circulation *Telegraph Herald* of Dubuque, Iowa, has been a leader in giving newspapers their "new look." (*Courtesy* Telegraph Herald)

ranged with a freedom of placement of elements that has been typical in magazine design. In effect, the page designer is thus reducing a complicated problem into several simpler ones, and is thus functioning like the electronics engineer who designs a television set so that it is composed of a small number of modules, each much easier to repair or replace than the multitude of small parts that make it up. A better parallel may be newspaper readers on the subway who fold their newspapers into halves, then quarters, and then perhaps to one-eighth the normal size so that they can focus their attention on only one item.

Once a page has been broken into rectangular modules, each module can be designed as effectively as an ad or a magazine page. With perhaps only one item to the module, the design can be simple and striking. Or, in the case where a module is to be made up of many small parts, the overall result is to give the impression of one large element. Each module contributes to a pleasing geometric pattern for the page, a pattern that often has a Mondrian effect (see Figure 16-8).

As shown in Figure 16-8, overall page appearance is enhanced by a variety of rectangular shapes ranging from extreme horizontals to extreme verticals; as in advertising and other design, squares are avoided because they lack interest. A lack of variety in shapes produces page patterns that are too obvious and static.

16-8 Rectangular modules are the most obvious characteristic of contemporary page design. (*Courtesy* Morning Call)

Many modular papers routinely give one module dominance, and often this module, complete with the largest illustration on the page, is placed near the optical center of the page. At other times modular papers seem to make an effort to grade news for their readers by placing the top story of the day in a module starting in the upper left, the key quadrant for design areas (Figure 16-9).

Making mods work for readers

While keeping the number of modules per page at a minimum, page designers can also perform some desirable reader services. One of the most important of these is the departmentalizing of news items: the grouping of two or more separate items into one module, each with its own separate heading but jointly carrying a departmental label, such as LABOR, STRIKES, or INFLATION. A common example of this technique is the *news brief* module, which is often carried under a heading referring to "today" or the day of the week (Figures 16-10 and 16-11).

16-9 Primary emphasis is usually placed at the upper left or at the optical center. (*Courtesy* Morning Call *and* Chicago Tribune)

16-10 Grouping of related stories and departmentalizing are helpful to readers. The *Chicago Tribune* summarizes the major stories of the day under departmental headings and refers readers to the detailed accounts. The *Columbus Citizen-Journal* groups economic stories at the top and crime stories at the bottom of this front page. (*Courtesy* Chicago Tribune *and* Columbus Citizen-Journal)

One of the weaknesses of modular design as compared with a traditional approach is the reduction in the number of separate items on a page, each of which could attract its own share of readers. Efforts to correct this weakness are concentrated on the news brief device and on magazine-like indexes (Figure 16-11). In looking at these indexes,

16-11 News brief modules, such as the "Monday" panel in this issue of the *Journal Herald* of Dayton, Ohio, are a way to include many intriguing items on a page while keeping optical elements to a minimum. Note also the top of the page: more items intended to lure readers inside. (*Courtesy* Journal Herald)

one must be impressed with the similarity of page one indexes to the hard-sell "teasers" that are common to newsstand magazine covers. It is the function of these indexes to get a reader (who might find the story that interests him or her on page one of a *traditional* newspaper) to go to an inside page to a particular story that meets his or her interest.

Use of borders Modules often have only white space for borders, but many contemporary newspapers are inclined to place borders around many of them, often in color. Geometric patterns are enhanced by these borders, but care should be taken to keep the borders from becoming heavy and obtrusive. Display type and illustrations can be totally confined within these borders, or they can be permitted to extend beyond them.

16-12 Mods can be set off with rules (lines), as in the *Morning Call,* or with white space, as above the large headline in the *St. Petersburg Times. (Courtesy* Morning Call *and* St. Petersburg Times)

16-13 The front page of the *Plain Dealer* of Cleveland sticks almost entirely to flush left headlines set in Cheltenham, along with striking contemporary design and use of illustrations. (*Courtesy* Plain Dealer)

16-14 When there are natural opportunities, contemporary newspapers sometimes create magazine-like titles for articles; "Scar Wars" is a good example. (*Courtesy* St. Petersburg Times)

Use of display type A primary characteristic of contemporary newspapers is greater freedom in the use of display type. Headline schedules may still be rather strictly employed with the result that headlines are standardized and perhaps monotypographic when all other characteristics of the page are contemporary (Figure 16-13).

In such cases the most used and most functional headline pattern is the *flush left*, or one of its modifications. Easy to write and set into type, the flush left pattern has become vitrually *the* basic pattern for American newspapers. This pattern has been modified to have the lines indented somewhat on the left, thus providing for some added white space around the type. Often accompanying this modification is a short line called a *kicker* above the main grouping. Figures 16-3 to 16-13 show several examples of flush left headings plus their variations. Also to be noted in Figures 16-3 to 16-13 is the willingness of many papers to let headlines slip into an *inverted pyramid* or *pyramid* form. In some cases, such headlines are originally written with the expectation that the flush left pattern would prevail, but changes are made when lines are being pasted into position in order to give better distribution of white space around the type lines.

Many front pages now have an even greater variety of headline patterns (Figure 16-14). These same pages often employ other tech-

niques that might be considered more radical for newspapers: variation in placement of headings, incorporation of artwork into headings, and varied type fonts in individual headings. A rather standardized pattern for contemporary heading is constructed from a one-word label that is given special emphasis with size and position, followed by smaller type in greater quantity and a different size (Figure 16-15).

16-15 These headlines in the *Morning Call* consist of a subject label followed by a subtitle, a system now used by many newspapers. (*Courtesy* Morning Call)

Headline capitalization and punctuation Most comtemporary newspapers use standard sentence capitalization for headlines. That is, each heading is treated as a sentence, and the beginning word plus proper nouns are capitalized. Many newspapers, however, capitalize every word in a headline, following a tradition of long duration. Some newspapers capitalize the main words, using lowercase for prepositions and articles. The use of all-capital headlines has virtually been eliminated.

Capitalization differs in that, although most headlines are skeletonized sentences, they are not ended with a period. In cases where one line of a headline is a complete sentence to be followed by another, it is ended with a semicolon. Commas are often permitted to substitute for *and,* and sometimes colons are used in the sense that they substitute for "say," e.g., Mayor, Council: Let's Debate.

Use of white space A central goal in the use of display type by contemporary papers seems to be the increased use of white space. Skillfully used, white space adds to the impact and potential of any visual display, including newspaper headings. White space between lines makes each line more legible, but then additional white space around the heading becomes essential to bind the lines into a single unit. Along with the willingness to use greater variety of placement and patterns for headlines and larger amounts of white space has come the need for greater appreciation of the effects of white space. It is imperative, for example, that readers know exactly which bit of text or which illustration the type is intended to accompany. Ruled lines can bind these items together, but often white space must do the job. As a general rule, the assignment of greater amounts of white space to the outside of the heading and lesser amounts between the heading and its related element will do the trick.

Use of photos and other illustrations Perhaps most striking of the differences between contemporary and traditional newspaper layouts are those involving the use of photos and other illustrations. Some of these differences are cosmetic and readily apparent to a casual observer, whereas others deeply involve basic attitudes regarding the functions of illustrations.

Most readily apparent is the greater size — a dynamic new magnitude — now commonly given to illustrations, especially photographs. Virtually all of the front page examples shown in this chapter illustrate a willingness — an insistence — of editors that illustrations be large and dominant. Full-page illustrations would once have been unthought of, but not today. Dynamic verticals that reach from top to bottom and spread over several columns are commonplace, as are half-page horizontals. The "large" two- and three-column photos of other eras seem to be microscopic in comparison with contemporary dimensions. See Figures 16-11 and 16-13 for some typical examples of contemporary sizes of photographs in newspapers.

Another rather obvious change has been an increased use of "nonphoto" illustrations, such as drawings and charts. Except for editorial cartoons and the comics, many newspapers historically ignored drawings as a means of illustrating the news. As Figures 16-14 and 16-16 show, drawings are finding an important place in newspapers, and charts and diagrams such as pictographs, bar graphs, and line graphs have joined weather maps and war maps as standard illustra-

16-16 The striking use of illustrations—artwork—is probably the hallmark of contemporary design. The surprint of type over photo at upper left and the special-effect halftones and bar graph at right are typical of efforts to give illustrations a more important role in newspaper design. (*Courtesy* Morning Call)

tions for many papers. Increased emphasis on diagrams (often called *graphics*) has come from the major news services as well as from local editors and artists. Writing in *AP Log*, Hal Buell of Associated Press said, "No doubt good graphics improve readability in a visual age. Well done, they show with great clarity exactly what happened. They provide information in easily understandable tabular form or in an instant show how subjects compare, or how they have changed. When well done, they put across the point quickly and with clarity." Note also in these examples that such techniques as combination reproductions, vignettes, and mortises are being used with good effect. These production techniques often have been considered legitimate only for ads, magazines, and other media and too involved or gimmicky for newspapers.

These changes are obvious to the eye. They represent, however, some basic changes in attitude about the use of illustrations in newspapers. One of these is the belief that illustrations are the best single means of attracting and seizing reader attention; it is natural that illustrations are increasing in size and usage. Another change relates to the role of the photograph: an appreciation of the artistic and symbolic roles that photos can play. The traditional spot news photo still gets plenty of attention, emphasis, and awards. News photographers who either by planning or by happenstance point their camera in the right direction at the right time to record the split second of an accident or disaster are well rewarded with contest ribbons and prime page position. But they are also winning awards and getting dominant display for their work when they capture a scene of beauty or a moment of emotion not tied directly to a news happening. The pages reproduced in this chapter show many examples of photos that can be called artistic as well as newsworthy.

Use of body type   The establishment of column widths for body type is one of the most fundamental and important layout decisions for any newspaper, not because of its effect on appearance but because it does affect income and readability.

As pointed out earlier, newspaper advertising income depends on column inches and agate lines, and the more columns there are on a page the more inches and lines there will be. Traditionally, the broadsheet was divided into eight columns that were 12 picas wide. As efforts to conserve newsprint by narrowing pages took their toll, columns shrank to 11.5 and 11 picas. Meanwhile, editorial departments were agitating for improvements in type readability that could only come from larger type, more leading, and *especially* wider columns. For many papers the solution has been a 6-9 format—editorial material presented in six columns and ads in nine. Some papers have six

16-17 Spreading five columns of type over the width of six columns is a technique used by many newspapers to add extra white space and draw attention. (*Courtesy* Lead Daily Call, *South Dakota*)

columns on page 1 and eight or nine columns on all other pages. Other papers have retained narrow columns throughout or have made wide columns standard. Some papers use only five columns; others use five, six, and nine.

Although the result of experimentation with column widths has been a hodgepodge, there is no doubt that there is a strong trend toward the use of wider columns for news display. Even the *New York Times*, with its traditional character, went to 6-9 in 1976. An increased appreciation of the value of white space has also permitted an increased use of a point of leading between lines and ample white space between columns. A common practice for gaining extra white space between columns is to spread type horizontally over one extra column, e.g., five columns of type over six columns (Figure 16-17).

Arrangement of Ads on Pages

So far, our examples of newspaper pages have been restricted to front pages, which usually do not contain advertising. Inside page layout, because of the complications caused by advertising placement, is especially difficult.

The placement of ads is done by the advertising department *before* news is placed on a page. Not only does the advertising department determine how many ads are to be placed on the page but it also determines the number of pages that are feasible for an issue. Thus, on

16-18 The three common arrangements of advertisements on a newspaper page. *Above left:* Pyramid to the right. *Above right:* Pyramid to the left. *Left:* Double pyramid.

days when there is heavy advertising, there are more pages for news. Newspaper carrier boys are familiar with the heavy midweek issues that are loaded with grocery store ads and the light Saturday issues caused by a diminished desire for advertising in the pre-Sunday issue. Following a predetermined ratio of advertising to news (e.g., 60 percent/40 percent) the advertising department arranges ads over the required number of pages. In placing the ads, pyramids are formed with larger ads on the bottom and smaller ones on top. The resulting arrangements can either be a *pyramid to the right*, with the upper left remaining for news; a *pyramid to the left*, with the upper right as the news hole; or a *double pyramid* with a center news hole. The insistence on these arrangements by advertising departments has been based on the insistence by advertisers that their ads be next to news. Only a pyramid can give all advertisers that desired juxtaposition.

Of these alternatives, news departments have favored the pyramid to the right because it leaves the main optical area (upper left) for news presentation. On some newspapers, notably those that now have art directors, there has been considerable pressure to have ads blocked off to form a horizontal line across the page. Modular inside page layout would be considerably easier if that were done, but there has not been much success in getting publishers to order the change. Computer-assisted placement of ads has also been developed to retain pyramids.

Figure 16-19 shows excellent modular layout on inside pages that offered a variety of shapes and sizes of news holes, and also shows how departmentalization as an aid for the reader is executed through the modular approach.

16-19 These two pages from the *St. Petersburg Times* show how modules can be used effectively on inside pages along with ads if ads are squared off horizontally. (*Courtesy* St. Petersburg Times)

Sectional Front Pages

Although contemporary page design is evident on all pages of many newspapers, it can perhaps be seen best in the front pages of sections or departments. For what perhaps are obvious reasons, there has been a greater freedom of design permitted for these pages, resulting in spectacular visual presentations.

In many instances, the news policies that cause retention of traditional makeup procedures for many newspapers are not kept in effect for these sectional pages. Newspapers that are traditional to the core when it comes to layout of the front page employ many nontraditional devices on the front pages of sections. Figure 16-20 shows sectional front pages of contemporarily designed newspapers, but Figure 16-21 shows sectional front pages from traditional newspapers.

The nontimely characteristic of many of the subjects being treated and the ability to display only one or perhaps a few items on the page contribute to the new look on these pages. Large dominant illustrations, extra white space, and other landmarks of contemporary design can therefore prevail for these pages though they may be missing from others.

16-20 Some of the most interesting newspaper page designs are found on section pages. The organization of the newspaper into standard subject-matter sections with their own front pages is developing into a strong trend. See also Figure 16-14. (*Courtesy* Chicago Tribune; Morning Call; Telegraph Herald)

16-21 Newspapers with traditional approaches to page layout are creating interesting and unusual sectional front pages. (*Copyright* © Washington Post. *Reprinted by permission from* Milwaukee Sentinel)

Editorial pages also can provide excellent examples of contemporary layout (Figure 16-22). Perhaps because they too are less timely—or perhaps because it is known that reader interest is low—the editorial pages of many newspapers show more design experimentation than any other. Wide variation in column widths, drawings, extra amounts of white space, and special headings are found on many editorial pages.

16-22 Extra design effort on editorial pages is traditional with newspapers. The results usually are good, as in these two pages. (*Courtesy* Journal Herald, *Dayton, Ohio*; Herald-Dispatch, *Huntington, West Virginia*)

The Traditional Approach to Page Layout

For some contemporary layout practices to be accepted, long-followed traditions must be set aside, and for some newspapers the abandonment of these practices is considered to be unwise. For example, the

New York Times is considered by many professionals and laypersons alike as the model of quality for other newspapers to emulate. For more than a century, the *Times* has built a reputation as the great recorder of all human events, a reputation that is of inestimable value. Reputation is built on character, and character, personality, and appearance are so intertwined that to change any of these could well endanger what has taken years of excellence to build. That such changes

16-23 Two newspaper giants, the *New York Times* in the East and the *Los Angeles Times* in the West, are representative of newspapers that deliberately maintain a traditional appearance for their front pages. (*Copyright © 1979 by The New York Times Company; reprinted by permission. Copyright 1979 Los Angeles Times; reprinted by permission*)

would be made slowly and carefully, if at all, is understandable. The front page of the *Times* (Figure 16-23) represents the facade of an institution that could never be torn down to incorporate changes which might or might not stand the test of time.

The *Los Angeles Times* (Figure 16-23) is another of America's great newspapers. Although its appearance has different roots than that of the *New York Times*, the giant of the West Coast has a similar investment in reputation that cannot be dealt with lightly. To suggest that either of these great newspapers totally adopt changing contemporary standards would be as unwise as suggesting that Rolls-Royce should try to reshape its product to contemporary design standards. It is equally unwise to suggest that, because their front page appearance is traditional, these newspapers have not changed, have not "progressed." Indeed these newspapers have changed, but not in areas that are important in retaining the character and reputation they both have achieved.

The list of newspapers that retain some or all of the traditions of layout that they have developed would be a long one, and no attempt is made here to develop such a list. For that matter, there are so many gradations of adherence to traditional practices that it is foolhardy to attach specific labels to specific newspapers. Even the most traditional newspapers employ some contemporary techniques. What is discussed here are the approaches to layout that are based on tradition (and remember, traditions are being made at any time). Examples of these traditional approaches are shown. Because it is especially important for the student, we try to emphasize the "whys" for these traditions just as we tried to emphasize the reasons for contemporary changes.

Some Basic Assumptions

Traditional layout practices begin with some important and basic assumptions. Among these are

1. News coverage is of overwhelming importance, and appearance must be secondary. This assumption is so strong that it leads to a belief that too much attention to appearance will probably be counterproductive.
2. Spot news is still the heart of a newspaper. Timeliness in presentation is also of such importance that makeup practices that slow the layout process cannot be accepted.
3. Pages must be treated as a complete unit, with all elements contributing to an overall harmony and unity.
4. Headlines serve a useful function of grading the news—telling the reader how important a story is—and their size and placement should help with this function.
5. Headlines must be standardized and restricted in order to obtain harmony among them and to permit maximum speed in writing and preparation.

6. The front page each day should be sufficiently similar to those of previous and following days so that they form a recognizable physical personality for the newspaper.

7. Illustrations primarily serve to amplify words. Depending upon how strictly these assumptions are followed, singly and as a group, there is a great variety of end products as the page reproductions in this section show.

An Editor's Layout Tools A newspaper layout editor works with three "tools": a *copy schedule,* a *headline schedule,* and a *dummy sheet.* The copy schedule lists the inventory of all the stories that have been processed and sent into print, the headline schedule is the inventory of the headline patterns the editor can use, and the dummy sheet is a scaled-down blank newspaper page on which story positioning will be shown.

Entries on the copy schedule (Figure 16-24) are made as stories are assigned to copy readers. In most cases, headlines are assigned at the same time, so when the copyreader is finished a full entry on the

COPY SCHEDULE

Slug	Headline	Story length (col. in.)	Total (col. in.)	Art	Typesetting	Page
COUNCIL	#4	6	6	—		1
EXPLOSION	#6-6	18	24	2-COL x 4 INCHES	2-COL	1
RALLY	#5-6	11	35	1-COL x 3 INCHES		

16-24 A typical copy schedule and dummy sheet.

copy schedule can include: a *slug* (a one or two-word description of the story); headline description; length of the story in column inches; a running total of column inches edited; a notation of any art (pictures) to accompany the story; and any special comments about the story. Some stories are set into type without headlines and are marked HTK (head to come). The headlines are not assigned on these stories because their relative importance will be determined by events still unfolding.

This part of an editor's work is monumental. With several pages under his or her control, the editor must evaluate stories quickly, assign a headline that will work into a page layout that has not even been conceived yet, and speed the flow of copy so that deadlines can be met.

Of special help to the editor is the headline schedule, which usually shows a sample of each headline as it would look in type, and gives the maximum unit count for each line of type. It also labels each headline, usually with a number, a letter, or a combination. By simply assigning and entering a number, such as #1, the editor is specifically identifying the many facets of a headline: type size, number of lines, arrangement of lines, and so on. The headline schedule thus helps make the editor's duties easier to carry out.

The headline schedule also is vital in another way. More than any other device, it sets the paper's appearance and outward personality. Policy judgments have already been made and incorporated into the headline schedule; there is, for example, no need to waste time deciding whether a 72-point banner (headline over six full columns) can be used; the headline schedule makes it available or it does not. The same is true about typefaces. Under time pressure, an editor cannot decide whether Bodoni or Garamond or Futura or some other face would be best suited for a particular story. All display faces must be carefully selected in advance and then specified in the schedule. A good headline schedule will be complete, providing enough basic news headlines to meet all needs, plus any special purpose headlines. Sports and other departments may have distinctive headlines of their own.

Headline Patterns

Most newspapers rely on *flush left* or *modified flush left*. Other patterns that may be specified in a headline schedule include the *stepline, hanging indention, inverted pyramid,* and *flush right* (Figure 16-25). Two-line steplines are formed by making the top line flush left and the bottom line flush right; if there is to be a middle line, it is centered. A hanging indention is formed with the first line flush left and the remaining lines indented uniformly at the left. The inverted pyramid is formed by centering all lines and having the lines decrease in length from top to bottom. Flush right is formed as the name implies.

Charter Suit
Asks State
Redistricting

**Representation
Called Unfair
And Unequal**

Flush left.

Wall St. Hails
Action by U.S.

Stepline.

Lottery cleanup
is promised

Inverted pyramid.

*Hempstead
runnerup
after 15-13
defeat by
Mason City*

Flush right.

Special headline forms may include one in which a rule is placed at the top and on both sides of the type (a *hood*) or one starting with a single subject word in large type followed by some smaller lines elaborating on the subject word (a *label*) (Figure 16-26). Label heads with their secondary lines are reminiscent of earlier headlines that relied

Mortgages
may reach
11 percent

Iran
Soldiers join demonstrators in protests against Bakhtiar

on several *decks* to form a single headline. Kickers are also, except for form, much like decks. Although many newspapers still use headlines composed of a top deck plus a second deck (Figure 16-27), few will include more than two (see *New York Times* page one for the exception). Special *jump* heads are also usually included in a headline

Sadat Reported to Be
Easing Stand on Pact
**Appears to Drop West Bank and Limit
Egypt's Demand to Return of Gaza Strip**

schedule. These are headlines given special typographical form and used over the continued (jumped) portion of a story.

To Jump or Not to Jump

As they swiftly put entries on the copy schedules, approve headlines, and do other preliminary chores involved in page layout, newspaper editors must be aware of a policy regarding carrying portions of stories from page one to an inside page. Some newspapers do not tolerate the practice, others encourage it, and some tolerate it but discourage it. Most studies indicate that there is a loss of readership of the jumped portion of a story, but a no-jump policy places restrictions on depth of coverage that many newspapers consider intolerable. At any rate, editors must have a policy in mind as they prepare a dummy.

Preparing the Dummy

With a completed copy schedule in hand, the layout editor is ready to put the pages together. If the preliminary work has gone well, there will be enough copy to fill the news holes (but not too much *overset*, wasted type). There will also be a sufficient variety of headlines assigned to stories so that a reasonably functional and attractive page can be created.

As layout editors position stories, they have two dominant considerations in mind. The first and most important of these is the importance of each story. They want the page to grade the news for the readers, to let them know what is most important. The other consideration involves appearance; the editors want each item to have *contrast*, but they also want the elements to *balance* (create a state of equilibrium), and they want the final result to be a *harmonious* unit.

Grading the News

In positioning the most important story of the day, an editor is likely to place it in the upper right-hand corner, a position that is contrary to design principles. This practice is a holdover from the early uses of banner headlines when editors thought it would be best to place stories in the right-hand column in such situations. It seemed unwise to start readers in column one with a headline, take them across the full width of the page, and then bring them back to column one to read the story.

More and more newspapers are shifting away from this tradition, especially in situations that do not involve headlines spreading over all or most of the columns. In such situations, the number one story is placed in the upper left quadrant of the page.

In any event, the top of the page is accepted as preferred for the most important stories, and the two or three most important ones are assigned to that area. In order to get contrast in the bottom area of a page, some strong display items, often of an *interesting* as opposed to *important* nature, are placed there.

The *nameplate* or *flag* (a newspaper's name as set in distinctive fashion) usually goes at the top of page one above all headings or art, but sometimes is moved to other positions. If the nameplate is placed at the top it often will have *ears* placed on each side. These are small display items, such as Scripps-Howard's lighthouse symbol, a weather box, or a symbol indicating the edition.

Achieving Desirable Contrast

As they place each story according to importance and interest, editors are also eager to have each story stand out, each trying to lure as many readers as possible. To accomplish this goal, the editors try to achieve contrast. As pointed out in earlier chapters, contrast comes from opposites: light and dark; large and small; tall and short; fat and thin; straight and crooked. It is the element that makes graphic communication possible: contrast between lightness and darkenss makes type and illustrations visible.

Because we start with a field of white, it is easy to fall into the trap of thinking that contrast automatically comes from dropping large dark areas onto this field. It is true that the first of these will give maximum contrast, but with consecutive additions, contrast is steadily reduced.

Contrast Among Headlines

With this in mind, two rules of contrast apply to headlines.

1. *Headlines should be separated by white space, gray matter, or illustrations.* Some newspaper makeup persons put teeth into this rule by insisting that two headlines never be placed together on a page. There are a number of ways to separate them. Spread leads provide gray matter between spread headlines and the headlines of stories below. Photographs, illustrations, and boxes serve likewise. Most makeup persons treat boxes as if they were illustrations because they perform the same functions in layout.

Separation of headlines on a horizontal plane is especially important. If two headlines of like size and style are next to each other horizontally, they form a so-called *tombstone*. Tombstones reduce the contrast for each headline so much that the reader can be tricked into reading the two headlines as one. Obviously these should be avoided.

2. *If headlines must be together, they must be individually distinctive so as to retain some contrast.* Their difference can be in type size, typestyle, or the typographical pattern of the headline.

Two spread heads in large type can be separated by a single-column head in smaller type. An italic head may be placed next to a roman, or a lightface next to a boldface. Boxed heads or feature heads can stand out from adjacent heads by white space and size-difference. Spread heads with a broad horizontal sweep are distinct from single-column heads in a vertical shape, but again difference in type size or style helps.

Contrast in Body Areas

The practice of changing the line measure for editorials is a good example of contrast in body areas. With lines in single-column measure on the rest of the page, editorials that are two columns wide get special visual attention.

Change of measure for contrast is not restricted to the editorial page, of course. Front-page feature stories and major interpretive efforts displayed under a *skyline* (a banner on a story above the nameplate) or a spread head at the bottom of the page are frequently given the additional eye appeal of wider columns.

The technique of spreading type over one more column than required (i.e., the 5 on 6) as discussed earlier has become increasingly popular for many traditional newspapers.

Special typographical devices—such as setting some paragraphs in boldface or italic, beginning paragraphs with a word or two in boldface, and inserting boldface lines (subheads) are also used to give some contrast in body type areas.

A Word of Warning

Contrast is essential to good design, but it can have undesirable aspects. Imagine a page with every headline set in a different face, and body copy varying widely among stories. There would be plenty of contrast, but the overall result would be distasteful. Effective contrast makes each component stand out on its own without destroying the equilibrium, harmony, and unity that are necessary for good design.

Newspaper makeup that concentrates so much on contrast that it neglects other parts of good design is called "circus makeup." It is characterized by spread headlines, often in excessively large type, all over a page with little or no thought being given to the total picture. Circus makeup creates an impression of action and noise—but so much from so many directions that the reader can barely see or hear any of it.

Balance is primary in the makeup of some newspapers and purely secondary for others. Newspapers trying to project a conservative, steady, and reliable personality are inclined to make balance dominant in their page design. "Shouters" may deliberately try to subordinate balance lest their readers think the day's news a trifle dull. Most newspapers try for a middle ground.

Balance on a newspaper page is acquired by placing relatively equal weights on both sides of an imaginary line splitting the page into vertical halves. Balancing opposite corners is also considered. When these weights are virtually identical, the makeup is in *formal balance*, or *symmetrical*. When they are only relatively alike, the balance is *informal*.

Headlines and illustrations have the most inherent contrast, which means they exercise the strongest influence on equilibrium;

therefore, their placement is especially important. A formally balanced newspaper page has every headline and illustration on one side of the page perfectly matched in weight and position by others on the opposite side.

But because makeup acts to grade the news for readers, formal balance demands that news stories develop in importance by pairs. Naturally, this is rare, and as a result formal balance is relatively uncommon in newspapers.

Functionally, in newspaper makeup, headlines are balanced by pictures, headlines of one pattern by those of another, and lighter elements by heavier elements placed closer to the center, like the heavier child sitting closer to the center of a seesaw.

Harmony in Newspaper Makeup

The makeup person is concerned with three kinds of harmony when laying out newspaper pages: (1) the general appearance of the pages must harmonize with the character or personality of the newspaper; (2) types must harmonize with each other; (3) special pages must harmonize with their subjects and readers.

Harmony of Appearance and Character

Because harmony in a paper's personality concerns the basic character, it is usually controlled by specific management policies. Only minor decisions on detail are made in this respect from day to day.

The range of headlines, the emphasis on illustration, and the preferred makeup patterns are a matter of policy. The makeup person must simply translate his or her news judgments into assigning headlines, display for photographs, and page arrangements that do not depart from the predetermined paths.

Typographic Harmony

Newspapers have more difficulty achieving typographical harmony than the other printed media do. The large size of the pages and the great number of individual units of type display almost require that the selection of display be *monotypographic* within any *section* of a newspaper. Some newspapers still have headlines in two or, at the most, three type families, but their ranks are steadily decreasing. Restricting the use of display type to one family assures harmony, and the numerous variations within any type family offer many ways to avoid monotony.

Type families can and should change from department to department. One family may be used for basic news pages, another for the sports pages, and perhaps another for the editorial page.

Harmony with Subject and Reader

Type families can be changed in different sections because their subjects and readers differ. The heavy sans serifs of a sports page may be inappropriate for an editorial page. Compare the typography of the sports and editorial pages of several newspapers; these pages have display faces that are completely different, but each is harmonious with subject and reader.

Changing Traditions

The makeup practices described as traditional in this section are constantly being sharpened and revised to improve the final product. Without totally discarding tradition and adopting complete new faces, most newspapers are integrating changes in their appearance.

These changes, many of which blur the distinction between what we have chosen to call contemporary and traditional practices, are

1. Reduction of the number of columns per page to six or five, thus permitting greater readability because of improvements in type size and line length. One-column headlines can be much more descriptive and are easier to write. Wider columns also offer mechanical and cost advantages. Hyphenation, the curse of typesetting, is reduced sharply. Fewer, longer lines means fewer justification problems and faster typesetting. Pasteup of pages is also easier.
2. Horizontalism—the tendency to arrange stories and headlines so they form horizontal masses. Fewer decks and fewer lines in headlines that are spread over more columns produce these horizontal shapes.
3. More and larger illustrations, with greater appreciation for their artistic appeal.
4. Legible headline patterns based on the flush left pattern and its variations.
5. More and better use of white space.

As one can readily see from this listing—and by looking at the reproductions of contemporary and traditional pages in this chapter—the major differences between the two groups are diminishing. There remain, of course, small or subtle differences, not only between the two groups but among the thousands of papers published in this country. Each newspaper in its own way is using graphic elements to get the most news into the mind of its readers in the best possible fashion. And that's the name of the game.

17 Designing Other Printed Literature

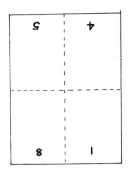

17-1 Flat sheet ready to fold to make eight-page booklet.

17-2 Folded sheet that will form eight-page booklet.

Some factors involved in producing effective graphic communications are beyond the control of the designer who is preparing materials to appear in the established media. The designer has to fit the layout to prescribed size limitations, and must use the printing process by which the medium is produced. The paper is predetermined as well as the ink, and this in turn affects the designer's use of continuous-tone artwork.

It is in the printing field outside the media that the communicator finds fewer restrictions and can exercise the fullest creative use of the principles of graphic communications. Here the communicator controls the selection of (1) printing process; (2) color; (3) paper; (4) nature of the fold; (5) size and shape.

Because this product goes directly to readers, it is referred to as *direct literature*. It may be mailed, distributed by individuals, or placed at convenient locations where readers can help themselves. The most common means of distribution is by mail, and, when so handled, the material is referred to as *direct-mail literature*.

Kinds of Direct Literature

These printed pieces take many forms, too many to be covered in this text. In broadest terms these pieces can be divided into two groups: (1) booklets and (2) flat or folded sheets.

Booklets Generally, the printed piece of direct literature comes from the printing press as flat sheets of paper, which may be folded and trimmed to become booklets. For example, Figure 17-1 shows a flat sheet with the folios (page numbers) as they would fall on one side. Take a sheet of paper, write the folios on it as shown, and fold it in the two directions indicated by the dotted lines. Folded properly, the paper should look like Figure 17-2. You can now carefully lift the leaves and place the folios 2, 3, 6, and 7 on the proper pages.

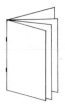

17-3 Folded and trimmed eight-page booklet.

Now refold the sheet and imagine staples driven through the "backbone" at the points indicated by the arrows in Figure 17-2. The staples should clinch parallel with and on top of the fold between pages 4 and 5. Next, imagine that the entire unit is compressed and that knives trim on the dotted lines as shown on the top and bottom edges and the fore edge in Figure 17-2. You can do this on your folded sheet, using two staples that you force through the backbone with your fingers and then taking scissors to the edges. You will wind up with what is shown in Figure 17-3, a folded and trimmed eight-page booklet.

What you have just produced is a *self-cover booklet.* A four-page cover can be printed (usually on a heavier paper) and the eight-page unit can be inserted before stapling and trimming. Then you have a *separate-cover booklet.* If the cover stock is so heavy that it makes folding difficult, it may first be processed with a scoring rule on special equipment.

Booklets are sometimes called *pamphlets* or *brochures.* Essentially the booklet is a small book and is made up of eight or more pages bound together and usually stapled. The booklet ranges in number of pages up to 36 or 40 and the number of pages must be divisible by four. The format itself may be either vertical or horizontal.

Books usually have more pages and are bound with more permanent covers. Books, moreover, are of a literary or scientific nature, whereas the content of booklets is more likely to reflect promotional interests.

Book format, which is traditionally standardized, has roughly three main divisions: (1) the preliminaries, or front matter; (2) the text; and (3) the references, or back matter.

The preliminaries include the *half title*, the book's first printed page, on which appears only the book's title; the *title page*, which includes the title and the names of the author and the publisher and the place of publication; the *copyright page*; the *preface*; the *acknowledgments*; the *contents*; the *introduction* when it is not a part of the text proper; and, often, a second half title. Tradition governs the order of these pages and whether they fall on a left or a right-hand page. *Folios*, or page numbers, are in lowercase or small cap roman numerals, appearing first on the opening preface page, although the actual numbering starts from the half title.

The text section contains the chapters; the reference section consists of appendixes, bibliography, glossary, and index. In text and reference sections the folios are in arabic, and may be either at the top or at the bottom of the page. *Running heads* usually appear at the top of each page, and the content is often different on the right- and left-hand pages.

Throughout, the progressive margins remain consistent although text on facing pages may run a line or two long or short depending upon makeup.

This description of book design refers to traditional formatting. However, as we saw in Chapter 6, book design may be altered considerably in the New Typography.

In the design of booklets, tradition and formality may also be applied in varying degrees (see Figures 17-4 and 17-5). Because of their

17-4 Formal layout of a spread in a booklet that describes specialty advertising. (*Courtesy Specialty Advertising Association International*)

17-5 Informal layout of a spread in a combination informative-promotional booklet. (*Courtesy nuArc Company, Inc.*)

usual promotional nature, booklets are more often of an informal design. Because a message unfolds through succeeding pages, as in a book, a continuity of style must be maintained by the designer, who works with units of individual pages or units of facing pages. The arrangement of elements in a booklet can differ from page to page. Cuts can bleed; copy block widths and margins can be varied; and display and color can be used with a free hand.

The front cover, often referred to as the *OFC* (outside front cover), will receive one of two types of treatment. In the case of an informative or literary booklet, it will be more conservatively handled with only a title set in type and placed formally or informally (see Figure 17-6). If the nature of the booklet is more promotional, display treatment of the cover may be more extensive, incorporating both visual and verbal elements (see Figure 17-7).

17-6 Conservative treatment of booklet cover. (*Courtesy Columbia Gas System*)

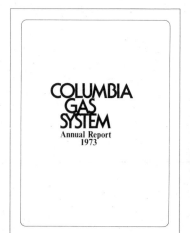

17-7 Display treatment of booklet cover. (*Courtesy nuArc Company, Inc.*)

Folders   The printed flat sheets delivered from the press do not always take the form of books or booklets. Many printed jobs are known as *flat pieces*. Several may be printed together on a large press sheet and then trimmed (cut) from it. Such flat pieces take many forms, such as letterheads, cards, announcements, posters, fliers, business forms, instruction sheets, envelope stuffers, and so on. These are often printed on one side only. The principles of design that were previously discussed apply to planning the message they carry.

We are, however, more interested here in those printed messages that are not finished flat but are, instead, folded. Such pieces are known as *folders*. The subject of folding is given a comprehensive treatment in Chapter 18, but certain implications in the folder have a direct bearing on information processing. This is primarily the result of the fact that, like booklets, folders consist of pages. The serial ordering of these pages is not so rigid as it is with booklets. Thus the design of folders presents some unique problems.

Human information processing is basically serial. When we present a message on one flat area, we hope that we can control information intake by guiding the eye through the message by means of visual syntax. Nonetheless, the reader may still look at any part of the total message at any time he or she wishes, but not when he or she reads a booklet. However, the problem arises again when we consider the folder.

Broadly speaking, the folder piece can be given any of several kinds of the so-called *letter fold*. Such pieces are usually about $8\frac{1}{2}$ by 11, 9 by 12, or $8\frac{1}{2}$ by 14 inches. A letter fold takes such pieces down to a size that will fit the No. 10 envelope, which is $4\frac{1}{8}$ inches deep by $9\frac{1}{2}$ inches wide. In addition to these more common-size folders there is the *broadside*, which is a jumbo folder, usually 19 by 25 inches up to 25 by 38 inches when it is flat (before folding). It unfolds to a smashing spread concentrated on one idea.

In Figure 17-8 are shown some common letter-fold pieces, which result in 4-, 6-, 8-, and 10-page folders. Only a few of the many possible treatments are presented, with particular concern to their effect in information processing. Try making these folds yourself with pieces of paper. The drawings indicate vertical formats, but the folder could also have a horizontal format.

Folder (a) presents no particular problems. Page 1 could be treated as a separate page, pages 2 and 3 separately or as a spread, and page 4 as a single unit. But folders (b), (c), (d), (e), and (f) offer more interesting possibilities. Consider, for example, (d). Take the folder you have made. Close it by swinging the left half to the right. When the reader opens it, he or she comes to a two-page spread; another opening reveals a four-page spread. The design of the same folder could be treated in other ways. Turn it back for front. Now consider what was the back as the front. Now it unfolds in a different manner. The order of the message and the designs given the pages may call for different treatments from folder to folder.

17-8 Common letter folds.

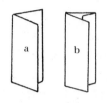

a: 4-page single fold;
b: 6-page standard or wrap-around

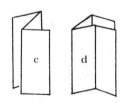

c: 6-page accordion;
d: 8-page standard, double parallel fold or fold within a fold

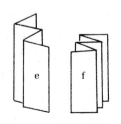

e: 8-page accordion;
f: 10-page accordion

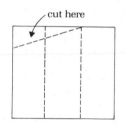

17-9 Angle-cut accordion fold.

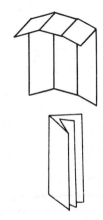

17-10 *Above:* Short-fold, 12 pages. *Below:* Off-center double parallel fold, 8 pages.

These considerataons do not exhaust the possibilities. Look at Figure 17-9. Take a piece of paper. Fold it as a six-page accordion. Before doing so, cut off a piece diagonally as shown. Note the step-effect that allows portions of page 3 and page 5 to be seen from the front.

Folds do not have to be equal as seen in Figure 17-8. Figure 17-10 shows what are known as a *short fold* and an *off-center fold*. To do the latter, lay a sheet in front of you. Bring the left edge toward the right but let it fall short, then crease; repeat and crease. As with the diagonal-cut accordion fold, an interesting tab or index step is visible.

What Kind of Printed Piece?

An important creative decision is the kind of printed piece to be produced. The following factors favor the use of a booklet:

1. Lengthy copy requiring continuity of presentation.
2. Need for a number of illustrative examples.
3. Highly technical material.
4. Catalogue material.

The folder, on the other hand, lends itself when these conditions exist:

1. A series of illustrataons is to be presented, as the number of different models of a product.
2. Short but crisp text is offered.
3. The unfolding naturally builds a climactic impression.
4. Production speed and economy are required. Booklet production means time-consuming, extra folding-and-binding operations, whereas folders can be *self-mailers*. With the latter, one section is left open for addressing and for the printing of postal *indicia*, an indication that the sender has a permit to pay postage at time of mailing in lieu of affixing stamps. Booklets are usually mailed in envelopes, thereby entailing the dual expense of envelopes and insertion.
5. *Imprinting* of, for example, various dealer names is called for. Such work can be done economically on the flat sheets before folding.

Standard Unit Sizes

An early step in planning the printed piece is the preparation of the dummy. At this point the designer must remember that the size of the piece has a significant effect on final production cost because manufacturers, in the interest of economy, produce certain standard sizes of paper, available through printers. Thus, only certain-sized pamphlets and other forms of direct literature can be cut advantageously from these stock sheets. These standard sizes are

Bond: 17 by 22 (basis), 17 by 28, 19 by 24, 22 by 34, 28 by 34, 34 by 44 inches.

Book: 25 by 38 (basis), 28 by 42, 28 by 44, 32 by 45, 35 by 45, 38 by 50, 19 by 25, 23 by 29, 23 by 35, 36 by 48, 41 by 61, 44 by 66, 45 by 68, 50 by 76, 52 by 76 inches.

Cover: 20 by 26 (basis), 23 by 35, 26 by 40, 35 by 46 inches[1]

Suppose an 8-page booklet, $4\frac{1}{2}$ by 6 inches, is being planned. What size stock can be used? Remember these points before solving this problem:

1. One-half inch should be subtracted from the short dimension of the stock to allow for press grippers, which hold the paper as it goes through the press. This is three-eighths of an inch on some presses. Printing can extend to, but not beyond, the grippers.
2. One-eighth inch should be allowed for bleed trim on every edge of the piece.

Thus, we can determine that 64 pages can be printed on a 25-by-38-inch sheet, 32 on each side, as shown in Figure 17-11. This means a total of eight eight-page booklets per sheet of paper.

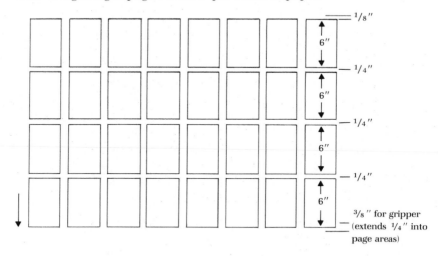

17-11 How 32 pages, each $4\frac{1}{2}$ by 6 inches, are imposed on one side of a 25-by-38-inch sheet. No pages at the head (gripper edge) can bleed. If head bleeds were essential, 28 by 42 sheets would be used.

---

[1] The basis size of cover stock (20 by 26 inches) is slightly larger than 19 by 25 inches, one half of the basis size of book paper (25 by 38 inches), to allow for *overhang covers;* that is, covers with dimensions larger than the inside of the booklet.

The finished booklet should be $4\frac{5}{8}$ by $6\frac{1}{4}$ inches to allow trim of one-eighth inch on top, bottom, and outside to open the pages. The fractions along the right side of the sheet in Figure 17-11 indicate trim allowances. As long as the print area falls at least one-half inch below the top of the sheet, 25 by 38 inches is adequate.

But when bleed pages are in the design, the printed booklet should be $4\frac{3}{4}$ by $6\frac{1}{2}$ inches. When trimming is done, the cut to make the finished $4\frac{1}{2}$ by 6 inches is then deep enough to ensure inclusion of the bleed art. The piece should be printed on a 28-by-42-inch sheet for bleeds.

Common sheet sizes

Size of piece (in inches)	Sheet size for trim	Sheet size for bleeds	Number of pages
$3\frac{3}{8}$ by $6\frac{1}{4}$	28 by 42	28 by 44	96
$3\frac{3}{4}$ by $5\frac{1}{8}$	32 by 44	35 by 45	128
$4\frac{1}{4}$ by $5\frac{3}{8}$	35 by 45	38 by 50	128
$4\frac{1}{2}$ by 6	25 by 38	28 by 42	64
4 by $9\frac{1}{8}$	25 by 38	28 by 42	48
$5\frac{1}{4}$ by $7\frac{5}{8}$	32 by 44	35 by 45	64
$5\frac{1}{2}$ by $8\frac{1}{2}$	35 by 45	38 by 50	64
$8\frac{1}{2}$ by $5\frac{1}{2}$ (oblong)	23 by 35	25 by 38	32
6 by $9\frac{1}{8}$	25 by 38	28 by 42	32
$7\frac{3}{4}$ by $10\frac{5}{8}$	32 by 44	35 by 45	32
$8\frac{1}{2}$ by 11	35 by 45	38 by 50	32
$9\frac{1}{4}$ by $12\frac{1}{8}$	25 by 38	28 by 42	16

A piece can be printed from other than standard-sized paper. Manufacturers make paper in special sizes, and quantities in excess of 5,000 pounds can be purchased economically. For small amounts, extra costs usually dictate fitting the design to a standard size.

Presses and envelopes are made to accommodate all of the standard-sized pieces. Special envelopes can be made to order. Both standard-sized letter and *booklet envelopes* are available through the printer.

Special Paper Considerations _____

In addition to size, certain other aspects of paper need the attention of the designer. These are (1) kind; (2) color; and (3) weight.

Kind of Paper Bond lends itself well to folders because of its good folding quality. It is also strong and durable. Offset prints well on its hard surface, but bond should be avoided for most letterpress work. Common weights

Equivalent basis weights of stock

Book paper Basis: 25 × 38	Cover paper Basis: 20 × 26	Bond paper Basis: 17 × 22
30	—	—
35	—	13
40	—	16
45	25	—
50	—	20
60	35	24
70	40	28
80	45	32
90	50	36
100	55	40
120	65	—
150	80	—

of bond that are in use are 20- and 24-pound, equivalent to the book paper weights of 50- and 60-pounds. Weight means the *basis weight*, the weight in pounds of a ream (500 sheets) of paper cut to its basic size.

Coated book stocks are high-priced and tend to crack in folding. Letterpress reproduction is best, but coated stocks are available for offset.

Uncoated book stocks are less distinctive than coated—and less expensive, enough so that in a long run the cost savings is substantial.

Offset stocks, which are also book paper, fold excellently, and are thus particularly adaptable to folders. The weights of 60-, 70-, and 80-pound are most commonly used.

Cover stock is particularly useful for the addition of separate covers to booklets and is also used for folders and pamphlets. Weights above 80-pound usually require scoring before folding.

Cover stock is also available in 90-, 100-, and 130-pound weights. No paper is made in weights above 150.

Color White has been the traditional color for paper since the earliest days of printing, and black ink on white paper will probably continue to be most popular in the future. But for some time interest in color stocks has grown. There are several reasons for this:

1. The contrast of color stock to white. With the bulk of printing done on white paper, messages on color stock attract attention.
2. Increased understanding of the psychological effects of color. As discussed, color stimulates positively and negatively. Skillfully used, color stock creates atmosphere and builds retention. Be-

cause black and white are in a sense the absence of color, they lack the psychological impact of printing in color ink on color stock.

3. Research in developing compatible inks and papers. Paper and ink manufacturers, with the assistance of psychologists, ophthalmologists, and lighting engineers, have uncovered pleasing combinations of color ink on color paper. Four-color process printed on a color stock has proved startlingly effective when the key color black is substituted by a dark color ink that is compatible with the paper.

The reading task is simplified when the message is printed color-on-color. There is less reflection than black-on-white. Many experts contend that this reduction in contrast is a welcome relief for the reader. Because the cost of color-on-color is not much greater, the continued improvements in paper and ink manufacture will no doubt mean an expanded use of color-on-color printing.

It is possible to match the color of some text stocks with cover stocks when this is desired. If a perfect match cannot be made, the designer would do well to consider a definite contrast between the two.

If a color stock is used for folders, all pages must, of course, be of that color. In the case of booklets, however, it is possible to use color stock for some of the pages, the number of such pages being divisible by four.

Even when a stock of one color is used throughout a booklet, it is possible to give some pages a different color by laying the color on the pages with ink. Offset printing is particularly adaptable to this technique. This applies to the printing of folder pages as well.

Weight   The weight of the stock used must be considered primarily because of its effect on mailing costs. This factor alone cannot, however, determine the weight. The nature of the message and the effect of the paper on the reader may require a stock of such substance that higher mailing costs can be justified. If a booklet carries a self-cover, consideration must be given to durability, which means that a substantial stock may be called for. Self-mailer folders likewise call for heavier paper.

Other Design Considerations _____

If the decision is made to maintain margins from page to page in a folder, the two side margins and the top should be about the same and the foot margin should be slightly larger. Such a decision is likely when the message is primarily verbal, as in Figure 17-12. Incidentally, on the four pages on the opposite side of those shown were the In-

TO OUR SHAREHOLDERS

We are pleased to enclose a check representing the quarterly dividend on shares of stock which you owned of record March 11, 1974. For those of you who have elected to participate in our dividend reinvestment plan, you will receive a statement of the amount of the dividends being reinvested for you into additional shares of common stock of the Company.

For the quarter ending March 31, 1974, the Board of Directors has declared a dividend of 37 cents per common share and the regular dividend on all of the outstanding series of preferred stock. The dividend on common stock represents an increase of 1¼ cents per share in the quarterly dividend rate, and raises the annual dividend rate from $1.43 to $1.48 per share.

For the 12 months ended February 28, 1974, earnings per average common share were $1.72, compared with $1.94, for the same period last year. Earnings for the two months of 1974 were 30 cents per average share, compared with 33 cents for last year.

Unusually mild weather experienced in the Company's service area during January and February, 1974, together with conservation measures of our customers, kept revenues for the two-month period below anticipated levels.

The Board of Directors, at the January, 1974, meeting, approved a construction budget of $144 Million for 1974, approximately $80 Million more than 1973's construction expenditures.

During January, the Company sold—at private placement—150,000 shares of 6⅞% Five-year Cumulative Preferred Stock, $100 Par Value. The proceeds from the sale were used to reduce the Company's short-term indebtedness, resulting from construction expenditures. Indications are that the next permanent financing—probably consisting of debt securities—will be about mid-year.

The Company continues to collect revenues, subject to refund, on rate increases applicable to retail customers, pending final decision from the South Carolina Public Service Commission. As stated in the Notes to Financial Statements of the 1973 Annual Report to Stockholders, the Company's right to place its retail rates in effect under bond was contested in Federal Court. A three-judge court upheld the constitutionality of the State statute and allowed the Company to continue its rates under bond. This ruling was appealed by the contestants to the United States Supreme Court. The Company has received notice that the Supreme Court has upheld the constitutionality of the South Carolina law by adopting the ruling of the three-judge panel.

The Annual Report for 1973 is to be mailed to all stockholders on or about March 22, 1974.

S. C. McMeekin
Chm. of the Board

Arthur M. Williams
President

March 21, 1974

This report is issued solely for the purpose of providing information. It is not intended for use in connection with any sale or purchase of, or any offer or solicitation of offers, to buy or sell, any securities.

SOUTH CAROLINA
ELECTRIC & GAS COMPANY
328 Main Street, Columbia, S.C. 29218

SOUTH CAROLINA ELECTRIC & GAS COMPANY

INTERIM REPORT
February 28, 1974

17-12 Margins on folder pages. (*Courtesy South Carolina Electric & Gas Company*)

come Statement and the Balance Sheet, each spread across two pages. What letter fold do you think was given the piece? The treatment of three equal margins and a larger foot margin may be given to booklets of 8 or 12 pages. If the booklet contains more pages, progressive margins are often followed throughout.

Folios are rarely placed on folder pages, and unless they are an aid to the reader, they are not used in booklets. If folios are used, a table of contents is generally included.

The decision of whether or not to print on the *IFC, IBC,* or *OBC* (inside front cover, inside back cover, outside back cover) of booklets is often determined by the nature of the contents. If the content is informative and the layout formal, these covers are often left blank, particularly if the piece carries a separate cover. If the booklet is promotional and the design less formal, the covers are often printed, particularly if the piece carries a self-cover.

Whether the folder or booklet is vertical or horizontal is a matter of option. Nonpromotional booklets that are formally designed are usually vertical in the tradition of the book. Promotional materials may be presented in either format. A particular advantage of the folder is that vertical and horizontal layouts are possible within the same piece. Consider the wraparound, six-page folder, for example. Page 1 may be

17-13 Bridging the gutter.

Bridging with art and a headline.

Bridging with space.

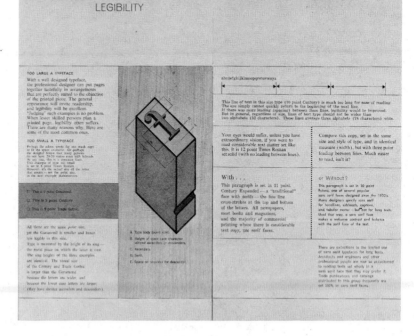

Bridging with a headline.

How long should a line of type be for easy reading? 15

There are, then, two typographies, as there are two worlds: and, apart from God or profits, the test of one is mechanical perfection, and of the other, sanctity—the commercial article at its best is simply physically serviceable and, per accidens, beautiful in its efficiency; the work of art at its best is beautiful in its very substance and, per accidens, as serviceable as an article of commerce. The typography of Industrialism, when it is not deliberately diabolical and designed to deceive, will be plain; and in spite of the wealth of its resources—a thousand varieties of inks, papers, presses and mechanical processes for

Stand at a distance from a building, and a sign a hundred feet long can be read without a twitch of an eyeball. But a newspaper headline held at arm's length not only requires that the eye move, even the head may have to swivel slightly.

The reading process is one of identifying the patterns created by words and phrases in type. The eye moves along the line, relaying these composite visual forms to the brain, where the abstract forms are decoded into meanings.

It becomes obvious that for continuous text, the proper length of line is that which enables the eye to grasp the units of pattern in the line with a minimum of eye movement; the muscles of the eye share with other parts of the body the reaction of fatigue from over-exertion.

Experience has resulted in general agreement that eight to ten words constitutes a basically readable line of type; this represents a line of roughly two alphabets or 52 characters in length. When a line goes longer than this, leading must be introduced between the lines to facilitate the eye's identification of the letter forms without confusion with the adjoining lines.

Lines which are shorter than this standard will obviously involve even less eye-strain; but they present a technical problem to the typesetter, for as the number of words diminishes, the fewer are the spaces in which he can distribute the necessary space to fill out his line. Where there are long words that are impossible to break (like 'stretch'), this often results in the uneven spacing that impedes legibility.

a vertical. Upon opening it, the reader may see a horizontal spread over pages 2, 3, and 4.

By bridging the gutter in a vertical format book, the designer can also present horizontal designs. Some of the techniques for doing this were shown in Chapter 15. Figure 17-13 shows spreads from booklets in which some of these techniques are applied.

Checking Press Sheets _____

Once a message is released to a medium, the opportunity for controlling the printed result fades. In the case of direct literature, however, there is a chance to check the printed piece as it comes from the press. At this point it is possible to find and correct *fill-in* or *plugging* of halftones and fine lines; streaks, slurs, and other blemishes; and improper makeready and inking.

Press sheets, or *press proofs*, are marked by an arrow that indicates change of position. The arrow is drawn to point out where type or art is to be moved. A circle is drawn around areas where makeready is faulty or where some other imperfection is spotted, and the proofreader's delete symbol draws attention to the circle.

One cannot be too careful in searching for errors in either verbal or visual copy before releasing it for publication. Information processing theory tells why. Things that we look at are usually within a familiar context which aids us in perception. Sometimes we see things that are not there; at other times we do not see things that are there, simply because of our expectations, which are guided by the context. Thus it is easy to misperceive.

One interesting study of proofreading confirms this interpretation. Subjects were asked to cross out each letter *e* in passages of prose. Analysis of results showed that the subjects were more likely to miss the silent *e* than the pronounced one. Further, the *e* in the word "the" was more likely to be missed than other pronounced *e*s. It was also found that the absence of an *e* that would have been silent is less likely to be discovered than the absence of an *e* that would have been pronounced.[2] It would seem that there is an interrelationship between visual symbols and acoustic coding. In any event, proofreading requires close attention.

---

[2] D. W. J. Corcoran, "Acoustic Factors in Proofreading," *Nature* 214 (1967): 851 — 852.

18 Paper: Selection, Folding, Binding, Finishing

By now it should be obvious that successful graphic communication is possible only when the desires of the user of any printing process are closely coordinated with the mechanics of the process. Obvious, too, is the fact that although the user may wish to think only in terms of the esthetic values, or utilitarian properties, or both, of printed material, these qualities cannot be separated from mechanics and cost.

The interrelationship of mechanics and desired effects come into still sharper focus with a study of paper selection and imposition—the preliminary steps in printing; and folding, binding, and finishing—the final production stages.

A discussion of these steps also highlights the need for comprehensive advance planning that takes into account all phases of printing production. For paper selection is affected by folding, binding is affected by paper, and so on. None of the steps in production can be separated from the others.

Paper Selection

Several important factors must be considered when selecting paper. Some of these factors are the immediate concern of the user; others are mainly of interest to the printer.

Paper shares full responsibility with type and illustrations in giving personality to any printed piece. Paper also contributes to the "voice" of the printed material. It can say quality or cheapness and speak loudly or softly. From the user's standpoint, this may be the most vital role of paper. But, although the color, weight, and smoothness must be judged according to their esthetic contributions, these and other characteristics of paper must be analyzed in other ways, too.

Practical properties, such as the ability to withstand age, are very important. Printed matter that is supposed to last for years may disintegrate long before its intended life span has expired if proper paper was not chosen. Or, faulty paper selection can cause printed pieces to fall apart at the folds before the material has completed its usefulness.

The cost of paper is always a determinant. Paper is priced by the pound, with the rate according to the kind and amount of processing needed to give it the desired qualities. Thus weight or thickness becomes significant, increasingly so if the finished product is to be mailed. A small difference in weight per piece can multiply postage costs by thousands of dollars if great numbers of pieces are to be mailed.

The user of printing is thus likely to be most concerned about these characteristics of paper: (1) the esthetic or psychological effect of its appearance and "feel," (2) its permanence, (3) its durability, and (4) its cost and weight.

Printers must share their customers' concern. But, because they are charged with the mechanics of production, they see these characteristics from a slightly different angle, regarding many other technical properties that have special meaning for them.

Printers must be aware of the opacity of paper, for example, knowing that appearance can be ruined if the inked impression on one side shows through to the other. They try to ensure that a printed piece is planned to fit a standard-size sheet of paper that matches press capacity. By so doing, they can minimize the unnecessary costs that increase through wastage from trimming.

A letterpress printer knows that only with a smooth-finish paper can fine-screen engravings be reproduced to a customer's satisfaction. The offset lithographer or gravure printer requires other special papers for good reproduction.

The chemical and physical properties of paper, such as acidity, porosity, and surface-bonding strength, must be checked. Papers with high acid content are fine for some work, but are not permanent enough for many uses. Ink spreads after contact with paper according to the porosity of the paper; surface-bonding strength determines a paper's resistance to "picking," the undesirable release of small bits of paper surface during a press run. If picking is excessive, press time can be lengthened because of the need for frequent cleanups.

Printers must always be conscious of the grain of paper. As paper is manufactured, the watery pulp is carried over fine wire cloth and the pulp fibers tend to lie in the same direction. In this way, the fibers give paper a grain, much like that in wood. Grain direction is important because it affects (1) the ease with which paper will run through a press, and (2) the folding and binding. In a magazine or booklet, for example, the grain should run parallel to the binding so that the sheets will lie flat when open. The bindery must always be consulted to be sure the grain is in the right direction for folding and binding.

The printer, then, in addition to the end-use properties of paper that may be apparent to the customer, must also consider (1) opacity; (2) sheet size; (3) special properties for particular printing processes; (4) capability of reproducing illustrations; (5) chemical and physical properties that affect presswork, folding, and binding; (6) grain direction.

It is therefore essential that the user of printing work closely with the printer in selecting paper for any job. A basic knowledge of kinds, weights, sizes, and finishes is important to permit the user to adapt his or her requirements to those of the printer.

Basic Kinds of Paper

Paper can be classified in many ways; for example, *wood* papers and *rag* papers. Most paper is made of wood pulp, but some is made of rags or a combination of both.

The cheapest paper is made by grinding bark-free logs into a pulp that is formed into sheets without benefit of any chemical action to remove impurities. This *groundwood* paper is commonly used for newspapers and disintegrates quickly because of its imperfections.

Wood-pulp papers of more permanence are treated to be rid of substances that cause fast deterioration. Called *sulphate, soda,* and *sulphite* papers, they are used for all kinds of printing.

A 100 percent rag content paper is virtually imperishable, but is so expensive that its use is limited.

To order paper, one must know its four basic classifications named by appearance and proposed use: *bond, book, cover,* and *cardboard.*

Aside from its use for bonds and stock certificates, bond paper is standard for office use. Because its primary application is for letterheads and typewriter paper, it has a semihard finish that is ideal for typing or handwriting.

As the name implies, book paper is used for books, but it also is the vehicle for virtually every mass-printed medium of communication. It comes in textures ranging from rough to a smooth gloss.

Heavy and durable, cover paper has been formulated to withstand the extra wear on booklet and magazine covers and is available in many colors and finishes. Publications are often "self-cover"—the cover is printed on the same stock and at the same time as the inside pages, but when special bulk or durability is desired, cover stock is specified.

Posters, stand-up advertising displays, and direct-mail promotion pieces are frequently printed on a stiff, heavy paper composed of several plies, or layers. Cardboard stock may also be referred to as *bristol board* or by a number of suppliers as *postcard.*

In addition to the basic classes, there are special papers for special uses. *Offset* papers have properties designed to compensate for the moisture and other problems unique in offset printing. *Gravure* or *roto* paper is especially made to absorb the large amount of ink applied in rotogravure printing. There are other kinds of paper, but most are variations of those already described. Much of the variety comes from giving standard papers different finishes or surfaces.

Paper Surfaces

Paper sheets are formed during manufacture when pulp is passed between rollers. This is called *calendering,* and the amount of calendering depends upon the desired degree of surface smoothness.

Paper with a minimum of calendering is called *antique* or *eggshell* and is widely used for books and brochures. It has substantial bulk and is rough in texture. Although it is not suitable for reproducing letterpress halftone illustrations, the nonglare surface of antique paper makes it desirable for lengthy reading matter. The bulk of antique papers is often reduced by additional calendering that is gentle enough not to eliminate the rough texture.

Fairly extensive calendering produces a smoother surface for paper called *machine finish.* Many magazines use this paper because of its good printing surface; *English finish* is very similar (slightly more calendering) and provides only slightly better letterpress halftone reproduction.

Supercalendered paper has been processed until its surface is slick enough to take all but the finest-screened letterpress halftone engravings. It also is popular for magazines.

Paper manufacturers, when confronted with the problem of finding a suitable surface for fine-screened halftones, developed *coated* papers. Originally these were brush-coated with a clay substance, and some still are, but most coating is now applied by machine as the paper is being made. Coated papers are expensive but essential for the finest quality of photographic reproduction.

Paper Weight and Sheet Sizes

Paper is priced by the pound but is sold in lots of a given number of sheets as well as pounds. Standard lots are a *ream* (500 sheets), a *case* (about 500 pounds), and a *skid* (about 3,000 pounds). A *quire* is one twentieth of a ream and a *carton* is one quarter of a case.

It would be impossible to identify paper's weight by that of a single sheet. Instead, this vital element of paper, usually called *substance*, is expressed as the number of pounds in a ream of sheets of a basic size. Hence, paper would be labeled "100-pound" if 500 sheets of the basic size weighed 100 pounds.

Unfortunately, the *basic* size is not the same for all kinds of paper. Generally, the basic size is the most suitable and efficient for most common uses of any particular paper. The basic size for bond paper, for example, is 17 by 22 inches because it will fit most presses and will cut into four $8\frac{1}{2}$ by 11-inch sheets.

Basic sheet sizes in inches are

bond: 17 by 22
book: 25 by 38
cover: 20 by 26
card (bristol): $22\frac{1}{2}$ by $28\frac{1}{2}$

These sizes must be kept in mind when ordering paper. Obviously, 500 sheets 25 by 38 inches will weigh a lot more than 500 sheets 17 by 22 inches of the same paper. The user of 20-pound bond who orders a 30-pound book paper expecting to get a sheet of more thickness will be shocked to find that it is, in fact, much thinner. (Equivalent paper weights are given in the table on page 339.)

In addition to the basic size, paper is available in many sizes said to be *standard* because they match press sizes or will cut or fold into standard-size booklets that, in turn, fit standard-size mailing envelopes. (Common sheet sizes are related to piece sizes in the table on page 338.)

Printers can use practically any size sheet of paper and cut it to fit a particular job. But when they do, waste results and, more importantly, a loss of efficiency occurs in each of the printing, folding, binding, and finishing steps that follow.

Imposition, Binding, Folding ⸻

Imposition and Signatures

As they produce booklets, magazines, books, or other such publications, printers ordinarily print several pages on a single sheet of paper. All of the type pages that are to print on one side of the sheet must be positioned so that when both sides of the sheet have been printed, the sheet can be folded and bound with the pages in proper sequence. This arranging or arrangement of type pages is called *imposition.*[1]

---

[1] See pages 331 — 332 and Figures 17-1, 17-2, 17-3. You arranged the type pages of a booklet in proper imposition when you followed the directions. You also created an eight-page signature.

Each printed and folded sheet is called a *signature* and it makes up one or more sections of the publication. Any section of a publication in which all pages of that section have been printed on one sheet is a signature. (Some impositions print two copies of each signature.)

The simplest of signatures can be two pages (one leaf printed on both sides), but ordinarily signatures range from four to 64 pages, in multiples of four. For booklets, books, or magazines, the most common signatures are 8, 16, 32, or 64 pages, and the two- or four-page units are treated as exceptions.

There are numerous kinds of impositions, especially for the great variety of intricately folded pamphlets and folders that are produced. In any case, the imposition a printer will use is dictated by the printer's press capacity and the folding and binding that are to follow.

The imposition a printer uses is extremely important to an editor, since much of the editor's planning for use of color and deadlines will depend on the kind of imposition that will be used.

For example, let us look at the problems of the editor of a small 16-page publication. If, as is typical, the printer plans to print half the pages on one side of a sheet and half on the other, the editor must know which pages go on which side of the sheet. The editor can then set separate deadlines for each unit of eight pages that must go on the press at the same time. Only when all eight pages are complete right down to the last plate and the last line of type is the form ready for the press.

If there is to be a color in addition to black on only eight pages, or fewer, the editor, knowing the imposition, can assign color only to those pages that fall on one side of the sheet. By so doing, the color is printed with only one additional press run; if one or more pages of color were to be assigned to each side of the sheet, two additional press runs would be required.

Imposition, therefore, is of great importance because press delays, missed publication dates, and unnecessary color costs can be avoided by a planner who knows what method the printer will use.

Kinds of imposition For most purposes there are two basic kinds of imposition. One of these is shown in Figure 18-1: half the pages in a signature are printed on one side of the sheet and the other half are printed on the back of the sheet. This method is called *sheetwise* and is preferred by most printers for most jobs.

In the other kind, all pages of a signature are printed on one side of a sheet for half the press run, and the sheet is then turned over for the same pages to be printed on the opposite side during the final half run. The sheet is then cut apart to form two signatures. Depending

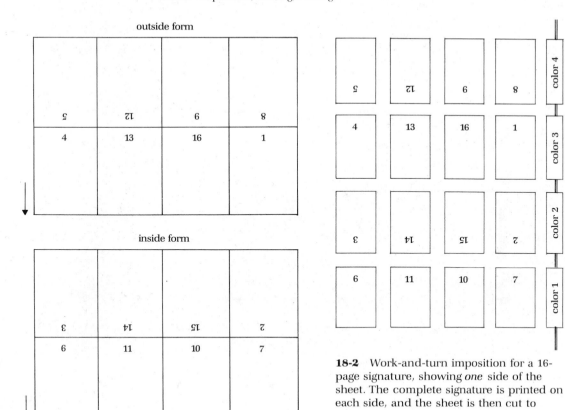

outside form

ς	ττ	6	8
4	13	16	1

inside form

ε	τ4	ςτ	τ
6	11	10	7

18-1 Sheetwise imposition for a 16-page signature, showing *both* sides of the sheet. Eight pages are printed on each side.

ς	ττ	6	8	color 4
4	13	16	1	color 3
ε	τ4	ςτ	τ	color 2
6	11	10	7	color 1

18-2 Work-and-turn imposition for a 16-page signature, showing *one* side of the sheet. The complete signature is printed on each side, and the sheet is then cut to make two signatures. This diagram also shows how fountains and rollers might be split to put four different colors on a signature in one press run.

upon how the sheet is turned before it is backed up, this imposition has three variations—*work-and-turn,* which is most common, *work-and-tumble,* and *work-and-twist.*

In work-and-turn, the sheet is turned so that the left edge becomes the right edge, but the front (gripper) edge remains the same. In work-and-tumble, the sheet is tumbled so that the back edge becomes the gripper edge when the sheet is being printed on the second side. In work-and-twist all edges are reversed. Because work-and-turn employs the same gripper edge for printing both sides, it is used much more than the other two techniques. Figure 18-2 shows a sheet that has been printed with this imposition.

It should be noted that the press used in Figure 18-2 would have to have twice the capacity as the one in Figure 18-1; it is capable of printing 16 pages at one time, and the press in Figure 18-1 will print only eight. Therefore, if a printer has a press large enough to print all

18-3 Split-fountain. Inks of different colors separated from each other in the ink fountains (wells at bottom) and transferred to rollers above. (*Printing Corporation of America*)

the pages required, work-and-turn will be used, but if the press capacity is only half of the number of pages needed, sheetwise imposition will be used.

The same figure shows a rather specialized printing technique which is of great importance to imposition. This is *split-fountain* or *split-color,* a technique that applies several colors to a sheet during one press run (Figure 18-3). Once a sheet has been printed in black, several colors can be added with one impression if they are planned to fall in "channels."

Although the procedure varies, the ink fountain is usually split into several compartments (four, in Figure 18-2), which carry different colors. From these, the inking rollers, correspondingly split, carry the colors to their particular pages. As many colors can be printed simultaneously as there are sections of the roller. To plan color according to the channels covered by each roller section the designer must know the location of each page in a form.

This technique is used extensively by magazines to satisfy the color requirements of advertisers at a minimum cost. Roller splitting for a one-time-only job may be too costly, but for magazines that can use cut rollers repeatedly it can offer substantial cost advantages.

Imposition and Web-Fed Offset

There has been a marked trend in recent years for many publications to change over from sheetfed letterpress or offset to web offset. Imposition and its effects on the use of color and planning vary considerably when multiunit web perfecting offset presses are used. As noted earlier, web presses are those fed from a roll rather than sheets, and a perfecting press is one that prints both sides of the paper at the same time.

In general, the typical four-unit and six-unit web offset presses used for magazine and book work offer much greater use of color at lower cost; the expense involved in running a second unit, for example, usually is considerably less than putting a sheet through a press a second time.

The availability of several units and the possibility of using more than one web gives great color versatility when using web offset. This wide variation makes it impossible to give a complete analysis of web offset impositions here; printers will provide imposition sheets showing page positions for each variation.

Wraps and Tip-Ins

Although good planning dictates a consideration of imposition and signatures, it is not always possible to produce a publication that will adhere to large signatures.

An advertiser, for example, will frequently insist that a magazine ad be on a special paper or other material. The ad must then be specially handled and inserted into the publication. In book work it is not unusual for the publisher to want a special glossy paper for reproducing the few illustrations to be used and to order the rest of the book printed on a cheaper stock.

In these and other cases where standard signatures cannot be used, the printer will most likely take care of the problem with a *wrap* or a *tip-in.* The former is a four-page insert placed around a signature before it is bound. Because they can be stitched into the binding with their signatures, wraps are as durably bound as the rest of the magazine or book. Wraps are a problem to the editor, however, because he or she must plan their location carefully in order to get the desired continuity of subject matter.

It is possible, but more time-consuming, to place four pages within a signature rather than around it. In that case the pages are simply called an *insert,* if they are in the center of the signature, or an *inside wrap* if they are between the center and the outside.

A tip-in is a pasted-in two- or four-page section. Most tip-ins are of two pages—a single sheet. They are given a coating of paste in a narrow strip along the inner edge that is used to "tip" the sheet into position. Tip-ins are not so durable as wraps or inserts because they are not stitched during binding, but they are frequently used.

Although these inserting methods are commonly used, their use is restricted to situations demanding such treatment. Only when substantial costs are avoided or imperative special effects are obtained should the use of units other than standard signatures be considered.

Folding, Binding, Trimming

When the printed sheets come off the press, the work of the printer, as such, is completed. The printer may or may not process the work further; basically, the remaining work belongs to the bindery, or finishing specialists.

18-4   Common folds for printed matter.

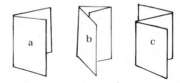

a: 4-page folder, single fold; **b:** 6-page standard folder; **c:** 6-page accordion

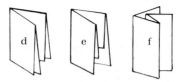

d: 8-page booklet or folder, two right-angle folds, also called French fold if printed one side and not trimmed; **e:** 8-page right-angle folder, first fold short; **f:** 8-page folder, two parallel folds.

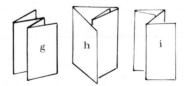

g: 8-page accordion; **h:** 8-page parallel folder, three-fold over and over; **i:** 8-page parallel map

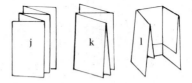

j: 10-page accordion; **k:** 12-page letter fold; **l:** 12-page broadside, first fold short

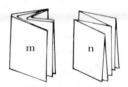

m: 16-page parallel booklet; **n:** 16-page broadside

In most cases, bindery operations begin with folding, an often underrated step in publication production. Sheets sometimes must be cut before folding, but this step is avoided whenever possible. Even with the best cutting, the knife "draws" the paper as it goes through a stack, and a variation in page sizes results. Unbound circulars using bleeds, however, must be cut before folding.

Kinds of folds The most commonly used fold, because of its use for books, booklets, and magazines, is the *right-angle* fold. Thus, a single sheet folded once becomes a four-page signature; folded again at a right angle it becomes an eight-page signature, and so on. An eight-page signature folded in this manner must be trimmed before the pages are free to be turned so that pages 2, 3, 6, and 7 can be read (as described on page 331).

A *French fold* is an eight-page unit made with right-angle folds and not trimmed. French-fold leaflets are often used in advertising and promotion work.

Parallel folds may be either *accordion*, where each succeeding fold is parallel but turned in the opposite direction, or *over-and-over*, where each fold is in the same direction. Like the French fold, both of these folds require no trimming. See Figure 18-4 for common folds.

Methods of binding Binding may be either a minor or a major contributor to the cost of any printing job. With simple leaflets binding can be skipped entirely; for an elaborate sales presentation book it may be the major cost element. This influence on cost makes binding an important part of production planning. Binding also has a direct bearing on planning in signature units. This point can be more clearly seen with a comparison of two commonly used binding methods.

Saddle-wire binding The most commonly used kind of binding, because it is inexpensive and adequate for many magazines and booklets, is *saddle-wire binding*. Signatures to be bound by this method are inserted one into the other, and wire staples are driven into the fold through to the center of the publication. As they are bound, the signatures resemble a saddle, hence the name.

18-5 *Above:* Saddle-wire binding. *Below:* Side-wire binding.

Saddle-wire binding has some special advantages. Because there is no backbone, only a fold, pages will lie flat. Inside margins can be small, because the binding does not infringe upon the page. Separate covers can be used but are not necessary. Saddle-wire binding is limited, however, in the number of pages it can accommodate. Generally speaking, it is usable only for publications up to about $\frac{1}{4}$ inch in thickness.

Side-wire binding Thicker magazines or booklets (up to about one-half inch in thickness) may be *side-wire bound*. In this sort of binding, signatures are stacked on top of each other and staples are driven through from top to bottom. Because these staples are inserted about $\frac{1}{8}$ inch from the backbone, they prevent side-wire publications from lying flat when open. A separate cover is usually wrapped around and glued to the backbone of side-wire publications. Figure 18-5 illustrates these two binding systems.

Once again, the effect of the mechanical operation on editorial planning should be emphasized. In this case, the pages that fall into each signature can vary according to the kind of binding. Except for the center signature, half the pages in each signature of a saddle-wire booklet come from the front of the booklet and the other half come from the back. Thus, in a 32-page booklet of two signatures, the outside or wrap signature contains pages 1 through 8 and 25 through 32. The center signature contains pages 9 through 24. On the other hand, all signatures in side-wire booklets have pages with consecutive numbering. Editors, therefore, must know which binding system is to be used as they complete the signatures to meet press deadlines.

The planner of a side-wire bound booklet or magazine must also allow a larger inside margin to compensate for the $\frac{1}{8}$- inch or more taken up by the binding.

Perfect binding   The development of durable and pliable plastic adhesives has increased the use of the so-called *perfect binding*. This is a much cheaper method than traditional book binding, yet it can be used for volumes as large as municipal telephone books.

No sewing or stitching is needed in perfect binding. Instead, the backbone area is roughened by grinding, the pliable adhesive is applied to it, and lining cloth is then glued to the backbone. Perfect binding is used for both paperback books (Figure 18-6) and hardcover books. This book is a perfect-bound hardcover book.

18-6   Perfect binding. Lining cloth is glued to backbone, then stiff paper cover is glued on.

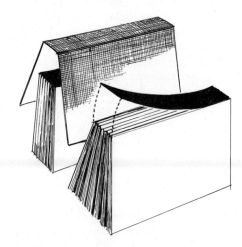

Traditional book binding   The traditional method of book binding, sometimes called *edition binding*, has been in use for centuries. Books bound by this method are *sewn* and *casebound;* as "case" implies, they are hardcover books. (Some sewn books are given paper covers, but this combination is not edition binding.)

After the signatures have been gathered, end papers are tipped (pasted) to the first and last signatures. Signatures are then sewn together (Smyth sewing), and the book is "smashed," or compressed before the three sides are trimmed. In Smyth sewing, signatures are saddle-sewn and sewn to each other at the same time (Figure 18-7).

Books are often *rounded* and *backed* after trimming. They are said to be backed when the backbone has been widened enough to compensate for the thickness of the covers to be added. When rounded, the backbone is made to form a slight arc. It is then reinforced with mesh and paper, which are glued to it, and the *case* (cover) is attached by gluing the end sheets to it.

18-7   Smyth sewing. Stitches hold the signatures together at the backbone.

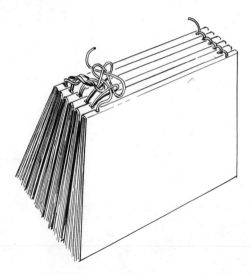

Loose-leaf and mechanical bindings   Scores of loose-leaf and mechanical binding systems are being used today, ranging all the way from student notebooks to elaborate catalogues and price books.

The chief advantages of these bindings are that pages open flat, may be of different paper stock and even different sizes, and there is no need to be concerned about signatures.

All the mechanical binding systems use more or less the same principle. Sheets are punched with holes along the binding edge and are then bound together by plastic or metal rings or coils that are slipped through the holes.

18-8   Steps from imposition to sewing of signatures.

(Courtesy New York Lithographing Corporation and Montauk Book Manufacturing Company, Inc.)

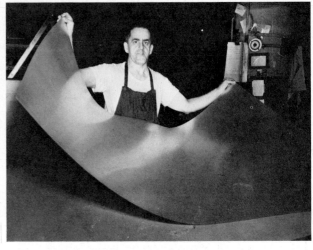

Exposed plate ready for developing and fixing.

Stripper lines up page negatives on a golden-rod flat according to folding and binding imposition. Light table enables him to follow ruled-up master form below.

Taking printed sheet out of delivery end of press.

Putting finished plate on press.

Banding skid of printed sheets
for delivery to bindery.

Cutting printed sheets according to specifications.

Skids of printed sheets ready to be placed on folding machines in background. Skid in left foreground holds stacks of sheets cut in half, each half containing a 64-page signature (32 pages on each side of sheet).

Smyth sewing signatures before binding. Spools of thread are at upper left. Stack of signatures is in front of each operator.

Some Special Finishing Operations

Some of the so-called finishing operations may be carried out by the printer, but many of them are the responsibility of a binder or a firm specializing in the particular technique. In many cases, finishing techniques are used to increase the utility of the printed piece, but they are often also employed simply to enhance visual appeal.

The following list is by no means all-inclusive, but it does present the more commonly used techniques.

Die cutting

Some printed pieces are much more effective if they are cut to special shapes. Any special shape—a company's product, a question mark, the outline of a state—can be made by die cutting. Several sheets of paper or cardboard can be cut at one time when *high dies,* very similar to rugged cookie cutters, are used. Some *steel-rule* cutting is done, however, on standard printing presses with only one or two sheets being cut at a time. For steel-rule cutting, the desired shape is cut into ¾-inch plywood with a jigsaw, and steel rules are cut and bent to fit the shape. The rules, when put into the cutout, are sharp enough and high enough to make the desired cut with each press impression.

Easeling

Finishers have stock sizes of easels, which are applied to display cards and other printed pieces so that they can stand on counters, desks, and tabletops. Either single- or double-wing easels are used, depending upon the weight of the board or the width of the base.

Embossing

Initials, seals, medallions, and other designs can be raised in relief on paper or other material by running the material in a press between a relief die (below) and an engraved die (above). Embossing may be either blind (no color applied) or printed. Inks or paints are applied before embossing. The major expense is in the making of the dies, but careful makeready is also required.

Gumming

Labels and other stickers may be gummed by hand or by machine either before or after printing. Machines can apply gum in strips of any number and in any direction. Many printing problems are avoided if gumming follows presswork.

Indexing

Indexing is a die-cutting process for providing the tabs needed on such items as index cards, address books, telephone pads, and so on.

Numbering

Most letterpress printers can easily and cheaply provide numbering because numbering machines can be locked in a chase with or without other plates and type matter. These machines can number consecutively or repeat.

Other printing processes require the use of special press attachments.

Pebbling

Any texture can be added to paper following printing by running the paper through rollers embossed with the desired design. Paper manufacturers offer a *pebble* stock, a paper with a textured surface, as well as other uneven finishes, but as a finishing term pebbling means the addition of *any* texture after printing. Linen and other clothlike surfaces are included.

Applying texture to paper as a finishing process instead of during paper manufacture eliminates the problems connected with running rough stock on letterpress machines.

Perforating Either the printer or the finisher can do perforating. If it is done by the printer, ink is carried to the paper at the perforating line because the sharp rule used is slightly more than type high. A perforating wheel is attached to the cylinder if the technique is to be done on a cylinder press.

The kind of perforating found on postage stamps is the work of a finisher who uses a rotary machine that punches rows of tiny holes. The purpose of perforating is simply to make tearing easy.

Punching Standard male and female dies are used to punch holes for the various styles of loose-leaf or mechanical binding.

Scoring Scoring, like perforating, is done to make tearing easier or to aid in folding. A sharp steel rule is used to cut the outer fibers of the paper slightly; if heavy stock or cardboard is being used, the rule may have to cut partially through the board.

Scoring should not be confused with *creasing*, a similar operation in which a dull, rather than sharp, rule is used. Creasing is also an aid to folding, but its other purpose is to make tearing more difficult, not easier. The blunt rule merely compresses the fibers, making the stock more durable at the fold.

To avoid confusion, it is wise to tell the finisher *why* the technique is being requested.

A Some Commonly Used Typefaces

The typefaces shown on this page and the following 12 pages represent designs commonly used for body and/or display in all forms of printed matter. They are set in a moderate size to show their suitability for different purposes. By analyzing the distinctive characteristics of various letters, students can quickly learn to recognize many of these common designs.

Avant Garde Medium _____

ABCDEFGHIJKLMNOPQRSTUVWXYZ
abcdefghijklmnopqrstuvwxyz
1234567890

P. T. Barnum _____

A B C D E F G H I J K L M N O P Q R S T U V W X Y Z &
a b c d e f g h i j k l m n o p q r s t u v w x y z
$ 1 2 3 4 5 6 7 8 9 0

Baskerville

ABCDEFGHIJKLMNOPQR STUVWXYZ&
abcdefghijklmnopqrstuvwxyz
$1234567890

Baskerville Italic

ABCDEFGHIJKLMNOPQR STUVWXYZ&
abcdefghijklmnopqrstuvwxyz
$1234567890

Benedictine

ABCDEFGHIJKLMNOPQRSTUVWXYZ&
a b c d e f g h i j k l m n o p q r s t u v w x y z
$ 1 2 3 4 5 6 7 8 9 0

Benedictine Italic

ABCDEFGHIJKLMNOPQRSTUVWXYZ&
a b c d e f g h i j k l m n o p q r s t u v w x y z
$ 1 2 3 4 5 6 7 8 9 0

Bernhard Gothic Medium

ABCDEFGHIJKLMNOPQRSTUVWXYZ&
a b c d e f g h i j k l m n o p q r s t u v w x y z
$ 1 2 3 4 5 6 7 8 9 0

Bernhard Gothic Medium Italic

ABCDEFGHIJKLMNOPQRSTUVWXYZ&
a b c d e f g h i j k l m n o p q r s t u v w x y z
$ 1 2 3 4 5 6 7 8 9 0

Bernhard Modern Bold _____

A B C D E F G H I J K L M N O P Q R S T U V W X Y Z &
a b c d e f g h i j k l m n o p q r s t u v w x y z
$ 1 2 3 4 5 6 7 8 9 0 ¢

Bernhard Modern Roman Italic _____

A B C D E F G H I J K L M N O P Q R S T U V W X Y Z &
a b c d e f g h i j k l m n o p q r s t u v w x y z
$ 1 2 3 4 5 6 7 8 9 0

Bodoni _____

A B C D E F G H I J K L M N O P Q R S T U V W X Y Z &
a b c d e f g h i j k l m n o p q r s t u v w x y z
$ 1 2 3 4 5 6 7 8 9 0

Bodoni Italic _____

A B C D E F G H I J K L M N O P Q R S T U V W X Y Z &
a b c d e f g h i j k l m n o p q r s t u v w x y z
$ 1 2 3 4 5 6 7 8 9 0

Bookman _____

ABCDEFGHIJKLMNOPQRSTUVWXYZ&
abcdefghijklmnopqrstuvwxyz
$1234567890

Bookman Italic _____

ABCDEFGHIJKLMNOPQRSTUVWXYZ&
abcdefghijklmnopqrstuvwxyz
$1234567890

Caledonia _____

ABCDEFGHIJKLMNOPQRSTUVWXYZ&
abcdefghijklmnopqrstuvwxyz
$1234567890

Caledonia Italic _____

ABCDEFGHIJKLMNOPQRSTUVWXYZ&
abcdefghijklmnopqrstuvwxyz
$1234567890

Caslon _____

A B C D E F G H I J K L M N O P Q R S T U V W X Y Z &
a b c d e f g h i j k l m n o p q r s t u v w x y z
$ 1 2 3 4 5 6 7 8 9 0

Caslon Italic _____

A B C D E F G H I J K L M N O P Q R S T U V W X Y Z &
a b c d e f g h i j k l m n o p q r s t u v w x y z
$ 1 2 3 4 5 6 7 8 9 0

Century Schoolbook _____

A B C D E F G H I J K L M N O P Q R S T U V W X Y Z &
a b c d e f g h i j k l m n o p q r s t u v w x y z
$ 1 2 3 4 5 6 7 8 9 0

Century Schoolbook Italic _____

A B C D E F G H I J K L M N O P Q R S T U V W X Y Z &
a b c d e f g h i j k l m n o p q r s t u v w x y z
$ 1 2 3 4 5 6 7 8 9 0

Cheltenham Medium _____

ABCDEFGHIJKLMNOPQRSTUVWXYZ&
abcdefghijklmnopqrstuvwxyz
$1234567890

Cheltenham Medium Italic _____

ABCDEFGHIJKLMNOPQRSTUVWXYZ&
abcdefghijklmnopqrstuvwxyz
$1234567890

Clarendon _____

A B C D E F G H I J K L M N O P Q R S T U V W X Y Z
a b c d e f g h i j k l m n o p q r s t u v w x y z
$ 1 2 3 4 5 6 7 8 9 0

Clarendon Semi-Bold _____

A B C D E F G H I J K L M N O P Q R S T U V W X Y Z
a b c d e f g h i j k l m n o p q r s t u v w x y z
$ 1 2 3 4 5 6 7 8 9 0

Cloister _____

ABCDEFGHIJKLMNOPQRSTUVWXYZ&
abcdefghijklmnopqrstuvwxyz
$1234567890

Cloister Italic. _____

ABCDEFGHIJKLMNOPQRSTUVWXYZ&
abcdefghijklmnopqrstuvwxyz
$1234567890

Cooper Black _____

ABCDEFGHIJKLMNOPQRSTUVWXYZ&
abcdefghijklmnopqrstuvwxyz
$1234567890

Craw Modern _____

ABCDEFGHIJKLMNOPQRSTUVWXYZ
abcdefghijklmnopqrstuvwxyz
1234567890

Dom Casual _____

ABCDEFGHIJKLMNOPQRSTUVWXYZ&
abcdefghijklmnopqrstuvwxyz
1234567890

Dominante _____

ABCDEFGHIJKLMNOPQRSTUVWXYZ&
abcdefghijklmnopqrstuvwxyz
$1234567890

Dominante Bold _____

ABCDEFGHIJKLMNOPQRSTUVWXYZ&
abcdefghijklmnopqrstuvwxyz
$1234567890

Egmont Light _____

ABCDEFGHIJKLMNOPQRSTUVWXYZ
abcdefghijklmnopqrstuvwxyz
$1234567890

Egmont Light Italic

ABCDEFGHIJKLMNOPQRSTUVWXYZ
abcdefghijklmnopqrstuvwxyz
$1234567890

Electra

ABCDEFGHIJKLMNOPQRSTUVWXYZ&
abcdefghijklmnopqrstuvwxyz
$1234567890

Electra Italic

ABCDEFGHIJKLMNOPQRSTUVWXYZ&
abcdefghijklmnopqrstuvwxyz
$1234567890

Electra Cursive

ABCDEFGHIJKLMNOPQRSTUVWXYZ&
abcdefghijklmnopqrstuvwxyz
$1234567890

Franklin Gothic

ABCDEFGHIJKLMNOPQRSTUVWXYZ&
abcdefghijklmnopqrstuvwxyz
$1234567890

Franklin Gothic Italic

ABCDEFGHIJKLMNOPQRSTUVWXYZ&
abcdefghijklmnopqrstuvwxyz
$1234567890.,-:;!?'

Futura Medium _____

ABCDEFGHIJKLMNOPQRSTUVWXYZ&
abcdefghijklmnopqrstuvwxyz
$1234567890

Futura Medium Italic _____

ABCDEFGHIJKLMNOPQRSTUVWXYZ&
abcdefghijklmnopqrstuvwxyz
$1234567890

Garamond _____

A B C D E F G H I J K L M N O P Q R S T U V W X Y Z &
a b c d e f g h i j k l m n o p q r s t u v w x y z
$ 1 2 3 4 5 6 7 8 9 0

Garamond Italic _____

A B C D E F G H I J K L M N O P Q R S T U V W X Y Z &
a b c d e f g h i j k l m n o p q r s t u v w x y z
$ 1 2 3 4 5 6 7 8 9 0

Goudy _____

A B C D E F G H I J K L M N O P Q R S T U V W X Y Z &
a b c d e f g h i j k l m n o p q r s t u v w x y z
$ 1 2 3 4 5 6 7 8 9 0

Goudy Italic _____

A B C D E F G H I J K L M N O P Q R S T U V W X Y Z &
a b c d e f g h i j k l m n o p q r s t u v w x y z
$ 1 2 3 4 5 6 7 8 9 0

Helvetica

ABCDEFGHIJKLMNOPQRSTUVWXYZ&
abcdefghijklmnopqrstuvwxyz
$1234567890

Helvetica Italic

ABCDEFGHIJKLMNOPQRSTUVWXYZ&
abcdefghijklmnopqrstuvwxyz
$1234567890

Kaufmann Script

ABCDEFGHIJKLMNOP2RSTUVWXYZ&
abcdefghijklmnopqrstuvwxyz
$1234567890¢

Kennerly

ABCDEFGHIJKLMNOPQRSTUVWXYZ&
abcdefghijklmnopqrstuvwxyz
$1234567890

Korinna

ABCDEFGHIJKLMNOPQRSTUVWXYZ
abcdefghijklmnopqrstuvwxyz
1234567890

Lightline Gothic

ABCDEFGHIJKLMNOPQRSTUVWXYZ&
abcdefghijklmnopqrstuvwxyz
$1234567890

Melior

ABCDEFGHIJKLMNOPQRSTUVWXYZ&
abcdefghijklmnopqrstuvwxyz
$1234567890

Melior Italic

ABCDEFGHIJKLMNOPQRSTUVWXYZ&
abcdefghijklmnopq rstuvwxyz
$1234567890

Trade Gothic

ABCDEFGHIJKLMNOPQRSTUVWXYZ
abcdefghijklmnopqrstuvwxyz
1234567890

Trade Gothic Italic

ABCDEFGHIJKLMNOPQRSTUVWXYZ
abcdefghijklmnopqrstuvwxyz
1234567890

Optima

ABCDEFGHIJKLMNOPQRSTUVWXYZ
abcdefghijklmnopqrstuvwxyz
$1234567890

Optima Italic

ABCDEFGHIJKLMNOPQRSTUVWXYZ&
abcdefghijklmnopqrstuvwxyz
$1234567890

Palatino

ABCDEFGHIJKLMNOPQRSTUVWXYZ
abcdefghijklmnopqrstuvwxyz
$1234567890

Palatino Italic

ABCDEFGHIJKLMNOPQRSTUVWXYZ
abcdefghijklmnopqrstuvwxyz
$1234567890

Scotch Roman

ABCDEFGHIJKLMNOPQRSTUVWXYZ&
abcdefghijklmnopqrstuvwxyz
$1234567890

Scotch Roman Italic

ABCDEFGHIJKLMNOPQRSTUVWXYZ&
abcdefghijklmnopqrstuvwxyz
$1234567890

Serif Gothic

ABCDEFGHIJKLMNOPQRSTUVWXYZ
abcdefghijklmnopqrstuvwxyz
1234567890

Souvenir

ABCDEFGHIJKLMNOPQRSTUVWXYZ
abcdefghijklmnopqrstuvwxyz
1234567890

Stymie Bold _____

ABCDEFGHIJKLMNOPQRSTUVWXYZ&
abcdefghijklmnopqrstuvwxyz
$1234567890

Stymie Bold Italic _____

ABCDEFGHIJKLMNOPQRSTUVWXYZ&
abcdefghijklmnopqrstuvwxyz
$1234567890

Times Roman _____

ABCDEFGHIJKLMNOPQRSTUVWXYZ&
abcdefghijklmnopqrstuvwxyz
$1234567890

Times Roman Italic _____

ABCDEFGHIJKLMNOPQRSTUVWXYZ&
abcdefghijklmnopqrstuvwxyz
$1234567890

Univers _____

ABCDEFGHIJKLMNOPQRSTUVWXYZ
abcdefghijklmnopqrstuvwxyz
1234567890

Univers Italic _____

ABCDEFGHIJKLMNOPQRSTUVWXYZ
abcdefghijklmnopqrstuvwxyz
1234567890

Vogue Bold _____

ABCDEFGHIJKLMNOPQRSTUVWXYZ
abcdefghijklmnopqrstuvwxyz
1234567890

Vogue Bold Italic _____

ABCDEFGHIJKLMNOPQRSTUVWXYZ
abcdefghijklmnopqrstuvwxyz
1234567890

Wedding Text _____

ABCDEFGHIJKLMNOPQR
STUVWXYZ&
abcdefghijklmnopqrstuvwxyz
$1234567890

Windsor _____

ABCDEFGHIJKLMNOPQRSTUVWXYZ&
abcdefghijklmnopqrstuvwxyz
$1234567890

Zapf Book Light _____

ABCDEFGHIJKLMNOPQRSTUVWXYZ
abcdefghijklmnopqrstuvwxyz
1234567890

Zapf Book Medium Italic _____

ABCDEFGHIJKLMNOPQRSTUVWXYZ
abcdefghijklmnopqrstuvwxyz
1234567890

B Specifications for This Book

The specifications that follow are the final ones. There were a few changes in the original specifications after sample pages were set and assessed. For example, the No. 1 head was originally specified for 16/16, which seemed too large, and the No. 3 and No. 4 heads were originally specified for Medium, which seemed too light.

The specifications cover general dimensions first, then the text type and text-connected specifications, and then all the display, beginning with *Chapter No.* At the end are the specifications for the running heads and folios, which, of course, were not set until the book was made into pages according to the dummies. The abbreviations in parentheses constitute the keying system set up by the editor who handled production of the book; these abbreviations, which are quite typical in form, were then used by the designer, the copy editor, and the compositor. (B/B = base to base.)

Trim Size: 7-1/2″ x 9-1/4″

Type Page: 35 x 46 picas

Margins: Head: 3/4″   Gutter: 13/16″

No. Lines to Chapter Opening Page: 33

No. Lines to Text Page: 44

Chapter Sinkage: 13 picas to first text line

Paragraph Indention: 2 ems   *Spacing:* French

Text Type: 10/12 Zapf Book Light x 26 picas

(UL) *Unnumbered List:* 10/12 Zapf Book Light Roman, flush left. Turnovers position flush left on same indent as NL TO's with 2-digit numbers; 18 pts. B/B above and below

(NL) *Numbered List:* 10/12 Zapf Book Light Roman. Numerals Zapf Medium. Numeral positions flush left followed by a period. Clear for 2-digit number, align on periods, 1 en space follows period to entry. Turnovers hanging indent: 18 pts. B/B above and below

(TT) *Table Title:* 9/10 Zapf Book Heavy Roman, initial cap only, centered x 26 picas; 18 pts. B/B below to table head

(TH) *Table Head:* 9/10 Zapf Book Medium Roman, initial cap only, centered x 26 picas; 2 pt. rule x 26 picas 6 pts. below, 6 pt. space below rule to table body

(TB) *Tabular:* 9/10 Zapf Book Light Roman. First column is flush left x 26 picas, 2 em space minimum between aligning column entries; 18 pts. B/B below to following table head. Position a 26 pica hairline rule 1 pica below last row of table body entries

(TN) *Table Notes:* 7/8 Zapf Book Light Italic, positioned flush left x 26 picas; 6 pts. space above to bottom hairline rule

(FN) *Footnotes:* (numbered) 8/9 Zapf Book Medium Roman, position flush left x 26 picas. Position a 26 pica hairline rule above FN

Art: Art is x11 picas maximum (marginal), 26 picas, or 35 picas. Art can bleed 3 sides (no gutter bleeds)

(LB) *Labels:* 8/9 Zapf Book Light Roman, position as indicated in art

(CP) *Captions:* 9/10 Zapf Book Light Roman (with Demi figure number), ragged right or ragged left x 8, x 26, or x 35 picas. 1 em space follows figure number. (Zapf Light Italic credit.) Head CP: all Zapf Demi

Glossary, Biblio.: 9/11 Zapf Book Light x 17 (17 + 1 + 17), TO's 1 em indent

(CN) *Chapter No.:* Zapf Heavy Roman, 15/16" numeral height. Position 1-1/2 picas sink from head; flush left x 26 picas

(CT) *Chapter Title:* 24 pt. Zapf Book Heavy Roman c. & l.c.; 7 pts. visual space between lines. Second line base aligns with CN. Total overall width for CN and CT x 26 picas. First 2 lines are flush left x 1 pica space from CN. Third line turnover is flush left x 26 picas. One-line CT's base align with CN. Break lines to make editorial sense, no hyphenation. First text line after CT sinks 13 picas from head, no paragraph indent

(1) *No. 1 Head:* 14/14 Zapf Book Demi Roman c. & l.c., flush left x 26 picas maximum, no hyphenation, break for sense. Position a 1 pt. rule base aligned with last line (2 pt. space to rule) to fill 26 pica overall width; 32 pts. B/B above first (1) head line, 20 pts. B/B below last line, rule. No paragraph indent after (1) heads

(2) *No. 2 Head:* 11/12 Zapf Book Demi Roman c. & l.c., flush right x 8 pica marginal gloss area, base align with first line of text; no hyphenation; 24 pts. B/B above. Text begins flush left

(3) *No. 3 Head:* 9/11 Zapf Book Demi Roman, initial cap only. Position same as No. 2 head except 18 pts. B/B above. Text begins flush left

(4) *No. 4 Head:* 10/12 Zapf Book Demi Roman, initial cap only; flush left x 26 picas. Follow with 1 em space and run in text; 18 pts. B/B above

(5) *No. 5 Head:* 10/12 Zapf Book Light Italic, initial cap only; flush left x 2 em indent. Follow with period and 1 en space and run in text; 18 pts. B/B above

(A) *A Head:* Word "Checklist": 14/14 Zapf Book Demi Italic, c. & l.c., flush left x 26 picas followed by checklist title, which sets 14/14 Zapf Book Demi Roman. 32 pts. B/B above, 24 pts. B/B below. Position a 1 pt. rule x 26 picas 6 pts. below A head

Running Head: 8/8 Zapf Book Light Roman. Left, all caps. Right, c. & l.c. 1 em space to right of and base align with folio. 2 pica sink from running head to first text line

Wording Left: Chapter title *Wording Right:* No. 1 head

Folio: 12 pt. Zapf Book Heavy Roman, 1 em space to running head. Flush top to head margin, flush left x 26 picas

Chapters start new right or left page

When 1 subhead follows another, maintain space below the superior head

Hairline space equals 2 units

Thin space equals 4 units

Thick space equals 6 units

APPENDIX

C Square-Inch Typefitting Table

Square-inch table

Type size in points	Number of words per square inch if set solid	Number of words per square inch if leaded 2 points
6	47	34
7	38	27
8	32	23
9	27	20
10	21	16
11	17	14
12	14	11

Bibliography

Arnheim, Rudolf. *Visual Thinking*. Berkeley, Cal.: University of California Press, 1969.

Bain, Eric K. The *Theory and Practice of Typographic Design*. New York: Hastings House, 1970.

Biggs, John R. *Basic Typography*. New York: Watson-Guptill Publications, 1968.

Bowman, William J. *Graphic Communication*. New York: John Wiley & Sons, 1968

Brown, J. "Information Theory." In *New Horizons in Psychology*, edited by Brian M. Foss. Baltimore, Md.: Penguin Books, 1966.

Burt, Sir Cyril. *A Psychological Study of Typography*. London: Cambridge University Press, 1959.

Chomsky, Noam. "Language and the Mind." *Psychology Today* 1 (1968), no. 9.

Click, J. W., and R. N. Baird. *Magazine Editing and Production*, 2d edit. Dubuque, Iowa: William C. Brown Company, Publishers, 1979.

Corcoran, D. W. J. "Acoustic Factors in Proofreading." *Nature* 214 (1967): 851–852.

Dondis, Donis A. *A Primer of Visual Literacy*. Cambridge, Mass.: M.I.T. Press, 1973.

Felten, Charles J. *Layout 4*. St. Petersburg, Fla.: Charles J. Felten, 1970.

Frank, Lawrence K. "Tactile Communication." The Journal Press: *Genet. Psychol. Monographs* 56 (1957): 209–215.

Garner, Wendell R. *Understanding Structure in Psychological Concepts*. New York: John Wiley & Sons, 1962.

Gombrich, E. H. "The Visual Image." In *Communication, A Scientific American* Book. San Francisco, Cal.: W. H. Freeman and Co., 1972.

Gregory, D. L. *The Intelligent Eye*. New York: McGraw-Hill Book Company, 1970.

Gregory, D. L. *Eye and Brain*, 2nd ed. London: World University Library, 1973.

Haber, R. N. "How We Remember What We See." *Scientific American* 222(5) (1970): 104–12.

Hayakawa, S. I. *Language in Thought and Action*. New York: Harcourt Brace Jovanovich, 1964.

Keele, Steven W. *Attention and Human Performance*. Pacific Palisades, Cal.: Goodyear Publishing Company, 1973.

Lindsay, Peter H., and Donald A. Norman. *Human Information Processing*. New York: Academic Press, 1972.

Nelson, Roy Paul. *Publication Design*. Dubuque, Iowa: William C. Brown Company, Publishers, 1972.

Paterson, D. G., and M. A. Tinker. *How to Make Type Readable*. New York: Harper & Row, 1940.

Robinson, David O., Michael Abbamonte, and Selby H. Evans. "Why Serifs Are Important: The Perception of Small Print." *Visible Language* 4 (1971): 353–359.

Smith, Frank. *Comprehension and Learning*. New York: Holt, Rinehart and Winston, 1975.

Smith, Frank. *Understanding Reading*. New York: Holt, Rinehart and Winston, 1971.

Tinker, M. A. *Legibility of Print*. Ames, Iowa: Iowa State University Press, 1963.

Tinker, M. A. "Recent Studies of Eye Movements in Reading." *Psychological Bulletin* 54 (1958): 215–231.

Zachrisson, Bror. *Studies in Legibility of Printed Text*. Stockholm: Almquist & Wiskel, 1965.

Glossary

Cross references are indicated by **boldface** within entries.

acetate Plastic sheet placed over mechanicals; copy that is to overlay copy on the pasteup or mechanical is affixed to the acetate.

agate Name for $5\frac{1}{2}$ point type; agate line is unit of advertising space measurement, $\frac{1}{14}$ inch deep, one column wide.

alignment *See* **baseline.**

ampersand The symbol &, meaning "and."

area composition Output of a photocomposing or cathode ray tube composing machine that is greater than a single column in width.

art Photographs, drawings, and hand lettering. Also pasteup of materials for camera copy, as in offset and rotogravure.

ASCII The American Standard Code for Information Interchange. The most common 8-level code used in computer word processing.

astonisher Name sometimes used for headlines that include a short line above and/or below the main lines. Also printers' slang for exclamation point.

author's alterations Abbreviated "AAs," refers to changes in proofs not caused by compositor's or printer's error. The publisher or author pays the charges.

author's proof Proof the author reads and marks "OK" or "OK with changes" and then initials.

backbone Portion of book binding between the front and back covers; the *spine.*

back lead The ability of a photocomposing or cathode ray tube machine to roll exposed photopaper back to a starting point for added exposures.

back slant The opposite of italic type stance; available through some cathode ray tube or photocomposing machines.

backup Duplicate hardware in electronic systems that can be used in case of breakdown.

banner Newspaper headline crossing the full width of the page. Also called *streamer* or *ribbon.*

bar graph A graph using varying lengths of bars to show relative quantities.

baseline (or *base*) Line on which center body rests; phototypesetter type families and sizes can be mixed since they all have common alignment or the same baseline. (See also **x-height.**)

basic weight The weight of a ream of paper at standard size (book 25 by 38; cover 20 by 26; index $25\frac{1}{2}$ by $30\frac{1}{2}$), also called "substance."

Benday process A method of applying shading and tinting (lines or dots) to line artwork.

binary digit The amount of information needed to resolve uncertainty between two alternatives. The number of alternatives determines the binary digits needed.

binding In a broad sense, any further treatment of stock after printing; includes cutting, folding, trimming, gathering, stitching, gluing, and casing.

bit Contraction for binary digit.

bleed An illustration filling one or more margins and running off the edge of the page.

blind keyboard machine A tape-perforating machine that does not display the copy.

blowup Enlarged type or picture materials.

blueprint (or *blue* or *blueline*) A fast proof on paper from an offset flat or negative; all printing is blue.

body type Type for main message; generally under 12-point size. Also called *text type.* Opposite of **display type.**

boldface (bf) A variation of a typeface that is heavier and darker than the fullface or lightface versions (as in all the **entry words** here).

bond paper A paper stock suitable for business purposes, such as letterheads and forms.

book Trade slang for magazine.

booklet Small book with either a self-cover or a soft cover.

book paper A paper stock for periodical printing as well as books and direct literature (promotion and so on).

box Printed matter enclosed in rules.

braces Symbols to embrace two or more lines: { }.

brackets Symbols to enclose words or other symbols: [ ].

break-of-the-book Allocation of space in a magazine.

broadsheet A full-size newspaper page format.

brownline or **Vandyke** Same as blueprint except printing is brown.

buildup An excess of ink sufficient to cause smudging or filling-in of letters.

bulk Thickness of paper, without reference to its weight.

bullet Large dot used as an attention-getter and sometimes as a divider.

burn To expose a photomechanical to a sensitized printing plate.

butted slugs Two or more linecaster slugs placed together to form a single line of type. Slugs must be butted when the printed line is to be longer than the machine can set.

byte A series of bits used to identify symbols—a series of 8 bits will identify 256 symbols; a series of 6 bits will identify 64 symbols.

calendering A rolling operation during papermaking that produces smoothness of surface. Super-calendered paper is rolled between polished steel cylinders to create an especially smooth surface.

callout Instructions to the printer written on mechanicals or other layouts.

caps and small caps CAPITALS (uppercase) and SMALL CAPITALS. Small capitals are the same height as lowercase letters in any typeface (the **x-height**) but have uppercase formation.

caption Text accompanying illustrations. Also used to describe the overlines or "heads" above newspaper illustrations.

carding A command in type composition by photocomposing machines and CRT machines, whereby spacing is provided between lines to enlarge the type area to a desired depth.

case A tray holding foundry type that is hand-set.

casebound A book with a hard cover.

case fraction A fraction that is a font character. (See also **piece fraction**.)

casting off Determining space required for the composition of typewritten manuscript.

cathode ray tube (CRT) A TV-like electronic tube used to create and then transmit images (words and pictures) onto paper, film, or printing plates.

channel The medium through which a message is transmitted in the communication process.

chase Metal frame to contain type and plates for printing or for molding duplicates.

clean proof A proof with error-free composition.

clean tape Tape containing only the necessary codes for operating linecasting, photocomposing, or electronic type-generating equipment with all errors and extraneous codes having been removed by an editor or a computer.

coated paper Paper to which a surface coating has been applied for a smooth finish.

cold type Type composed by other than traditional methods (**hot type** or **foundry**)—namely, photocomposition, pastedown, or "typewriter methods." The latter type is printlike in varying degrees.

collage A combination of several distinct pictures into a composite picture. (See also **montage**.)

collotype *See* **photogelatin.**

colophon Symbol or trademark identifying a printer or publisher.

color print Color photograph viewed by reflected light as compared with a transparency, which is viewed by transmitted light.

color separation Process of preparing separate primary color plates that, when printed in register, produce a full-color illustration.

column inch One inch of depth in one column of a publication.

combination Line and halftone combined into a single illustration. Also a run of several different jobs at one time on one press.

command In electronic systems a communication from one part of the system to another—e.g., a keyboard stroke to put material in storage or to forward it through the system.

composing stick A device in which foundry type is assembled by hand and justified into lines.

comprehensive A hand-drawn layout or dummy, carefully prepared and finished to approximate the piece in print. May also be a hand-painted presentation of a cover.

contact print A print on photo paper from negative or positive in contact, as opposed to enlargement or reduction.

copy Text or art to be printed or reproduced.

copyediting Correcting, improving, and marking copy to be printed.

copyfitting Determining (1) space required for copy, (2) amount of copy to be written for allotted space, (3) size of type to accommodate an amount of copy in an allotted space.

copyreading Reading copy for errors and marking copy for printer.

copy schedule An inventory sheet kept by copy desk chief of a newspaper; contains sufficient information about each item for a dummy to be made.

core memory The computer memory that holds program and type-element information that is being processed.

coquille board A textured board used to produce shading in drawings.

counting keyboard machine A tape-perforating machine that signals the operator when hyphenation and justification directions must be punched into the tape.

cover stock Special paper suitable for covers of booklets.

crash A breakdown in computerized electronic systems.

crop To mark artwork or photographs indicating which portions are to be reproduced.

CRT Cathode ray tube.

cursor On VDT screens a small block of light that locates on the screen the character(s) being affected by the keyboard.

cut A **photoengraving** (line or halftone) for letterpress printing.

cutlines Text accompanying illustrations. (See also **caption**.)

cutoff rule A rule that prints a line used horizontally across columns in newspapers to separate items and guide the reader.

cylinder press A press on which paper is held to a cylinder that revolves, rolling the paper across a flat, inked letterpress form to receive impressions.

Datanews The high-speed digital news service of United Press International.

Datastream The high-speed digital news service of Associated Press.

dead matter Printing materials (type and illustrations) no longer needed (foul matter).

deep etch Special offset technique for long runs in which plates are made from film positives instead of negatives.

dial-in To indicate to a hard-wired logic photocomposition or cathode ray tube machine the format specifications by setting the controls.

die-cut A printed piece cut into special shape by dies made by shaping steel blades into the desired form.

digital Information in binary digit (0 and 1) form.

dingbat Typographic decorative device such as a bullet or star.

direct image master Short-run offset plate, usually of paper or plastic, and made without photographic negatives or positives.

directory In electronic systems a listing of all files stored in memory.

diskette In electronic systems a storage medium resembling a 45-rpm recording. (Also called *floppy.*)

display type Type larger than body.

doctor blade The blade on a gravure press that wipes excess ink from the plate before the impression.

double-burn The exposure of light in succession through two separate **flats** or **mechanicals** onto the same **plate**; in many cases one flat contains halftones and the other contains line copy.

doubleprint A surprint, for example, a black line appearing on a tone area.

downtime Unproductive time caused by failure of electronic equipment.

dropout A halftone without dots in unwanted areas; produced by a number of photomechanical means.

dummy Proofs of text, illustrations, captions (or measured holes for each element), and display pasted into position on sheets in specific page arrangement for compositor's guidance in making up pages. In newspapers and magazines the elements may be sketched in place.

dump To release copy from a video display terminal's screen to the perforator.

duotone A two-color reproduction of a halftone from separate plates. When two plates are made from a single black-and-white photo (one high-key carries color, the other normally carries black) it may be called a *duograph.*

ear Small amounts of type, illustration, or both on either side of a newspaper nameplate. Also refers to the hook on the letters *r* and *g.*

electrostatic printing A technique of affixing a printed image in powder form on paper by means of electrostatic charges.

electrotype A metal plate cast from a wax mold of the original type page.

ellipses Three dots signifying omission as in a quote.

em (short for **em quad**) Nonprinting square of a metal type body of any size; designates a square white space of any point size in phototypesetting. Also measure of amount of type composition.

embossing Pressing a relief pattern of type, art, or both into paper or cover materials.

en A metal quad half the width of a mutton (em quad). Also refers to white space half as wide as an em of white space.

end papers Paper glued to the inside covers of a book; often left blank but may contain printing.

engraving A printing plate etched by acid from photographic or other copy; a copper plate into which letters are hand-etched in reverse for printing invitations, calling cards, and so forth. Also a synonym for a cut or photoengraving.

ephemera Printed material of a transitory nature, generally materials other than books.

exception dictionary A computer memory store of hyphenation codes for words not amenable to the logic algorithm for breaking.

face The printing surface of type or plate. Also the name for a specified type.

fake process color Full-color reproduction from a black-and-white photo, effected by the engraver's manipulation of four separate negatives so that they represent the respective primaries and black. (*See* **process color**.)

file management A computer program that organizes input within memory so that it may be retrieved for further use.

filling in Building up of excess ink to a point where letters plug or close up.

first revise A proof of type with corrections made after first proofreading.

fit Space between characters; can be altered to tight or loose in phototypesetting.

flag Nameplate of a newspaper.

flat A vehicle for holding film positives or negatives in position for exposing onto **plates**. Offset flats are usually **goldenrod** paper; photoengraving and gravure flats are usually glass.

flatbed press A direct-from-type (or engraving) press using either platen or cylinder to print from a flat, as opposed to curved, type form.

flat color Simplest form of spot color; each color stands alone, solid or screened—colors do not overlay each other to form additional colors.

flat piece A printed sheet delivered to a customer unfolded.

flexography A relief printing method using liquid fast-dry ink on rubber plates.

flop To reverse art laterally—image, when printed, is opposite from original.

floppy *See* **diskette**.

folder A printed piece with one or more folds; also a machine that folds printed flat sheets.

folio A page number.

folo head Headline over a small story related to, and placed directly following, the main story.

font All the letters and characters in one size of a typeface.

form Metal type and photoengravings locked in a chase ready for printing or preparing a duplicate, either a mat or a metal or plastic plate.

format The shape, size, and style of a publication; also the typographic requirements for composition, such as line length, typeface, size, and so on.

formatting In electronic systems the capability of specifying typographic composition requirements with terminal keystrokes.

foundry type Hand-set type.

fullface The standard or normal weight and width of a typeface.

furniture Metal or wooden material used to fill in large nonprint areas of a letterpress form.

galley A metal tray for storing metal type. Also a term for a galley proof.

galley proof Proof from type in a galley; also refers to a proof from phototypesetting of type matter not made into pages.

gang To run several jobs on one press at a time. Also, to make several engravings—all at same enlargement or reduction—at one time.

gauge See **line gauge.**

goldenrod Opaque golden-orange paper that serves as the vehicle for an offset **flat.** (See also **mask**.)

Gothic type Those faces with, generally, monotonal (noncontrast) strokes and no serifs; also called **sans serif,** *contemporary,* or *block letter.*

Greek golden mean An elegant and universal ratio manifested in natural growth and development and applicable to graphic design.

grid A division of design space into orderly and regular rectangular areas that serve to contain printed elements, thereby establishing a structural relationship among them. Also, a ruled pasteup sheet.

gripper edge The edge of a sheet held by the gripper on the impression cylinder press or sheet-fed rotary; it represents an unprintable $\frac{3}{8}$ to $\frac{1}{2}$ inch.

gutter The inside margin of a page at the binding.

halftone A reproduction made from a photograph, wash drawing, and so forth. Gradation of tone is reproduced by a pattern of dots produced by the interposition of a screen during exposure.

h&j Hyphenation and justification; codes for hyphenation and justification incorporated into perforated tape produced by a computer that has been fed idiot tape or produced from a counting-keyboard perforator; such codes may also be **on-line.**

hanging indention A typesetting style; the first line is full measure with succeeding lines indented from the left.

hanging punctuation Typesetting style in which smaller punctuation is to the right of the right-hand margin of lines of type.

hard copy A printed, usually typewritten, record produced (1) simultaneously when the message is perforated onto tape, or (2) as printout from a computer that has prepared composition tape. Used for editing purposes.

hardware The actual computer and its other "hard-to-the-touch" components. (See also **software**.)

hard-wired logic Wired-in capacity of an automated phototypesetter or CRT to perform certain mathematical and logical functions. Such machines are not programmable and can perform only their wired-in functions.

hed sked A headline schedule, the newspaper inventory sheet showing all headlines the newspaper normally uses.

highlight The lightest portion of a photo or other art or reproduction of same. To highlight a halftone is to remove mechanically or photographically the dots in certain areas. Such a halftone is called a highlight or dropout halftone.

hot metal *See* **hot type.**

hot type Type composed by machine from molten metal; sometimes includes **foundry type.**

IBC Inside back cover.

idiot tape Perforated tape without h&j codes. (Also called *raw tape.*)

IFC Inside front cover.

image (verb) To expose a type element photographically.

image conversion Any of several techniques for adapting hot metal composition to film negative images for making offset or roto plates.

imposition The location of pages in a form or on a sheet so that when the printed sheet of the signature is folded, the pages will fall in proper order.

impression The pressure of type or plate against paper in printing. Also, "impressions per hour" refers to the number of sheets being delivered.

imprint To run a printed piece through another press to add information such as a name or address.

indent To set one or more lines in from left or right margin; one em indent from left of first line signifies a paragraph start.

in-house Printing production systems located in, and part of, an editorial operation.

initial A large letter used to start a copy area.

insert A separately printed piece placed in a publication at the time of binding.

intaglio Process of printing from depressed areas carrying ink.

interface To hook various text-processing devices directly via hard wire in lieu of using perforated tape for intermachine communication.

IPS Information processing system; a biological or man made system capable of accepting information, interpreting (processing) it, and reacting after making a decision.

italic Type that *slants right*; counterpart to roman posture, which is upright.

jet printing Plateless printing system using fast-moving computer-driven ink jets to put an image on paper.

jig A customized ruled pasteup sheet marked for columns, margins, and so on. (See also **dummy**.)

jim dash A short dash (about three ems long) used between headline decks in some newspapers.

jump To carry over a portion of a story from one page to another. Also the continued portion of the story.

justify To space or quad out a line of type to make it full to the right margin.

K A designation of computer capacity, each K representing 1,024 bytes.

kerning Reducing space between letters so that one extends over another, i.e., placing an *i* under a *T*. Sometimes used as a general term for tight letterspacing.

keyline A **pasteup** or **mechanical** on which lines are drawn to show where art, tint blocks, and so on should be stripped into the **flat.**

key plate The printing plate in color printing that is laid first and to which others must register.

kicker A short line of type above and/or below the main part of a headline; used mainly for feature story headlines.

laser Light beams used to scan photographs, full pages, and symbols and send the scanned results in digital form to cameras, to typesetting equipment, and to platemaking equipment and from point to point, as with AP laser photographs.

layout Often used as a synonym for **dummy.** A pattern, roughly or carefully drawn, to show the placement of elements on a printed piece.

leaders A row of dots used to guide vision across open areas of tabular material.

leads (pronounced "leds") Thin metallic strips used to provide extra space between type lines. (See also **linespacing**.)

legibility That degree of visibility which makes printed matter read easily and rapidly.

letterfold The basic fold given to business letters and to most direct literature.

letterpress The traditional system of printing from raised (relief) areas.

letterset A printing process similar to offset but without the use of water.

letterspacing Adding or subtracting units of space between characters in phototypesetting.

ligature Two or more letters joined together as a single unit, such as *ffl, fi, ff, ffi, æ*, or *œ*.

line In advertising, an agate line; in illustrations, artwork and plates composed only of extreme tones as opposed to halftone illustrations.

linecaster A machine, such as Linotype, which casts type in line units.

line conversion A relatively new technique of converting photographs to line illustrations for special effects.

linecut An engraving, usually on zinc, containing no gradation of tone unless applied by Benday or similar means.

line gauge Printer's ruler marked off in picas and other printing units of measure.

line printer A high-speed impact printer that produces hard copy of computer-stored information.

linespacing Adding extra space between lines of type; reduction of space is possible in **photocomposition.** (See also **wordspacing**.)

lithographic conversion Lithographic printing of plates originally made for letterpress. Plates can be chalked and photographed directly or proofs can be pulled and photographed.

lithography A system of printing from a flat surface using the principle that grease and water do not mix. (See also **offset**.)

lockup The securing of type, engraving, and furniture in a form before plating.

logotype Originally a hot type term for two or more images, especially letters, on one type body; today refers to any brand, corporate or store name consistently appearing in a certain typeface; the logotype, or logo, may also include art, such as a trademark or a trade character, or a particular design.

long-term memory (LTM) Human "permanent" memory of vast storage capacity and very long duration, perhaps a lifetime.

lowercase Small letter, as distinguished from a capital.

lower rail In type composition, the normal weight and posture of the size in use.

LTM Long-term memory.

Ludlow Typograph A typecasting machine usually used for display type; molds are hand set in lines and then the line is cast as a single slug.

makeready Preparation of page forms or plates in letterpress printing to make certain that impression is even and light when paper is impressed against the inked forms or plates.

makeup Arrangement according to design of type, illustrations, and other elements into pages.

mark up To put composition instructions on copy or layout. As a noun, refers to ad layouts so marked. Also, to give command codes to a photocomposition machine or computer indicating typographic formats.

mask A sheet of opaque paper used to prevent light from striking the **plate** while making offset or engraving plates; areas are cut from the mask so that the desired images will be positioned in windows and thus exposed on the plate. Masks may also be made photographically on film. (See also **flat, goldenrod**.)

matrix A mold of a typecasting machine from which a type character or other element is cast.

Also the sheet of papier-mâché or composition material used as a mold in stereotyping.

measure Page, line or column width expressed in picas.

mechanical Camera-ready copy with type and pictures positioned on illustration board or heavy paper, keylines drawn to show positioning of other elements, trim marks drawn, and instructions written in margins. One or more overlays may carry additional copy and art with instructions for positioning to the keylines. (Also called **pasteup**.)

mechanical binding Type of binding using plastic, metal spirals, or rings instead of traditional sewing or stapling.

merge On dual screen VDTs, the ability to select the best from two stories to form one story.

mezzotint An illustration that has been given a textured impression through the use of a special halftone screen.

microprocessor A single chip computing device, having the capacity of a minicomputer.

miniature A small **layout** prepared as a preliminary to executing a full-scale layout.

mixing Placing two or more typefaces, typestyles, or type sizes within a line, matched to common alignment.

moiré A pronounced screen pattern that results from the clash of dot patterns when two or more screens are used; corrected in full-color and duotone work by changing screen angles.

monitor printer *See* **line printer**.

Monotype A typecasting machine; casts single letters rather than lines and uses both a tape-punching unit and a casting unit to do this.

montage A combination of several distinct pictures into a composite picture; usually called a **collage** unless the edges of the component pictures are made to blend into each other.

mortise A cutout area in a halftone that permits the insertion of type or other matter; if the cutout is from outside edges, it is usually called a **notch**.

nameplate The name of a newspaper, usually at the top of page 1.

negative In photography, engraving, and photographic printing processes, the film containing a reversed (in tone) image.

nonpareil A size of type, 6-point.

notch A portion cut out from one or more edges of an illustration.

numerals Numbers within a font, either lining (or Modern), that do not extend below the baseline (1234567890), or Old Style (or nonlining) that extend below the baseline (1234567890).

OBC Outside back cover.

OCR **Optical character recognition.**

OFC Outside front cover.

Offset A lithographic printing method in which the inked image transfers from plate to rubber blanket to paper. Often called indirect or photo-offset **lithography.**

on-line Electronic text processing machines that are directly connected via hard wire.

optical alignment The projection of certain letters beyond the left margin to give a more aesthetic appearance, for example, the stem of a capital *T* aligned with the left stem of an *N* in the succeeding line, with the *T* cross stroke left of the margin.

optical character recognition (OCR) Scanning of typewritten or printed characters, followed by the conversion of the message to magnetic or perforated tape or electronic signals.

overhang cover A cover that, after trimming, projects beyond the dimensions of the inside pages.

overlay Transparent paper or acetate flap placed over a **mechanical** or art to protect it; or to give **photomechanical** instructions; or to carry images to be combined on the same plate with images on the key mechanical.

overset Type that is set but not used.

page proof Proof of type matter in page form together with illustrations or with holes left for them.

parameters Specifications for photocomposition or CRT composition; the details of formatting.

pasteup A layout board with visual elements (proofs from hot metal or cold type composition) pasted on it (and often also on one or more overlays) in exact positions; the pasteup is then photographed to make printing plates. (Also called **mechanical**.)

patch To correct photocomposition by pasting in reset matter on the paper or stripping it into the film; also reset material to be pasted in or cut in.

patent base A frame locked up in a letterpress form and to which duplicate plates less than type-high may be attached by hooks.

perfect binding A method of binding books with paper in lieu of case and flexible glue instead of stitching.

perfecting press A press capable of printing on both sides of a sheet or web at the same time.

photocomposing Automatic, repeated exposure of a **flat** on a single offset or wraparound plate. Each printing impression from the plate results in several copies of the same image.

photocomposition Type composed by exposing negatives of the characters on film or paper.

photoengraving Letterpress plate used to reproduce line or halftone materials.

photogelatin process A screenless printing process using gelatin plates, especially suitable for reproducing tone illustrations. (Also called *collotype*.)

photomechanical Film positives of type, line art, and halftones positioned on transparent film base from which a single film negative is made.

photostat A photocopy, either positive or negative (reversed in tone), same size, enlarged, or reduced (usually called *stat*).

pica Standard unit of linear measurement (12 points); approximately $\frac{1}{6}$ of an inch.

pi characters Special characters or symbols not found in most type fonts.

pictograph A graph using pictures of objects to show relative amounts of data.

piece fraction A fraction made on a phototypesetter by using numerals plus a slash or a hyphen between superior and inferior numerals. (See also **case fraction**; piece and case fractions should not be used together in composition.)

pie chart An illustration showing a circle divided into segments to show relative quantities of statistical data.

plate An image carrier, usually metal, which transfers ink to paper or other printing surface.

platen press A flat-surfaced relief press. Paper is supported on one surface, type on the other. The two are brought together for impression.

PMT (photomechanical transfer); a processor for automatically making enlarged or reduced photoprints from line copy, including type, or screened photoprints (**Veloxes**) from continuous-tone copy such as photos. The photoprints are placed on the **pasteup.**

point Printer's unit of measuring size of type and rules, border, spacing material; there are 12 points to a pica and approximately 72 points to an inch. As unit of measurement for thickness of cardboard, equals $\frac{1}{1000}$ of an inch.

posterization A special technique for reproducing halftone illustrations in which the two absolute tones (white and black) are combined with only one middle tone.

press proof One of the first copies off the press; it offers a final opportunity to make changes in the job.

process color The reproduction of continuous-tone color originals by separating out each color and recording it on film; plates are made from these films to carry the respective colors to paper.

program In electronic systems, the "thinking" or decision-making processes of which equipment is capable. (See also **software.**)

progressive proofs Proofs of process color plates; each color is shown separately, then in combination with each other. For four-color process a set of *progs* would show seven printings.

proof A trial printing of type, negatives, or plates, to be checked for possible errors.

quad In hand composition a less-then-type-high spacing material used within lines; an em quad is the square of the type size. In electronic composition spacing created by moving the escapement system without exposure of type elements. In automated composition, quad left is the same as flush left and quad right is the same as flush right. Quad center is centered.

queue In electronic systems a listing similar to a directory or a lineup of material held in memory for processing.

quick print Efficient, automated printing based on electrostatic platemaking and offset printing.

quire Usually 25 (sometimes 24) sheets of paper of the same size and quality.

quoin A wedge-shaped device used in locking up letterpress forms.

ragged left Opposite of ragged right.

ragged right Composition in which all lines of type are aligned at the left but are of different lengths and thus uneven or ragged on the right.

rated speed The capacity of a photocomposition or CRT typesetting device expressed in lines per minute, usually based on 8-point, 11 picas (approximately 30 characters and spaces per line).

raw tape *See* **idiot tape.**

ream usually 500 (sometimes 480) sheets of paper of the same size and quality.

redundance Excess of information needed to make a decision.

register Placement of forms, plates, or negatives so that they will print in precise relation to or over other forms, plates, or negatives, as in color printing.

reproduction proof A proof on special paper of exceptional cleanness and sharpness to be used as camera copy for offset, rotogravure, or relief plates (usually called *repro*).

retrieval The recall of information from **LTM** to **STM.**

reverse Reproducing the whites in an original as black and the blacks as white.

reverse lead *See* **back lead.**

roman A type characterized by serifs; also refers to vertical type commonly used for typesetting as distinguished from *italic*.

rotary press A press that prints as paper passes between a cylindrical impression surface and a curved printing surface.

rotogravure Printing and printing presses using the rotary and gravure principles; **intaglio** process.

rough A preliminary layout not in finished form.

routing Cutting away of excess metal from non-printing areas of engravings or duplicates.

rule A strip of type-high metal that produces a line on paper; rules vary in width. Also the printed line itself (phototypesetters, CRT typesetters, and strike-on machines can create such lines). Also, the black adhesive-backed tape pasted on mechanicals to photograph and print as a black line.

run The number of copies to come off the press.

running heads Titles or heads repeated at the top of book and publication pages, usually followed by or preceded by folio. (When at the bottoms of pages they are *running feet.*)

saddle-stitch To fasten a booklet together by stitching or stapling through the middle fold of the sheets.

sans serif Type having no serifs. *See* **Gothic type.**

scale To find any unknown dimension when enlarging or reducing original art for reproduction to size.

scanner An electronic machine that "reads" visual images and produces by means of electrical impulses reproduction materials. Some scanners can produce black-and-white negatives (or positives) from black-and-white photos or composed characters; others can produce screened or unscreened color separation negatives (or positives) from color photos (prints or transparencies); some can read mechanicals or pasteups and produce printing plates for offset or letterpress. There are also scanners that read materials and send them via wire or radio waves to other locations. (See also **optical character recognition.**)

score To crease paper or cover stock to facilitate folding without breaking.

screen Cross-ruled glass or film used in cameras to break continuous-tone copy into halftone dots. The number of lines per linear inch on the screen governs the fineness of engraving or reproduction. Also a tint block or flat tone.

script Types that simulate handwriting in which letters appear to join.

scroll On video display terminals, to roll the text material up across the face of the video tube for reading; permits seeing previous input that has gone off the screen. (Similar to rolling paper up or down in an ordinary typewriter.)

second generation In **photocomposition,** used to describe electro-mechanical units incorporating rotatable lenses. (See also **third generation.)**

self-cover A cover that is part of one of the signatures of a booklet and of the same paper.

series The range in sizes of a typeface.

serif The finishing cross stroke at the end of a main stroke in a type letter.

set width The width of a character plus the small amount on either side to keep it separate from other characters in composition; measured in units; can be increased or decreased in phototypesetting.

sheet-fed Referring to presses that accept sheets, not rolls (webs).

sheetwise An imposition calling for printing half the pages in a signature on one side of the sheet, the other half on the other side.

short-term memory (STM) Human memory of short duration and limited capacity; information quickly forgotten unless moved to **LTM.**

side-stitch To fasten sheets together sideways through the fold.

signature A number of pages printed on one sheet of paper; when folded and trimmed, the pages fall in numerical order. A book signature may contain 8, 16, 32, or 64 pages.

silhouette Reproduction of art or photo with background removed.

silk-screen process A process of printing by which ink or paint is "squeegeed" through a stencil-bearing silk screen to the paper beneath.

slave terminal A terminal with no storage and processing capability of its own.

slug A line of type from a linecasting machine. Also, between-line spacing material of metal 6 points or greater in thickness. Also, the word or two to identify a story.

small caps *See* **caps and small caps.**

soft copy Copy seen on a video display device.

software The programs that direct the operation of a computer as it performs mathematical and logical functions. (See also **hardware.**)

split-fountain printing In printing, the ink receptacle (fountain) can be separated into compartments corresponding to segments of the ink roller, which has also been split. By putting different colors in each fountain segment, more than one color can be printed from a form during one press run.

split page A magazine page that is part advertising and part editorial.

split-roller *See* **split fountain printing.**

split screen The feature on some VDTs that permits display of two stories in side-by-side columns.

spot color Any color printing other than process printing.

square indention A newspaper headline pattern in which all lines are uniformly indented from the left; a modification of the flush left headline.

square serif Types basically **Gothic** in nature but having monotonal serifs.

stand-alone Electronic text processing machine that is not on-line.

stereotype A letterpress duplicate metal plate (flat or curved) made from a mold similar to cardboard.

STM Short term memory.

stock Paper or cardboard.

straight matter Text copy composed in normal paragraph form; contrast with tabular matter.

strike on Cold type composition produced on machine that resembles a typewriter.

strip The computer function of removing **h&j** codes from wire-service tape and inserting new h&j codes in a second tape.

stripped slug A type slug that is shaved underneath; it can then be mounted at any angle on base material that brings it type high.

stripping Affixing film negatives or positives to a **flat.** Also, cutting linecast slugs to less than type height. *See* **stripped slug.**

substance A term for the basis weight of paper.

surprint A combination **plate** made by exposing line and halftone negatives in succession on the same plate.

syntax The relationship of verbal (sometimes visual) elements arranged so that they impart information clearly.

tabbing Composing copy in even columns within a specified line measure.

tabloid A format that is half the size of a **broadsheet.**

teletypesetter An attachment that automatically operates a mat-circulating linecasting machine from perforated tape.

Text A typeface with an "Old English" look. Also any body type (written with lowercase *t*). Also the body of a book excluding front and back matter.

text-processing system Combination of various electronic composition gear that puts author's original copy into type on photo paper or film.

thermography A printing process that produces a raised impression simulating an **intaglio** engraving. An image is put on paper in the usual way; it is powdered while wet, then heated so that powder and ink fuse to a raised image.

third generation In **photocomposition**, used to describe totally electronic units that utilize **CRT** technology. (See also **second generation**.)

thumbnail A miniature **layout.** Also a half-column photoengraving.

tint block A photoengraving used to print tints of any percentage of color. Also refers to the panel printed from a block.

tip-in A single sheet or partial signature glued into a book or magazine. It is often of smooth stock used for halftone printing whereas remainder of publication may be printed on a cheaper stock of paper.

tombstone The typographical effect that results from side-by-side placement of two or more headlines too similar in size and face to stand as separate units.

transparency A color photograph that may be viewed by transmitted light. (See also **color print**.)

trim mark Right angle marks on a mechanical to show the four corners of the printed sheet after it has been trimmed; the marks are cut off when the piece is trimmed.

TTS code A six-level digital code used for teletypewriters and in many computerized typesetting systems.

type high In letterpress printing, .918 inches, the desired height for all elements in a form.

typo A typographical error.

unit A measurement of set width, usually 18 per em of the type size.

uppercase Capital letter.

upper rail In type composition the **boldface** or *italic* alternative that is available for the size in use.

VDT Video display terminal.

vellum Originally a calfskin or lambskin prepared as a writing surface; now used to label a paper stock with a good writing surface.

Velox A screened photographic print similar to a **photostat** positive, but usually sharper in definition.

video display terminal (VDT) A cathode ray tube keyboard-operated device for viewing material as it is keyboarded into or drawn from computer storage.

video layout system (VLS) A video-screen, keyboard-control unit-system for area composition of advertisements up to $\frac{1}{2}$ newspaper page width and full-page depth.

vignette The treatment given a photograph or halftone so that edges fade away into the background without breaking sharply.

visual STM Human memory of very short duration in which information is held long enough to ascertain whether it is useful.

watermark A faint design or lettering pressed into paper during its manufacture that can be seen when the sheet is held up to light.

web-fed A press that prints on paper fed from a roll.

white print A photocopy (contact print or enlargement) from a negative (halftone or line).

widow A short line at the end of a paragraph; always to be avoided at the top of newspaper or magazine columns or book pages, but its presence elsewhere may or may not be disliked.

wire strip Elimination of typesetting codes from stories transmitted by a wire service such as AP or UPI.

wordspacing Adding or reducing units of space between words in **photocomposition.** (See also **linespacing.**)

word wrap The capability of a VDT to end each line with a full word. Adding a word to any line will push as many words forward as necessary to make room, perhaps involving several lines. The change of characters is instantaneous.

work-and-tumble A system resembling **work-and-turn** except that the sheet is turned so that a new edge is grabbed by the grippers.

work-and-turn A system of printing both sides of a printing piece on one side of a sheet, then turning the sheet so that its gripper edge remains constant and the sheet is printed on the reverse side.

work-up A fault in relief printing that causes a spot to be printed because spacing materials or blank portions of type slugs have risen high enough to gather ink.

wrap An insert into a magazine or book. Unlike a tip-in, it is wrapped around a signature.

wraparound press A relief press (sheet- or web-fed) that utilizes a shallow-etch curved plate made from a **flat** similar to that used in offset.

wrong font (wf) A letter or character that is of different size or face from the type that was specified.

xerography A dry system of printing based on electrostatic principles.

x-height The height of the center body of lowercase letters, excluding ascenders and descenders. The bottom of the x-height is on the **baseline.**

zinc A photoengraving, line or halftone, made of zinc.

Index